W9-BZJ-043

The Holy Spirit & Counseling

Marvin G. Gilbert
and
Raymond T. Brock
Editors

HENDRICKSON
PUBLISHERS
PEABODY, MASSACHUSETTS 01961-3473

Copyright © 1985
Hendrickson Publishers, Inc.
P.O. Box 3473, Peabody, MA 01961-3473
All rights reserved
Printed in the United States of America
ISBN 0-913573-14-0

The Holy Spirit & Counseling

Marvin G. Gilbert
and
Raymond T. Brock
Editors

Table of Contents

EDITORS' INTRODUCTION

Early in my graduate education I received an exciting exposure to those personality theorists whose thoughts have significantly shaped the face of academic and applied psychology. Allport's and Adler's thoughts regarding the unavoidability of motivation in understanding behavior had a particularly strong impact upon me. We do what we do, these theorists claimed, because we are motivated to do so, whether we are reading an introduction to a new textbook or writing the same.

The purpose of this introduction is not to "sell" the idea of motivated behavior; rather, it is to share some of the experiences and struggles which have motivated this project. Both of us agree that these two volumes will be more understandable if the underlying motivation and assumptions are addressed overtly at the beginning.

The aforementioned graduate education in psychology and counseling came after I had completed an undergraduate degree in Bible. From that context, stepping into a completely secular graduate school classroom was a novel, exciting experience. In the back of my mind rang all of the warnings—shouted enthusiastically from pulpits—about the evils of secular psychology and its inherent spiritual dangers. Yet, the theories proved to be enlightening, stimulating, and surprisingly consistent (in places) with Scripture's perspective of humanity. During my master's degree study, I made a commitment to myself to seek all that I could learn, yet to view it all, including personality functioning, from a biblical perspective. Thus, like Trueblood, I found a *place to stand* which allowed (in fact demanded) a true psychological eclecticism with God's Word serving as the unifying thread.

In this light, I read of Man's depravity *à la* Freud, and could say "amen." I read of Man's greatness and glory in Carl Rogers and Rollo May, and heartily agreed. I embraced that part of Maslow's teaching which emphasized the necessity for commitment to a purpose or cause greater than one's self in order to achieve a self-actualizing way of being; I saw that cause as Christ Himself. The self-fulfilling prophecy theories of Leon Festinger and G. H. Mead sounded amazingly like the words of Solomon: "as he thinks within himself, so he is" (Prov. 23:7).

Thus, graduate school became a spiritual refinery in which those beliefs and values which I had previously found no need to question were examined and integrated (on a trial and error basis) with those threads of truth which I could accept from secular psychology and counseling theory. Missing from this developing integration, however, were the beliefs which contribute most to the uniqueness of my theology; that is, belief in the active role of the Holy Spirit, the transcendent Third Person of the Trinity. I had developed an understanding of how Christianity and psychological theories can interrelate, but I found little opportunity to judge the "fit" between a Pentecostal theology and those secular theories.

A large portion of the reason for this lack of integration was the non-existence of a corpus of integrative literature which, ideally, could have provided direction for study and reflection. Generally, it seems that those who write of the ministry of the Holy Spirit do so either with a theological aridness or with an appalling lack of psychological sophistication. Conversely, those who write with psychological sophistication (even from a biblical-Christian perspective) rarely, if ever, mention God's transcendence in general, or the Holy Spirit's ministry in particular.

The motivation for these volumes, initiated for me in graduate school, has only become more clearly defined for both of us in recent years. We are regularly involved in counseling with singles, married and engaged couples, and families. Frequently, clients approach us with great (and often unrealistic) expectations that we will produce immediate, miraculous change because we are "Spirit-filled" counselors. It has been a continuing struggle and growth producing experience for both of us to define—at least crudely—what it means to be a Spirit-filled counselor, counseling in a Spirit-filled manner.

Thus, these two volumes hopefully represent a seminal effort to provide a working definition of "Spirit-filled" counseling and psychotherapy. They also represent an attempt to combine two words which have not always been compatible: "Pentecostal" (or Charismatic) and "scholarship." The reader should be forewarned, however, that the combination is not perfect. There are occasions in these volumes where little integration is possible—or even desirable. If the fit were perfect, if the concepts of psychology and theology fit exactly, there would be little need for such a book, or for the non-theologians who wrote it.

These two volumes have been written with two groups of readers in mind. First, they will be of interest to Pentecostal or Charismatic believers, specifically those who are involved in providing pastoral and psychological care. Of course, such a classification crosses quite freely many denominational and ecclesiastical boundaries. Second, they will appeal to non-Pentecostal believers who accept—even embrace—the possibility that God can and does guide and empower His servants as they attempt to minister care to people in distress and pain. Included in this second group are those who may be curious about what Pentecostal theologians, counselors, and psychologists have to say about the Holy Spirit.

This project has a clear focus: integration of psychological and theological truth. Obviously, these books will never replace secular texts on theory (Volume I) and application (Volume II). We believe, however, that there will be much in these books which will prove useful to the non-Pentecostal and even to the non-Christian. Where psychotherapeutic theories are discussed, they are presented with clarity and with sufficient depth to be of interest to those who are simply looking for a concise presentation of the prominent theories in the field. Volume II will be of particular interest to those who want to review the literature in one or more areas of application and practice.

Thus we share a large part of ourselves with you, the reader, both directly in our own chapters, and indirectly, "behind the scenes," in editing the contribution of others. It is with a mixture of confidence and apprehension that we present previously private thoughts, unstated struggles, questions, and biases. We do so with a firm conviction that what is written in these volumes *needs* to be written; this integration is an idea whose time has come.

Marvin G. Gilbert, with Raymond T. Brock

NOTE: Throughout this volume we have attempted to limit the number of gender-designating pronouns and other forms of sexist language. However, when the context indicated the need for a singular noun or pronoun, we chose to use a masculine term, rather than "his or her," "he or she," or other more cumbersome conventions. We trust that this choice results in a more readable text. We also trust that this choice is not offensive to the reader; no offense or irresponsible disregard for current editorial style is intended.

THEOLOGY

INTRODUCTION

When Dr. Marvin Gilbert first mentioned to me his dream, which is culminating in this book and the projected second volume, I was delighted. For more than a quarter of a century, I have been involved in a ministry of counseling in Pentecostal-Charismatic circles. With theological training completed at Central Bible College in Springfield, Missouri, and Phillips University in Enid, Oklahoma, I have taught in Assemblies of God colleges in Illinois, Texas, Missouri, and Nigeria, West Africa.

It was when I was in my first year of teaching at Southwestern Assemblies of God College in Waxahachie, Texas, that the need for counseling as a ministry first dawned on me. I noticed that at the end of each school day there would be students waiting to talk to me before I left campus. The conversations related not to class materials, but to personal problems the students were facing. The variety of problems spanned the whole spectrum of human emotions. For the first time, I became aware of the fact that the school had no one specifically trained to counsel the students. This realization motivated additional formal studies in counseling, guidance, and psychology at the University of Colorado in Boulder and at the University of Tulsa. Later I became a licensed psychologist in the state of Missouri and a clinical member of the American Association for Marriage and Family Therapy.

Thus, it was from the standpoint of a psychologist and family therapist that I approached this project. The operation of the Holy Spirit in my ministry has been essential. Whatever has been accomplished is the result of the interaction of the Holy Spirit with the training and skills I have tried to continue to develop through the years. I would not begin to do what I do in counseling and psychotherapy if I were not acutely aware of the presence of the Holy Spirit in therapy sessions.

I have shared this personal information to indicate why we decided to introduce Volume One with a theological overview of the ministry of the Holy Spirit in the life of the believer in general and the counselor in particular. This section contains and effectively communicates a message that is relevant both to the Christian who is a counselor in a professional or paraprofessional role and to the counseling pastor in a religious setting.

We invited Dr. Del Tarr, President of California Theological Seminary in Fresno, California, to write the first chapter, "The Role of the Holy Spirit in Interpersonal Relations," because of his unique training and experience in cross-cultural communication. His extensive travels around the world have given him unique insights into interpersonal relations in areas where culture and religion collide as well as interact.

Tarr asserts that "there is a realm of competence that surpasses human competence: where secular resources are exhausted and the sacred can be utilized." He draws vividly on American, African, and oriental concepts to illustrate his thesis. His references to the uniqueness of right and left hemisphere brain functions are noteworthy as he explores the "fan of perception" in communicating ideas within a culture as well as across cultures. His concluding emphasis on listening to the voice of the Spirit in the counseling interaction is both academically and spiritually sound.

In the second chapter, Dr. William Menzies discusses "The Holy Spirit as the Paraclete: Model for Counselors." He writes from the standpoint of historical theology; he has been both an undergraduate and graduate level professor of theology for a quarter of a century. He is Vice President for Academic Affairs (elect) at the California Theological Seminary. Currently, he is Interim President of the Far East Advanced School of Theology in Manila.

Menzies first looks at the relationship of the Holy Spirit to the Triune Godhead. Then he turns his attention to the relationship between the Holy Spirit and counseling and observes that "it is not easy always to distinguish what the Holy Spirit does *for* the counselor from what He does *through* the counselor." Therefore, counselors should, "continually seek to model their lives after the gentle Spirit." Although Menzies, as a theologian, is not academically trained as a counselor, his insights into the relationship between the Spirit and counseling are superb. I heartily agree with Him: "the counselor has available to him, in moments of great need, information and insights that are not naturally available....the wise counselor will be eager to cooperate with the Holy Spirit."

Dr. Stanley Horton is an internationally known scholar in theology and biblical languages; he is a professor at the Assemblies of God Theological Seminary. In Chapter 3, "The Gifts of the Spirit," Horton discusses the gifts of the Holy Spirit that are available to the Christian counselor. He looks first at the purpose of the gifts in the body of believers and how they are uniquely suited to enhance the ministry of the counselor in both secular and religious settings. He reviews the nine gifts of the Spirit discussed in 1 Corinthians 12:8–10; he highlights those that are especially useful in therapeutic interventions, and notes their relationship to the *agapē* love of 1 Corinthians 13. He concludes the chapter by illustrating directly the relationship of spiritual gifts to counseling.

As you read this initial section of the book, invite the Holy Spirit to lead you into all the truth He desires to share with you about Himself, about Jesus Christ, and about your ministry in counseling and psychotherapy!

Raymond T. Brock.

1

THE ROLE OF THE HOLY SPIRIT IN INTERPERSONAL RELATIONS

Del Tarr

INTRODUCTION

His hair had not yet grown out to normal length for he had been a disciple in the Hare-Krishna temple at New Orleans. That episode was only the last of a series during a seven-year period in the counter-culture. Drugs, mushrooms, and many forms of hallucinogens were accompanied by experimentation with the occult. His mind was not clear. This tall, thin, young man was in a desperate state of confusion and fear. Surprisingly, he had been reared by missionary parents overseas where he had developed an appreciation for the value structures of many foreign peoples. He was a sensitive and very intelligent young man, and was, in some ways, artistic.

And there he sat with a small group of youth leaders about his own age, uncomfortable, but participating in a conference led by qualified academic notables discussing contemporary New Testament teaching principles. He did not really belong, though in the informality of dress and relaxed mannerisms of the group, he did not stand out. His way had been paid by a Sunday School class which knew of his struggles. He had come unannounced, and in these first sessions he was relatively unknown. That session's teacher recalls that the evening's atmosphere was charged by the sweet but overpowering presence of God. The lesson plan was abandoned as the participants broke into soft singing and intense personal worship.

Another of the guest lecturers, an observer in this session, stood to his feet and asked for the attention of the group. His words were heavy and penetrating, but compassionate: "I have a message from the Lord for someone here tonight." The message was astonishing in an environment of believers and Christian leaders. The details emerged slowly, but when blended together they painted a mosaic describing exactly this troubled young man. It was a picture of his life, his longings, and the heartbreak that he had shared with no one present. Unknown by anyone in the group, he was not even a qualified participant.

The message was clear: "God loves you. He is calling to you because He has not forgotten you." The speaker continued, "You have wondered if there is really a God and yet you are running from Him." Another young man stood to his feet and asked the group to pray for him saying that he was in the midst of a spiritual struggle. The leader thanked him for his honesty and encouraged him to open his life to God, but told him tenderly, yet clearly, that he was not the one to whom the message was directed. "There is someone else," said the man acting as God's prophet. At this statement, the tall, thin young man identified himself as the person fitting the description and acknowledged that, in fact, it could fit no other. The group prayed and administered the grace of God through the supporting hands of sympathizing brothers and sisters in the Lord. It was the beginning of a long road back to mental and spiritual health for a soul on the verge of destruction—to a new life of working out his salvation.

I bring the reader to a different focal point, however, in this story: the guest lecturer. Could such an educated person, with an earned doctorate, be sensitive enough and vulnerable enough to the Spirit of God to know what would be humanly impossible to know? Does the Holy Spirit of God really seek human instruments through which to show His power? Can interpersonal relations be influenced by such a person in contact with God's Spirit?

THE NEED FOR SYMBOLISM

The essence of this chapter is related to the preceding story. It explores the role of the Holy Spirit in interpersonal relations; specifically, how Divine influence might impact the methodology of human communication processes in the life of a Christian counselor.

Theology (Man's words about God) describes God as ultimate; He transcends the realm of finite reality that we inhabit. Thus, no finite reality can express God directly and properly. Whatever we say about God or to God needs to have special meaning and is often best expressed symbolically. Tillich (1958) stated that God must be expressed symbolically because symbolic language alone is able to express the ultimate. The language of faith is the language of symbols.

But modern Man is becoming "symbol-less." Western civilization prides itself in what it calls being "free from superstition"; much of that pride is good. Pragmatists like William James defined a rational way of reasoning and problem-solving. This has helped to lead us away from the errors of a superstitious way of thinking. However, the modern Westerner does not understand the extent of the grip of "rationalism." Rationalism has destroyed our capacity to respond to our own psychic needs for symbolic thinking, and indeed, for symbols themselves.

If we have lost the capacity to react to symbols and to use symbols, then we are at the mercy of a technological world that has dehumanized the spiritual realm. Our moral and spiritual tradition is disintegrating and we now pay the price of separation from the universe around us.

Symbolization was a prominent construct in Jung's (1964) analytic psychology. Jung believed that a sense of wider meaning of one's existence raised one beyond mere getting and spending. Symbolic thinking, related to the supernatural forces of the cosmos, was a vital part of the ancient Judeo-Christian world view. While some of these traits remain as vestiges of modern American or Western thought, the "technicalization" of modern society based upon humankind's rush to be scientific and "objective" has dimmed our senses to the needs of our souls to believe in the God of the supernatural. The traditional belief in their role as sons and daughters of the Father-Spirit provided some of the American Indians (e.g. Pueblo Indians of the southwestern United States) with a perspective and goal that reached beyond their own limited existence. This belief provided a framework for the unfolding of their personality and permitted them a fuller life. Many social scientists would describe the life of the Pueblo Indian as infinitely more satisfying than that of people in our contemporary American cultures.

Modern men and women in a consumer society do not recognize themselves; they have come to believe that they are merely cogs in the machine of life, which has no inner meaning. Evidently, however, those who dare to believe in the Bible seem to find inner solace and strength in life. They achieve this advantage by believing in something beyond themselves: an "ultimate reality" that accepts the supernatural as a necessary part of a balanced, healthy psyche. Many psychologists and anthropologists are reexamining the traditions and belief structures from which Western culture emerged (Eliade, 1965; May, 1960). They are asking questions about why Western civilization seems to have robbed our lives of a needed dimension that can be related to the realm of our spirits. An example of such questioning may be seen in Jung's (1964, p. 89) statement:

> We have never really understood what we have lost for our spiritual leaders unfortunately are more interested in protecting their institutions than in understanding the mystery that symbols present. In my opinion faith does not exclude thought (which is man's strongest weapon).... We have stripped all things of their mystery and numinosity: nothing is holy any longer.

I have lived with the Mossi and the Ewe tribesmen of West Africa and have learned their languages. I have listened to them talk about thunder being the voice of God. I have seen their great fear of the indiscriminating lightening bolts, which they are certain represent judgment upon sinful behavior. I have heard them describe the spirits of rivers, mountains, trees, and the animals that live in the forests. I have heard them talk of voices that speak from rocks, plants, and animals. They have intimate contact with nature. While I do not agree either scientifically or theologically with all of their definitions of their animistic world, I have noted the tremendous emotional energy that this symbolic connection between the supernatural and the natural provides them. While Africans may need help to modify some beliefs in the origins of supernatural phenomena, they certainly do not need me—from the West—to tell them that there are no such powers, or that they should not believe in the supernatural.

In the West, reason tells us that we have "conquered nature." Yet, despite our own reassurances, Westerners are painfully aware that neither our rational religions nor our philosophies are providing us with those powerful, animating ideas, that would, in turn, give us the security needed to face the present world conditions and our own condition in it.

Many modern Christians are not much better off, for they have put their church and the Bible between themselves and their unconscious; between themselves and a belief in the supernatural. In fact, it is now popular to debunk most of the miracles recorded in the Bible—to explain away the supernatural as being irrelevant to their "religious" life. Such Christians, whether Catholic or Protestant, are too concerned with the daily round of buying and selling and learning and becoming up-to-date in this age of consumerism to attend to or to value the supernatural. However, "the meaning of life is not simply explained by one's business life nor is the deep desire of the human heart answered by the bank account" (Jung, 1964, p. 102).

The spiritual renewal experienced in most established denominations during the second half of this century transcends sectarian ecclesiastical parochialism. Hundreds of thousands of Christians, turned off by idols of materialism, are reaching out to the Creator. They want to believe in the supernatural and to allow the Holy Spirit to be their Guide in life. They are searching to find a balance between their desire for the new world of technology and their old needs to be in harmony with the universe.

Pentecostals—or, using the newer term, Charismatics—are people who believe in the supernatural. A belief in the Holy Spirit and His supernatural intervention into the thought process, including the thought processes of a counselor with a client, is seen as mysterious by some. It is perhaps described as spurious by less generous critics. Yet those individuals who can speak and communicate and counsel from a deep consciousness of their role in life as children of God can inject into any interpersonal dialogue and communication event a sense of direction, security, and confidence that others seek.

MAKING ROOM FOR THE SUPERNATURAL IN INTERPERSONAL RELATIONS

Sociologists and anthropologists are interested in noting and attempting to explain how societies (people groupings) divide the elements in their value systems and make sense out of their world. This is known as a "world view." Durkheim, the French father of modern sociology, laid the groundwork for a much used and revised sociological theme. This has come to be known as the dichotomy between the sacred and the profane, or *the sacred and the secular* (Eliade, 1968).

This chapter purports that our technological society tends to dehumanize the individual, especially limiting the concept of what is "sacred." I believe that there is a growing resistance to becoming an unfeeling machine. I can see a movement of people seeking another dimension of reality. It is part of our reaching to touch again the Creator God; we need contact with the supernatural.

One part of the many-faceted group of seekers in the spiritual realm is the traditional Pentecostal movement, which started at the beginning of the 20th Century in America. Its adherents might be accused of lacking academic sophistication in the early years of their existence, but they cannot be accused of neglecting to return to the primitive New Testament beliefs. They are characterized by a willingness to accept the promise of God's Word that Man has the potential of being influenced by the Holy Spirit. The "sacred" has remained very vivid in both theory and practice for Pentecostals. However, they do not pretend to be the only authorities on understanding the Person of the Holy Spirit. Their belief in the enabling of the Holy Spirit makes a difference in their relationships with others, whether on an informal personal level, or on a professional level such as that of counselor and client. The sacredness of this supernatural ingredient, however, demands time and "space" inside the Pentecostal believer's usual secular mode of thinking. Let me illustrate "spiritual space needs" with a parable from the third world.

People on the savannah of West Africa live much closer to the middle eastern lifestyle and in an ecological environment more similar to that of Christ's day than most Westerners imagine. This story illustrates both an event in the Scriptures about Jesus and the present topic.

> An old man was walking down a road near a public school in which the children were playing football (soccer) during the lunch hour. The man was very old and had outlived all his kinfolk, leaving no one to care for him properly. He was hungry and looked about wondering how he might find something to quiet the gnawing pangs of hunger in his stomach.

> Because the soccer game was raising quite a hubbub, and the attention of the children seemed to be on the game, he deftly caught the leg of a rooster near the road and quickly put it into the sack he was carrying on his shoulder. Alas! One of the students saw him and in the typical West African fashion began raising the alarm: "Thief, thief. There is a thief."

> All of the children stopped playing football and ran to the old man and surrounded him, crying out their accusations. The school teacher, who was resting and eating his lunch, heard the noise and came from the school room. He made his way through the students to the old man, addressed him in the honorific due to one of his age, and said, "Papa, what is this noise and what is this accusation I hear?" The old man looked at the teacher intently and replied, "Please look in

this sack with the eye of an old man and see that there is nothing to the students' accusation.''

The teacher removed the bag from the old man's shoulder, opened it and looked inside. Then, with a wave of his hand, he chased the children away and said, "Go back to your game, children. There is no rooster in the sack.''

The children ran off back to the school yard, but the teacher took the old man by the shoulder and guided him to his classroom and shut the door. In the privacy of the room, the teacher admonished the old gentleman for having stolen the rooster. Then he took out some coins from his pocket and gave them to the old man and said, "Go buy yourself something to eat, Papa. What a terrible thing you have done today. You must never do this again.''

The teacher took the rooster and let it out the back door of the classroom and chased it into the field so that the children would not see it. Then he admonished the old gentleman again and sent him on his way.

I find a marked relationship between this parable and the story in the New Testament of Jesus being confronted with the woman taken in adultery. This latter story has long perplexed theologians. When the school teacher in the African parable looked in the sack, he of course saw the rooster. If he would have let the students' acccusation stand, the old man would have been so shamed that, according to African custom, he would have taken his own life before sundown. When the school teacher chased the children away and then admonished the old man privately, he saved the old man's life just as certainly as Jesus saved the life of the adulterous woman—and also saved her soul. Christ, too, chased the children (Pharisees) away; His statement, "he that is without sin amongst you, let him first cast a stone at her'' (John 8:7), has made that story live for two thousand years.

The element that makes both of these stories relevant revolves around the word *withdrawal*. Greenleaf (1977) stated that one of the greatest attributes of a servant leader is the ability to withdraw in the very moment when the whole world is clamoring for a decision—just like the Pharisees and the school children. To look in the bag with the "eye of an old man" was indeed an invitation to the school teacher to seek another answer to the obvious. Greenleaf believed that by stooping to write in the sand Jesus chose to withdraw and reduce the stress right in the middle of the event itself in order to open His awareness to creative insight, and to divert the attention of the men from the woman's shame.

The communicator, the friend, the counselor, the good neighbor—anyone who wants to do good for others—can learn the art of making "space" for the Holy Spirit to function in the mind and perception. These "spaces," or Greenleaf's "areas of withdrawal," do not need to come only from the inspiration of the Holy Spirit. My point is that a quick decision, based on past knowledge and experience and habitual thought patterns, too often crowds out a better, alternative solution. I am clearly affirming my belief that a better solution may be obtained from the supernatural via the Holy Spirit. My experience informs me that the supernatural takes time, requires faith, and sometimes demands great courage.

The scientific mind may not allow this alternative action; after all, Western scientific knowledge is perhaps the highest expression of the linear mode of thinking. Until recently our culture lacked the objectivity which would allow us to consider how another world view could relate the realm of the spiritual to human consciousness. In the East, theories of consciousness and human thought processes have generally entered the relevant disciplines of their societies. Examples of this can be readily found in Hinduism, Buddhism, Yoga, and even some forms of Islam (especially Sufism).

Interestingly, Western science has recently conducted important studies of brain functions. In particular, there has been considerable research conducted on the two cerebral hemispheres and their apparent different relationship to analytical and sequential thinking in the left hemisphere, and synthesis and holistic thinking in the other. These results have led some scientists to conclude that many people in the West have been "disadvantaged" by our propensity to reward left hemisphere thinkers (Bruner, 1962). They claim that we are creating a system that rewards its makers (people who are hyper-analytic, linear, and rational) to the partial exclusion of those who tend to think predominately in the right hemisphere (people who are arational, spacial, and intuitive).

Here is an example of a certain parochialism that is largely cultural, and thus insidious in nature. One is reminded of the classic statement attributed to Maslow (1969): "if the only tool you have is a hammer, you tend to treat everything as if it were a nail." I am not suggesting that an expectation or reliance on the Holy Spirit to help solve people's problems is more closely related to Hinduism or Buddhism than it is to Western ideology. I am suggesting, however, that primitive Christianity with its strong reliance on the sacred and the supernatural is philosophically distant from modern Western thought, even for the modern "evangelical" Christian. Our cultural standards and educational systems have tended to crowd out other possibilities or alternative ways of thinking by their "hammer" of inordinate reliance on Aristotelian, Euclidian, linear logic.

An emphasis upon religious experience—and specifically the role of divine intervention in counseling—necessitates stepping back from the linear "grid," i.e., a deviation from following only the script of learned remedial behavior. Such an emphasis represents a strong attempt to look in the tool chest for a different kind of tool. The procedures of the Spirit-filled counselor/communicator are surely incomprehensible if "comprehension" is restricted to the mode of verbal logic generally taught and practiced in the West.

Someone who has learned to yield to the world of "Holy Spirit consciousness" has tapped another reality outside the province of language and rationality. This shifts from the normal analytical arena, where things occur in sequence and on a line, to a more holistic gestaltic perception. It is not enough for someone simply to have had a "mystical" experience for this ability to accrue. Indeed, the Scriptures clearly talk of "walking in the Spirit" and "being led by the Spirit" (Rom. 8:1, 14; Gal. 5:16). This denotes duration and a learning process, as God the Holy Spirit seeks to teach us to beome like Christ. Spirit-directed living has as its result not a separation from humanity, but deep involvement in interpersonal relationships.

This can be partially accomplished by both the study of and the willful understanding of the cognitive processes of good communication theory. Plus, a heightened awareness of the many dimensions of nonverbal communication must be attained. But the real issue—the central focus of this chapter—is that a realm of competence exists that surpasses human competence; in this realm secular resources are exhausted and the sacred can be utilized. I speak of unusual empathy, understanding, trust (and the encouragement of reciprocal trust) as the Holy Spirit Himself becomes the medium and encouraging environment who allows two or more people engaged in dialogue to flow and resonate together.

Lest I be misunderstood, let me emphasize that I am not speaking of the powers of the occult, or their practices. I do not refer to conjuring of spirits, or attempting to discover information from the dead, or anything associated with the unscriptural practices of necromancy. Here I am specifically talking about the healing of psychological scars, the discovery of solutions to vexing or perplexing problems, the building and solidifying of relationships between family members. To attempt to manipulate the Holy Spirit into becoming the "all seeing eye" and "source of all knowledge" of past, present, and future events is outside of New Testament scriptural guidelines. Later chapters deal with some of the more specific areas of the enabling gifts of the Holy Spirit in communication and counseling; such an explanation is not necessary here.

It may come as a surprise to some to discover that those who rely on the Holy Spirit from an orientation of New Testament practice and belief are not always making noise or being excited and exuberant about their religious experience. A life lived in the realm of Holy Spirit consciousness possesses great breadth and variation. Worship in non-liturgical forms may indeed have more spontaneity and unpredictability than traditional conservative or ecumenical forms. But the critics of Pentecostal worship have been quick to seize upon the visible "noisy" expressions that are only a part—a small part—of the total experience of those who choose to live in the Spirit. The analogy of artists from the Oriental schools of painting and woodcarving can serve as an effective illustration.

The Western person, whether artistically trained or not, is struck by the quantity of empty space remaining on a canvas of a completed Oriental painting. Space for the Oriental is not an absense of something; it is a real entity, a commodity to be used just like any other object in the real world. The Japanese call this concept *ma. Ma* is not to be lightly employed. Think of the last time you saw a Japanese painting. Often a beautiful picture of a bird, a blooming limb from a tree, or a kimono-clad woman will be the central focus of the picture and all around the centerpiece is the emptiness of *ma*. For many Orientals, the Western insistence on "cluttering up" the depictions of nature is an unnecessary bother. Orientals believe it detracts from the central message.

The person who wants to maximize the potential guidance of the Holy Spirit to enhance the ability to understand, communicate, touch, teach, exhort, correct, reprimand, or encourage will find that the Spirit of God often helps one relate to others in dialogue by simply withdrawing and allowing space (like *ma*). The Spirit of God can impress upon the intellect a better meaning, understanding or solution.

The work of the famous Japanese artist, Hokosai, further illustrates this concept. From his early youth until his death at the age of 90, Hokosai created flower and bird prints in a series of wood block prints and canvasses which featured Japan's famous landmark, Mt. Fujiyama. In all of these priceless treasures *allowing space helps to tell the story.*

The story of Elijah in the Old Testament illustrates this concept in his spiritual search for God. The prophet did not find God in the wind or the earthquake or the fire, but in the "still small voice" (1 Kings 19:11, 12). This depicts a relative absence of distracting phenomena impinging on his physical senses. Both the *ma* and the "still small voice" illustrate how one might allow the Holy Spirit to permeate human experience and lead to a dependency on another dimension of reality—the operation of the Holy Spirit in the life of the counselor.

INTERPERSONAL RELATIONS AND COMMUNICATION

The discipline of communications has undergone vast changes in the last two decades, moving from *speech,* as its old designation (where it was largely influenced by and classified as one of the humanities), to the new influence of the behavioral and social sciences. This is quite a shift! "How to talk to people and how to interrelate with people" was often the topic reserved for speech teachers. Speech as a discipline traditionally concerned itself with the content of the message. This, no doubt, naturally developed because of the great emphasis placed on the speaker and the acquisition of language skills by educational systems. When one considers the thousands of hours in a normal lifetime that are spent learning to speak and spell correctly, to construct sentences, to understand grammar, syntax, artful composition, colorful visual imagery and all of the related skills, it is no small wonder that the performance of the speaker has predominately centered around *what* was being said rather than *who* received the message.

The modern discipline of communications has moved from content orientation to audience-centeredness. Thankfully, a number of years ago, communicators began to realize that the perception of meaning is not truly in words; it is *in people*. Modern communication theory consequently is helping us become much more effective "meaning makers." Thus, in preparing to speak or write (i.e. transfer meaning from one person to another), the meaning-maker concentrates on the perceptual field and world view of the *audience*, whether it is one person or a hundred. This audience-centeredness naturally leads to a new and different emphasis in the art of communication. We are now ready to inspect closely how knowledge of the process of communications will add to the thesis of this chapter.

COMMUNICATIONS THEORY

You may have heard the old joke about the two men who met again after not seeing each other for twenty years. They had been very close friends in their youth. After the usual pleasantries and exclamations of how good it was to see each other again, one man inquired of the other man's wife and asked, "How's Mary?" The response from his old friend was, "Oh, don't you know? Mary's in heaven." To this, the first man reacted with sudden emotion by saying, "Oh, I'm so sorry!" He then tried to recover, realizing that it did not sound right to say that he was sorry that Mary was in heaven. His next statement did not ameliorate the situation at all as he said, "I guess I should say that I'm happy." He then flushed with embarrassment, realizing that it might sound like he was happy that Mary was dead. He tried unsuccessfully to recover from his predicament with, "What I really mean is I'm surprised!"

The word "run" in American English has at least ninety distinct meanings. A foreigner learning the American language is amazed to find the great number of choices available for that one word. Much of language usage is similar; this prompts me to present a simple communication model. Communication models have evolved rapidly in the past twenty years. Models and graphs help Westerners represent in visual form our linear mode of "meaning making." The model presented on page 16 is adapted from Ross (1974) and Brembeck and Howell (1976). In my opinion, it is a succinct and clear representation of the problem we all face in talking. The model explains why people constantly misunderstand each other, even though the words they employ might be common words.

No one practices good ccommunication naturally. We have to work very hard to communicate well, and even then misunderstanding is inevitable. This model illustrates communication between two individuals, but the principles would also be valid for a larger group.

As in the old joke above, friend A and friend B had many different meanings in their minds for the words *death, sad, happy*, and *surprised*. Though neither of them would have to look these words up in a dictionary to give a definition, the fact that true meaning resides in the mind or perceptual field of people, and not in words, is perhaps the largest single reason why misunderstandings occur

Figure 1

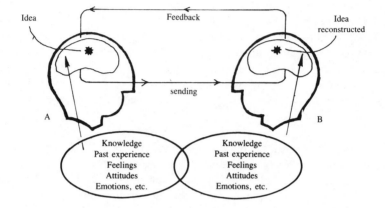

in communication for all people—not just friends A and B.

Suppose that a male counselor (person A in the model) desires to speak with a male client (person B) who is suicidal. The counselor uses words that he has already internalized and which in his own mind represent assigned meaning or meanings (the * idea in the model). Not all words have as many meanings as the word "run," yet all it takes is for a word to have two or three different assigned meanings for a potential misunderstanding to exist. This is called a person's *fan of perception.*

Because the client also has a fan of perception that probably differs from the counselor's, the counselor must not make the common error of believing that meaning is in words. That common error would lead him to believe that all he must do is choose common words and the client will understand.

What is in a person's *fan of perception?* Hundreds of thousands of ideas (meanings-concepts) attached to electrical neurons somewhere in the complex cell structure of the brain. The culture-language system has *assigned* symbols (words) to those ideas. Because all learning is metaphorical, where all new things must be related to old things, the *fan of perception* is full of meaning separated into thousands of categories. Each society and its particular language structure determines for its members what phonetical sound or sight system is used to "tag" or identify a meaning in the person's mind. This model describes the mass of meaning with such words as attitudes, feelings, past experiences, knowledge, etc., for each individual in the culture or subculture. These big value words act as transitors or filters through which incoming information is decoded and put in the proper bin or slot in the mind—much like a person sorts the mail into "boxes."

Any person acting as a source of communication encodes from a perceptual fan by selecting and sorting through a "file box," and then a message is sent.

Figure 2

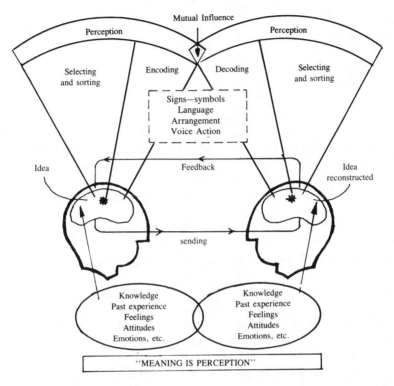

The listener decodes the message by selecting and sorting it in an attempt to reconstruct the idea. Only if some mutual influence (shared meaning) occurs do we say that real communication has taken place. Let us examine a hypothetical event in the communication between counselor and suicidal client to illustrate this process.

The counselor wants to talk about the word "God." The counselor is a Christian and has a well-developed and positive concept of God. Suppose the counselor has a wonderful father who treated him with love, respect, and responsibility. Psychologically, we know that the person who served as the father-symbol in the counselor's youth made a great impact on his idea and perception of what God is like. Suppose the suicidal client, however, experiences quite a different decoding pattern. In his perception, the concept "God" is perceived through the memory of a father who was often drunk, who was a wife-beater, and who often abused the client and his siblings. The communication model states, "meaning is perception." The perceptual meaning for the word "God" in the client is obviously going to be quite different than that of the counselor. The counselor, then, must take time either to find out what the client has in his "meaning box" for the word "God" or he must try to influence the client to comprehend the counselor's category for "God" before *comm-uni-cation* (making the meaning common) can transpire.

Good communication can only happen when the idea that the counselor has in mind can be reproduced in the mind of the client with sufficient similarity for mutual understanding to occur. Responsibility for successful communication in this transaction obviously rests with the counselor. The counselor must not make the mistake of assuming that if he says "God loves you" that there will be any similarity between what the counselor encodes (intends) and what the client decodes (understands). The counselor may value God and have a warm understanding of what His love is. The client, on the other hand, may believe that God is unfair, unjust, and exploitative. If he does not explicitly hate God, talking about "God" may elicit feelings of perplexity, anxiety, or even fear.

You will note that the model shows verbal and nonverbal feedback occurring in all communication events. Suppose that the counselor did not try to attend to the perception of the client, and simply spoke the words, "God loves you." If the counselor had any sensitivity at all, he would probably see the client frown or cast his eyes to the side or down; he might even shake his head or verbally challenge or question the counselor's statement. This "feedback" should immediately show the counselor that he had encoded improperly vis-à-vis the client's *fan of perception* of the word "God." The counselor should then *re-code* the message—perhaps by choosing some other words—or take another tack altogether. The counselor/communicator takes the time to learn about the client so that when he encodes and speaks about God and His love, a way can be found to break through the values, attitudes, stereotypes, and past experiences of the client so as to evade much misunderstanding.

In this sense, the counselor who is "walking in the Spirit" has a decided advantage. Listen to the Apostle Paul in 1 Corinthians 2:11-12; it looks as if he had studied this communication model!

> No one can really know what any one else is thinking or what he is really like, except that person himself. And no one can know God's thoughts except God's own Spirit. And God has actually given us His Spirit (not the world's spirit) to tell us about the wonderful, free gifts of grace and blessing that God has given us. In telling you about these gifts we have even used the very words given to us by the Holy Spirit, in words that we as men might choose. So we use the Holy Spirit's words to explain the Holy Spirit's facts. *(Living Bible)*

Amazing! Paul clearly said that in doing God's business we can expect the Holy Spirit to help us with word-choice to get inside the *fan of perception* of our audience so that "mutual influence" can occur. Paul closed this passage with words of encouragement and wonder at the seeming miracle of it all. "But strange as it seems, we Christians actually do have within us a portion of the very thoughts and mind of Christ" (1 Cor. 2:16, *Living Bible*).

THE HOLY SPIRIT IN NONVERBAL AWARENESS

Inside of the relatively new interdisciplinary subject of speech communications is the even more recently developed subfield of nonverbal communications. Third world and/or preliterate societies (developing nations without written languages) have not developed the emphasis of the Western world on literacy and literariness. They might be termed aural/oral societies. In these areas of the world the spoken word is much more important than it is in literary societies of both the East and West. To the extent that aural/oral societies are underdeveloped in their literary distinction, most are fully developed in their use and practice of nonverbal communication. For these people—in Asia or Africa, the Pacific Islands or the Indian population of South and Central America—there is, running parallel to oral language, another language of nonverbal communication. Many times the *agendum* for a particular speech or communication event resides in the nonverbal element.

Again, the literary linearity of the West inhibits us from perceiving this significance. We tend to be somewhat illiterate in our own nonverbal communication systems. This is not because we are any less capable of understanding these more subtle systems; it is only that we have lost a part of the older world. Many in the modern industrialized West have become insensitive to the forces of nature that previous generations knew so well.

Nonverbal awareness in communication is related to the intuitive side of human beings. This type of knowledge may be contrasted with the analytical aspect of knowing, which is the type of knowing we have stressed most in our educational processes. Some counselors, especially Gestalt therapists (e.g. Perls, 1969), have encouraged their followers to become keenly aware of the nonverbal behavior of their clients. "What is your body telling you?" "What is the tone of your voice saying?" These are typical questions a counselor may use to help a client focus on nonverbal message systems.

Interpersonal understanding is greatly enhanced if we are first aware of another side of each of us. The Holy Spirit can help the believer develop these abilities. The Spirit will enhance what has been learned in the formal study and application of communication theory. But beyond human education and academic preparation, the Holy Spirit will supernaturally use natural cognitive preparation and competencies if our motive is to bring others to a knowledge of Christ and His Kingdom.

However, only when we are willing to develop another side of our consciousness can the Holy Spirit maximize our own natural abilities. I emphasize again that Western thinking tends to be related to the left hemisphere of the brain; the tendency is to filter everything through a linear, mechanistic world view. The mathematical, literal side of our *formal* training and our *informal* culturalization limit our perceptual skills, unless we are willing to back away from our left hemisphere "computer-type thinking." In no other way can our right hemisphere—our more intuitional potential—be developed. If we are willing to forego the need to categorize and label an individual quickly (especially from first impressions), we can develop our natural understanding of nonverbal communication and also learn to sharpen our interpersonal sensitivity.

To summarize, we must resist trying to interpret everything from the more external visible cues ordinarily conveyed in verbalized language. Here the believer can ask the Holy Spirit to fill in the *deliberate* space; the space the believer has allowed "around the edge of the painting." Can competent professionals, sincere lay counselors, and clergymen learn to attenuate the volume of their normal sensory systems to develop the new dimension (and enabling) of the Spirit? We must if we, as Christian believers, are to be effective counselor/communicators.

COLLIDING WORLDS

The scene is West Africa; the days are enormously hot and hostile. Dust from the Sahara desert filters down through the air everywhere. The evenings are beautiful as the burning yellow ball in the sky descends, casting delicate pastel colors on the landscape. Suddenly, it is night. The dry air cools rather quickly and those of us accustomed to more temperate climes find this a good time to work and study and visit.

On one such full moonlit night my shortwave radio told me of the escapades of the U.S. astronauts as they actually walked and cavorted on the moon. I had been reading for weeks about this important space shot which most of the modern world was watching via television. A large portion of what we term the preliterate world had also been listening to their transistor radios and had been contemplating it, even if not clearly understanding. And such it was on the night of one of the early moon landings. Gathered around me in the darkness were many African friends—neighbors I had come to know and love. We sat with our backs against the warm mud bricks, which had retained the heat of the day's horrible sun. We sat looking at the moon. In the distance drumming and dancing could be heard. Our conversation drifted from the usual topics to what I had recently heard on the radio from a shortwave station in Europe. It described strangely clad men walking on the surface of the bright ball we could all see from where we were sitting.

I began to explain about the force of gravity (no easy task in an African vernacular which does not contain much sophisticated scientific jargon). I tried to tell about the special car that had been created at great cost so that the astronauts could cover a great distance on the moon. The Africans were amazed at what mankind has been able to do. They shook their heads; third world people often wonder how other nations can be so advanced technologically while they seem to be left so far behind. And yet, were not these people around me human beings, just like those walking on the moon? If one of them would say to me, "You told me man can go the moon. I am a man, send me," how could I explain to him all he would need to do and learn to prepare for a moon walk? How could I tell him that, while he has a head, two feet, two hands, two eyes and a nose, just like the men walking on the moon, he also is lacking many things which would take a long time for him to learn? Would he be willing to pay that price even if someone were willing to finance it for him? Would he have the capacity to learn, now that he is already an adult? Could he accomplish the enormous task of someday walking on the moon? In comparison to the sophisticated, competent moonwalker, isn't my African friend really someone from another world?

One is reminded of the words of the Apostle Paul where he talked about the natural human being not receiving the things of the Spirit of God, for they are spiritually discerned and in its natural state humanity cannot really perceive correctly (1 Cor. 2:14). How do you explain the relationship of experience and belief? It is most difficult to tell professional counselors that there is a realm of reality—a consciousness—that they have never touched. Their specialization has itself excluded them from easily perceiving it! They have habitually attenuated a part of their own human capacity by the very nature of their learning and experience. The education which led them through linearity (Western cognitive processes) excludes another way of "knowing."

Now, let me tell *such a* person that there exists a realm of "knowing" by the help of God's Spirit, where it is possible to "unhitch" the usual way of *understanding.* This task may be akin to telling the African sitting near me in the dark that, though he is physically like the moonwalker, he lacks many skills and perception. Let us not despair, however. Christ said, "He that seeketh, findeth" (Luke 11:10). The knowledge of the Spirit comes to those who are first born of Him and then seek to learn to "walk in Him." Contrast this gift of God with the obligation to conform solely to the paradigms of the intellect that filter experience only through the gate-keepers of past experience, knowledge, and attitudes.

RESONATE TO COMMUNICATE

One of the characteristics of a good communicator is the ability to influence the cognitive and affective aspects of the audience. Professional marketing research analysts boldly tell us how to sell a product or idea to the American market by using psychological persuasion. These analysts sell their findings to media producers, some of whom make the television commercials which flood our screens. Research presented by these professionals is sometimes frightening; it can be manipulative because the human thinking processes have become well-known in the last few decades. Commercials that sell find a way to "resonate" with the beliefs and value structures of a high percentage of their target audience.

Schwartz (1974) illustrated modern communication methods related to the media on this topic. Schwartz stated that when the string of a guitar is plucked in the vicinity of a piano, the particular wave length vibration of the string "sounding" will create a sympathetic dynamic vibration on the piano string tuned to the same tone of the guitar. This is known as resonance. The reader may know people who are skilled in communicating and who, it seems, are able to "affect," invisibly and unconsciously, the interest and motivation of those listening. This analogy of resonance enhances the previous analogies of Spirit-related interpersonal relationships.

I believe that God created mankind for His purpose and joy. He wants to communicate and reestablish fellowship with His creation. In that pursuit, He has chosen to use other "beings" (not angels) as instruments of His divine power. As a Spirit-filled believer, I accept His command to be a witness for Him (Acts 1:8). I also can expect that the Holy Spirit will help me to "resonate," to reach out and touch the need in someone's life! I see this avenue as a direct possibility of how God's Spirit in the life of a counselor can lead a client to growth and conflict resolution in a way not possible in the natural.

How comforting to know that the Spirit is available for a professional counselor working with those needing to modify their behavior, or to a housewife talking to a friend over the back fence, or to a teen-ager seeking to share the positive nature of the Kingdom with school friends. The Holy Spirit will take our abilities, studied skills, and accumulated wisdom and add His own enablement that will utilize—but go beyond—our own natural talents and learned abilities. He thus gives us an added edge so we can touch and minister and bless (resonate and "contaminate"[1]).

HELP IN LISTENING

The Holy Spirit not only helps us as the source communicator in an interpersonal event, He also abides to help us listen and understand (decode). In fact, there are times when this element is more important than any other. Listening is related to what was previously stated about "withdrawal." Too often, the Church militant has been depicted as a tactless bull in a china shop. It must be understood that the role of the Holy Spirit in interpersonal relations is not only active but passive as well.

The usual intellectual channel of thinking can only recognize what is familiar. That fact makes anything unfamiliar often unrecognizable, or it at least stimulates the need to *make* something recognizable. Frequently, this leads to a distortion of the intent of the symbol used by the source. As we grow, learn, and mature, our left hemisphere also becomes one of the greatest barriers to effective learning. Thus, we become intellectually apathetic when confronted with something new. We tend to prefer the old, habitual pigeon-holes; we make judgments too quickly about where to put incoming information. We make listening errors when we overuse the habitual categories.

It is better if we "let the jury deliberate" a little longer, continuing the cue-search to make a more appropriate judgment about which "bin" or "file" to use for identification and classification. We have all met people who continually misunderstand us because of the disease called "hardening of the categories." If we should try to talk to them about a topic which they do not understand or about which they have inadequate knowledge, they will quickly generalize and "pigeon-hole" (we all love to do this), thus blocking a fuller explanation, which might have produced a better final categorization. What should we do when we discover that someone is an atheist? Should we immediately define that person by that single category? Probably not. We must realize that we need a perceptual file with many tabs or "files" for "atheists". There are no two alike! I have had to go back to people more than once—embarrassed—to modify my original opinion because I spent energy on quickly filing them away in my classification system instead of really listening to them.

In Matthew 18, Christ exhorted us to "be converted and become as little children." The lesson here is not only about guile, simplicity, or being malleable, as we often hear stated, but it is also about *perception*. A child's file system is *growing* and is not very ego-involved. Jesus' words indict our habitual system of perception as inadequate. He talked often of deafened ears and covered eyes (Matt. 13). Why? Because His own people *thought they KNEW* what the Messiah was to be, but their eyes and ears could not make room for new belief. They did not listen or perceive; old habits of perception—"hardening of the categories"—limited their vision. But the Master turned to His disciples and said, "blessed are your ears for they hear". To the same group, He stated that when the Holy Spirit had come, "He will lead you into all truth" (John 16:13). Blessed Holy Spirit, You are available!

Please consider that when Christ admonished His disciples and hearers to become as little children, He was inviting them to become like children in perception; children who have not yet filled their life with habituated categorizations. The Spirit-led person can become like a little child and bypass some of the model-building tendencies of the person who categorizes too quickly. Instead, the Spirit-led individual allows the Spirit to give hints or cues about perceiving and understanding another person in a communication event.

Christ was a master communicator. In Mark 13, Christ instructed His disciples not to plan every minute detail of what they were going to say in the event that they were called before kings and magistrates. He was obviously telling them that if they tried to follow the map (the prepared script) too closely, they would not be free to listen to promptings and cues of the Holy Spirit. If we can only break the restraints of our "map following," we will be freed from the usual in favor of the unusual. Thus, the Holy Spirit can help the teacher, counselor, or friend to make an "end run" around the usual answers that are stored—learned and prepackaged—in the mind. Thus a mode of interpersonal communication is available which is not normally achieved by the firing of neurons associated with the word-object mechanism of the brain.

Summary

I have not assumed that every reader accepts as a "given" that the Holy Spirit as described in the New Testament exists, or desires to influence humanity. Nonetheless, I must and do believe both of these presuppositions in order to attempt to write about the Holy Spirit and His relation to the supernatural.

Sharpening our sensitivities to His subtle and gentle capacity to influence our effective communications is one way He wants to be the "paraclete"—our helper who "stands along side" (see Chapter 2). If the Holy Spirit already knows the content of the perceptual fan of our target audience, then He can help us "resonate" with that person effectively and personally. Come, teach us, O Holy Spirit!

[1]To pursue the topic of *resonance* in interpersonal relations, see Lamb (1965, pp. 137ff.). He introduced the word "contaminator" to describe individuals who have special natural powers, usually described as someone with a magnetic personality. Lamb felt that probably the biggest "contaminator" of all time was Jesus Christ.

2

THE HOLY SPIRIT AS THE PARACLETE:
MODEL FOR COUNSELORS

William W. Menzies

INTRODUCTION

A fundamental message of the Bible proclaims that the Holy Spirit desires to assist all believers in the discovery of ways for living the Christian life to its highest potential. This includes equipping believers for fulfilling important ministries necessary for doing God's will in this world. What the Bible teaches us about the personality and activity of the Holy Spirit offers a remarkable example for the counselor.

One may define counseling as a specially devised relationship in which one person, through knowledge and experience, serves to guide another through a process of clarification and resolution of basic life-problems. This is a specialized form of "helping" people. We will explore in this chapter the special role that the Third Person of the Trinity plays in this "helping" process.

THE PARACLETE

It is exclusively in John's writings that the Holy Spirit is referred to as *paraklētos* or "paraclete." This word, found commonly in extra-biblical writings in the Hellenistic age, had a legal connotation. It referred to a person who was a "helper in court," one who filled the role of advocate, petitioner, advisor, defender, or counselor. In the New Testament, this legal usage does not exhaust the meaning attached to that term. It is true that in 1 John 2:1, the single passage in which *paraklētos* is used of Christ, the courtroom inference is quite clear. Also, in the Gospel of John it occasionally carries this legal connotation (see e.g., John 15:26; 16:7–11). However, such passages as John 14:16 convey a much broader meaning. We might translate that verse to read something like this: "And I will ask the Father, and He will give to you another Helper to be with you forever" (Behm, 1967). As we shall see, Jesus promised the Holy Spirit would abide with believers to aid them in an amazing variety of ways in a whole range of life-situations. The Holy Spirit, then, would seem to be of a particular significance for the ministry of counseling, which we have defined as a specialized form of "helping."

In the passage just cited, John 14:16, Jesus told His disciples that He would send *allon paraklēton,* "another Helper." This tells us that Jesus Christ was sent into the world as the initial *paraklētos* and that the One whom Jesus would send would be of the same essence as Himself. Therefore, the "Second Helper" would be not merely a vague, impersonal force in the universe, but He would in fact be personal and, like Christ Jesus, fully God.

Ephesians 1:3–14 pictures what might be called a distinction in functions within the Persons of the Trinity. God the Father is described (vv. 3–5) as the One who conceived the plan of world redemption before time began. God the Son (vv. 6–12) is featured as the central agent effecting the plan of world redemption. The last two verses speak of the Holy Spirit as the Person within the Godhead who applies the fruits of the finished work of Christ to the created order until the end of time. The Holy Spirit, then, since the resurrection and exaltation of Christ to the Father's right hand, is the "down payment" of the Coming Age; He brings reality into our confused and broken age! What Jesus—the First Helper—accomplished, the Holy Spirit—the Second Helper—was dispatched to make vivid and real. He is to apply the fruits of that achievement to mankind (Schweizer, 1978).

God's method is incarnational. Jesus came into the world (John 1:14; Phil. 2:5–9), but when His earthly mission was completed, He went away. He came as God visualized, localized. As Luther said, "Infinity was compressed into finitude." But, with the mission of Jesus accomplished, a new era was dawning. This new era would be marked by the presence of the Holy Spirit. God the Spirit would make the blessings of Calvary available on a universal scale! On the Day of Pentecost, Peter recognized that what the prophets had anticipated had now come (Ladd, 1974)! No longer would the Holy Spirit be available to and minister through only a select few individuals on particular occasions, as was true in Old Testament times; rather, the Helper would be poured out "on all flesh" (Acts 2:17). The incarnational principle is now operative in a new dimension. God's method is to fill believers with His Holy Spirit to accomplish His mission in this world! Can you see why Jesus attached so much importance to His sending of the Holy Spirit into the world upon His return to the Father? Now Jesus is our great intercessor (Heb. 7:25), but the Holy Spirit has been sent into the world as the vivid presence of God among us!

We will explore various ways in which this wonderful Helper actually is available to believers today, particularly in the context of counseling. His Person and activity are in a real sense a model for Christian counselors. We shall see, however, that it is not always easy to distinguish what the Holy Spirit does *for* the counselor from what He does *through* the counselor.

REACHING OUT

Jesus told His wondering disciples on the night before His crucifixion, "But

I tell you the truth: It is for your good that I am going away. Unless I go away, the Counselor will not come to you; but if I go, I will send him to you'' (John 16:7, NIV). Jesus promised to send the Holy Spirit to them so that they would not be alone. He was teaching them that in the Era of the Spirit, the mighty presence of God would be immediately available to believers at any time or place, through the special ministry of the Holy Spirit. Jesus is the ''sender'' of the Spirit.

Historical Perspective

Jesus announced that the Father would send the Spirit (John 14:26). So it is that both Father and Son are pictured as sending the Spirit into the world. In the centuries immediately following the Apostolic Age, the leaders of the Church were preoccupied with basic questions, such as ''How can God be One Being, but consist of three centers of personality?'' The ''sending'' of the Spirit was employed by these early scholars to picture the interpersonal relationships within the Godhead—the Holy Spirit eternally ''proceeding'' from the Father. So, early creeds, such as Chalcedonian Formula and the Athanasian Creed employed this language, attempting thereby to demonstrate strong confidence in the full deity of the Holy Spirit. There were others in that day who taught that the Holy Spirit was somehow subordinate to the Father and the Son. The language of ''eternal procession'' seemed to ensure the concept of equality of being within the Godhead. Apparent differences within the personalities of the Godhead were understood by orthodox Christians from that time onward to be functional, not essential.

So it was that by A.D. 451, with the adoption of the Chalcedonian Formula, both the Eastern and Western wings of the Church accepted the terminology of the eternal procession of the Holy Spirit from God the Father. The Western Church in A.D. 589 added what is called the ''filioque'' clause to the creed, adding ''and the Son,'' so that the Holy Spirit is stated to proceed eternally from both Father ''and the Son.'' The significance of this is that it establishes a strong connection between the work of the incarnate Christ and the work of the Spirit, so that life in the Spirit is perceived as necessarily flowing out of a relationship with Christ. Pentecostals and Evangelicals eagerly say ''amen'' to this, recognizing that such a statement echoes biblical teaching.

Fortunately this question about the ''procession'' of the Spirit was dealt with by early leaders. We do not have to redefine continually the nature of the Trinity in every generation, thanks to the care with which earnest scholars addressed this issue long ago. However, in their preoccupation with the question of the Trinity, they seem to have missed an important point. The ancient Church said very little about the mission of the Spirit in the world (Menzies, 1979; Morris, 1971). But, did not Jesus say, ''I will send Him *to you*'' (John 16:7)? In a very real sense, since the outpouring at Pentecost, the Holy Spirit, has been ''heaven's missionary'' in the world. He has come to abide with us (John 15). Through His gentle, persuasive ministry people are awakened, convicted, regenerated, sanctified, anointed for service, and in many other ways refreshed and blessed.

The most wonderful gift Jesus could give His disciples was the Holy Spirit. The love of God is expressed not only by the incarnation and sacrificial death of Christ, important as this "divine invasion" is, but also by the sending of the Holy Spirit. God, by nature, therefore, is One-who-reaches-out. Just as Christ came to seek and to save that which was lost (Luke 19:10), so the Holy Spirit has been given to help us in our infirmities (Rom. 8:26). The startling truth is that God does not really need us; He is complete in Himself. But, His loving nature is exhibited in reaching out to the whole created order to redeem and to restore. In this important sense, God the Spirit becomes a model for us. The counselor is called upon to be a special kind of missionary, reaching out to those who hurt. He is to be an agent of reconciliation (2 Cor. 5:18-20).

The Personal Paraclete

The Holy Spirit is personal. That is, He possesses attributes of intellect, emotion, and will. First Corinthians 2:10 tells us: "The Spirit searches all things, even the deep things of God" (NIV); this demonstrates the intellectual activity of the Spirit. The Holy Spirit may be grieved (Eph. 4:30), which is evidence of emotionality. He exercises self-determination; He distributes gifts as He chooses (1 Cor. 12:11), which affords evidence of volition.

The Holy Spirit is pictured throughout Scripture as engaging in activity appropriate to persons. He speaks (John 16:13), He teaches (John 14:26), He bears witness (John 15:26), He is creative (Gen. 1:2), and He persuades (Gen. 6:3; John 16:8).

To the foregoing could be added a whole catalog of additional evidences to support the contention that the Holy Spirit is personal. There is one quality, however, that bears special attention because of the implications to be derived for the ministry of counseling. The Holy Spirit is *gentle*.

We have already emphasized that God reaches out. This is love in action. However, because God is personal, this means that He deals with other persons (including us), in a noncoercive way. He respects the integrity of personhood in each of us. Although He is not wanting any to perish (2 Pet. 3:9), and extends a gracious invitation to "whosoever will" (John 3:16), God the Spirit ministers by *gentle* persuasion, not compulsion (John 16:8-11). And, He can be grieved (Eph. 4:30). This means that persistent resistance can eventually drive away the tender ministry of the Holy Spirit. Evidently this is what Paul referred to in Romans 1:18-32, where he pointed out the disaster that befalls those who harden their hearts. So it is with the Christian counselor. A counselor can be effective only as he or she is a noncoercive, accepting, and responding friend. The responsible counselor cannot force ministry on an unwilling client, indeed, one must be supportive and helpful, not ruthless and domineering.

One other matter merits attention in this connection. Because the Holy Spirit is *gentle*, not forcing Himself on anyone—even believers—a whole realm of life in the Spirit exists that is available *only to those who ask* (Harper, 1981). In teaching His disciples to pray, Jesus carefully instructed them to repeat what we have come to call "The Lord's Prayer" (Luke 11:2-4). But what is often overlooked are the following verses, where Jesus taught His disciples to pray persistently and earnestly. But, for what purpose? *To receive the Holy Spirit* (Luke 11:15). The best thing the Lord could do for His disciples was to show them how to enter into the Spirit-energized life. For a very long time, many earnest Christians were taught that all that God had for them came with New Birth. Now, a great host of believers are discovering that the gentle Holy Spirit will *fill* believers with His presence, if they ask in faith. This baptism in the Spirit, described in at least five places in the Book of Acts, is not the same thing as New Birth, although on occasion it might occur almost simultaneously (Harper, 1981).

Because the Holy Spirit is personal, we should not expect His full blessing to occur mechanically or automatically (Marshall, 1978). Thus, it is highly appropriate to seek God for all He has promised in order to equip us for the tasks of life. Counselors, then, should continually seek to model their lives after the *gentle* Spirit. And, because He is personal, we should expect it necessary to seek His counsel and blessing in the fulfillment of the counseling ministry, expecting that He will invade the need-situation with His power, as we invite Him.

THE PARACLETE'S CENTER OF ATTENTION

"He will bring glory to me by taking from what is mine and making it known to you" (John 16:14, NIV). This statement by Jesus provides evidence that the work of the Spirit centers in Christ. The Holy Spirit draws attention, not to Himself, but to Christ. His mission is to glorify Christ. One might picture this as a manifestation of the interpersonal expression of love within the Triune Godhead. As Christ sends the Spirit into the world, so reciprocally the Spirit glorifies Christ in the world. His ministry is built upon the finished work of Christ and is a necessary sequel to this fact (Williams, 1971). There is no division within the Godhead. The next verse (15) affirms that whatever belongs to the Father belongs to Christ. It is highly appropriate, then, that whatever belongs to the Father and the Son is made available to believers through the ministry of the Spirit.

All of history points to the Cross and the Empty Tomb where Christ Jesus triumphed over everything that destroys; including Satan himself. The mission of the Holy Spirit is to point people to Christ, the propitiation for the sins of the world (Rom. 3:25). The Holy Spirit is consistently identified in the New Testament as the agent of regeneration, or New Birth, but this activity of the Spirit presupposes the prior work of Christ, the Redeemer. Without the achievement of the incarnate Christ, the Holy Spirit's task would not be meaningful. There is a marvelous interplay between the roles of the Father, Son, and Spirit in bringing deliverance to suffering mankind.

Some years ago, the great British Pentecostal leader, Donald Gee, was asked by a friend, "What would you say, Brother Gee, is the main meaning to you of the baptism in the Holy Spirit?" His response was, "the Holy Spirit has made Jesus very, very real to me." This is a way of saying that the ministrations of the Spirit inevitably point to Christ.

What special significance does this have for counseling? First, we would do well to model our ministry to others on the "Christocentric" principle. This does not mean that we will not discover fresh ways of introducing people to the Person and work of the Holy Spirit—after all, for so long He has been the neglected person in the Godhead—but, we will ever be mindful that our primary task is to bring people into vital contact with the Redeemer, the risen Lord. All the blessings of heaven are mediated to us through the work of Christ. This means that the Christian counselor will allow nothing to divert any primary objectives away from the "healing center," Christ Jesus Himself. Even on those occasions when a client may be encouraged to seek earnestly to be filled with the Spirit, the counselor must always insist that the client keep a mind focused on the Giver—Christ—and not on any blessings or feelings that may be associated with the giving of spiritual gifts (Horton, 1976).

One additional implication should be observed. The counselor does well to acknowledge that training in psychological theory and clinical techniques offers no guarantee of adequate strength or wisdom to "give" help to a client. Optimum functioning occurs when the counselor plays the role of a catalyst in the healing process. Just as the Holy Spirit does not draw attention to Himself, so the counselor must (or should) humbly stand aside, pointing the client to the One who alone has the power to deal with the fundamental problems of humanity. In this way it is possible to bring into play the skills of the trained counselor to help clients clarify their needs, while creating an environment in which the deepest inner needs may be met by the Lord. This stance can set the counselor free—knowing that performing the impossible is not expected. Rather, the counseling task is circumscribed within the appropriate boundaries of this Christocentric understanding.

WHOLENESS

"I have come that they may have life, and have it to the full" (John 10:10, NIV). Jesus expressed this truth while teaching about His role as the Good Shepherd. Abundant living is possible only through the death of the Shepherd, He tells us (John 10:14). God intends that we be fully alive. Paul supplied a vivid contrast between the subexistence of the unregenerate person and the infusion of new life for those who are saved by faith through grace (Eph. 2:1–10). Jesus came to make abundant living possible; this is God's grace manifested. Faith is the response which opens the door to the new life in Christ (Eph. 2:8–9). But, the activity of the Spirit actually applies the work of Christ to the individual believer

(John 3:5-6). He gives life and ministers *wholeness* to people.

A Psychological View

Psychologists use such terms as "integration of personality" to describe properly functioning human beings, persons who are characterized by the resolution of inner conflict. William Glasser (1965) has sought to recover a definition of wholeness as the ability to accept responsibility for one's own behavior. Such definitions of wholeness have good biblical bases. For example, Titus 2:12 employs a term to describe vital Christian living in the present age, a term translated in the NIV as "self-controlled." This word carries the notion of "marshalling of one's energies in a single direction." In effect, this is not unlike the concept of an integrated personality. And, certainly Glasser's goal of bringing an individual to the level of maturity at which responsibility for life could be accepted has repeated and overwhelming support throughout the Scriptures. God deals with us as responsible beings from beginning to end. This is a worthy goal which Christian counselors should set before themselves in dealing with hurting people.

Inner Wholeness

In the Christian life, one aspect of wholeness needs to be mentioned which might be phrased the "two-dimensional life in the Spirit." First, the Holy Spirit engages in an "interior" ministry. This begins with regeneration and continues by means of the indwelling Spirit who conforms us increasingly to the image of Christ. Another word for this is sanctification (see Lovelace, 1979); that is, the continuous process by which the Holy Spirit convicts believers of sin and monitors their lives against the standard of the life of Christ. Galatians 5:16-18 picture the important role of the Holy Spirit in this quiet and unobtrusive task of making us to *become* what we *are* in Christ. We can foster this process daily, through a devotional life which makes abundant room for reading the Bible, the mirror of the soul (James 1:23), and for prayer, which is talking and listening to God.

All of the noble virtues of the fruit of the Spirit (Gal. 5:22, 23) are really various aspects of love, the chief mark of the Christian. It would not be improper to say that the goal of sanctification is to bring God's people into a full understanding and experience of love. There is no fear in love (1 John 4:18). Perfect love drives out fear. Talk about therapy! The counselor will do well to pray for discovering ways of cooperating with the Sanctifier—the Holy Spirit.

Expressive Wholeness

The interior dimension, sanctification, is an important feature of the work of the Holy Spirit. As vital as this function in the Christian life is, it does not exhaust the full range of the Spirit's possibilities for the believer. John 7:37-39 tell of a dramatic moment in the life of Jesus. At the Feast of Tabernacles, just a few months before His death, Jesus interrupted the most sacred moment in the week-long festival, when the priest poured out a goblet of water drawn from a nearby spring, and had the people conclude with the singing of Psalm 150. In sharp contrast to the physical water that flowed from the priest's vessel, Jesus shouted aloud, "If a man is thirsty, let him come to me and drink.... Streams of water will flow from within him" (NIV). He was speaking of the promised Holy Spirit.

The imagery here is *expression*. God is articulate and expressive (Heb. 1:1–2). It is His nature to communicate. The very concept of creation and incarnation report this outflowing of God. God not only communicates, He moves with power against the forces of darkness. This, too, is an aspect of His expressive nature. Mark, in his Gospel, pictures Jesus as confronting the demonic world, triumphing over the best the devil could do (e.g. Mark 1:21–27). Jesus commissioned His followers to establish the Church after His withdrawal into heaven, but He insisted that prior to their going—as they made disciples of all nations (Matt. 28:19, 20)—that they wait in Jerusalem until the Spirit would be given to them (Luke 28:49). They would need "expressive power" to accomplish the assigned task.

Summary

Paul and John primarily picture the Holy Spirit as the "indwelling Spirit," which is really a way of describing the inner ministry of the Spirit. But in Luke and Acts, there is a very different, complementary emphasis. Acts 1:8 tells us about this: "But you will receive power when the Holy Spirit comes on you; and you will be my witnesses" (NIV). In the Acts narrative, little attention is given to the cultivation of the virtues of the Christian life, the fruit of the Spirit. Luke seems to assume that this is occurring without discussing it. His attention is focused on the *empowering* of the Church to penetrate the darkness of the pagan world with the redemptive message of the risen Lord (Horton, 1981). The Apostolic Church is described in terms of powerful expression, of the ability to move against terrible obstacles, of great deliverances, healings, and miracles. This was a Church alive and vibrant!

How can we put this together? Paul and Luke were contemporaries, travel companions, and close friends. Each certainly was acquainted with the other's emphases. Rather than seeing them offering conflicting messages, is it not better to see them featuring different aspects of a greater reality? Indeed, both sanctification (being) and anointing for ministry (doing) are important. Love and power both have a place. As Christian counselors we will do well to bear in mind that, first, for our own personal life, the Holy Spirit is present to make us more loving and to equip us for effective service. Further, we will also want to see the counselee as a candidate for the full blessing of the Spirit. While so many in our world are just now discovering this "two-dimensional life in the Spirit," we would be shortchanging impoverished Christians if we did not help them enter into this fuller life (Marshall, 1978).

THE SPIRIT OF TRUTH

The counseling process depends in various ways upon truth. An important task confronting the counselor is to secure from constructive interaction with the counselee the possible sources of the distress being experienced. Truthfulness is essential for this process to be meaningful. Although Christian counselors cannot guarantee that clients will be so forthright, we are not without some remarkable possibilities supplied by the Holy Spirit to aid us in this therapeutic ministry.

After all, John 17:17 tells us plainly that the Holy Spirit is "the Spirit of truth." What does this mean? Let us explore several dimensions of this topic in terms of implications for the counseling process.

The Word and the Spirit

Second Timothy 3:16, 17 is an axiomatic statement about the inspiration of Scripture. "All Scripture is God-breathed." The action of the Holy Spirit guarantees that the words of Scripture are the words of God (2 Pet. 1:21). This assures the counselor that the Bible can be trusted as the repository of prophetic and apostolic truth.

Equally important to knowing that the Bible is a trustworthy book is the reassurance that the Author, the Spirit of truth, is also present on the *receiving* end of the revelatory process. Any one reading the Word with an obedient and faith-filled heart, can know that the Holy Spirit is available to help understand divine truth. The natural person is spiritually blind (1 Cor. 2:14), but the spiritual person is aided by the Spirit of God to understand God's message (2 Cor. 3:14–18). This is not a brief for neglect of aids for Bible study; rather, this assures us that in the task of unlocking the treasures of God's Word, we are not without divine help.

All Truth is God's Truth

John 16:13 records these words of Jesus: "But when he, the Spirit of truth, comes, he will guide you into all truth" (NIV). This certainly does not mean that without the discipline of study the believer is guaranteed virtual omniscience. A possible paraphrase would be, "He will help you recognize that which is true." This may be expressed metaphorically as a kind of "holy radar," which gives to the spiritually sensitive person a means for rendering judgments on the mass of descending information, thus assisting that one in sorting out that which corresponds to reality from that which is deficient. For example, in spite of spiritual blindness, it is possible for an unbelieving scientist to discover valuable truths about God's creation. This does not make the truth he has discovered less valuable. The Christian needs special assistance to recognize truth when it does come, regardless of the medium through which it is expressed.

As an example, consider the world of psychology. The astute counselor will be discriminate in developing useful techniques. Whether or not Carl Rogers or Sigmund Freud were Christians is incidental: if insights they uncovered for counseling are valid, why should the Christian counselor not employ them? Certainly, there is considerable worth in nondirective counseling. Cannot the Christian counselor profit from this, without having to accept all of the naturalistic-humanistic assumptions and implications of Rogers's theory and methodology? Likewise, Freud did a great service to the disciplines of psychology and counseling by pointing out the importance of the subconscious. B. F. Skinner may have something of value to tell us about behavior modification, even if the package in which it is housed is completely naturalistic and disclaims any theological base.

The Spirit and the World

Usually the Holy Spirit is pictured as ministering to believers. However, John 16:8-11 outlines for us one instance in which the Holy Spirit ministers to those outside of Christ. His mission is to "convict," "convince," or "persuade." This might be called "spiritual surgery." The Holy Spirit always takes the initiative in the salvation of mankind. Repentance and faith are appropriate *responses* to the conviction of the Spirit, but it is the Spirit who must first confront the unbeliever. To be sure, the Holy Spirit uses human instruments to deliver the facts of the gospel (Rom. 10:14-17), but it is His function to cause the gospel to make an impact on the individual.

This mission of conviction outlined in John 16 touches three categories: (a) "sin"—making individuals aware of their guilt, (b) "righteousness"—the very embodiment of righteousness is Jesus Christ, and (c) "judgment"—disclosing people's ultimate responsibility for their own behavior.

The wise counselor will be eager to cooperate with the Holy Spirit at the right time so that the conviction of the Spirit may initiate a "godly sorrow that leads to repentance" (2 Cor. 7:10, NIV). Indeed, without question a fair proportion of the problems counselors face contains at least some spiritual dynamics. Conviction ought to lead to confession and repentance, a spiritual catharsis. The fruit of this process is peace (Phil. 4:7). An important role of the counselor is assisting the penitent person to *accept forgiveness*. Some earnest and sensitive Christians have great difficulty in believing that Christ does truly forgive and forget. Fairly common is the need to remind believers of the truth expressed in Romans 8:1: there is no condemnation to those who are in Christ Jesus; believers have been set free from the bondage of sin through the work of the Holy Spirit.

Help for the Counselor

Entrance into full life in the Spirit makes available to the Christian counselor special resources that flow from the Spirit. Among the nine manifestations of the Holy Spirit in 1 Cor. 12:7-11 are three that bear an obvious relationship to revelation, or the disclosure of truth. These are "the word of wisdom," "the word of knowledge," and the "discernment of spirits." Although the context of Paul's discussion of the gifts of the Spirit concerns the body of Christian believers who have come together for corporate worship, it does not appear that such manifestations are expressly limited to worship services (I have even seen gifts of the Spirit manifested in church board meetings!). And, as Williams (1971) has pointed out, the content of such gifts of revelation need not be limited to deep matters of faith, such as reinforcing the biblical teaching about salvation or sanctification. They may even relate to rather mundane matters. Saul found the lost donkeys through the exercise of the word of knowledge (1 Sam. 9 & 10). It should be observed, too, that any Spirit-filled believer has access to *all* of the gifts as need arises and as the Spirit chooses.

Since an entire chapter is devoted to the gifts of the Spirit (see Horton, Chapter 3) it will not be necessary here to elaborate. Let it be sufficient to state that the counselor has available, in moments of great need, information and insights that are not naturally available. The Spirit may grant supernatural insight into the root of the client's problem, and whether or not a client is telling the truth. He may give a flash of inspiration that provides a solution to a vexing problem. He may enable the counselor to discern the spiritual condition of the counselee. The exercise of such gifts of knowledge appear repeatedly throughout the Scriptures (see e.g., Peter's encounter with Ananias and Sapphira in Acts 5:1-11).

THE INNOVATIVE SPIRIT

God the Spirit is characterized as being *creative* from the first verses of Genesis (1:1, 2). Throughout the Scriptures, the Holy Spirit is pictured as coming upon individuals to help them meet new situations in a fresh way. Patriarchs, judges, prophets, and kings experienced the inspiration of the Holy Spirit to aid them in meeting a bewildering array of needs (Horton, 1976). With the coming of the Pentecostal outpouring, the creative Spirit came to abide in the lives of all believers.

The Spirit's presence marked the New Testament Church with diversity, spontaneity, and freshness. Although there are clear patterns evident that furnish general boundaries for the work of the Spirit (see, e.g., the cautions and limitations placed on the public exercise of spiritual gifts at Corinth: 1 Cor. 11-14), it is equally clear that the activity of the Spirit is not exhausted by the citations in the New Testament. A principle which seems to surface is that *the Spirit is available to invade need-situations creatively.*

In Acts 6, a problem arose in the Jerusalem church for which there was no precedent to guide the young congregation. The minority, those who were Greek-speaking Jewish Christians, felt that they were being discriminated against by the majority of Aramaic-speaking Christians. The leaders, evidently led by the Spirit, instituted what appears to be the principle of a board of deacons to care for the distribution system for the poor. That all seven chosen for this task had Hellenistic names seems to disclose a great concern to demonstrate Christian love. What a lovely solution to what could have been a troublesome problem!

Spirit-led people can rely on the Paraclete to aid in solving all kinds of problems. A counselor facing a particularly baffling counseling situation can expect in faith that the Holy Spirit is able to bring to one's mind a novel approach, a new combination of methods, a way of adapting to the uniqueness of the individual or group.

Several years ago, I found myself in a situation which called for a form of group counseling. I wrestled with the problem of how to generate a climate in the group that would furnish an effective setting for dealing with the problem. I believe the Holy Spirit led me to a very simple, but effective, solution. We decided to have breakfast as a group on a weekly basis. Those breakfast meetings became a useful means for dealing with the problem at hand. But far beyond meeting the immediate need, they proved to be the basis of a long-lasting, deep kinship of spirit in the group. I attribute the success of that venture to the prompting of the innovative Holy Spirit.

THE ENABLING SPIRIT

Prayer

The Christian who has engaged in counseling for any length of time eventually encounters baffling circumstances that challenge all available resources. We can rest assured knowing that there is a remarkable channel available to the Source of power and wisdom. It is called prayer (MacNutt, 1977). We may engage in various forms of petition and call on God for assistance.

Supplication is acknowledging one's dependence on the Lord. It is out of that well-spring that positive achievement comes. Paul's admonition is highly appropriate to those engaged in the awesome responsibility of counseling others: "Do not be anxious about anything, but in everything, by prayer and petition, with thanksgiving, present your requests to God" (Phil. 4:6, NIV). Keeping the channel open to heaven is an important kind of preparation for any kind of spiritual ministry, certainly including personal ministry to others in a counseling relationship.

There is another form of petitionary prayer, *intercession*, which is petitioning God on behalf of another's need. As Andrew Murray beautifully pictured it, prayer changes the future in a way we cannot fully understand. James 5:16 reminds us that "the prayer of a righteous man is powerful and effective" (NIV).

Jesus placed a high priority on prayer; He spent whole nights in conversation with the Father. The entire 17th chapter of John is devoted to His intercession for the disciples. If our Lord placed such value on the ministry of prayer, should not those engaged in the strategic ministry of counseling take very seriously the life-changing implications of continual intercessory prayer for those entrusted to their care?

Now, it is great to know that the Paraclete is present in a very special way to help Spirit-baptized believers in the very important responsibility of prayer.

> In the same way, the Spirit helps us in our weakness. We do not know what we ought to pray, but the Spirit himself intercedes for us with groans that words cannot express. And he who searches our hearts knows the mind of the Spirit, because the spirit intercedes for the saints in accordance with God's will (Rom. 8:26, 27, NIV).

Baptism in the Spirit opens the door to a new level of praying—praying in tongues. When we reach the limits of our rational capability, the Spirit can enter into our praying, helping us to intercede on an entirely new level. Since this Spirit-energized kind of praying is available to the counselor, we would be missing out on an important spiritual resource if we ignored this possibility. The entire counseling enterprise should be bathed in prayer—both rational and supra-rational. It is clearly a principal means by which the Paraclete works in the counseling situation to effect healing.

Power

The incarnate Lord moved about in His public ministry of preaching, teaching, and healing, chiefly in the power of the Holy Spirit. Acts 10:38 states that "God anointed Jesus of Nazareth with the Holy Spirit and power, and...he went around doing good and healing all who were under the power of the devil, because God was with him." Although Jesus was God in flesh, He chose to identify deeply with humankind, so that He could be a genuine model for believers of all ages (Heb. 2:17, 18). Paul tells us that Jesus—who required no act of robbery to be on a plane of equality with the Father—chose to divest Himself of the glory which was rightfully His, entering this world on a very humble level, deeply identifying with the sufferings of humanity, even dying the most inglorious death imaginable in that age, crucifixion (Phil. 2:5-9).

What did this mean, to choose not to display His "glory"? Glory is the outshining of the inner reality. So, Jesus, in emptying Himself of His right to display His inner reality (deity), chose to live among humanity primarily in the anointing of the Holy Spirit. Only on rare occasions, such as the Transfiguration, did that glory burst through (Luke 9:28-36). So it was that Jesus could tell His disciples that they could expect to do "even greater things than these, because I am going to the Father" (John 14:12, NIV). With the outpouring of the Spirit at Pentecost, the power of God was made available to believers to fulfill that promise of our Lord!

CONCLUSION

Indeed, the book of Acts is witness to the empowered Church moving against the forces of darkness in the ancient world. There is no reason to believe that this possibility ended with Acts 28, for the Spirit was given to abide with us until the end of time. All of the potential wrapped up in the presence of the Paraclete, His gifts and graces, are still available to earnest believers in our day. He has come to anoint for service (Acts 1:8).

In ministering to the hurts of troubled persons, there are occasions when only the supernatural delivering power of God will effect the desired result. Some counselors happily are discovering powerful resources for ministering at a deep level, helping people to achieve an inner healing that might not otherwise be possible. Spirit-filled counselors are not left to their own devices. They can expect God to *enable* them to accomplish His healing task. The Paraclete has come!

3

THE GIFTS OF THE SPIRIT

Stanley M. Horton

THE PURPOSE OF SPIRITUAL GIFTS

What is the great purpose of the gifts of the Holy Spirit in this age? The Bible gives us the answer. Turning to 1 Corinthians 14 we see an emphasis on edification. In verse 26 we read, "Let all things (with respect to the gifts) be done unto edifying."

This calls for the constructive upbuilding of the believers, both as a group and as individuals, through the ministry of the gifts of the Holy Spirit. The Greek verb *oikodomeō*, translated "edify," literally means to build. It is used of building cities, monuments, temples, palaces, and houses. It can be used to connote building up again or restoring. Frequently it functions in a figurative sense of building the Church as a spiritual temple, or of building up, strengthening, and establishing individual believers. The corresponding noun, *oikodomē*, is similarly used of building as a process, as construction, and of building up and strengthening spiritually. As Paul tells the believers in Corinth, "you are God's building *(oikodomē)*."

Christ As A Builder

Ever since God formed the first man and, as the Hebrew says, "built" the first woman, God's purposes have always been constructive. He is a Builder (Heb. 11:10). Jesus contrasted Himself to the thief who comes to "steal, and to kill, and to destroy" (John 10:10). The promise of Jesus is "I will build my church" (Matt. 16:18). The Bible shows He does this by giving life through the Spirit and by manifestations of supernatural power through the gifts of the Spirit.

Too often we misunderstand what Jesus meant by building His Church. In defining the word "church," *Webster's Collegiate Dictionary* gives as the first meaning "a building for public especially Christian worship." The second meaning is "the clergy or officialdom of a religious body." The third meaning is a little better, "a body or organization of religious believers," but it includes a denomination as a part of this meaning. Actually, the New Testament word "church" (Gk., *ekklēsia*) is never used of a building, organization, board, denomination, program, or set of activities. The New Testament usage of the word shows it means "an assembly of citizens," and the emphasis is always on people. The word is used of a confused mob that rushed pell-mell into the Greek theater at Ephesus (Acts 19:29, 32), and it is used of a "lawful assembly" (Acts 19:39). The same word is taken over to describe the assembly of citizens who are believers set free by Christ; it describes the local body, the whole number of believers in a city or a province, and the totality of believers of all places and times (Eph. 1:20–23; 2:19–21). The attention, however, is never on the group as a group, but on the individual persons and their relationship to the Lord and to each other.

The Gospels show Jesus doing His work of upbuilding, encouraging, strengthening, and establishing believers through His teaching and healing ministry. He gave himself in teaching the great crowds that followed Him, even when He was physically weary. Unflattered by the size of the crowds, He saw them as individuals with needs; "he was moved with compassion on them, because they fainted [were weary and harassed], and were scattered abroad, as sheep having no shepherd" (Matt. 9:36). As the Good Shepherd, Jesus knows each one of His sheep (John 10:14); even one lost sheep that strays away is important (Luke 15:3–7).

As he taught the crowds, Jesus was always open to questions. When they pressed in upon Him, He was aware of the touch and the faith of one poor woman with an issue of blood (Luke 8:42–48). He gave some of His greatest teaching privately to individuals like Nicodemus and the woman at the well. During the miraculous feeding of the multitude, each man, woman, and child received more than enough to satisfy his or her hunger. His miracles of healing were never on a mass production basis. He dealt with the afflicted as persons, each according to need, and when necessary He strengthened their faith in a variety of ways, always calling for an obedient response.

Upbuilding Through the Early Church

Now the Gospels only show us what "Jesus *began* to do and teach" (Acts 1:1). The Book of Acts shows what Jesus (through the Holy Spirit) *continued* to do and teach, not only through the Apostles, but through all the believers. Acts emphasizes the work of the Holy Spirit and demonstrates how the gifts of the Spirit built the Church both spiritually and numerically. Persecution did scatter the believers, but it only spread the gospel, increased the number of assemblies, and encouraged the boldness of believers. In between such times there were always times of rest and quiet when the churches were built up, "and walking in the fear [reverence, respect] of the Lord, and in the comfort [encouragement] of the Holy Ghost, were multiplied" (Acts 9:31). All of this adds up to the sum that when believers were in right relation to the Lord in their daily living, the Holy Spirit, through operation of His gifts, brought them encouragement and met needs. Through them, the needs of others were met so that they were added to the community of believers. The Church was thus a supernatural community, living in relation to their resurrected Lord who ministered *to* them and *through* them by the supernatural working of the Holy Spirit.

Unfortunately, some people have supposed that there was some kind of "bump" at the end of the first century (after all the Apostles died), which the Church passed over, resulting in a cessation of all the gifts and the miracles of the Spirit. But when we examine the structure of the Book of Acts we see it has a formal introduction, but no formal conclusion. What Jesus continued to do and teach by the Spirit through the believers in the Book of Acts was meant to continue throughout the history of the Church until Jesus comes again. Acts 3:19 (esp. in the Gk.) shows that until He comes we can enjoy the same kind of times of refreshing portrayed by the Book of Acts. Such spiritual refreshing will require repentance—a change in our basic ideas and attitudes—but once we are willing to accept it in faith, it is fully available to us. Surely, in a day when so many churches are feverishly trying to build up their number and counsel their members by human methods, we need to return to a new dependence on the supernatural gifts of the Holy Spirit. Surely, the One who created us, knows us. He loves us. He, by His Spirit, is sufficient for His own work. Through the gifts of the Spirit He wants to upbuild, encourage, strengthen, and establish us. He has set the gifts and ministries of the Spirit in the Church, and He wants us to be agents of their power and blessing. Without them, any counselor is reduced to what humanity has been able to do and teach; this is certainly a dramatic reduction of therapeutic potential.

BIBLICAL OVERVIEW OF SPIRITUAL GIFTS

Since the Holy Spirit is an infinite Person, He can deal with each one of us on an individual basis with a variety of gifts to meet our needs. Each gift actually belongs to a class of gifts expressed in a variety of operations or workings designed to meet the variety of human needs. Three Bible passages deal with the gifts and ministries of the Holy Spirit. Each one gives us important truths. Ephesians 4:11–16 list gifts given to establish the Church and bring the Church to a point of maturity where each member can minister gifts of the Spirit and contribute to the upbuilding of others and the Church. First Corinthians chapters 12 through 14 discuss specific gifts by which members of the local assembly may minister to their own needs as the Holy Spirit wills. Then Romans 12:3–8 give another list of gifts of the Spirit which provide further guidance concerning their use.

The Gifts of Ephesians 4:11–16

The gifts of Ephesians 4:11–16 are actually gifts of *Christ*. But when we compare the various lists of gifts in 1 Corinthians 12:8–10; 12:28, 29, 30, with Romans 12, we discover that they parallel the gifts of the Spirit, and involve diverse ministries of spiritual gifts.

The apostles, prophets, evangelists, and pastor-teachers listed in Ephesians 4:11 are *ministries* rather than offices (the only local church offices mentioned in the New Testament are those of the elder-bishop and of the deacon). Ephesians 4:8 echoes Psalm 68:18 to show that the risen and ascended Christ gave these ministries as gifts to the Church. Ephesians 4:9, 10 form a parenthesis to indicate that the One who ascended is the same One who came down from the higher parts of heaven to the lower parts; that is, to the surface of the earth, to be born of a virgin, and to live and die for us. Paul is actually making an analogy, using the common custom in which a conqueror would take captive a host of captives who were skilled and give them as gifts to his friends. This is why most of the teachers, doctors, lawyers, and skilled workers in Rome were slaves. Thus, our ascended and exalted Lord Jesus has taken men and women captive to himself and given them as gifts to the Church to perfect, or rather mature, the believers. Being so perfected, the believers can effectively do the work of ministry, and by serving one another, build up the Body of Christ.

Paul further pointed out that through these ministries the whole Body will achieve a maturity in which its members will no longer be spiritual babies swept this way and that by every wind of teaching that comes along. Instead, every believer will continue growing and will receive from Christ the gifts necessary for the upbuilding of their fellow believers and for the attracting of others to Christ.

Apostles. If those who minister as apostles, prophets, evangelists, and pastor-teachers are to be effective, they must be taken captive by Christ. The Apostle Paul called himself a servant—literally a slave—of the Lord Jesus Christ, so did Peter, James, and Jude. Thus they exemplified the kind of servant leadership Jesus demands. Jesus pointed out that the leaders of this world like to lord it over others. They love to play the tyrant. But it must not be this way among Christ's followers. He said, "whoever wants to be great among you, let him be your servant; and whoever wants to be chief among you, let him be your slave" (Matt. 20:25–28). Those who are taken captive by Christ will not exalt themselves. Their one desire will be to exalt Jesus and minister to the members of His Body, the Church.

The New Testament indicates that there were several kinds of apostles. The first group of twelve Jesus chose after a night of prayer were trained for a special ministry and leadership (Luke 6:13; Acts 1:20, 25, 26; Matt. 19:28; Rev. 21:14). A second group of seventy were also sent as apostles with the same commission, and they experienced the same results (Luke 10:1–12, 17). Others named as apostles include Paul, Barnabas, Andronicus, and a woman, Junia (Rom. 16:7; Acts 14:4, 14). These apostles, however, were all firsthand witnesses to the resurrection and teachings of Jesus; Paul was the last of them (1 Cor. 9:1; 15:5–8).

The Bible does, however, indicate a continuation of apostolic ministry through the Holy Spirit and His gifts (Acts 5:32). In 1 Corinthians 12:18, 28, we see that just as the various parts of the human body are all necessary for its proper functioning and are all set in the body for a specific purpose, so God has set in the Church apostles, prophets, teachers, miracles, helps, governments, and various kinds of tongues. Again, these are not "offices," but are ministries intended to be continuing vital parts of the Church, just as eyes, ears, hands, and feet are continuing vital parts of our natural bodies. We still need apostolic ministry that will establish and build up bodies of believers through the miracle-working power and gifts of the Holy Spirit.

Prophets. The word "prophet" means speaker; specifically, a speaker for God. Some of the first New Testament prophets, along with the apostles, expounded those truths that were mysteries in Old Testament times (Eph. 3:5). Thus, they helped lay the foundation for the Church (Eph. 2:20).

Others, like so many Old Testament prophets, wrote no books, but God used them to challenge the people by bringing illumination and practical application of truth already given. This was truth which had been or which was then being included in the written Word, the Old and New Testaments. Acts 15:32 gives an example in the ministry of Judas and Silas, who as prophets encouraged, challenged, and confirmed or strengthened the believers.

Though prophets occasionally foretold the future (Acts 11:28; 21:11), this was not their normal function. Nor was there ever anything like fortune-telling involved. Further, prophets never provided a substitute for believers seeking the will of God for themselves.

The gift of prophecy was not limited to those who were regularly used in such a ministry. The gift is emphatically made available to all believers (1 Cor. 14:31). Prophecy is defined (not as foretelling the future, but) as speaking for God by the inspiration of the Spirit in *edification* to upbuild spiritually; in *exhortation* to encourage, awaken, and challenge; and in *comfort* to cheer, revive, and encourage (1 Cor. 14:3). In the variety of its expression, it may illuminate mysteries of the gospel, but more importantly, it will stir people to conviction, to devotion, and to action.

Evangelist. The word "evangelist" refers to one who spreads good news, that is the Good News about Jesus Christ, who has come, not to condemn the world, but to save it (John 3:17). Prophets traveled to churches encouraging, and strengthening believers. The evangelist's emphasis, however, was to reach unbelievers. Philip *the evangelist* went to a city and then to an individual who did not know the Lord (Acts 8:6–8, 12, 35). Timothy, though his gift was primarily that of a teacher, was also challenged to do the work of an evangelist (2 Tim.

4:3). However, some, like Philip, are especially gifted as evengelists and that becomes their primary ministry.

Pastor-Teachers. Throughout the New Testament, the term "pastor" (Eph. 4:11) is translated "shepherd," and refers to a ministry, not an office. It is combined in Ephesians 4 with the ministry of teaching. The Hebrew word for "shepherd" means a "feeder." In the Early Church, the Elder (also called Bishop, meaning overseer or superintendent) was the chief administrative officer of the local church and directed its affairs. The pastor-teacher usually stayed at one location for a while to feed the believers the good food of God's Word. He explained it and helped them understand, assimilate, and apply it. In a changing world, he helped them relate the truths of the Bible to their daily living. Then, after bringing believers to the point of maturity that they, too, could be teachers, he would move on to help others. Apollos is an example; he was teachable (Acts 18:26). Then he went on as a teacher to "water" what the Apostle Paul had already "planted" in Corinth (1 Cor. 3:6).

The Gifts of 1 Corinthians 12:8-10

The nine gifts listed in 1 Corinthians 12:8-10 are usually thought of as "the" gifts of the Spirit. Actually, they seem to be classes of gifts with a variety of expressions. The Bible shows they are to be exercised one at a time by any believer, but only as the Spirit wills. We see also that these gifts are ministered through individuals to meet the needs of others in the Body, or to meet needs of the Body as a whole. Paul also makes comparisons with the human body to show that different gifts and ministries of the Spirit through individual belivers are necessary for the upbuilding and growth of the church as the Body of Christ.

To Whom Do the Gifts Belong? We must not presume to try to minister these gifts according to *our* view of what is needed. Nor is it ever safe to assume that we "possess" a particular gift, or that we are free to develop it as we see fit. All of these gifts are produced, operated, and made effective by "the one even the same Spirit as He distributes them individually to each one (men and women) as He wills" (1 Cor. 12:11, my translation from the Gk; cf. Heb. 2:4).

Why this emphasis on the sovereignty of the Holy Spirit in each individual manifestation or operation of the gifts of the Spirit? He knows the things and the will of God (1 Cor. 2:11; Rom. 8:27). Like Jesus, He knows what is in us (John 2:25).

Oswald Chambers (1965) emphasized that self-diagnosis is usually wrong; we cannot know our real needs, and we cannot depend on what others tell us about their needs. We must learn to depend on the Holy Spirit to minister the gifts as He wills. The Bible certainly tells us to seek the best gifts (1 Cor. 12:31); yet, only the Holy Spirit knows what is really best in each situation.

Notice also that these gifts are the gifts *of* the Holy Spirit—they belong to Him. They mean nothing unless He energizes and administers them. We never come to the place where we can manifest genuine gifts of the Spirit without total dependence on and response to Him. Nor do the gifts become ours in the sense they cannot be taken from us. When the Bible says the gifts and callings of God are without repentance, it is talking about Israel (Rom. 11:28, 29). This means that those gifts and callings, once given, remain available. Actually, both individual Israelites and the nation as a whole often lost the blessings of God through unbelief—and so can we (Heb. 3:18; 4:1, 2). But, when we come back in faith, we see the same Holy Spirit still making the gifts available through faith and distributing as He wills, i.e., as He sees what the real need is. Sometimes He distributes a single gift to a particular individual for a brief ministry in an assembly. Or, He may choose someone for a prolonged ministry of one or more of the gifts. Thus, it is important to remain open to the Spirit, ready to respond in faith and expectation.

The nine gifts of 1 Corinthians 12:8-10 are often grouped by some Bible teachers as gifts of revelation, power, and utterance or communication. But the Bible simply lists them and gives no more description of them in this passage, though chapter 14 gives details concerning the gifts of tongues and prophecy.

A Word of Wisdom. The first listed is a word of wisdom. This is a specific declaration of divinely given wisdom or counsel to meet a need. It neither makes us wiser, nor does it render us free from mistakes. Rather, it grants us the Holy Spirit's insight into a need and into the Scriptures for their proper application to the need. Acts 6:2-4 and 15:13-21 show how a word of wisdom brought guidance to a body of believers. Jesus promised the word of wisdom to help us against those who oppose us in spreading the gospel (Luke 21:3-15). The Book of Acts on many occasions records how such a word of wisdom was supplied (Acts 4:8-14, 19-21; 6:9, 10; 23:6).

A Word of Knowledge. Since knowledge is a necessary basis for wisdom, the gift of the word of knowledge is listed next. It involves a word, or declaration of divinely given knowledge. Again, God does not impart a great stock of knowledge at once, any more than He gives us a great supply of wisdom. This gift grants an insight necessary to meet a need detected by the Holy Spirit.

Some have identified the word of knowledge with a kind of clairvoyant ability to locate lost articles or to diagnose the nature of illness or disease. But this has little, if any, biblical grounds for support. When the Bible speaks of God-given or Spirit-given knowledge, it is usually the knowledge of the things of God and Christ (2 Cor. 2:14; 4:6; Eph. 1:17-23; Col. 1:9, 10), including knowledge of the truth of the gospel and its requirements (1 Tim. 2:4; Heb. 10:26; 1 Pet. 3:7; 2 Pet. 1:5, 8). Such knowledge leads to good works out of a good, noble, praiseworthy way of life (James 3:13) and forms part of the Holy Spirit's way of teaching us and guiding us into all the truth (John 14:26; 15:26; 16:13). Peter gave this kind of word of knowledge at the house of Cornelius and later at the Jerusalem Council (Acts 10:47, 48; 15:7–11).

Faith. Now, wisdom and knowledge will not be effective unless they are, by faith, put into faithful, obedient action. Biblical faith always involves more than a mental attitude. I used to think that if I could "squeeze up my mind" and "squeeze out the doubts," that would leave faith. But a biblical faith involves a personal trust in a personal God, a trust that brings an obedient response to His Word and promise. The New Testament word for faith could be translated "faith-obedience." The Old Testament word means faithfulness and involves commitment to the one true God.

It should be obvious, then, that the gift of faith does not raise the faith of the gifted individual to a superior level any more than a word of wisdom makes one super-wise. Rather, it makes one a channel for ministering faith to others so that they will trust God and commit themselves to Him in obedience and faith, just as Abraham did when his faith was counted for righteousness (Gal. 3:6).

Many have experienced faith imparted by the Holy Spirit in a song, prayer, testimony, sermon, or a simple one-to-one sharing. Preaching is especially important; when it fails to generate saving faith, few will be saved. Paul's preaching encouraged others to receive the Holy Spirit through the (obedient) hearing of faith (Gal. 3:2, 5). United prayer became a channel to receive faith that brought a new outpouring of the Spirit in Jerusalem and a new boldness to speak God's Word (Acts 4:31).

Gifts of Healing. The Greek speaks not of a *gift* of healing, but of *gifts* of *healings*. Some interpret this to mean that the Spirit gives a supply of gifts of healing to one person at one time, and to another person at another time. They assert that Peter's words at the Gate Beautiful, "such as I have give I thee," mean that he had a supply of gifts of healing available to dispense to the sick (Acts 3:6). However, "such as I have" in the Greek is singular and means Peter had received a particular gift of the Spirit to give to *this* lame man. The text does not indicate that Peter or any of the other apostles possessed a reservoir of healing gifts. They had to receive a fresh gift of healing from the Spirit for each sick person to whom they ministered.

We should note, too, that 1 Corinthians 12:8–10 concerns itself with gifts available through individual members of the local assembly. God heals in other ways as well. We are told for example, to call for the elders of the church (James 5:14, 15). But as the Spirit wills, He can use any believer to minister a gift of healing to the sick.

Workings of Miracles. As in the case of the gifts of healings, both nouns are in the plural in the gifts of workings of miracles. "Miracles" is the plural of the Greek word *dynamis* translated "power" in Acts 1:8. In the plural, however, it usually means "deeds of mighty, supernatural power." These are direct divine interventions to meet human need. Some suppose they break natural law. Not at all! Drop any object you may be holding. The law of gravity says it will fall toward the earth. Put you hand under under it and catch it. You did not break the law of gravity. The weight you feel shows that the law is still operating. But your hand has enough power or strength to counteract the pull of gravity. So God does not break natural laws. He simply puts in His hand and by His mighty power accomplishes what we cannot do. In fact, He is able to do whatever He wills, and He may even use or speed up natural processes to accomplish His mighty acts.

Palma (1974) pointed out that the biblical use of "workings" chiefly concerns the activities of God or Satan. Examples might be the judgment of blindness on Elymas (Acts 13:9-11) and the casting out of demons. Others would include nature miracles, but, as Gee (1963) stated, nature miracles are practically absent from the Book of Acts and the Epistles. For example, at Malta Paul was given divine assurance of the preservation of his life and the lives of all on board the wrecked ship. But they escaped to land, not by a miracle, but by swimming or paddling on pieces of board (Acts 27:23, 43, 44). Workings of miracles are still available, not on our demand, but as the Spirit wills. They give witness to God's power, God's sovereignty, and Christ's ultimate victory.

Prophecy. We have already discussed the regular use of the gift of prophecy in the ministry of the prophet who has been taken captive by Christ for that ministry. But in 1 Corinthians 12-14, prophecy is encouraged above other gifts because prophecy always edifies, encourages, and upbuilds the believers. By it the mysteries of the gospel are illuminated.

We should also be warned against any supposed prophecies that are negative, discouraging, or vindictive. God did call Jeremiah to a six-fold ministry, four parts tearing down, and two parts "to build, and to plant" (Jer. 1:10). But the gospel is *Good News*. The New Testament ministers were occupied with building, planting, and watering. As noted above, Paul describes the gift of prophecy in terms of *edification, exhortation* and *comfort*.

Discerning of Spirits. Because false prophets and teachers abound, the next gift mentioned is the discernings of spirits. In my book, *What the Bible Says About the Holy Spirit* (1976), I noted:

> The plurals indicate a variety of ways in which this gift may be manifest. It involves
> a "distinguishing between" spirits.... In fact, the word *discerning* involves forming
> a judgment and is related to the word used of judging prophecy. It involves a

supernaturally given perception, differentiating between spirits, good and evil, true or false, in order to make a decision.

John says we are not to believe every spirit, but must put them to the test (1 John 4:1). Sometimes, a gift of the Spirit is needed to do this. Actually, the Bible speaks of three spirits, the Spirit of God, the spirit of man, and the spirit of the devil (plus the evil spirits or demons associated with him). In the operation of this gift in the local assembly or gathering of believers, it would seem that the spirit of man might be the chief offender. Even with the best of intentions, it is possible that some people will mistake their own deep feelings for the voice of the Spirit. Or, because of excessive zeal or spiritual ignorance in not knowing how to yield to the Holy Spirit, one's own spirit may intrude.

Like the other gifts, this one does not raise an individual to a new level of ability. Nor does it give anyone the power to go around looking at people and telling of what spirit they are. It is a specific gift for a specific occasion. Some examples may possibly be found in Acts 5:3; 8:20–23; 13:10; 16:16–18. (pp. 276–277)

Tongues and Interpretation. By the gift of tongues (kinds or families of languages), believers edify or upbuild themselves spiritually (1 Cor. 14:4). This is not wrong, for we need spiritual edification if we are to help others. But in the local assembly, the need is for the edification of others. Thus, the gift of interpretation is needed in the public meetings to relate the meaning or essential content of the utterance in tongues.

The Apostle Paul limited the manifestation of the gift of tongues in the public meeting only to give opportunity for other gifts, such as prophecy, which would bring greater edification. At the same time, Paul made a practice of exercising the gift of tongues, and did so more than all the Corinthians. Yet, in the assembly he would rather speak five words with his mind and understanding than speak 10,000 words in an uninterpreted tongue. Thus we can assume that he exercised this gift primarily in his private devotions. Many today find that private daily exercise of this gift still offers a means of receiving edification and strength from the Holy Spirit. Paul set the example also by praying and singing in the Spirit (in tongues) and by praying and singing also in his own language. Sometimes, when it seems we are unable to pray, if we just let the Spirit give us tongues, He will bring refreshing, and we will soon be praying in our own language with a renewed freedom and power.

Other Gifts

Some writers take the nine gifts of 1 Corinthians 12:8–10 as the totality of the gifts of the Spirit. In one sense, perhaps they are. But when we consider the five lists of gifts given, it appears that the Bible is not concerned with counting gifts or drawing lines between them. Rather, the Spirit offers a wide range of gifts and ministries to all the unique needs of the assembly. Gifts such as administration, ruling, ministry, giving, helps, mercy, and exhortation all are concerned with service and outreach (though other gifts such as prophecy, faith, miracles, and healings also contribute to outreach).

Administration. The gift of administration or governments is expressed in the plural and indicates a variety of expressions of the gift to give spiritual help to church leaders or adminstrators. The term implies giving wise counsel to others. The early church expected their leaders to be full of the Holy Spirit and wisdom. They were to depend on the Spirit's gifts, not their own leadership ability.

Helps. The gift of helps or helpful deeds enables one to help the weak (Acts 20:35), and to devote one's self to acts of kindness (1 Tim. 6:2). The same word was also used as a term for a chief accountant. This gift would thus help the seven deacons chosen in Acts 6 to do their work (the word *tables* in Acts 6:2 means money tables). Deacons, however, also ministered to the weak, the sick, and the poor by helpful deeds. So both meanings describe their work.

Service. The gift of ministry or service (Rom. 12:7) describes both the ministry of the Word and the ministry of deacons. It also depicts the service involved in preparing a meal, of the ministry of reconciliation, and of the distribution of help to the poor. Thus, the Spirit's help was available for every avenue of service of the church.

Exhortation. Though exhortation is part of the gift of prophecy, Romans 12:8 lists it separately. By this gift, the Spirit challenges, appeals, conciliates, encourages friendship, and unifies the local body of believers. Through exhortation the Spirit keeps the hope of Christ's coming before us and urges us to walk in the light of that hope.

Giving. The gift of giving or sharing helps us give to the needy without belittling them or making them feel under obligation. This is not a gift just for the rich, however. The Bible urges the poor to work with their hands so they can share with the needy as well. The outpouring of the Spirit on the Day of Pentecost brought all believers into a participation in this gift (Acts 2:44, 45; 4:34, 37). They shared with simplicity, sincerity, and generosity, even though no one put them under any pressure or obligation to do so.

Ruling. The gift of ruling involves not only directing, but caring and giving aid with loving concern. It shows that leadership was not to be a matter of domineering over others but of service. The gift of ruling helps leaders care for souls. It helps them set the example and stir the whole assembly with a concern to help one another under the leadership God has given them.

Mercy. The last, but perhaps most important gift in the list of Romans 12:6–8 is mercy, which Jesus himself gave priority (Matt. 25:31–46). The gift of showing mercy involves gracious acts of compassion in the personal care of the needy, the sick, the hungry, and the naked (the Gk. does not mean stark naked or nude; rather, it means they have insufficient clothes). Mercy also includes the same kind of concern for those in prison, whether in literal prisons or in the "prisonhouse" of sin. The Bible emphasizes that God is rich in mercy. Thus the gift brings His mercy to those in any kind of need, whether it be physical, financial, mental, or spiritual. Some perform deeds of mercy out of a sense of duty, but this never accomplishes God's purpose. Only the Spirit enables deeds of mercy to be done with cheerfulness, gladness, and graciousness.

GIFTS OPERATED IN LOVE

Now all these gifts of the Spirit are important, but even more important is the manner in which they are administered. This is why the Holy Spirit put the love chapter in the middle of the discussion of the gifts in 1 Corinthians 12–14. Love is not presented as an alternative to the gifts of the Spirit, but it shows that God wants to see the gifts ministered with love. As Bittlinger (1967, p. 75) pointed out, God wants love to guide and control the expression of the gifts. He also desires the gifts to be channels for the expression and manifestation of His divine love. God's love purposes the gifts to build up the believers. Thus, He asks us to seek both love and the gifts.

In the King James version (KJV) "charity" means love. It represents the Greek word *agapē*, which in the KJV itself is translated *love* 86 times and *charity* only 27 times. The KJV also translates the corresponding verb *agapaō* as *love* 135 times. Earlier versions such as Tyndale's and the Geneva Bible (preferred over the KJV by the Pilgrims and Puritans who settled in America) translate *agapē* as *love* in 1 Corinthians 13 also. This is important because "charity" today is all too often used of cold, impersonal gifts to the poor. It belittles them as "objects of charity." How different this is from "the love of God...shed abroad in our hearts by the Holy Ghost which is given unto us" (Rom. 5:5)!

Love is never included among the *charismata*, the spiritual gifts. It is a *fruit* of the Spirit. As with all the fruit of the Spirit, we must cultivate it and give it opportunity to grow and develop.

> It is obvious that neither salvation nor the baptism in the Holy Spirit automatically bestows all the fruit of the Spirit in one's life. On the other hand, the Holy Spirit does not wait to bestow His gifts until we are spiritually mature. God did not wait to use the Corinthians and give them gifts until they got rid of their failures, divisions, and lack of love.
>
> Even today we see God is using people who have not fully heeded Peter's Pentecostal plea to save ourselves from a crooked generation (Acts 2:40). Pentecostal power is not a guarantee of Pentecostal godliness or of Pentecostal love and compassion. God wants both (Horton, 1980, p. 20).

The Bible does not say, however, that gifts without love accomplish nothing. Giving all my possessions to feed the hungry poor might do them a great deal of good. Giving my body to be burned as a martyr, or as a testimony to my faith might inspire the faith of a great many others. But if I do it without love it will profit *me* nothing (1 Cor. 12:3).

God's use of us in the manifestations of gifts obviously does not suggest that He approves of everything we say or do. God seeks to use believers as soon as they are converted to Christ. Thus, the Holy Spirit does not wait until we are mature before He gives gifts. Even a "babe in Christ" can minister gifts in the highest degree that the Spirit wills. But His choice of us does not excuse immaturity, lack of love, or a failure to let Christ be formed in us. In God's eyes it is more important to *be* something than to *do* something. We may impress people with gifts and miracles, and then stand before God as a meaningless zero, with all our works receiving no reward. Even if I remove mountain after mountain and have not love, "I am nothing" (1 Cor. 13:2).

GIFTS OPERATED UNDER OUR CONTROL

This emphasis on love, a love which includes all the fruit of the Spirit, precedes the emphasis on edification in 1 Corinthians 14. Love always edifies, always builds up (1 Cor. 8:1). Thus, love will cause us to be courteous in the expression of the gifts, giving opportunity to others, not interrupting when others are being used to minister. Then there will be no confusion, but all will learn and all will be comforted and encouraged (1 Cor. 14:31–33).

If there is confusion, then it is our fault, for 1 Corinthians 14:33 tells us that God is not the author of confusion. Some suppose that because the Spirit gives gifts severally as He wills, we must jump up and manifest the gift as soon as the Spirit moves on our hearts and minds. But the Spirit does not treat us as if we were machines. He makes us fellow-workers with the Lord. He often impresses us with a gift for which opportunity will come later. In fact, if we hold steady, the Holy Spirit will deepen the impression and make the manifestation of the gift even more effective when the proper opportunity does arise. The Holy Spirit does not just "pull our strings"; we can wait until our gift can be expressed without causing confusion, for "the spirits of the prophets are subject to the prophets" (1 Cor. 14:32). Like Paul, we need to serve God with our own spirits, as well as in the Holy Spirit (Rom. 1:9).

It is important to recognize also that all of these gifts are manifest not merely through individuals, but in relation to a group of believers. When we become Christians we do not go off into orbit by ourselves. We are baptized by the Spirit into the Body of Christ, into the assembly of believers. Then Christ baptizes us into the Spirit, saturating us with His presence (1 Cor. 12:13).

Every Believer Gifted—Every Believer Contributing

Paul, in 1 Corinthians 12, emphasized that different parts are necessary to the human body, and each part is dependent upon the other. Likewise, in the local assembly we are individually and collectively members of the Body of Christ. Each and every believer should have a gift and ministry with its own unique operation. All are needed, so there are no grounds for envy, dissension, or contention. The gifts and ministries are given and directed by the Spirit, who expects us to respond with the intent of bringing good to the whole body. There is no room for pride on one hand or self-depreciation on the other; rather, as we work jointly with the Spirit, He will help us have a real concern for each other as individuals. We will feel one another's hurts and rejoice in one another's successes. Instead of playing politics or trying to seek our own advantage, we will work to bring harmony and will learn to function together for the glory of God.

Three more things need to be said about the gifts of the Spirit. First, in the Early Church spiritual gifts were manifested in an atmosphere of expectation and hope. Pentecost was a harvest festival where first fruits were offered. Thus, the believers looked ahead to the spreading of the gospel through the whole world and to the culmination or consummation of God's plan of redemption in the Second Coming of Jesus Christ. This made them even more conscious of the necessity of carrying out God's plan and doing His work through the power and gifts of the Holy Spirit. They saw that this was the only way to break down barriers between sexes, peoples, nations, and races so that by the power of the gospel all could be made one in Christ. *Maranatha*, "Our Lord, Come!" was their watchword. We are not to exercise the gifts and ministries of the Spirit with our eyes focused only on immediate or practical needs. Through the expression of the gifts, we become part of the outworking of God's great plan of redemption, part of the fulfillment of the promise of blessing on all the families of the earth (Gen. 12:3).

Second, let us not forget that the Spirit has come to abide, to settle down to stay, both in the hearts and lives of individual believers, and in the midst of the local assembly. He is present with us whether we feel anything or not. His work in and through us does not depend on our emotional state; it does not matter if we are fully conscious of His presence or not. Even if there are no visible or special manifestations of His gifts, He is still present to guide and help us. Some people teach that we need a new revelation or special guidance from the Spirit every day of our lives. But this was not the case with New Testament believers. Most of the time they simply carried out the work God assigned and faithfully went on with the business of living without spectacular interventions. When the Spirit stopped the Apostle Paul from preaching in the Roman provinces of Asia, He gave him no further guidance for some time. In faithfulness to his calling, he traveled through Mysia to the borders of Bithynia before the Spirit gave him any further guidance. Yet as we are faithful, we can be sure that the gifts and ministries of the Spirit are always available to us in our work and worship.

Finally, even though God does not wait until we are mature to use us, the Holy Spirit is holy, and He wants to use us as holy vessels. This does not mean we must spend a great deal of time perfecting ourselves. The kind of growth and maturity we need comes through the exercise of a combination of the fruit and gifts of the Spirit in the service of Christ and His Church. The saint (literally, the holy dedicated, consecrated one) does more than spend time in study, prayer, and devotion. The "holy one" does that, but he is also busy working for the Lord. A good illustration may be seen in the holy vessels of the Tabernacle and Temple. They could not be taken into an Israelite's kitchen or dining area and used to cook with or eat from. They were separated from ordinary use. But that was not what made them holy. They did not become holy until they were actually used in the service of the Lord. Our holiness, then, is not merely a matter or separation from evil, though that is necessary. It is a separation for and a dedication to God and His service just as it was for the prophets, priests, and kings of Old Testament times. But the New Testament shows us that every believer is a king and priest unto God, and we may all prophesy as the Spirit wills. Prophets, priests and kings in the Old Testament were also anointed with oil, symbolic of the Holy Spirit. Along with this, God gave the reality of the anointing of the Spirit. We read that when the prophet Samuel anointed David with oil, the Spirit of the Lord literally came into David from that day "upward" (1 Sam. 16:13). His was an abiding, growing, continuing experience. So today, the baptism in the Holy Spirit is the entrance to a growing, continuing anointing of the Spirit that brings His gifts and ministries.

THE USE OF SPIRITUAL GIFTS IN COUNSELING

Since we are urged to desire spiritual gifts (1 Cor. 12:31; 14:1), we need to keep ourselves open to the moving of the Spirit with eager expectation and childlike faith. The Holy Spirit is eager to bless us with needed gifts. But He will never force himself on us. He wants us to cooperate with Him in a spirit of Calvary love.

Some of the gifts which may be particularly relevant in a counseling situation are: the word of wisdom, the word of knowledge, and the discerning of spirits. When evil spirits or wrong human spirits are involved, the Holy Spirit can help us distinguish between them. He can also reveal from the Scriptures guidance and help.

If the need for counseling arises out of a need for healing, then gifts of healing are available. God is able to heal our bodies, our spirits, our minds, and our memories.

The gift of prophecy is normally manifest to build the local body—the assembly. However, in its exhortation, edification, and comfort, the counselor may receive insight for helping others.

Then let us not neglect the daily exercise of the gifts of tongues as a "prayer language.'' Early in my teaching experience I learned this important lesson. I was asked to teach a training course for a week in a church 80 miles away. By Thursday, after teaching in Springfield all day and driving over winding roads to teach for two hours each night, I felt exhausted. I cried to the Lord, telling Him I didn't know how I could be of help to the people. He reminded me that "He that speaketh in an unknown tongue edifieth himself'' (1 Cor. 14:4). I let the Spirit give me tongues during that 80 miles to the church. That night was the best session of the week. Surely the same spiritual principle can be effectively applied by the exhausted, weary counselor who feels that he or she has nothing left to give.

Tongues, then, can edify the counselor spiritually in private prayer. We will be more in tune with the Spirit and more open to receive other needed gifts from the variety the Spirit has available to help us in spiritual ministry.

COUNSELING

INTRODUCTION

The second section of the book focuses attention on the *role of the Holy Spirit in the personal life of the counselor.* The human instrument—the counselor or psychologist—must become the channel through which the Spirit operates in the therapeutic situation. If the personality of the counselor is as important in counseling and psychotherapy as research indicates, it is essential for the Spirit-filled counselor to be a whole, healthy person who is also willing to be led by the Holy Spirit. Human limitations place restrictions on the operation of the Holy Spirit in counseling because God has chosen to channel His intervention to hurting souls through finite human beings.

Those who seek to experience—and enjoy—the intervention of the Holy Spirit in a ministry of counseling must carefully examine their own identity and be open to the free flow of the Holy Spirit in both private and professional life.

Rev. M. Allen Groff is the author of Chapter 4, "The Holy Spirit and the Devotional Life of the Counselor." He is a graduate of the University of Tulsa and currently is pastor of Oak Cliff Assembly of God in Dallas, Texas. For more than a quarter of a century Groff has maintained a thriving counseling ministry in conjunction with his pastorates in Oregon, Oklahoma, and Illinois. He continues to be active in ministers' institutes and marriage and family workshops in the U. S. and abroad. As a counseling pastor, Groff indicates that the ministry of counseling needs to be an "overflow" from the personal spiritual life of the counselor. He draws on the devotional life of Jesus as a model for Christian counselors and psychologists to emulate in their personal lives.

"The Personal and Spiritual Growth of the Counselor" is the subject addressed by Dr. Mark Stocks in Chapter 5. He approaches his topic by investigating the integration of faith and learning in the development of a person empowered by the Holy Spirit to counsel God's people. Apparently Stocks has been greatly influenced by Dr. Bruce Narramore and Dr. John Carter. These individuals were Stocks's mentors at the Rosemead School of Professional Psychology, a division of Biola University, where he completed his Psy. D. degree. The faculty at Rosemead has pioneered the study of the integration of theology and psychology. Stocks notes that the Christian "develops maturity as the result of a deepening relationship with Christ individually (one-to-one) and as the result of increasing quality of human interaction." Stocks is an assistant professor of psychology at Evangel College and is engaged in private practice as a licensed psychologist in Springfield, Missouri.

In Chapter 6, I examine a problem which can strike counselors at any age if they "become weary in well doing." In "Avoiding Burnout Through Spiritual Renewal," I discuss the symptoms of burnout and pinpoint some of the causes of burnout I have detected in pastors and counselors. Strategies for avoiding burnout and for finding renewal through the intervention of the Holy Spirit are offered. I have taken the liberty to draw on my experiences as a missionary, counseling pastor, and psychologist to illustrate some of these processes. Many of these concepts have been learned in my experiences as chairman of the Behavioral Sciences department and former director of the counseling center at Evangel College, and adjunct professor of pastoral counseling at the Assemblies of God Theological Seminary.

The final chapter (7) in this section was contributed by Dr. Jack Rozell, pastor of The Neighborhood Church in Bellevue, Washington. He discusses "Lay Counseling in the Local Church." Lest it appear that the Holy Spirit limits His ministry to professionals in the helping professions, this emphasis on lay counseling has been included to illustrate the breadth of scope within which the Holy Spirit can function in a ministry of counseling in the spiritual community. Rozell has been uniquely used of the Lord in devising a strategy for involving laypersons in an active counseling ministry under the supervision of trained pastors and professional counselors. He illustrates the application of "Agape Therapy" by using his experiences at The Neighborhood Church as an example. Rozell is a former professor at Northwest College in Kirkland, Washington, where he taught while completing his Doctor of Ministry degree at Phillips University in Enid, Oklahoma.

Despite the diversity of topics addresssed in this section, a single, unmistakable message is communicated: the counselor who seeks to know the intervention of the Spirit in the counseling session *must first know God intimately*—must experience "Spirit-filled" as a living reality and not just as a catch phrase which may impress some clients. My hope is that the Spirit will use this section to initiate or renew that reality in the life of the reader.

Raymond T. Brock

4

THE DEVOTIONAL LIFE OF THE COUNSELOR

Allen Groff

INTRODUCTION

The Spirit-filled counselor is one so used by the Holy Spirit that counselor and counselee both recognize that God is not simply an adjunct to the process—He *is* the process. Certainly, skills developed by study and training are desirable, but those are inadequate without God. Omitting God leaves the Christian counselor without the plus-factor which is not only expected, but needed by the person seeking support from a Pentecostal helper.

A Personal Challenge: Spiritual "Overflow"

Some time ago, a British colleague, Eric Lavender, responded to my invitation to address our staff in a weekly meeting. His theme struck a responsive chord in my heart when he stated that genuine ministry is only that which results from the minister's own personal "overflow." Hope that the Christian faith is God's answer to human need and human problems truly can be birthed in the overflow of one's own vital, intimate relationship with God. With spiritual resources undergirding the counseling process, the counselor can move from theoretical admonition to realistic goals. Without such spiritual reserves, it is predictable that early or late, a person will suffer defeat in the role of helper or counselor.

Constant involvement with others at the intense level required for effective counseling takes its physical, emotional, and spiritual toll, often leaving the counselor a victim of burnout. The variety of ills and problems one can face in a day, coupled with the awareness that total healing has not occurred for everyone, contributes to feelings of fatigue, cynicism, futility, and frustration. A healthy devotional life serves to ward off such needless wreckage. Probably every Christian counselor would echo an immediate and pious "Amen" to such a thought, but, without making a blanket accusation, I suspect that much pursuit of the devotional life is motivated more by anxiety about a given person or situation than by trust that God is indeed our "very present help" (Ps. 46:1).

Internal Spiritual Preparation

In his presentations, German theologian Helmut Thieckle makes much of Jesus moving from His devotional life to His meeting of human need. This observation holds true again and again as we read the Gospels. It is not surprising then, that to support and encourage anxious followers who have just been told that they will be hauled before governors and kings to give testimony, He told them not to worry about preparing speeches (Matt. 10:18–19). Rather, He instructed them to prepare themselves for the encounter; their preparation would, like His, lie in their own intimate devotional life. And as certain as those early disciples were that Jesus' warning of emergency situations would be realized, we, too, can expect that we will experience such times of crisis. The assurance of victory lies not so much in precisely determining our destiny so we can plot a strategy beforehand; rather, we must simply keep ourselves spiritually prepared so we will not be left gasping from the shock of crisis. Yet the opposite of Jesus' model regularly occurs in the Christian helper who spends little time in spiritual preparation, yet who goes running for assistance from God *after* being confronted with human need.

Spirits communicate so well that there are few actors adept enough to fool forever the troubled people who find their way to the Christian counselor's door. In only a short time people will sense whether or not they are simply dealing with another academic degree stamped out in the humanistic mold, or if they are in the presence of one who projects a well-founded faith that declares ''the Lord is my helper'' (Ps. 121:2).

''Relationship'' is one of the most used words in counseling. So much, if not *everything*, hinges on relationships. To relate to others at an optimum level, the Christian counselor must maintain a personal, vibrant relationship with God. This is the central relationship that affects all others. This being true, the only way to stay free of a gnawing, free-floating anxiety regarding one's own up-to-date relationship with God is to maintain an adequate devotional life. It is doubtful that another chapter on the topic will add much weight to conviction concerning the matter, but perhaps the mind and heart can be quickened by the model of the ''Wonderful Counselor'' (Isa. 9:6).

THE UNSEEN, PRIVATE DEVOTIONAL LIFE OF JESUS

Jesus resisted and taught strongly against the prayer model commonly found among the Pharisees. He directed, ''And when thou prayest, thou shalt not be as the hypocrites are: for they love to pray standing in the synagogues and in the corners of the streets, that they may be seen of men. Verily I say unto you, they have their reward'' (Matt. 6:5). He then instructed, ''But thou, when thou prayest, enter into thy closet, and when thou hast shut the door, pray to thy Father which is in secret; and thy Father which seeth in secret shall reward thee openly'' (Matt. 6:6).

Among other references, Mark gives insight into the Lord's practice when he related: "And in the morning, rising up a great while before day, He went out, and departed into a solitary place, and there prayed" (Mark 1:35). And Luke stated: "He withdrew himself into the wilderness, and prayed" (5:16). The authority with which He spoke, and which so amazed His enemies (Mark 1:27; Luke 4:36), was obviously the result of being fortified by the direct communication with His Father while in secret prayer. Small wonder we read that He stated, "My Father and I are one," for He spent so much time in conversation with the Father that He picked up His very heartbeat.

In Matthew 14:23, we find, "And when He had sent the multitudes away, He went up into a mountain apart to pray; and when the evening was come, He was there alone." We can only surmise what took place in that meeting, but it should not be surprising that He is next found walking over a stormy sea to calm His terrified disciples. The miracle of calming the tempests of both nature and the human heart issued from His private spiritual discipline. To hear Him say to a disciple, "Simon, Simon, behold, Satan hath desired to have you, that he may sift you as wheat: but I have prayed for thee, that thy faith fail not" (Luke 22:31–32), is only to realize again how specific and personalized His private prayer life really was.

Implications of the Private Model of Prayer

The implications, of course, are patent as we consider what happens in the life of any individual who follows Jesus' example of private prayer. It means to be armed with a confidence generated by recent communion with The Chief Counselor. Such communion will also provide insights into counselees' concerns and will permit the counselor to offer hope and healing to the anxious and despairing. Honestly being able to tell people immersed in trouble that you have prayed for them that their faith would be quickened in their crises will almost always bring new hope.

How regrettable that the hidden aspects of relationship to God sometimes seem like a waste of time to those who find themselves as "public" people. In hidden prayer, Jesus experienced something in His life and ministry that apparently no other outlet could provide. Thus, He urged His followers to make His own example of "closet" devotion a part of their lives. There is so much that can be accomplished in us only through such a pursuit. Who is there that can string proper words together in public prayer that would ever be found publicly confessing sins of lust and pride or selfishness and hypocrisy, which sap spiritual strength and growth? It just is not done. However, such conditions do often exist, and ignoring them will leave one powerless, while the heart and mind grow weak with the accumulated clutter of secret sin. In no way does this intimate that Jesus had sin, confessed or otherwise, in His own life. His call to the closet summons us to strip our souls before Him and be rid of unspeakable, concealed sins, which are so ugly and opposed to the nature of God.

The closet of devotional prayer also liberates one to address and grieve over the needs of lives touched by divorce, dishonesty, infidelity, or perverse sexuality, and to bind the "strong man" (i.e. Satan) in a manner which would most likely never be done publicly. To deal with matters concretely in private gives an assurance and higher degree of authority when actually confronting the situation.

Also, in private prayer, the vague references to God's blessings frequently offered during public utterance take substance in joyous, grateful recollection of a loving Father's generous hand. Private prayer encourages heightened thanksgiving for God's blessings: a companion to love and who loves, comforts and satisfies; children who are healthy and growing; for a nose that can detect the scent of warm cinnamon rolls as you come home hungry from work; friends who are faithful; a puppy that thinks you're "it"; for sunshine after a long winter—the list is endless. In corporate worship gatherings, such a list might find some response, but generally it would evoke yawns, if not impatience. However, alone with the Giver of "all good and perfect gifts" (James 1:17), we can delight ourselves and our Lord in an outpouring of gratitude. The sense of well-being it brings inspires confidence as we move back into the mainstream of those who are blind to such blessings and provisions.

Perhaps the most important thing that happens in private devotions is that we are not praying for general "consumption"—we can keep our mouths shut and allow God to speak to us! It is a rare corporate gathering that can, or will, tolerate an atmosphere of meditation. However, if prayer truly allows God and humanity to converse, where is conversation if a person persists in a Carsonesque monologue? (After all, is not "active listening" supposed to be one of a counselor's skills?) Failure to allow time for God to answer questions, to give direction or to solve problems allows imbalances to develop. For a devotional life to take wings, there must be listening as well as talking. It is tragic to flop around like a wounded bird with the use of only one wing, when with the balanced power of interaction with God, we could see the miracles our hearts tell us are really possible as a result of prayer. Until one truly believes that God not only hears, but that He speaks, a pernicious, spiritual anemia will devitalize the spirit. Effective ministry will be slowed or stopped, while the undiscerning disciple muddles on, wishing things were different, yet talking on and on in a one-sided conversation. Things most likely never will be different until Jesus' model of unseen, private devotional life is part and parcel of one's own dedication to God and His service. Daily practice of the priority rediscovered by disciples of every generation, "service follows devotion," can mean the difference between enriching relationships in ministry and dull, frustrating experiences.

THE SEMI-PRIVATE DEVOTIONAL LIFE OF JESUS

There were other times when a few close friends observed Jesus praying. When

He called disciples to follow Him, some realized that the distance at which they would follow would be determined by themselves. Out of all the people in the world, He chose twelve men to train, and from that group came an inner circle of three—Peter, James and John. Of these three, John bore the name "beloved." Apparently these three men intuitively understood the principle to be articulated later by James, "Draw nigh to God, and He will draw nigh to you" (James 4:8). In all probability there was some resentment or misunderstanding about the special intimacy enjoyed by the "Sons of Thunder" (cf. Matt. 20:24) and by Peter, but it apparently never deterred the trio from following Jesus nor intimidated their Lord.

As a boy, I enjoyed a marvelous relationship with my maternal grandmother. There was always something special between us that was known and discussed by the whole family. When, at age 17, I joined the Armed Forces and was away my first Thanksgiving, most of the family was together and my absence was not only noticed, but a lively conversation erupted regarding my suspected favorite place with my grandmother. A happy, nonthreatened saint, she let the attack continue to a certain point, whereupon she ordered, "Hold it! I am not partial to him—He's partial to me!" Then she elaborated by presenting some irrefutable facts. She continued, "On my birthday and Mother's Day, he always remembers to bring or send me a gift. No other grandchild does that. When he was home and had special places to go or occasions that were meaningful, he always invited me to share them. None of the rest have ever done that. He's the only grandchild who ever writes or calls. See what I mean? He's partial to me!" Well, she made her point and the subject was changed, never to be brought up again.

That's the way it was for the disciples' relationship to Jesus. Those aware that nearness to Him would be determined by their own initiative were privileged to enter into some of the high and holy moments experienced spiritually by their Master. Luke 9:28-36 relate the semi-private devotional session Jesus had on the Mount of Transfiguration. These amazing events included a radiant alteration of His countenance as He prayed, and the appearance of Moses and Elijah, also in glory, who conversed with Him concerning the approaching Passion Week. That devotional period climaxed with, of all things, the disciples hearing the proclamation of God concerning their Master.

The intimacy developed by Peter and the two sons of Zebedee not only afforded them the privilege of witnessing the transfiguring power of prayer, but made them accessories to the agonizing prayer of Gethsemane. While their minds reeled under the tension of the battle being waged (and they moved through the experience in a blur), they still learned that prayer can be an exercise in devastation. There was nothing easy about it. Great burdens must be wrestled until victory comes—as it ultimately did. And when it did, Jesus endured the treachery, the trial, the desertion, the cruel beatings, and ultimately the crucifixion as the only calm, collected person in the whole incredible uproar!

Again, semi-private devotions incorporate one of God's grand provisions for communion with Him—singing. It was the night of betrayal and Jesus and the Twelve were in the Upper Room, celebrating Passover. Before the evening ended, the Lord took the elements of Passover and instituted a new feast. The striking note is that with all that drama going on—and they were but moments from plunging into the most earth-shaking event the world had ever experienced— Jesus concluded by leading them in a hymn (Matt. 26:30). Thank God for this vignette provided of that semi-private devotional setting, which reveals singing as a part of the Lord's devotional practice. That Christianity is a singing faith is universally known. To assume that it is the norm for one's personal devotional life would probably be questionable, but I am always heartened when I hear of friends, or read of great men and women of God who testify that the hymnbook is a part of their devotional equipment. Songs, whether in the Spirit or with the understanding (1 Cor. 14:15), express something that transcends regular verbalization. The impact made upon the worshiper by singing is probably more powerful than is usually considered (Eph. 5:19; Col. 3:16).

Some years ago, a young friend was stricken by a heart arrhythmia that deprived his brain of oxygen. It looked for days as if he would die, but he finally stabilized in a severely comatose condition. After many weeks, he recovered consciousness. He had the power of speech but his memory was totally irradicated. Walking, reading, writing, and even the identity of his wife and children had to be relearned. The damage was indescribable. But a mutual friend, his pastor, made a startling discovery one day when they were driving. The pastor, who loved to sing, without thinking began to hum a gospel chorus. Spontaneously, the brain-damaged young man started singing it, word and tune-perfect! His conscious memory could not recall his pastor's name, but deep, deep in his unconscious the times he had adored his Master with that song came rising to the surface of his consciousness with no effort! Another striking event happened on that ride; after singing for a little while, the young man began to pray in the Spirit. Then he asked his pastor, "What was that? I do that every now and then." When my colleague related that to me I wept with a new appreciation of what Paul was describing when he said, "For if I pray in an unknown tongue, my spirit prayeth, but my understanding is unfruitful" (1 Cor. 14:14). In the life of our young friend, the prayer of the Spirit was independent of the brain's limited capacity.

Far-reaching effects resulted for those who fellowshiped with the Lord in His visible, semi-private devotions. John, the beloved, authored five of the books in our New Testament Canon. Peter was not only known as the chief Apostle, but he penned two beautiful epistles himself, while James became one of the early Christian martyrs.

Reading the Scriptures occupied many of Jesus' devotional hours. While we would most likely place such activities for ourselves in the model of total privacy, for Jesus it would have been semi-private because of the lack of available

Scriptures. They certainly would not have been in the home of a poor carpenter. But wherever and however He learned to read, Jesus read and meditated in the Scriptures until they became a vital part of Him. His careful attention to the written Word made Him invulnerable to the attacks of His enemies. In the early rounds of temptation by Satan, He escaped the trickery of the master deceiver (who used Scripture) by replying, "It is written again..." (Matt. 4:7). Having lived in the Old Testament, He was thus equipped to triumph over a potential spiritual coup. Later, when he found Himself in conflict with the Pharisees, who had accused Him of transgressing the tradition of the elders, Jesus did not deny the accusation; rather he tied their hands with a counter-question, "Why do ye also transgress the commandment of God by your tradition? For God commanded, saying, honor thy father and mother: and, he that curseth father or mother, let him die the death" (Matt. 15:3-4). That He had schooled Himself in Scriptures as part of His devotional life is a model we should not overlook or take lightly.

THE PUBLIC DEVOTIONAL LIFE OF JESUS

That powerful incidents took place in public as a direct result of Jesus' private life before the Father cannot be escaped. When finally it was time for Him to leave His family and proceed with fulfilling His mission, Jesus was drawn to the waters of baptism. And what a service it became! Luke reported, "Now when all the people were baptized, it came to pass, that Jesus also being baptized, and praying, the heaven was opened, and the Holy Ghost descended in a bodily shape like a dove upon him, and a voice came from heaven, which said, Thou art my beloved Son; in thee I am well pleased" (Luke 3:21-22). I have been present at and have participated in some memorable baptismal services, but never one with such supernatural accompaniments as are listed here.

In His earthly ministry, our Model Counselor epitomized living out scriptural direction, including public, corporate worship. The Psalmist had long since extolled public devotional gatherings, especially as found in Psalm 95, verses 1, 2, 6, and 7, where the plural is used in acts of worship: "O come let *us* sing unto the Lord; let *us* make a joyful noise to the Rock of *our* Salvation. Let *us* come before His presence with thanksgiving....O come, let *us* worship and bow down; let *us* kneel before the Lord *our* Maker. For He is *our* God; and *we* are the people of His pasture,..." (emphasis is the author's).

Since we know Jesus' familiarity with Scripture and His dedication to live a holy life, it should not surprise us to read: "And He came to Nazareth, where He had been brought up: and, *as His custom was, He went into the synagogue on the sabbath day*" (Luke 4:16, emphasis added). Jesus was able to actively participate in public worship because His personal sanctuary was always previously in order. Consequently, when He stood up to read from Isaiah, He ultimately set the place afire with conflict. "The Spirit of the Lord is upon me, because he hath anointed me to preach the gospel to the poor; he hath sent me to heal the brokenhearted, to preach deliverance to the captives, and recovering of sight to the blind, to set at liberty them that are bruised, to preach the acceptable year of the Lord'' (Luke 4:18–19). His life was so enmeshed with the Father, that whether alone in meditation, with a few friends in prayer, or in a corporate worship setting, His flow was directed God-ward.

It is no puzzle that ''common'' people and those in trouble sought Jesus as counselor. Even in public, His compassion and love for people was communicated in moving, verbal expressions, and the openness of His own spirit reached their condition. As Jesus broke down and wept, the crowd attending Lazarus' funeral exclaimed to one another, ''Behold how He loved him!'' (John 11:36). Then, moving naturally and easily from that display of emotion, He began to pray: ''Father, I thank Thee that Thou has heard me. And I knew that Thou hearest me always: but because of the people which stand by I said it, that they may believe that Thou hast sent me. And when he thus had spoken, he cried with a loud voice, Lazarus, come forth'' (John 11:41–43). The whole Christian world knows that Lazarus did, in fact, come forth!

Surely no one present at the feeding of the five thousand ever forgot the miracle of the fish and loaves (Matt. 14:15–21). Every generation since has taken account of what happened after that extended service led by Jesus. (I have a friend who remarked once that probably the only reason there was food on the premises was that the little boy with the fish and bread had heard Jesus before and knew He preached a long time!) Reluctant to send the people away hungry, He took that pitifully inadequate lunch, and ''he looked up to heaven and blessed, and brake the loaves, and gave them to his disciples to set before them; and the two fishes divided he among them all. And they did all eat, and were filled....And they that did eat...were about five thousand men'' (Mark 6:41–44). Once again, when Jesus prayed in public, things happened.

SUMMARY AND APPLICATION

We have now recounted three areas of a model life of devotion. How do these apply? The evidence is too striking to disregard; there must be some correlation between the personal appeal of Jesus to troubled people, the miracles that took place when He prayed, and the facts of His devotional life.

It would be easy to ''cop out'' by attributing it all to His divinity, but that is exactly what that would amount to—a ''cop out.'' This is expecially true in light of His promise, ''He that believeth on Me, the works that I do shall he do also; and greater works than these shall he do; because I go unto my Father'' (John 14:12). This solemn word from Christ was surely not intended as some elusive, impenetrable mystery. The mystery is not so much that there is little evidence to verify the promise, but that so many who know it are unwilling to become a model of the ''well integrated'' personality, i.e., the integration of a personal devotional life with public service or ministry. We can so easily give assent to the belief that if the private life is charged with constant intimacy with God, then ministry to the troubled will have miraculous results. However, the "rub" is not in assent, but in practice! Scarcely anyone I talk to these days wants another "seven easy steps" to anything in God's kingdom. Rather, pure minds must be stirred up to a fresh realization that effective ministry to the sick and hurting requires returning to the elementary performance of what too often gets postponed—i.e., prayer, reading of God's Word and adoration of our Lord. An effective devotional life will lead to dynamic relationships both on this earth and in heaven.

The Spirit-filled counselor's ultimate assistance does not come from the latest thought of leaders in the counseling or psychological field, but is anchored in "Thus saith the Lord." There is no way to escape the cause and effect here: "Jesus answered and said unto them, Ye do err, *not knowing the Scriptures, nor the power of God*" (Matt. 22:29, emphasis added). Knowing the Scriptures and God's power are as inseparably linked as flesh and blood, and they still interact in harmony to bring life and health. If one knows and believes the Scriptures and can rightly put them into practice, real power *can* be released.

A worthy goal is for counseling to be as food to a hungry soul. For that to happen, the counselor's own soul needs to be full, for who can give what he does not have? In his awful suffering, Job was able to declare, "I have esteemed the words of His mouth *more than my necessary food*" (Job 23:12, emphasis added). Jesus challenged the devil by stating that real living did not come by just keeping fuel in the engine: "Man shall not live by bread alone, but by every word that proceedeth out of the mouth of God" (Matt. 4:4). That statement, itself, was a quotation from the Old Testament (Deut. 8:3), which Jesus knew so well.

In our desire to impart sweetness to lives gone sour, we must make sure we have ample supply ourselves. When we do, then we can state with the psalmist: "How sweet are thy words unto my taste! Yea, sweeter than honey to my mouth" (Ps. 119:103).

What of the conflict that "sizzles" our brains when we believe the time has come to confront? How shall we arrange the proper setting and make it "come off" like it is supposed to? The effect being sought can often be facilitated by application of Scripture: "Is not my word like a fire? saith the Lord; and like a hammer that breaketh the rock in pieces?" (Jer. 23:29). When with the confident handling of God's Word we bring an individual "to task," clarity for the counselee and solid ground for the counselor is assured. Unlike the orator and debator, who seem to take pleasure in elaborate use of words or clever mental gymnastics, the counselor does not get far in effecting life-change by argument or even by logic. But, "the Word of God is quick, and powerful, and sharper than any two-edged sword, piercing even to the dividing asunder of soul and spirit, and of the joints and marrow, and is a discerner of the thoughts and intents of the heart" (Heb. 4:12).

Thank God! His Word stands ready in every generation to help helpers. Decades ago I stood at the door of a church one Sunday, greeting worshipers as they left. A young man would noticeably get out of line to let others pass by until finally he alone remained. Having watched that process, I sensed that he had more to say than "goodbye," and that, whatever his problem, it was weighing heavily on him. So I cheerfully greeted him without taking his hand in the goodbye mode and moved back down the aisle, talking as I went, with him following. When I got to the front pew, I sat down and motioned for him to join me. Then I took his hand and said, "What can we talk about, Steve?" With that he began to weep and said, "Oh, Pastor, I have fouled up so bad!" Then he sobbed out a story of betrayal to his own desire to maintain a pure life. When he finished, together we moved from the pew to the altar where I took the Bible and read again, "If we sin we have an advocate..." (1 John 2:1). And I weep again, all these years removed, remembering the forgiveness and sweetness that came with the application of "wherewithal shall a young man cleanse his way? By taking heed thereto according to thy word" (Ps. 119:9). And it still works!

Very recently another young man, a non-Christian heavily involved in the drug culture, shared his astonishment when he learned that Christians practice celibacy except in marriage. Having for some years been given to promiscuity, he sought to quarrel about it; such a lifestyle seemed unreasonable to him. But when the same Word which showed him the way to eternal life also revealed the way to live here on earth, he too, "cleansed his way...according to thy Word" (Ps. 119:9). When we are not only familiar with what God has to say on a given subject, but also believe with conviction that it is not debatable, problems cease to become issues; they have already been settled in the light of what God has said. The Bible will always be the lamp for wandering feet and a light to obscure paths (Ps. 119:105). "The statutes of the Lord are right, rejoicing the heart: the commandment of the Lord is pure, enlightening the eyes" (Ps. 19:8).

A Pentecostal pastor is probably no more sensitive than the Spirit-filled professional counselor to the reality that the immediate need of a non-Christian who has come for counseling, is really to find Jesus as Savior. A young convert reported to me what some of his friends said after attending a funeral I had conducted for a suicide victim—one of their group. Curious, he had asked them what they thought of me. They grudgingly thought I might be all right, but they felt that I "was recruiting." I have no intention of denying it. Though I would never want a person to feel I was "getting my soul for the day," I thank God that "I am not ashamed of the gospel of Christ: for it is the power of God unto salvation to every one that believeth; to the Jew first, and also to the Greek" (Rom. 1:16). The keen distinction between the Spirit-filled craftsman and the humanist is not so much their training in personality theory and management; rather, it is where they are rooted—in Freud, Skinner, Maslow, Carkhuff, Rogers and company—or on the *Solid Rock*, God's Word.!

Based on Jesus' example, the essential elements of a Spirit-filled counselor's devotional life are clear: establishing a relationship with God so consistent that it is intimate, and practicing private devotions that are so saturated with easy conversation and adoration that public worship unashamedly continues where the last private expression ended. Such a devotional life will result in human relationships which evidence the presence of God that has been accompanying the counselor all the while. We can then expect that lives which have been marred by sin and its effects, emotions that have gotten away from their owner, guilt that is unbearable for its weight, will all have been brought into the presence of someone who can deal with such things effectively: a devotional-practicing, Spirit-filled counselor and Our Lord!

5

PERSONAL AND SPIRITUAL GROWTH

Mark Stocks

INTRODUCTION

The role of growth in the experience of everyday life can hardly be overestimated. We are either growing or dying; there is no neutral holding pattern. Counselors and psychologists are particularly interested in the personality dimension of growth and development. While the physical body matures mainly along genetic lines, the personality develops along uniquely individual patterns of expression in communication, emotionality, and motivation. Growth in these areas cannot be measured in inches or pounds, but must be evaluated in light of behavioral principles, moral law and divine revelation.

Historically, maturity and psychopathology were not well understood. If a person were particularly mature and had social stature, he or she was revered as being wise—a sage to be consulted. Conversely, those individuals suffering from what we today call mental health problems were condemned as being demon possessed, or at best "strange." The possibility that becoming wise or mature involves some lawful principles is suggested poetically in the book of Proverbs where the young man is enjoined to search out and follow wisdom wherever "she" goes (Prov. chs. 8 & 9). However, it has not been until the twentieth century that a scientific effort was made to discover the principles of psychological growth, maturation, and psychopathology. Now Western culture—in its optimism—seems to believe that if the principles of maturity and "self-actualization" can be delineated, humanity can still save itself from terrestrial suicide. Unfortunately, while science has become an exercise in optimism, our meaning in life has died through adherence to existentialism. We talk as though the problems of Earth will be solved, but live as though there is no tomorrow.

Christianity seems to proffer another view: live for eternity and do not plan for tomorrow in this life. One's motivation is highly impacted by the way life is perceived. With no tomorrow, there is no hope; thus there is no reason to change. A belief in eternity does not result in a lack of responsible motivation, as critics claim; rather, it frees us to review our alternatives and to choose the way we will live life based on eternal absolutes. A professor in a psychotherapy techniques class once told me that he preferred to work with Christians because, as he put it, "There is more hope." He was not referring to the power of his own belief in the Christian's ability; instead, he was referring to the power of the Christian client's belief in the goodness of God who works all things together for good (Rom. 8:28).

Christianity and the activities of psychotherapy and counseling seem to fit together hand-in-glove. However, many people, both Christians and non-Christians, do not agree with this apparent fit. Much of the debate centers on the differences between individual, personal growth and Christian, spiritual growth. Are issues such as self-actualization and self-realization valid in a Christian context? What are the natures of spiritual growth and personal growth, and what do they have to do with psychotherapy and counseling? This chapter presents a perspective that I have adopted while struggling with some of these basic questions. I am presenting what I believe to be an integrative understanding of the relationship between psychology and theology in theory and practice. This represents no final solution; but rather, it offers a base from which to view the issues.

Some notes need to be made in reference to the following discussion. First, I have made no distinction between the activity of counseling and the practice of psychotherapy. Debates rage over this issue and I am making no judgment as to the validity of the arguments. Second, I am writing from a vantage point of a doctorate in clinical psychology. I believe, however, that the discussion will benefit readers at different educational levels and from varied academic disciplines because the fundamental thesis is foundational to all of Christianity.

NATURE OF PSYCHOTHERAPY AND COUNSELING

The essence of psychotherapy and counseling is growth, growth which eventually leads to maturity and an ability to fulfill one's individual and interpersonal needs. That is, given its present state, the practice of counseling and psychotherapy offers sophisticated methodologies for enabling individuals who have problems in living to grow through their difficulties and mature into complete persons. Whether the immediate goal is as complicated as psychoanalysis or as simple as relaxation training, the larger goal is wholeness or completeness. Paradoxically, this is a state which may never totally exist in this life. In any case, the meaning of wholeness is indelibly etched on the hearts of all mankind.

Given that the essence of psychotherapy is growth and the goal is wholeness, three general statements can be extrapolated. First, psychotherapy is a process, not an act. That is, while medication is used in some cases and behavior modification techniques are employed for various specific problems, actual change involves a developing awareness of the self, which enables a person to adjust internally, and allows him or her to change external circumstances to meet idiosyncratic needs and desires. This emphasis on process is explained more fully later in this discussion. Suffice it to say now that just as human beings are not totally objective and intellectual, so psychotherapy cannot be a purely intellectual, objective experience if it is to meet human need.

The second statement suggested by the idea that personal growth and psychotherapy are synonymous activities is that growth, at least the kind of growth in which therapy specializes, is fundamentally interpersonal in nature. This should come as no surprise; help from another person is why the client comes into therapy. However, the ramifications of this statement are far-reaching. If we say that growth through therapy involves both content and process, then we must define maturity, the result of growth, as fundamentally an interpersonal issue. In essence, psychotherapeutic treatment is founded upon a relationship which has as one of its goals enhancing the depth and quality of the interpersonal process through changing communications. The content of therapy concentrates on the specific problems brought by the client. The process of therapy, in contrast, involves adjusting the way the client expresses problems interpersonally, i.e., changing those self-defeating ways of resolving conflicts in order to meet needs. Thus we define maturity as an interpersonal issue, while concomitantly defining psychopathology as problems in interpersonal relating. Issues of interpersonal relatedness, therefore, can be seen as both the means and the end of therapy. While this is obviously not true for those patients who have physically-based problems, it does include the physically ill person's attitudes *about* the illness.

The third implication has been woven throughout the previous two statements. The activity of interpersonal relating—mental health functioning and psychopathology—is an expression of the total person. This, too, seems obvious. However, the primary emphasis in psychotherapy lies in emotional development. It is for this end that modern psychotherapy came into being. Freud had a desire to be able to heal the emotions damaged as a result of trauma and distortion. Although as a medical doctor he desired a truly "scientific" method and believed that eventually mental illness would be controlled like physical illness, the method he finally adopted involved an intense, albeit one-sided, relationship. This was the best way he knew to emphasize the emotional dimension, the source of distortion. On the whole, his method has changed only in terms of varying emphases of technique. The focus on emotional processes remained. That there is such a need for a focus on the emotional processes seems to be a function of society, the family and ultimately the impact of humanity's separation from God. That is, the unity of our personality has been violated by the sin of Adam. Society and family reinforce the fragmentation via imposition of distorted expectations.

While it may appear that I have digressed from an initial focus on the idea of wholeness to an emphasis on emotions, this is actually not the case. As educated individuals, we work very hard on our intellectual development. Our emotional defenses allow us to believe that since we have our doctrine and philosophy in order, we have our lives basically together; when we struggle with problems, we think the solution lies in learning more. We fool only ourselves with such beliefs. The New Testament book of James is a great handbook for psychologists and counselors. The message of James can be summed up in the question, "If you have it together, why don't you act like it?" The gap between intellectual comprehension and committed activity is primarily a function of emotional investment. The essence of Christian maturity, then, lies in the need for one's emotions, intellect and behavior all to be expressing the same message—a *whole* message by a *whole* person.

Throughout this section I have equated personal growth and Christian or spiritual growth. I have done so as the result of specialized training and a considerable amount of personal questioning. When I first entered the field of counseling, I was fresh out of graduate school with a master's degree. I was employed by the state of Ohio in a substance abuse program. Being a committed Christian and being interested in maintaining my integrity on all fronts, I found myself in a great deal of internal turmoil. The conflict essentially raged over the question of how God fit into the practice of counseling. Being faced fairly consistently with some rather extreme situations, and feeling very inadequate—and at times totally helpless—I would try periodically to "witness" to clients, saying, in effect, "Christ is the answer." But nothing changed for me or for the people I was working with. As a result I found myself in a quandary: Christ is indeed the answer, but why did God not change the situation when He was so asked? Ultimately, I concluded that *God is more interested in changing the people in the problem than changing the situation in which the difficulty exists.*

The specific processes by which people change, I concluded, are essentially the same for the Christian as they are for the non-Christian. The one intervening, determining variable in the process occurs in the person's access (or lack of access) to God, the Creator of the change process. The issue for me then focused on a relational context: Man to God, and man to Man. This has become my understanding of therapy and subsequent growth.

While I have loosely covered a variety of issues in this section, the primary focus has been on three simple assumptions: (a) psychotherapy and counseling are specialized situations for enabling people with problems in living to develop maturity in specific areas of their lives; (b) personal growth and development is an ongoing process; and (c) the essence of the change process involves issues of interpersonal relationships. For the remainder of the chapter, I will focus on three basic questions, one of which has already been briefly addressed. First, what is the relationship between personal and spiritual growth? Second, what is the nature of interpersonal change in such a process, and subsequently in psychotherapy? Third, what is maturity for the Christian and how is it different from maturity for the non-Christian?

Personal and Spiritual Growth

A delineation between personal (psychological) and spiritual growth is evident throughout Christian literature. Conversely, modern secular literature, which emphasizes humanity's spirituality (e.g. humanism and existentialism) stresses our wholeness as both spiritual and psychological/physical beings. Consequently, several questions arise, the most obvious of which involves whether or not the secular concept of spirituality is identical (or even akin) to the Christian concept by the same name. A second, more fundamental issue is related to philosophical/theological questions concerning whether or not "natural" processes and "spiritual" processes are different or essentially the same. The answer to both questions would seem to be found in an examination of the nature of humanity and the nature of the change process.

The Nature of Humanity

At some level, a counselor must define the nature of Man (in the generic sense) and how that nature affects, and is affected by, the routine of life. In general, there are three approaches to defining the nature of Man: (a) Man is morally good, (b) Man is evil or morally bad, and (c) Man is morally neutral (neither good nor evil). On one hand, to stress humanity's positive nature or goodness sensitizes the counselor to focus on a client's potential for self-improvement. On the other hand, emphasizing pathology leads to focusing upon the negative, weaker side. The idea that Man has potential for both positive and negative actions is not a new insight. However, having the potential for good and evil does not necessarily mean that Man is neutral in nature. Christianity stresses the facts that we are made in the image of God and are fallen from that lofty position. Any theory utilized by a Christian counselor or psychotherapist must therefore recognize and give equal treatment to both aspects. The essence of changing and growing lies in a maintenance of the inherent process in Man by which the individual's personality moves toward fulfilling its positive potential. This might be described as actualizing the image of God.

In emphasizing the *process* over the *content* of Christianity in counseling, I am simply trying to balance the emotional and intellectual dimensions of humanity. I am portraying psychotherapeutic intervention as an intricate walk, where the process is fostered even while content is conveyed. Directing attention to the process simply means growth develops from the inside out. What, then, is this process and how is it fostered?

The Nature of Process

The concept of process is difficult to define. It connotes ongoing movement, change, and development such as one might see in a river. A river develops from a stream, is maintained (as a whole) by boundaries, has an end (the ocean), and encompasses a variety of levels or depths. One cannot take a slice of water and call it a river. Nor can a river bed in itself be accurately called a river. The idea of a river lies in the wholeness of the concept involving content, movement, and direction.

Gendlin (1964), a one-time associate of Carl Rogers, described the nature of process, and subsequently the nature of change in psychotherapy, as a series of occurrences in a human relationship in which movement (change) is recognized as an internal, viscerally felt event. As a person focuses on internal feelings and listens to them expressed aloud in the presence of another person, the internally blocked issue or conflict moves toward completion (i.e. resolution) and internal change occurs. The nature of the mechanism that initiates and maintains such movement is highly speculative, but is worth considering as a potential model or explanation of the growth process.

Gendlin[1] postulated an in-process internal frame of reference or internal perspective as the basic level of human personality. This in itself is not unique. As previously noted, however, this internal data level is described as a feeling process, i.e., inwardly sensed and viscerally felt. This internal frame of reference is what Gendlin called the direct referent of experience and as such it contains felt meanings: ideas and feelings unique to the individual. Such felt meanings function implicitly as part of motivational content in thinking and behavior. They provide for the expression of the most fundamental functioning of human personality. The *implicit* felt meanings exist internally as the result of interaction between everyday life and one's internal frame of reference, but they remain incomplete until they are expressed in speech or behavior. When felt meanings interact with verbal expression, the meanings become *explicit*. Work, behavior, and speech are completed communications of meaning. Completion, in this context, refers to a communicated existential statement of one's being. Thus, these implicit meanings are not hidden conceptual units, intellectual in nature; rather, these can be seen as an internally patterned readiness for organized interaction on the part of the whole person. Just as physical life is an interaction between the body and the environment, so psychic life, or experiencing, is an interaction between feelings (felt meaning) and the symbols which complete or carry the feelings forward. Gendlin's use of the term "feelings" in this context refers to one's unique phenomenological perspective and is not solely tied to emotions. That is, "feelings" refer to the whole person and not to a single dimension of experience.

Even as life is continuously occurring, so experiencing is continuous, albeit as an implicit process. The ongoing interaction between internal feelings and events, others' behaviors, and external occurrences, enhances the process. Consequently, others' responses are very important to this process, because they provide the events which carry forward (complete) the felt meanings. This would seem to be logical, since human (interpersonal) activities affect human processes more effectively and powerfully than do non-human events. Only if there are events can there be an ongoing interaction process. If responses from another person are not forthcoming, then some feelings are not carried forward and those aspects of experiencing cease to be in process. Thus, according to Gendlin, the importance of others for experiencing cannot be minimized for at least several reasons: (a) events available for interaction are different when one is alone and when one is with another; (b) others influence the manner in which experiencing occurs; and (c) rejection of a person by another ignores the person's felt meanings and those meanings are not carried forward. Others' responses are thus the fuel and the vehicle for the completion of feelings.

Perhaps an example at this point would be helpful. Two men go to a play, a murder mystery. One observes the performance in relative composure and reflects on the meaning of murder in today's culture. The other person, though, becomes extremely anxious, although he cannot specifically say why. After the play, the two sit down to talk about it. The apparently unaffected individual glibly discusses the critical dimensions of the play and its relative merits as a cultural statement. The second man, however, finds it difficult to talk about the details without referring to a friend who had been murdered some years ago. As the first person listens, the troubled man begins to realize the dramatic affect that his friend's death had on him and his present lifestyle. This realization allows him the freedom to feel less anxious and to discuss the play from a more objective, cultural perspective.

The felt meaning for each individual in regard to the play was unique and was affected by the individual's defenses and history. One person obviously had incomplete, frozen feelings, which were only brought to awareness through a relatively innocent occurrence—the play. As the person focused on the feelings and talked about them in the context of his own meanings, and as his friend listened and did not interrupt the flow, the full ramifications of that person's feelings were realized. Subsequently, he was able to acccept those feelings as part of his own experiencing and respond appropriately to the immediate situation. He was then able to continue living free of the conflict related to this particular event. The other individual may or may not have had incompleted felt meanings associated with parts of the play. If he did, the meanings were not sufficiently activated to cause him the same disruption as occurred in his friend. The two men were in the same situation with different felt meanings. The result was seen in different reactions, one person in conflict and one person unmoved. The conflict was resolved through communication and acceptance.

People are capable of completing the feeling process on their own, at least to a certain degree. However, even this is a result of interaction with other persons. An individual experiences interpersonal events before developing a "self," e.g., mother and child exist in interaction with each other before the child is aware of a "me" and a "you." These interpersonal events interact with the person's (child's) felt meanings. In time, the child develops the ability to respond intrapersonally to its own feelings. The responses then carry forward personal felt meanings. However, to the extent that the individual cannot carry feelings forward, another person becomes necessary. Others are important not for their assessment or attitudes, but because their responses (assuming they are appropriate) carry forward or complete the individual's felt meanings.

Spiritual Application of Gendlin's "Process"

Gendlin's somewhat complicated description of "process" seems to portray human spiritual interaction. That is, just as the Holy Spirit is biblically likened to a wind, unseen and unheard, yet always moving (John 3:8; Acts 2:14), the process level—the basic level of personality—is described as a moving, flowing river of personhood uniquely organized but commonly shared by all. There are many similarities, and some differences, in the conceptualization of the Spirit and personality process. Essentially, the biblical description of the Spirit is an illustration used as an attempt to communicate that things of the Spirit must be seen through spiritual eyes. As such, the analogy of the wind and the Spirit may not be a strictly valid one. Similarly, the image of a river may not do justice to the concept of process. However, the key to life in the Spirit is openness. Likewise, in this model, the key to growth lies in the ability to hear and be heard.

How then does Christian spiritual growth fit into this conceptualization? The answer seems to lie in the person of Jesus Christ; He who is both Man and God. How does Man relate to God? Man relates to Him on a personal level through Christ, who, because of His work on Earth, has become mediator between Man and God (1 Tim. 2:5). Thus the human spirit interacts with God through Christ on the level of the Holy Spirit or the Spirit of Christ (Rom. 1:9). Therefore, Christian spiritual growth might generally be defined as the completion or carrying forward of felt meanings having to do with God. Given that God is involved in all areas of a person's life, spiritual growth is potentially part of every event. This occurs via individual interaction with the self (e.g. meditation), with other Christians in fellowship, and with God in prayer and worship. For the Spirit-filled believer, then, tongues, which "edify the self" (1 Cor. 14:4), might generally be understood as an ongoing series of interpersonal events which potentiate some felt meaning completion, the heavenly language being the result of "listening in" to God's side. This process is good—and perhaps even necessary (1 Cor. 14:39); however, in itself, it is not enough. Fellowship and openness with other Christians is not only a privilege, it is a necessity for growth.

If all this is true, then it would seem that counselors and psychotherapists (as relationship specialists) are unnecessary appendages in the Church. Ideally, this might be true. However, to the Church's discredit, the emphasis on Christian, human interaction has been minimal. Rather, correct doctrine has been the focal point of primary interest. Intellectual development has been perceived as being more important than the development of interpersonal relationships. Differences among and between churches appear to have had more impact on the way we see life than the power of Christian love.

In brief, to this point I have stated that counseling or psychotherapy is a specialized arena for personal growth, where the fundamental task concerns interpersonal relationships. I have applied to spiritual growth a theory of process and change which seems to account for many of the factors suggested as necessary for individual development. I have discussed the concept of process from what is generally interpreted as a secular viewpoint, that is, a viewpoint which is non-spiritual in language and reference. It would therefore seem to be helpful to address the relationship between psychology and theology. Since this is a hotly debated field with many participants, I will simply express my thoughts and perspectives, along with those of writers who have impressed me and helped form my thinking. The first part of this discussion addresses some of the theological-philosophical bases of my orientation. The second part discusses the concept of maturity, that is, the goals of therapy from a psychology-theology integrative perspective.

THE RELATIONSHIP BETWEEN PSYCHOLOGY AND THEOLOGY

Personal Struggle

As I related earlier, my initial struggle with the psychotherapy-Christianity issue was founded in the conflict between my psychology training and much of my upbringing and subsequent Christian commitment, along with a felt responsibility to "witness" that "Christ is the answer." Endemic to this conflict was my understanding, or rather lack of understanding, of the change process. I understood Christian witnessing to be a matter of proclaiming the truth, a combination of prophetic swerve and salesman-like persuasion. I eventually came to understand that my need to witness was born not of evangelical zeal, but rather of my feelings of helplessness over the enormity of the problems that people brought to my office. As I began to study the issues in depth, I found that the primary emphasis in Christianity was on the quality of one's relationships and only secondarily on evangelism. The salvation message was appropriate when the person was ready to hear it. It was not, however, a magic exit door out of situational conflict and problems in living.

Thus, I began to make human interaction the focus of my assessment and intervention. The interpersonal relationship issue became the pair of glasses through which I viewed the psychology-theology issue. The question of what these disciplines had in common seemed to be answered. Nevertheless, the question of *how* they were different was not settled until I had done some further study and reflection.

Psychological-Theological Differences

A variety of writers have addressed the issue of the relationship between theology and psychology. Christian writers' attitudes toward this relationship vacillate between denying the validity of scientific, empirical data to embracing without question such findings. Secular writers usually communicate in neutral terms unless they have a specific bias. Generally, however, the nature-spirit conflict, i.e., the philosophical foundations in question, remains in the background for most writers. The impasse seems to have a resolution in an article by Larzelere (1980).

Larzelere proposed that Christianity and psychology basically ask different questions. He suggested that the disciplines differ on all but one of six levels of scientific inquiry. The six levels are: (a) the *Data level*, which includes all admissible elements of information; (b) the *Hypothesis level*, where initial generalizations are suggested which tie together the elements of data; (c) the *Specific Proposition level*, where several hypotheses are pulled together with research results, and empirical laws and models are suggested; (d) the *Linkage level*, where processes of induction and deduction are utilized to begin to synthesize the data in a wholistic view; (e) the *General Proposition level*, where all general models and theories are delineated; and (f) the *World View level*, where basic assumptions and values are posited. All information through the General Proposition level is open for research, revision through new information, and general argumentation. The World View level, however, is not subject to the direct empirical process of confirmation/non-confirmation. Basic assumptions and values are chosen by the individual. Christianity generally exists on the World View level and is not provable in an empirical sense. However, it does offer a foundation of values from which the other levels can be understood.

The problem with many well-intentioned Christian writers seems to come from a misunderstanding of the levels at which the various theories exist. Anything that smacks of behaviorism or psychoanalysis is automatically viewed as wrong because Skinner and Freud denounced religion. However, the theories of behaviorism and psychoanalysis actually exist on a General Proposition level. Further, the principles utilized by Skinner and Freud do appear to be valid and do stand up to examination, albeit with some variations in emphasis and language. While Skinner and Freud specifically have written about Christianity in negative terms (e.g. *Beyond Freedom and Dignity*, 1971; *Totem and Taboo*, 1913/1955), they technically have passed the bounds of their information and moved to the World View level. Theologically, they have attempted to discover the creator of nature by looking at natural principles. In so doing, they deny divine revelation.

This does not mean that natural principles are invalid for Christians, only that one cannot arrive at the infinite through study of the finite. Principles delineated through research and theory are of interest and are useful to psychology and subsequently to Christianity. These are the mechanisms which offer insights into how people grow, develop, and learn. Too frequently, though, Christian writers have been content to condemn the principles on the basis of their association with non-Christian writers. Non-Christian writers have been content to condemn

Christianity on the basis of theory. In so doing, both the Christian and the non-Christian are outside the bounds of their respective disciplines.

Underlying this statement is the oft quoted maxim, "all truth is God's truth" regardless of the interpreter or discoverer (Holmes, 1977). The unity of truth has been claimed by Christianity since it began. However, the focus has often been lost (Carter & Narramore, 1979). How we see the world (the World View Level), affects how we approach the data and affects what will be done with the results, namely, how we interpret. However, the information (the Data level) remains unchanged regardless of our description. In many ways, Christians have bought the theorist's World View level description. Simply because a theorist claims a World View based on research, this does not make the espoused World View true. Christians therefore need not fear psychology; God has ordered all truth, even psychological principles.

Thus, we can say that principles of human activity are issues essentially apart from the theological-philosophical interpretations of the same. "The Earth is the Lord's and the fullness thereof" (Ps. 24:1). As Christians, we can accept the principles of psychology even while we eschew the non-believer's philosophy.

FOUNDATIONS OF INTEGRATION

I have noted that the essence of psychotherapy has to do with interpersonal interaction—human relationships. Further, I have stated that the process of psychotherapy and growth is an ongoing process of a relationship which develops in terms of its quality and depth. Finally, I have proposed that psychology addresses the mechanisms of human growth and development. As such, it has no argument with Christianity, which addresses the World View—the underlying values and assumptions. Both are expressions of God's truth in life.

An obvious conclusion is that psychotherapy is concerned with human relationships. Is Christianity also thus minded? The answer is an obvious yes! The fundamental responsibility of the Christian is what has been termed "The Royal Law": "Thou shalt love the Lord thy God with all thy heart, mind and soul,...and thy neighbor as thyself" (Matt. 22:37–39). In the interplay of life and humanity, love is portrayed as the beginning and end of all relationships and the foundation for all actions (1 Cor. 13). This, then, is to be the foundation and the goal for the Christian psychotherapist, to love and to aid the development of love. This does not mean that the end product is totally achieved; rather, the process toward the goal is uninhibited. In a broad sense, maturity equals love. From a more limited perspective, maturity is the road which eventually leads to the actualizing of a person's ability to love and be loved.

From a secular standpoint, Sullivan (1953) stated: "One achieves mental health to the extent to which one becomes aware of one's interpersonal relations" (p. 87). In Christianity *and* psychology, the interpersonal dimension is clearly stressed as the foundation upon which people find satisfaction in life. What, then, is the content and subsequent direction of such a focus specifically from the "integrated" Christian perspective?

According to Carter (1974a), mature persons in a psychological and biblical sense are integrated, have a purposeful or goal-directed quality about their lives and are open to themselves and others. Carter utilized the concept of self-actualization to express the idea that mature individuals are continually developing their mind, body, and emotions toward becoming fully functioning persons. "Biblically it [development] is the same; that is, the process is parallel but the content is different" (Carter, 1974a, p. 95). The process of maturing is a human one, and is thus the same for the Christian as it is for the non-Christian. However, the content of assumptions at the World View level differ radically.

As Carter explained it, the dimension of humanity that is to be encouraged to develop is the *Imago Dei*, the Image of God in humanity. Non-Christians are capable of actualizing this image to a degree and potentially may become relatively healthy persons. This is so because the Image of God in us exists despite Adam's fall, albeit with distortion. In contrast, Christians, as redeemed, maintain an inherent potential to actualize the Image to a greater, more complete degree since they have a relationship with the source of the Image, God Himself. "Since he is related to the creator of the universe, he [Man] becomes more in harmony with the divine pattern and purpose in both himself and the World" (Carter, 1974a, p. 95).

This then is the direction of the process, an active development of the Image of God in people. The non-Christian talks about developing the personality utilizing such terms as ego defenses, congruence, creativity, authenticity, and regression. Some of these terms do indeed describe aspects of the Image of God in Man. They obviously do not refer directly to God or to the nature of His Image *per se*. Rather, they are "objective" terms which simply describe functions. Christianity addresses the same dimensions utilizing the vocabulary of a Christian culture. Thus when the non-Christian speaks of enabling the emotional growth of an individual through acceptance, authenticity and the confrontation of reality, the Christian talks about the development of truth and grace as one identifies with Christ (Carter, 1974b) and being transformed through the renewing of the mind (Rom. 12:2).

The concepts of truth and grace generate much theological fascination. To stress truth over grace is to live under the law. Issues of right and wrong result in lists of dos and don'ts. On the other hand, to emphasize grace over truth is to encourage license and sinful acting out. People echo a distortion of freedom claiming that a truly loving God will forgive all and save all without punishment. One side stresses responsibility at freedom's expense and the other side emphasizes mercy at the expense of justice. Maturity may be defined as a balance of these two concepts; a lack of balance is a distortion of the Image of God. Despite this apparent all-inclusive intellectual perspective on the content of maturity as a concept, the actual focus of Christian development remains a person—Jesus Christ. The Gospel of John (1:14, 17) portrays the personality of Christ as the perfect blend of truth and grace with the implication that they were the essence of Christ's personality, and thus of His ministry. Therefore, as we interact with Him and continue to have our mutual felt meanings completed through this interaction, balance in our personality develops, we become more like Him. Once again, the real emphasis of growth lies in interpersonal relations. To grow spiritually is to increase in one's ability to relate to and identify with Christ intellectually, emotionally, and behaviorally—as a whole person.

Summary

While the process orientation seems to exist as a reality for human beings, the content or rationale—that in which we say we trust—differs from person to person. The non-Christian must look exclusively to human interaction for personal development and fulfillment. The Christian, however, develops maturity as the result of a deepening relationship with Christ individually (one-to-one) and as the result of increasing quality of human interaction.

This, then, may be viewed as the meaning of Christian psychotherapy. As with most therapies, the fundamental focus lies in all issues affecting the therapeutic relationship (therapist and client). But the Christian therapist also attempts to understand how the Christian client distorts his or her relationship with Christ. The assumption underlying this concept is that a client's emotional stance toward Man regarding issues of dependence and independence will reflect the conflicts and subsequent distortions of the way he or she tries to fulfill needs, e.g., attempting to manipulate God. While it is true, at least from a psychoanalytic perspective, that a client's references to God are in reality often disguised references to the therapist and/or the client's parents, this is not always the case. Sensitivity to an honest questioning and searching, along with subsequent sharing, teaching and confrontation of distortion, is an ongoing process in all therapies. The same activities in the context of a person's perception of God is merely an adaptation of the Christian client's value system.

MATURITY AND THE THERAPEUTIC RELATIONSHIP

The Need for the Therapist's Growth

Unstated in the last section is the assumption that the therapist not only knows theology on an intellectual level, but also lives theology in a personal, growing, maturing manner. That is, the therapist has begun and is continuing to integrate faith and profession. An aspect of therapy as yet unpresented, but generally assumed throughout this discussion is the necessity for the therapist to be intimately involved in the maturing process in his or her own life even while attempting to facilitate growth in the lives of clients. In psychotherapy, the only available tool is the personhood, i.e., the personality of the therapist. A distorted, segmented personality in a therapist produces and encourages distortion and fragmentation in clients. It is only to the extent that the therapist is familiar with the growth process and walks in it personally that he or she can facilitate growth in clients. This is not to say that the counselor necessarily must have experienced the same or even similar problems as those of the clients. Rather, the therapist must simply have faced and be currently facing the issues of life that are part of the personal growth process. In terms of the therapeutic relationship, this means that the therapist must maintain integrity in dealing with his or her own emotional issues as they affect and are affected by the emotional vicissitudes of the people seeking help.

A Case Study Illustration

While this is not a textbook in therapeutic techniques, a brief case example might illustrate the interface of counselor growth and client development that occurs in the therapeutic relationship. A young woman named Jan[2] came to me for therapy some years ago in order to find relief from a nagging depression and lifelong inability to develop long-term relationships with people on anything but a superficial level. Insofar as a clinical diagnosis was concerned, she was generally labeled as having a histrionic personality disorder. While her history is not an issue in this discussion, it can be noted that she had experienced a variety of heterosexual and homosexual relationships throughout her life, none of which lasted for any length of time or provided any consistent level of satisfaction. Within the five years or so prior to her beginning therapy with me, she had become a Christian. This had provided a certain amount of comfort and peace along with a very great amount of guilt and rage. She perceived God as a demanding, angry parent who wanted her to stop doing the only things in life she enjoyed doing, and to become a perfect housewife and mother—a prospect she both abhorred and longed for. She could not imagine herself married for any length of time, and she was unable to picture any kind of close relationship without sexual involvement of some sort. Thus, she resented men for their demanding attitudes, especially sexually, and feared women for what she described as their power over her life. Because of her emotional needs, she would get too close too quickly to the women in her life. As a result, she would feel overwhelmed and panicky.

The first problem in her therapy was establishing a "therapeutic alliance," or a working relationship. According to Langs (1973), this covers a relatively brief period in which the client comes to believe that the therapist is actually trying to help find what the client wants and needs. Jan offered some unique difficulties in developing such a relationship. Other than the general difficulty of developing a quality relationship based on trust and openness, the sexual dimension presented a barrier. Since all barriers or defenses offer both an opportunity for growth and an excuse for failure, it was important for me to recognize the conflicts in her and the concomitant potential conflicts in *myself* with her. Since she was physically attractive and prone to use her attractiveness manipulatively, the establishment of a successful therapeutic alliance would be at least partially predicated on my ability to understand how her attractiveness affected me.

Initially, therapy seemed to move along well. Yet, after a period of time, I began to notice that something was wrong in our sessions. She talked about negative issues and relationships with people who had used and abused her. Periodically, I would make what I thought were brilliant observations and subsequent interventions. But nothing seemed to "click." I became somewhat troubled over my apparent inability to make contact with her. I talked it over with several therapists, and I prayed about it. I did notice that I looked forward to our sessions, although that did not strike me as unusual; I look forward to almost all of my counseling sessions. Yet there was something different about this one. Finally, during one session she stated that she did not believe she could continue therapy. When I asked why, she stated that she just didn't feel comfortable with me. She clarified this by stating that she felt "icky" when she tried to talk to me about her problems. I had the presence of mind to say that I was glad she had shared those feelings with me and if she wanted to find a therapist with whom she could be more comfortable, she was welcome to do so.

She did return and continued therapy with me. Before our next session, however, I realized that I had some issues to work through myself. I noticed that my initial feeling about the last session was one of depression; I felt rejection. It was not until a supervision session that I began to understand what was occurring in me. As I explored my feelings and thoughts in relation to this client, I eventually acknowledged a subconscious attempt on my part to attract her to me. Thus, when she stated she could no longer work with me, I immediately interpreted it as a rejection of my masculinity. In other words, on a subconscious level, I was asking her—a lesbian—to acknowledge my male identity. This was impossible for her to do with her very confused sexual identity.

Having recognized these dynamics, I had to ask myself some fundamental questions. Did I need such acknowledgement from this woman? My answer was simply, No! God made me male; I am a man and her response or lack of response to my attempts to attract her did not and does not change that fact. The fact that I wanted her to be attracted to me affirmed her femininity and my masculinity implicitly, but I did not need a response in order to maintain the affirmation. I had seen her homosexuality as a challenge to my masculine identity. As such, this particular incident was a primitive power struggle on my part as a male to control her sexuality. Her use of the word "icky" allowed me to associate the sexual element to the conflict since she had previously described her feelings about male sexuality utilizing that same term. Having realized my conflict and having resolved it, I was free to deal with her on a new level (i.e. as a person *wholly* motivated to help her) and thus was able to facilitate her growth in a relationship free of my unspoken conflict.

This particular episode could be interpreted in a variety of ways. The point I wish to stress, though, involves the process orientation and the conflict resolution which enabled therapy to continue. First, note that the issues all occurred in the context of a relationship, my relationship to my client and her relationship to people in general and men in particular. Second, notice that there were no confrontations about morality and immorality, right and wrong. The focus was on her feelings and the freedom to be herself and get her needs met while she was trying to grow up. Third, notice that the process moved from a focus on her to a focus upon myself and back to a focus on her. Conflicts have to be dealt with as they arise. They cannot be ignored simply because the therapist is expected to have all personal conflicts resolved. Thus, as I became aware of conflict in the therapeutic relationship, I dealt with the only part that I could change and take responsibility for—myself!

Finally, note that when my conflict was sufficiently in focus for me to comprehend the issues, I resolved it by choosing to believe the truth: I am a male regardless of how this female responds to me and I do not need to control her sexuality in order to help her change. The truth is used to resolve conflict, but only after the process is assisted by openness and honesty. God's grace grants me the freedom to look into all the cracks and crevices, to allow the issues to arise to awareness, even though anger, hate, fear—and sexuality—may be part of the upsurge. Once such elements of personality are visible, the truth points to the heart of the problem and to the resolution: a confession of (agreeing with) the truth. Conflict resolution is not possible without both process and content dimensions in full operation. A morality orientation (truth only) cuts the process side short with a "just do it" attitude. A non-content perspective (grace only) never has any foundation upon which to base decisions about how to look at the issues. Both aspects are needed.

CONCLUSION

The fundamental thesis of this discussion has been the belief that personal and spiritual growth and the resulting maturity are founded on interpersonal relationships. Thus, while it may be possible for an individual to be mature as a person and immature as a Christian, the reverse is not true. This would seem to be the idea behind 1 John 4:20, where the statement is made that the person who says he loves God but hates his brother is a liar. One can argue about non-Christians' capability of experiencing real love, and therefore their capacity for maturity. It is a fact, however, that the person who claims to be a mature Christian and who claims to love God is lying when he exhibits disdain and competitiveness in relationships at home or in business. The spiritual and the personal dimensions exist on the same plane and affect the expression of the whole person. A person cannot be spiritual without being personal, and vice-versa. The spiritual dimension is the internal, essential expression of the "person-who-really-is"; external behavior merely reflects the state of the spiritual, internal Image of God.

What then shall we say about the Holy Spirit and His role in this process? The Bible portrays the Holy Spirit as a Person in His own right (Eph. 4:30; 1 Thes. 5:19) who is particularly sensitive on a feeling level. He is a separate personality, and yet is one with the Father and Son. As a mystery of the Church, the doctrine of the Trinity is beyond a concrete description capable of doing justice to its essential character. It seems, however, that as the One who "completes the meanings" in the growth process, the Holy Spirit is the actual essence of God's personhood. Robinson (1928) described the spiritual growth process as the pressure of "spirit on spirit," specifically, God's Spirit on Man's spirit. He works internally and of His own accord, although His operation is always the will of the Father.

The present age is the period when God works primarily through the Holy Spirit for the work of convicting, comforting, guiding, and leading us into all truth. Listening to the Spirit is synonymous with growing; as we listen to Him, the incomplete meanings of our personality are unfrozen and wholeness ensues. It is a lifelong process of being attentive and sensitive to the process. It requires an understanding of how the Spirit's voice differs from other voices which would interfere with His. That is, selective listening requires a humanly unnatural tuning of the internal ear to God. Growth aims toward understanding and recognizing the various competing internal voices with the result that a person hears as God hears, sees as God sees, and speaks as God would speak because the individual's personality accurately reflects Christ. We do not become Christ—we do not lose our identity; we simply become an expression of the reality that is God's desire in concrete situations. This is what doing the will of the Father is about.

The model of therapy for generating spiritual and personal growth that has been presented is somewhat speculative and obviously unverifiable in an empirical sense. The Holy Spirit, as is true of the human spirit, is not a tangible mass to be manipulated, or even a scientific law to be validated statistically. He lives in the area of what the existentialists refer to as the "Ground of Being." Fundamental to the spirit of Man and the Spirit of God is love—committed relatedness.

Psychotherapy is not a panacea for all ills. It is, however, a microcosm of individual growth, which in many ways recapitulates the parent and child interaction patterns. It enables a focus on the individual's self-defeating styles, which encourages self-awareness and freely selected change. God is part of the therapeutic process; He will personally (via principles of human relations) point out the negative interactive patterns which the client maintains toward Him if we as therapists are willing to look for them in ourselves first. The Holy Spirit heightens a person's felt-meaning for the sake of awareness and understanding and subsequent change. As we come to see life the way God sees life, we become free to choose His way.

¹ My thanks to Dr. John Carter of the Resemead School of Psychology for explaining these concepts primarioy via his (1974a) article.
² Names and events have been altered in order to maintain confidentiality.

6

AVOIDING BURNOUT THROUGH SPIRITUAL RENEWAL

Raymond T. Brock

INTRODUCTION

Although it has been only within the past few decades that the terms "burnout" and "mid-life crisis" have received special attention in the religious and mental health communities, transitional crises are phenomena of ancient origin. In Isaiah 40:31, the prophet alluded to the problem and offered a promise of renewal several hundred years before the coming of Christ: "But they that wait upon the Lord shall renew their strength; they shall mount up with wings as eagles; they shall run and not be weary; and they shall walk and not faint". It is not God's will for those upon whom He has placed His call to be caught up in the throes of burnout. Rather, He wills, through the operation of the Holy Spirit, to bring renewal and healing to those who have become weary in well doing; to guide them through the morass of problems that can lead to weariness in the work of the kingdom.

Burnout has been defined by Edelwich and Brodsky (1980, p. 14) as a feeling that comes when a person perceives that "a job is a job is a job....We can use the term 'burnout' to refer to a progressive loss of idealism, energy, and purpose experienced by people in the helping professions as a result of the conditions of their work." From the standpoint of the educator, Pines said that burnout is "physical, emotional, and attitudinal exhaustion. It begins with feelings of uneasiness. The joy of teaching begins to slip away. Not just for a day or a week, but permanently" (in Hendrickson, 1979, p. 37). To this, Hendrickson (1979) added, "burnout is a response to circuit overload; it is the result of unchecked stress" (p. 37). Faulkner, from the pastoral perspective, stated that burnout happens to ministers when they run out of fuel. He saw burnout as a part of the grief process related to unfulfilled goals in the ministry: "We have not become all we think we should have become and therefore we deny the hurt" (Faulkner, 1981, p. 11).

Symptoms

When examining symptoms of burnout or mid-life crisis, it is difficult to distinguish them from symptoms of depression (Collins, 1980; Maher, 1983). In fact, depression appears as both a cause and an effect of burnout and mid-life crisis. With so much overlap in symptomatology, it is not possible to make clear-cut diagnostic distinctions between burnout and mid-life crisis. Thus, it is appropriate to consult theories of emotion and personality to attempt to determine what is happening to the individual who is withdrawing into such symptomatic behavior. Several constants have been observed in the literature that deserve attention.

Sleep Disorders

Basically three types of sleep disorders may be related to burnout: sleeplessness, fatigue following adequate sleep, and interrupted sleep.

Sleeplessness. Insomnia, the inability to go to sleep, is a prime indicator of stress, be it conscious or unconscious. It must be corrected or it will become a chronic problem (Edelwich & Brodsky, 1980). Physical, emotional, and spiritual relaxation techniques can help ease the symptoms, but determining the problems leading to sleeplessness is of primary importance in *avoiding* burnout. Diagnosis must precede renewal not only to resolve an immediate crisis but to forestall future occurrences. The writings of David are replete with references to his struggle with sleeplessness and the exhaustion—both physical and emotional—that accompanied these night time bouts (e.g. Ps. 55:17; 63:5–8). Fortunately, he also writes of discovering spiritual renewal as he brought his thoughts into spiritual perspective.

Fatigue following adequate sleep. Fatigue follows both sleeplessness *and* adequate rest if the mind has not been at peace. Some people report adequate hours of sleep but experience a residual sense of fatigue. Not allowing for sufficient sleep can be the result of neurotic-based obsessive compulsive behavior. If one is deprived of the normal rest that occurs during adequate sleep, the unseen emotional stress reveals itself in perpetual feelings of fatigue. I have observed that a person is susceptible to temptation, maladaptive behavior or so-called attacks of the devil under these primary conditions: fatigue, hunger, and when running a low grade fever without having discovered the presence of a virus or the common cold.

Psychological studies have established that the average person needs eight hours of sleep a night, although there are some who require nine and others who can survive on seven (Czeisler, Weitzman, Moore-Ede, Zimmerman, & Knauer, 1980; Meier, Minrith & Wichern, 1983; Silverman, 1982). A few notables, such as Winston Churchill and Henry Kissinger, have demonstrated a metabolic ability to survive on less sleep, but these persons are few and far between. The person who cuts his sleep time below what his metabolism requires sets himself up for the fatigue that leads to depression and burnout. The Sermon on the Mount addressed this problem with cautions not to worry and to let tomorrow take care of itself (Matt. 6:25-34). Paul added a similar warning in Philippians 4:6-9.

Interrupted sleep. A special sleep disorder that portends burnout or a schizophrenic episode is the interrupted sleep phenomenon; a person falls asleep quickly, wakes up and lies awake for several hours, only to go back to sleep shortly before the necessary awakening hour. The feeling of fatigue—to the point of exhaustion—that comes with this form of sleep disorder is a clear signal that a change of thinking and behavior is urgent. Otherwise, burnout or a full-blown emotional problem is imminent.

Psychosomatic Disorders

"Psychosomatic disorders" is a broad term used for symptoms that range from minor physical maladies to major physical problems that have emotional or psychological causes. In minor forms these symptoms include frequent colds, headaches, dizziness, diarrhea and other similar maladies. If these initial symptoms go unchecked, the result can be such major problems as peptic or duodenal ulcers, colitis, asthma, back pain, chest pain and some forms of arthritis.

In the psychosomatic disorders, the pain is real and the damage is physical, but the origin of the problem is inappropriate thinking and attitudes. Even when surgery is used to correct the acute symptoms, the problem will recur in healthy tissues in other parts of the body unless the attitudes and perceptions change.

Self-Concept Disorders

The person experiencing burnout frequently finds that his or her self-concept drops to a new low. Feelings of guilt and incompetence finally lead to a sense of inadequacy. Wagner (1975) has demonstrated that a healthy self-concept is formed through an interaction of feelings of belonging, worth, and competence. When a person begins to question these, he or she is subject to burnout. And, when other factors converge that precipitate burnout, the self-concept is attacked on all three fronts and becomes subject to distortion.

When Paul cautioned the Romans not to think more highly of themselves than they should, but to think "soberly," he was addressing the problem of pride in the church (Rom. 12:3). A kindred problem of inappropriate thinking is that of thinking too lowly of one's self with the resulting depreciation of self and development of an inferiority complex. It does no violence to Romans 12:3 to caution against both thinking too highly *and* too lowly of one's self. Rather, Paul essentially admonished believers to think sensibly, sanely, rationally, and adequately of themselves without the distortions that come from either pride or depreciation of self.

Depression

Depression, as a symptom of burnout, is frequently a blend of anger, fear, and guilt. Hurt often develops into frustration which itself breeds fear. If not checked, these feelings may lead to anger, which fosters feelings of hostility. Hostility, in turn, may generate aggressive behavior. When fear and anger lead to overreaction, guilt is the unhappy product. Alienation from God, self, and others results. Depression, then, is a signal that a change is needed in life and it becomes an opportunity to deal with the hurt, fear, anger, and guilt that are seething in the soul. If these primary emotions go unchecked, depression results, leading to despair—that sense of hopelessness called *anomie* (Coser & Rosenberg, 1967; Sawrey & Telford, 1968). This is frequently followed by an abnormal state of inactivity as the black cloud of melancholy collects overhead, stirring feelings of dejection, gloom, and discouragement.

Depression manifests itself in the human personality as a slowing down of activity. There is a loss of enthusiasm for living, often a loss of appetite and lowered sex drive. Feelings of worthlessness and sinfulness develop into guilt, further lowering the self-esteem. Then come the vague bodily complaints as psychosomatic symptoms emerge along with the disruption of sleep patterns previously discussed. Escape may be sought through television, drugs, alcohol, or thoughts of suicide.

It is important to realize that depression is different from normal mood swings. Moods may fluctuate when hormonal or situational factors lead to a slowing down of activity. Death of a loved one, setbacks in attaining career goals, and being uprooted through change of location are normal and lead to mild depressive episodes of an exogenous (external) nature. It is the endogenous (internal) form of depression, however—where there is no apparent cause—that is a function of burnout. This may begin with a situational trauma but lingers abnormally, indicating that something is wrong in the person's thinking.

Causes

Why do counselors suffer burnout? The question plagues those who watch as Christian and non-Christian, professional and paraprofessional counselors fall prey to this malady in increasing numbers. A number of causes have been identified by research (Conway, 1978; Faulkner, 1981; Ragsdale, 1978). In presenting an overview of these causes of burnout, I have chosen to use the young male counseling pastor as an illustration. However, most of the content of this section can be applied to a counselor in any setting or of the opposite sex.

The young minister, fresh out of Bible college or seminary, is challenged with noble ambitions and enthusiasm for the ministry. He throws himself into the work of the ministry with abandon and with little thought of his own limitations or his need to measure time and energy appropriately. Then the perennial problems of Christian service emerge. There is a *lack of criteria for measuring ministerial* accomplishments. The minister soon discovers that what he considers his personal goals may not be the same as those of his official board, the local congregation, area ministers, district officials or denominational leaders. The ambiguity of measurement criteria leaves him adrift because what is high on the list of expectations of one set of critics is low on or completely absent from the "measuring stick" of another group of observers. Ambiguity leads to a flurry of change with the subsequent depletion of energy and enthusiasm.

The problem of excessive activity, not balanced with adequate rest and personal development, is compounded by the *low pay, high demands and the heavy responsibility of the ministry*. Suddenly, the young minister feels cornered. He is pleasing no one, including himself. He lacks sufficient funds to bring about change and is in dire need of leisure time. Thus, he burns out; not from overwork, but from over-worry, over-fear, or over-resentment.

Along the way he discovers that, in most denominational settings, there is *very little upward mobility to more prestigious churches*. He is stuck in a place that does not challenge his abilities. This may be compounded by *insufficient opportunity for creative planning*. He works on new ideas and shares them, only to find that the inertia of tradition impedes progress—he feels rejected. Even when he is convinced that the new plans are the result of fervent spiritual intercession, they are not received with the enthusiasm Moses had at Sinai with the second set of stone tablets. Squelched, the young minister is tempted to shelve his creativity and slip into the mode of the *status quo*. Even if an idea finds mild acceptance, there may be inadequate funding for the innovative idea, so it is left in the planning stage to collect dust, while feelings of rejection insidiously mount in the young minister's soul.

High public visibility, which always accompanies the ministry, is frequently coupled with *popular misunderstandings as to the mission of the minister*. Too frequently there is not a clear understanding of what the minister is expected to do. Even if the church board has an adequate job description, there are individuals in the congregation who have never read the document and do not intend to. The suspicion with which innovations are met is frequently the capstone of the burnout syndrome and results in a paranoia that comes from being "shot down" one time too many. This scenario is replayed with alarming frequency.

STAGES OF DISILLUSIONMENT

Researchers have isolated several stages of disillusionment in the development of burnout (Edelwich & Brodsky, 1980). These stages are relevant to ministers as well as mental health professionals and educators.

Loss of Enthusiasm

The beginning of the ministry, in response to the call of God and the approval of ministering brethren, launches a period of high hopes and high energy. This intial period is high on ambition but low on reality. Unrealistic expectations lead to setting inappropriate personal and congregational goals. Through preaching, teaching, counseling, and committee work, these goals are alluded to, described, and defined. But when enthusiasm is high and response is low, a vacuum of discontent develops. Unless the goals are reassessed in view of the realities of the situation, stagnation sets in.

Stagnation

With stagnation, the minister is still on the job, but the job is no longer thrilling. I have seen this happen frequently when a pastor has led a congregation through a growth period, either in terms of numbers or a building program. When the church moves into the new building or succeeds in filling an old facility, the let-down is demoralizing. With no new fields to conquer, the minister is tempted to do as Alexander the Great did as he looked from the mountains of India into China: he wept because his men would not move to another conquest. He became depressed and died in his early thirties.

Burnout can be averted in the stagnation period by reassessing goals, reevaluating priorities, and redistributing energy. If this does not occur, frustration is the inevitable result.

Frustration

In frustration, the minister questions his effectiveness in doing the job. Congregational inertia or lack of measurable results lead to a questioning of personal effectiveness or to a questioning of the job to be done. Frustration is that point reached when life tells you "NO!" Conflict offers alternatives, but frustration is a dead end. What does the minister do when the congregation does not respond to his leadership or moves at a snail's pace? Frustration offers three alternatives: surrender, withdrawal, or creative change (Schmidt & Brock, 1983).

Surrender. The first temptation in frustration is to surrender, to give up. This is, of course, emotional suicide and the death knell to an effective ministry. Whether the minister stays with his congregation or moves to another charge, the residual aftermath of surrender lingers in his mind and raises cautions and hesitations in the new location. This, in turn, impedes his progress.

Withdrawal. The opposite of surrender as a response to frustration is withdrawal. This is the temptation to flee the scene. Knowing there is no way the situation will go away, the minister decides to make a rapid exit, hoping to recoup his emotional losses in a more favorable setting. Calculated withdrawal may well be the best measure of gallantry in war—even spiritual warfare—but if it becomes a habit, it leads to a gypsy-like existence that speaks loudly of personal instability. Knowing when to withdraw and when to stand firm is a measure of maturity. Paul has told us that there is a time to stand, but to stand girded with the armor of the Christian soldier (Eph. 6:13).

Apathy

Unless frustration is handled creatively (as discussed later in the chapter), apathy will result. Chronic frustration on the job leads to burnout when the minister stays on the job because he needs the income and sees nothing else as a viable option in life. We have already discussed what happens in the stage of apathy: sleep disorders, psychosomatic illness, self-concept distortion, and depression. At this point, burnout is complete. There are, however, other options.

BURNOUT ASSESSMENT

Several instruments have been devised to help in the assessment of burnout. Edelwich and Brodsky (1980) offered a "Planning Board Exercise" designed for people in the helping professions (p. 21). Faulkner (1981) adapted some of Gary Collins's work into a questionnaire entitled, "Are You Burned Out?" The classic instrument in this field is still the Holmes-Rahe Scale (Holmes & Rahe, 1976). This scale ranks life change units with a numerical value allowing a person to indicate the stressors experienced during the previous twelve months and add up a total score (Coleman, 1979). I have used this scale effectively as an informal observation in counseling youth and adults. I have found that those whose units were excessively high frequently experienced an illness or accident in less than a year. And, it was not unusual for the trauma to be serious enough to require hospitalization.

RENEWAL

Studies using the burnout assessment inventories emphasize the need to learn how to deal effectively with the inevitable crises of life. In addition, anxiety, conflict, frustration—as discussed earlier in this chapter—are very common experiences of those in the helping professions.

In coping with these stressors, it is essential to make corrective decisions which are reality oriented as well as spiritually motivated. At times, the options will be clear; at other times resolution will come only by prayer and fasting (Foster, 1978). Such resolution will generally lead to life changes, such as a change of location, a shift of professional role, or an alternation of attitude and perception. *Constructive creative changes* bring relief from the stress and revitalize the person for continuing the work of the ministry. Rediger (1982) has suggested the *AIM* prescription: *A* for awareness, *I* for input, and *M* for management.

When life says "No," the battle may be lost but the war has not. The minister and counselor are advised to take courage in the Lord and "dig in their heels"; they must also lower their profiles and reconstruct ideas through *creative change*, patience, and love. An awareness of "Who is the Lord of the harvest" must be renewed. When we remember it is Christ's Church, His ministry and His harvest field, as the people of God we can content ourselves with being co-laborers with the Lord (1 Cor. 3:9).

Plans rejected at one meeting can be laid aside momentarily to let the ideas incubate in the subconscious of both the minister and the ones with whom he is sharing the ideas. At another time these ideas can be dusted off and reworked with the insight that such mental incubation brings. Frequently, the revision receives a more favorable response with the heightened excitement that comes because the time is more appropriate. With a lowered profile and personally reduced demands, the minister finds he can adjust the pace of his movement to match that of his congregation and the atmosphere of the community. He can then lead his people on to victories he believes have been inspired by God and worked out in prayer and meditation.

If, however, self-appraisal leads to an awareness that burnout is a possibility in life and ministry, it is time to "take charge of life." This simply means determining what needs to be changed in life and devising a strategy to bring about the desired change. It is most appropriate to ask the Lord to help in initiating a strategy of self-change. The decision to take charge—to cope or to change—must be made by the one desiring to change, not by someone else. It must be a personal commitment, not a result of external pressure. After this personal decision has been made, it is appropriate to ask the Lord to help in devising the plan by which the change can be implemented. It is also appropriate to ask the Lord to strengthen the awareness that the change is being implemented as an act of worship unto the Lord (Col. 3:17).

As the fruits of the self-change program are demonstrated, there comes satisfaction with perceived accomplishment. This change in attitude will have a tremendous influence on the way the counselor or pastor perceives life and approaches other people (Schmidt, 1978, 1983).

How then does the minister or counselor break the cycle of impending burnout? By prayerfully taking steps of specific intervention in light of one's call from God. The following is a partial list of specific intervention possibilities.

Leave the Ministry

This is the intervention of lowest value, for it removes the minister from the career of choice, ostensibly one that was God-given. This decision requires much soul-searching to determine if this is really the way to plan the remaining years of life. If one is convinced that the ministry was entered for the wrong reason or with inadequate motivation, training, or personality foundation, one may well make this choice. But it should be the last option considered. For most, there are better alternatives to burnout.

Change the Type of Ministry

Redefining the type of ministry is a challenging opportunity for self-growth and spiritual maturity. For too long, many of us have believed that the only way to fulfill the call of God was in the pulpit. But there are diverse dimensions to the ministry—multiple ministries in the metropolitan centers show the need not only for the preaching pastor, but for specialized ministers to work with youth, music, education, adults, children, counseling, and administration. No doubt new portfolios will be developed as the Church adapts to spiritual changes by increasing its specialties. Embellishment will also need to be made in the existing styles of teaching, evangelistic, and missionary ministries.

Take Advanced Training

One of the easiest ways to fall into the burnout syndrome is to stop growing professionally. This is true of both the church and community counselor. There are times it is wise to take additional courses at a nearby college or university. Even if no advanced degree is in focus, the mental stimulation of continued education and the social interaction with people who are pursuing knowledge can be invigorating. Sometimes it is wise to study in a field other than the undergraduate major, simply to broaden the perspective. At other times, it may be wise to consider a long-range plan of adding courses that would ultimately lead to another degree, certification, or license.

If additional formal training in a degree-granting institution is not feasible—or desirable—continuing education experiences are a necessity. Mental stagnation can set in if new input is not assimilated with the routines of ministry, counseling, and living. Seminars and workshops are held in metropolitan centers on such a regular basis that it would be impossible to take in all of them; however, selected attendance at conferences of special interest can be extremely beneficial.

Expand Life Outside of Ministry

Commitment to Christian service is a high and holy calling; nevertheless, a balanced life requires more than service to the church. There is a need for involvement in community and civic activities as well as a need for personal recreations and hobbies to keep life balanced and in touch with the whole community. Research has shown that neither men nor women enjoy a recreation in retirement that they did not at least dabble in during the pre-retirement years. It is important—as an admission that aging will come to all of us—to maintain hobbies and recreations throughout the active ministry years that will add pleasure and meaning to life when time is more plentiful and energy (and possibly money) will not be as abundant as before.

Participation in civic clubs and community social activities is good for both the church and the pastor. Such participation allows the minister to be seen as a total person with civic awareness. It also broadens opportunities for witnessing and for having spiritual influence in elements of society where the values of the Kingdom of Heaven need to be introduced. When kept in balance, these times need not be perceived as time off, but as an extension of the ministry outside the walls of the sanctuary.

Take a Vacation

Everyone needs change. The change which occurs through a vacation can add a new dimension to ministry and marriage. One of the mistakes ministers make is to tie their vacations to ministry or church conventions. These events are not a vacation and should not be labeled as such! A vacation should be just that—a time away from the regular routine for recuperation and re-creation of body and mind as well as spirit.

Compulsive addiction to the work of the ministry is not a mark of spirituality. A congregation must be taught to survive in the absence of the pastor even as a family must be taught to survive in the absence of either or both parents. Total dependence on the pastor is not healthy in bringing lay leadership to the fore. Learning how and when to delegate responsibility is an art that the Holy Spirit can teach the pastor who is more interested in building the Kingdom of God than his own status in the congregation. It is also a principle which Jesus taught to the Twelve and the Seventy disciples.

Too often, I find ministers who feel guilty when they take time off or are involved in legitimate leisure. This is not a guilt that comes from God. Rather, it is part of the obsessive-compulsive behavior that leads to neurosis both in the parsonage and the congregation. Leisure does not have to be idleness, but it does need to offer a sufficient change of pace so that the total person can be revitalized for the work of the Lord. And, vacations need not be expensive—just well planned within the budget and interests of the family.

Take a "Working High"

Seminars, workshops, and retreats fall into the category of a "working high." These go beyond the continuing education experiences suggested above and include conventions of the church on local, sectional, state, national, and international levels, that broaden the base of fellowship and increase awareness of what is going on in the global religious community. The same principle certainly applies to the counselor who attends special seminars and conventions. The change of pace provided by these events can revitalize both the marriage and ministry through the sharing of professional and private goals.

Reassess the Day Off

Everyone needs time off from work. God taught us that in the creation sequence, and gave Israel strict laws to illustrate the concept. Since Sunday is the heaviest work day of the week for the minister, it can in no way be termed a day off. So what can be done with the day(s) off? When I ask this question, I am frequently faced with stares of unbelief. "What day off?" is the typical reply. Or if the minister names a day of the week, I ask his wife what he does on his day off. He blushes as she frequently tells of the office and hospital calls that carve the day into another day on the job with little or no time or space for a re-creative change of pace.

It is a misinterpretation of the example of Christ and His teachings to conclude that a minister must be on call twenty-four hours a day, seven days a week. Proper planning can allow the minister time for self, spouse and children without neglecting the congregation. With a multiple staff, the days off can be staggered. In the smaller congregation, a "deacon-on-call" plan can be implemented to handle emergencies. With experience both as a pastor and as a clinician, I have found that people will honor the day off of a pastor, counselor, or psychologist if it is handled without apology or guilt.

A real temptation for those of us in the helping professions is to train people to depend on us. Unfortunately, we teach our clients or counselees not to respect our humanity. A pastor or counselor can train people to make their contacts in a professional way at professional hours, or they can unwittingly be trained to call around the clock. The pastor who sees himself as a shepherd of God's flock will give the congregation a sense of self-reliance although he will always be available for emergencies. The pastor who is having trouble with his identity or self-concept finds it is ego-building to have people depend on him. But this is more a function of personal ego need than a desire for spiritual ministry to the congregation. Here, again, the Holy Spirit can guide us in dealing with this precursor of burnout.

The day off should include time for personal recreation, for couple revitalization, and for interaction with the children. The age of the children will have much to do with the choice of the day, but the minister is advised to take a day off and concentrate on family togetherness. This same concept needs to be carried into the nights during the week so that not every night is involved in ministry, while the home is neglected. How horrible it would be to lose a member of the minister's household because of compulsive attention to church activities!

Redefine the Ministry

With the proliferation of responsibilities in ministry, it is often important for the minister to refine the job description and limit it to areas of potential specialization. Concomitantly, other responsibilities must be effectively delegated to others—either laypersons or clergy—who can carry out those responsibilities.

It has been my practice when counseling with pastoral couples to encourage them to list their duties and to rank them in the order of preference. I then encourage them to cut the list in half and to delegate selected areas to other qualified individuals. The result has generally been renewed ministry and revitalization of marriage commitments as these Christian workers have redistributed their energies into fewer activities that are more consistent with their call and personal gifts. This has freed them to pursue personal, couple, and family goals; this enriches both the marriage and the ministry. It has also attracted others to the ministerial team, increasing the efficiency of spiritual service to the Church.

Alter the Perception of Ministry

The intervention of the Holy Spirit is essential, but some ministers consciously need to alter their perception of the call God has laid on their lives (Brock, 1976). I discovered this in a personally traumatic way.

One day I was called by a medical doctor who asked me to visit one of his patients—one of my fellow clergymen—and to minister to him spiritually. This Spirit-filled doctor said, "I can't put my finger on it, but there is more to his problem than the physical symptoms I have diagnosed." I made an appointment and went to his patient's office. We shared informally and then I told him I had come to minister to him at his doctor's request. He was delighted. As a minister, he was open to being ministered to.

I anointed him with oil (James 5:15) and began to pray. But no English words would come. So, I began to pray in the Spirit. As I did, the Lord revealed to me what had to be said. I stopped praying, moved to the other side of the desk, and said: "The Lord would not let me pray for your physical healing. He told me that physical healing was not your problem. He revealed to me that your greatest need is a healing of your perception of His call upon your life. Your physical ailments are only a symptom of a deeper spiritual problem." He broke into sobs and wept for some time. As he regained his composure, he said, "You are exactly right. That is what the Lord has revealed to me, too. But Ray, I would rather die than change!"

Six months later I visited my friend in the hospital after he had suffered a paralyzing stroke. He could not talk, but as I entered the room, tears rolled down his cheeks. We both knew what was happening. I wept through his funeral because I knew he had made the choice not to change his perception of God's call or alter his driving, compulsive lifestyle.

It is better to change than die when that is consistent with God's will. Yes, a healing of perception may be necessary for us to change our view of the ministry and flow in the mainstream of what God is doing. Such a refocusing of perception can help us determine what He wants us to be, to become His hand extended at a given point.

GUIDANCE OF THE HOLY SPIRIT

A primary function of the Holy Spirit in the life of the believer is that of leading or guiding into all truth (John 16:13; 14:16, 18). That is why the Holy Spirit was sent in the first place (Brock, 1983). It is the ministry of preventative guidance that allows the Holy Spirit to help the Spirit-motivated counselor to avoid the pitfalls that lead to burnout. When sensitive to the will of the Father and the Son, the counselor (pastoral or professional) is open to the intervention of the Holy Spirit. But, when involved in what Shakespeare called "much ado about nothing," he or she falls victim to the pressures of life that culminate in the symptoms called "burnout."

It is important to take all of the known precautions: getting adequate rest, following good eating and exercise routines, and being alert to impending illnesses or infections. A counselor is only mortal and must learn to live within the limits of a finite physical body. God is not pleased when His people push themselves beyond the limits He has set for us. I still remember the advice given to me by Inez Spence, the Dean of Women at Evangel College for many years: "When the Lord gives you an ounce of strength, He does not expect you to expend a pound of energy." Whether we like it or not, we live in a sin-cursed world and until it is reconstituted at the end of the age, we must live within its limitations and admit our own finiteness.

In Chapter 3, Horton described the ministry gifts available to the counselor. Of special importance to the counselor desiring to experience renewal instead of burnout are the gifts of knowledge, wisdom, discernment and faith.

Knowledge

God gives us knowledge as the Holy Spirit recalls to our minds the things of God and of Christ already revealed in the Scriptures. He also is able to activate our recall of the discoveries of mankind in scientific research and observations (Collins, 1977; Crabb, 1977). The Holy Spirit will bring information to our attention, both from Scripture and research, so we owe it to ourselves to study both God's Word and professional books and journals. This permits us to have a breadth of information available for the heightened recall of the Spirit (Brock, 1974). The Holy Spirit is not obligated to reveal to us that which is available unless we have made adequate spiritual and professional preparation for His intervention. But, He will remind us of the needed information—both sacred and secular— when we are close to Him and ask for His heightened recall abilities.

Wisdom

Horton (Chapter 3) indicated that wisdom involves a proclamation or declaration of divinely given knowledge. God does not give a large amount of wisdom at one time. The gift involves both human knowledge as well as spiritual knowledge and is available to the Spirit-filled counselor for both one's professional and personal life.

Scripture indicates that the Spirit made up for human limitations in the lives of the New Testament saints, but He did not give them what was available to them unless they used their God-given talents of reason and observation. He is able to help us take information learned in one setting and transfer it to another setting where it will assist us in functioning more adequately for Him. He also gives us insight into the needs of clients and into Scriptures that are applicable to the counseling situation.

Discernment

Discernment is a special intervention of the Holy Spirit to help the counselor differentiate not only between spirits (the Spirit of God, the spirit of Man, and the spirit of the devil or demons), but also between good and evil or truth and falsehood (Horton, 1976). The Holy Spirit can caution us against decisions that would lead to excesses; He can urge us to investigate alternatives in the decision-making process. Since burnout results from inappropriate decision-making, this intervention of the Spirit of God is vital in avoiding burnout or recovering from its effects.

Faith

When we know that we are in tune with His purpose, faith in the faithfulness of God and the ability to claim His promises gives us the courage and tenacity to stay on the appropriate course of action in the counseling session, even though it may not appear to be the most logical way to go from a purely human point of view. As Horton has noted in Chapter 3, faith involves more than a mental attitude—it is "faithful, obedient action."

HEALING OF PERCEPTION: A PERSONAL CASE STUDY

I shall never forget my first encounter with burnout. My wife and I had been on the mission field for almost three years when I became ill. After a series of medical interventions over a period of several months, I was admitted to the Sudan Interior Mission hospital in Jos, Nigeria. After extensive examinations, the missionary doctor said to me, "I will give you thirty days to make your plans. You can either reserve a ticket back to the States or order your coffin. I really don't care which you do!" This was just the kind of shock therapy I needed at the time. When he left the room, I remember turning my face to the wall in desperation and being very vulnerable to the Lord. In the delirium of my fever, I remember saying, "Lord, it's not fair. I have given my life to You and now You are going to kill me. It isn't fair! I want to know why."

Now, I realize that God has never promised to answer "why" in this life, but I was desperate. By His grace He honored my request. I heard the voice of God, somewhere in my fevered head, saying: "It is none of your business!"

The message was clear, distinct, and succinct. I could handle that in my weakened state. I remember responding, "All right, Lord, if it's Your business, get with it!" I went to sleep for the first hour of natural sleep in more than six months. When I awakened several hours later, the fever was gone, the EKG was clear, my blood pressure was normal, and a pathological blood condition was gone. I was still extremely weak, but I immediately began the process of planning furlough.

When I arrived back in the United States, the medical problems had all cleared except the malaria, which has continued to crop up periodically to remind me of my need to be sensitive to the Lord and His will. Although the doctor in Africa told me I would not be able to minister again, I was back on the missionary itinerary trail in a couple of months and have been in active ministry ever since. And, that was twenty-eight years ago.

For me, the renewal came when I realized that it is *God's* business and *His* kingdom. I have experienced several physical upsets in my ministerial career since that memorable day in Africa, but I have been able to look back on each of them as a time when I momentarily lost sight of the fact that I was involved in *His* work, not mine.

Such experiences have led me to an insight that crystallized when I was dealing with the clergy brother whose doctor sent me to minister to him. It was in that prayer of discernment that the Lord first brought to my mind the phrase ''healing of perception.'' As I reexamined Christian service, this concept has changed my approach to spiritual and physical stamina.

One of the best ways I know to view burnout is to see it as a faulty perception of God's will and purpose. All of us function within the parameters of our perceptual field. If we have a faulty perceptual field, we run into problems because our perception is not consistent with reality. Just because we perceive a situation in a given way does not mean it is necessarily so (Goldstein, 1980). And it is just as possible to have a faulty perception about spiritual things as it is to experience error in our sensory modalities.

We need to seek the Holy Spirit's help in analyzing what the will of the Father actually is for our lives. Then we can ask Him to assist us in the adjustments necessary to bring our lives into line with His purpose. It is this correction in life, a change of trajectory in forward movement, that allows a minor adjustment early in the course of Christian service to bring us closer to the goal of God's purpose and to keep our lives on course.

Sometimes the healing of perception requires us to get more information; sometimes it involves rearranging our perceptual field so we can see things in a new and different perspective. But, it is the good pleasure of the Holy Spirit to guide us in these changes of perception. The process brings healing to our minds which allows us to be renewed in body, soul, and spirit.

When we allow ourselves to move in God's will, in God's place, at God's time, we can live with His blessing and freely draw upon His great resources. If, however, through faulty perception, lack of wisdom, or overt rebellion, we veer from the course that He would have us to follow, burnout can be an expected result. It is only as we stay on a course guided by the Holy Spirit that we can expect Him to lead us into all of the truth that the Father wants us to know. Then we can expect Him to empower us that we might magnify the Christ whom the Spirit has come to exalt.

7

LAY COUNSELING IN THE LOCAL CHURCH

Jack V. Rozell

A BRIEF OVERVIEW

At first glance the ministry of lay or paraprofessional counseling appears new, but careful examination brings the realization that both the concept and the practice are as old as the Church itself. It is, however, true that the labels "lay counseling" and "paraprofessional counseling" are relatively new to the Church. It is also true that some of the methodology through which this ministry is expressed is also new.

Biblical Foundation

The foundation for the concept and expression of lay counseling is clearly biblical. It is inherent in the call Jesus gave to His disciples to love (Matt. 22:34–40; John 13:34–35). He taught them that their effectiveness in bringing healing to a hurting world was directly related to their willingness to help, give care, and love. Paul tells us that the essence of ministry itself is love (Eph. 4:11, 15, 16). Lay counseling that is patterned after biblical concepts and principles is a formalized expression of the essential love function of the Church as dictated by Jesus and amplified in the New Testament epistles. It is a commitment of lay persons to be trained, supervised, and released to minister love in specific ways to hurting persons.

Literature

Only a little literature directed specifically at paraprofessional or lay counseling existed prior to 1960. In fact, there is not even much literature on the general theme of pastoral counseling before 1960. However, the 1970s witnessed a significant increase in writings dealing with pastoral and lay counseling. Presently, a considerable amount of material is available. However, there is still a need for more literature in the field that has a solid biblical base and gives models, concepts, principles, and "how to" guidelines.

I believe the increase in publications in recent years has been encouraged by several factors. It has been nurtured by a growing awareness that the lay population is the Church's greatest resource besides the Person and work of the Holy Spirit. It is also due in part to the willingness of clergy to train and release lay persons to ministry. Along with these factors is an increasing appreciation and respect by the secular counseling world for the Church's potential and its healing role in helping people (Targett, 1972). Finally, as lay persons have discovered that they are effective as healing agents, their excitement for this expression of ministry and their demand to be trained has created a need for resources and opportunities. (A list of resources for lay counseling, written from both Christian and secular perspectives, is included at the end of this chapter.)

Current Emphasis

The current emphasis on lay counseling is intense and growing; it appears that it will continue in the future. The Church is serious about doing the Kingdom work of loving (Matt. 22:34–40; 28:16–20). The only answer to the overwhelming love need in our hurting world is for the laity resource to be mobilized, trained, and released to multiple ministries. The Church will then be following biblical principles and will become the love force God intended it to be (Matt. 9:35–38). The Church, then, is being built, victory is assured, and Satan's power-hold on lives is being broken (Matt. 16:18, 19).

More and more, church leaders are recognizing the role of the pastor-teacher as the equipper (Eph. 4:10–12). As this leadership function is clarified and refined, increased effectiveness in the function of the saints will follow (Eph. 4:12, 16). The result *in the Church* will be unity, maturity, stability, and continuous growth in love. The impact of the Church *in the world* will also be love. This, of course, will bring renewal, healing, and wholeness to those who will receive it.

The biblical assumptions for paraprofessional or lay counseling are the same as they are for other ministry expressions within the Church. Sometimes this has not been recognized. This may be the result of two things:

1. The terminology used in counseling in the Church resembles that used in the professional, non-church world. To some, this has been intimidating and has given an impression that what is being done is non-Christian. This assumption, however, is not necessarily true.

2. The Church's adoption of non-Christian counseling concepts, models, and methods—without purifying their false and untruthful aspects—has also contributed to the unwillingness of some to accept the validity of the ministry of counseling.

The purifying process is called integration and is essential for any methodology the Church uses. We must never seek to do God's work with the world's techniques. This does not mean that we never use a method or technique that the world uses, but it does mean that we examine its truth content according to Scripture before we use it.

Underlying Assumptions

Five basic assumptions underlie a biblical approach to lay counseling. In this section we will identify them and show how each is basic to lay counseling.

The Sovereignty of God

God is the Sovereign Creator, Redeemer, and Lord of all and has revealed Himself in nature, history, and His special redemptive acts. The life, death, and resurrection of Jesus Christ is His final and ultimate act of revelation. God brings us an understanding of His revelation through the Holy Spirit and the illumination of His inspired and infallible Word. This assumption tells us that God is redemptively involved in the affairs of humanity and that assurance and stability are experienced in life now and in the future as a person relates to Him properly.

God the Giver of Truth

Truth is a unity originating with God. He has revealed truth to us partially through nature (Rom. 1:21), and completely and ultimately through His Son (John 14:6). He is now making truth known to us through His Holy Spirit (John 16:13) and His Word (John 17:17). These facts give lay counselors a positive perspective and hope; they need never be fearful or defensive in reference to what any academic discipline or pursuit of knowledge has to say. Lay counselors are on the offensive as they exercise their responsibility to examine theories, techniques, and models of counseling according to the truth. In this process, they are able to: (a) identify the truth and possess it, (b) recognize the false and disown it, and (c) refrain from using theories until they are validated in reference to God's truth. As Figure 1 demonstrates, this approach is especially useful in examining therapeutic models.

Figure 1

INTEGRATION: DETERMINING TRUTH

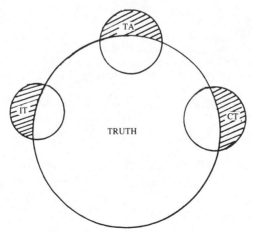

The large circle represents *Truth* with a capital *T*. The small circles represent
the pursuit of Truth by various disciplines. For our purpose, they represent such
various therapeutic approaches as Transactional Analysis (TA), Integrity Therapy
(IT), and Cognitive Therapy (CT). The area of overlap is the amount of Truth
in the specific approach. However, no effort is made in this figure to show the
actual truth content by degree of overlap. The outer area of the smaller circle
represents theory—or even non-Truth. If it is theory, it is viewed without
commitment until proven biblically consistent. If untrue, it is rejected entirely.
This approach gives Christian lay counselors the assurance that Truth can be known
(1 Cor. 2:19; John 16:13). It also sets them free to embrace it even if it comes
to awareness through a non-Christian source.

The Priesthood of Believers
All believers are priests. This assumption gives us a ministry model; the Model
is Jesus Christ Himself! He was God's High Priest (Heb. 2:17) representing God
to humanity and humanity to God. We are to follow His example (1 Pet. 2:9;
Rev. 1:6).

Love in the Life of Believers
Agape love is the essence of life and experience for believers. Modeled and
made available to us by Christ, this love is to be expressed both in relation to
God and to people (Matt. 22:34–39). This God-kind of love is the major theme
of the New Testament and reflects the nature of God. Therefore, agape love should
be the natural expression of His children because they share His nature (2 Pet.
1:3, 4; Matt. 5:48). Agape love is therapeutic; that is, it heals, it gives assurance
(Rom. 8:38, 39), and it provides lay counselors with a functional definition for
their relationships with counselees. Consider 1 Corinthians 12:31–14:1 for
practical ways in which it can be expressed. William Barclay defined agape love as:

> The spirit which says: "no matter what any man does to me, I will never
> seek to do harm to him; I will never set out for revenge; I will always seek
> nothing but his highest good." That is to say, Christian love, agape, is
> unconquerable benevolence, invincible good will. It is not simply a wave
> of emotion; it is a conviction of the mind....it is a deliberate achievement
> and conquest and victory of the will. (1969, pp. 21, 22)

This definition easily demonstrates how this love provides an ethical standard
for the counselor in any relationship to the counselee. One filled and motivated
with agape love will never take advantage of or "use" another person.

The Effectiveness of Non-Professional Counselors
This assumption provides a clear message: non-professionally trained counselors
can be *as* effective and sometimes *more* effective than professionally trained
counselors *if* they relate to the counselee with high levels of accurate empathy,

non-possessive warmth, and genuineness (Truax, 1970). This assumption is based on research reported by Carkhuff (1965), Truax (1970), Rogers (1967) and others during the 1960s. Their studies demonstrated that effective counseling is not due to the level of professional training of the counselor, but rather the quality of the relationship established with the counselee (cf. chapter 9 by Greve).

These three qualities (often called the Therapeutic Triad) that are so essential to effective counseling relationships were defined by Truax and Carkhuff (1973) as follows:

> 1. *Accurate empathy.* This involves relating to the counselee in such a way that he or she recognizes and acknowledges genuine concern.
> 2. *Non-possessive warmth.* This quality involves accepting the counselee without conditions.
> 3. *Genuineness.* This condition is defined by the openness or realness of the counselor in the relationship with the counselee.

The beautiful, interesting characteristic of these three qualities is that each is expressed in agape love. For example, merciful love is empathetic. *Mercy* involves feeling what the other person feels. Jesus is the merciful High Priest because He is so completely identified with us (Heb. 2:17, 18; 4:14–16). God's mercy encompasses accurate empathy and much more.

Grace has often been popularly defined as "God's unmerited favor." It is the experience of receiving His kindness and love even though it is undeserved. Obviously, God's grace includes non-possessive warmth, but goes far beyond it, even to the Cross.

Finally, truth in Scripture can be viewed as objective (i.e., seeing things as they really are) and subjective (i.e., relating truth to oneself, or being transparent or genuine). Subjective truth, then, includes the third aspect of the therapeutic triad. Agape love not only rejoices in truth, but seeks it (1 Cor. 13:6; Eph. 4:15).

When an agape love relationship is established with a counselee it embodies accurate empathy, nonpossessive warmth, genuineness and much more. This quality of relationship results in healing (see also Gilbert, 1979).

THE ROLE OF THE HOLY SPIRIT

The Holy Spirit's presence and work in the counseling process gives the Christian counselor an immeasurable advantage. Consider the following: (a) the Holy Spirit is God, (b) He is a person, (c) He is the third Person of the Godhead, and (d) He not only works in and through the counselor, but also in the counselee. This means that God, who is Agape Love, is the third party in that counseling relationship. The possibilities in this setting are far beyond what we can ask or think (Eph. 3:20). By the way, the context of Ephesians 3:20 is a prayer for agape love. This is an appropriate prayer for every counselor.

Having considered the assumptions of Christian lay counseling and the role of the Holy Spirit in counseling, it is now time to define Christian counseling from my perspective. The reader will observe that the definition shows that Christian counseling is a work of agape love as directed by the Holy Spirit. Formally defined, Agape Counseling or Agape Therapy is

> an agape relationship between the counselor and one or more counselees in which the counselor uses all of the resources available to him (human and divine) to bring renewal, healing, wholeness, and maturity to the counselee. (Rozell, 1983, p. 19)

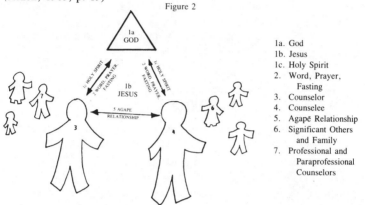

Figure 2

1a. God
1b. Jesus
1c. Holy Spirit
2. Word, Prayer, Fasting
3. Counselor
4. Counselee
5. Agapē Relationship
6. Significant Others and Family
7. Professional and Paraprofessional Counselors

This definition is conceptually shown in Figure 2. The various resources in the counseling process are identified numerically. In one sense, all of these are divine resources because the source and success of everything is in God. However, for my present purpose, I consider numbers 1 and 2 as divine resources, and 3 through 7 as human resources. It must be remembered, however, that the human is only fully effective when touched by the divine. Also, in some situations with non-believers (or even believers), not all of these resources are always being used.

Resource 1: God

Unless God is involved in Christian counseling, it is not "Christian." Obviously, much could be said regarding this, but my purpose here is only to identify resources with some suggestion of application. As our Father, God gives us provision and both present and future security.

God, the Son—Christ Jesus—is our Savior and Lord. As Savior, He is the only remedy for sin; as Lord, He secures us in our relationship with the Father and assures us of eternal life. Jesus gives us our model of agape for counseling. Therefore, we need to imitate Jesus (Eph. 5:1, 2). He always related to others in a therapeutic way. As the Holy Spirit indwells us, fills us, and works through us, He enables us to do the love work or ministry of Jesus. He not only helps us to understand who Jesus is (John 16:13), but He gives us enabling gifts (1 Cor. 12:31–14:1) to do His work and to bear spiritual fruit that make us like Him (Gal. 5:22). The counselor needs to have an intimate and maturing relationship with God in all of these aspects.

Resource 2: Prayer, Fasting, and the Word of God

We will never know in this life why the Almighty Sovereign God has chosen to work through the prayers of His people, but this awareness should honor us, humble us, and drive us to unceasing prayer. No resource so dramatically impacts the counseling process as prayer. Prayer releases the power of God. Effective Christian counselors are praying counselors. They know the discipline of intercessory prayer. They not only pray for themselves, but for their counselees. It may be that the most essential skill the counselor has is the skill of effective praying.

Fasting cannot be separated from prayer and the Word of God. It demonstrates our desire to place priority on things that are spiritual; it is directly related to healing, renewal, and ministry in the Scripture (e.g., Isa. 58:6–12). The Scriptures give us a number of reasons for fasting:

1. It imitates Jesus (discipleship) (Matt. 4:1–2; 1 Cor. 11:1).
2. It demonstrates spiritual priorities (Gal. 5:16; Ps. 35:13).
3. Jesus expects us to fast. It is seen and rewarded by the Father (Matt. 6:2ff.; Isa. 58:6–12).
4. It expresses devotion to the Lord (Matt. 9:14–17).
5. It prepares us for ministry in renewal, power in faith, revelation, and decision-making (Matt. 17:21; Mark 2:18–22; Acts 9:9; 14:23).

The Word of God is essential for effective Christian counseling. It is divinely inspired and infallible. As such it gives us true concepts and principles that are essential for meaningful living. The lay counselor not only needs to know the Word of God, but counseling should be patterned after it so the counselor can clearly impart the Scriptures to the counselee. The Word is the counselor's authority; it is what the Holy Spirit uses when appealing to the counselee for change.

Resource 4: The Counselor

It has been correctly said, "What you are is more important than what you do." This maxim is especially true in the counseling process. Counselors who speak truth but live otherwise will find their lives speak so loudly that their counsel cannot be heard. I had a seminary professor in homiletics who used to say repeatedly, "preaching is you." The same can be said of counseling, or any Christian ministry for that matter. We should learn to agape-love ourselves, to bring ourselves into love maturity in Christ, to focus on our love quality of being. The ministry that follows will express love.

Resource 5: The Counselee

It is true that the only person we can change is our self. In order to change we must see the need to change, have a model for change, and make a commitment to change. Everything else in the counseling setting may be primed and ready, but unless the counselee wants to receive healing, find renewal, experience wholeness, and move into greater maturity, effective counsel cannot take place.

Resource 6: The Agape Relationship

Lay counselors have repeatedly asked me through the years how they could be more effective in meeting counseling needs. They often say, "If I only knew,..." implying that the key to effective counseling is knowledge. My response is not to negate the importance of knowledge, but to remind them that it is not only what the counselor *knows*; it is also the *relationship* that brings healing in counseling. Agape relationships are therapeutic!

Resource 7: Significant Others

Others play an important role in the counseling process, both in the life of the counselee and in the life of the counselor. These others are referred to as *significant others*. They may include family members, members of the Body of Christ, or other friends. Sometimes the spiritual family is more significant than the biological family. The effectiveness of the biological family may be limited due to the hurts and broken relationships of the past. In contrast, the deep bond of spiritual life we share in Christ may enhance the role of spiritual family members. The wise and loving lay counselor will seek God's guidance in allowing each of these resources to be experienced in the counseling process to its fullest potential.

Resource 8: Professional and Paraprofessional Counselors

Other counselors—whether professionals, paraprofessionals, or specialists (e.g., medical doctors, lawyers, financial consultants)—are also important counseling resources. The lay counselors (and especially the supervisory personnel) need to be acquainted with the professionals around them and to learn to work with them. This can bring "the best" of resources to bear upon the counselee's need. It helps the lay counselor avoid the pitfall of trying to accomplish a task beyond his or her qualifications. And finally, it fulfills an agape commitment to the counselee, which is to use all of the available resources to bring healing, renewal, wholeness, and maturity.

What One Church is Doing

If someone had told me in 1975 that the lay counseling ministry of The Neighborhood Church would grow to its present size, I would have responded in disbelief. Neighbors Who Care, as the program is called, has provided training for hundreds of lay counselors from over 100 organizations and churches. About

50% of those trained have been from The Neighborhood Church.

Each week lay counselors give from four to six hours to love hurting people in one-to-one, marital, family, and group counseling settings. Counselees have come from all walks of life and with a wide variety of needs. From 60% to 70% have come from outside of the church family. At the time of this writing, the average number of new counselees per month is about 20 to 25. Approximately 200 to 225 fifty-minute counseling sessions are held monthly. The counseling center has 9:00 to 5:00 daytime office hours, is open two evenings per week, and on Saturday mornings.

Support groups have been organized for engaged couples, alcoholics and their families, remarried spouses, children of divorce, women who have been emotionally, physically, and sexually abused, and persons who are experiencing bereavement.

Motivation

The program began when our Senior Pastor suffered from total exhaustion. The church was growing, but he was overextended in his responsibilities. His recuperation took two years, during which time he was very limited in ministry. While the pastor recovered, Dr. Ray Vath, a clinical psychiatrist in the church body, and I began the Neighbors Who Care lay counseling ministry. Dr. Vath has served as a consultant, trainer, and member of the Neighbors Who Care Advisory Council. Because of my training in pastoral counseling and my availability, I was appointed as part-time director of the ministry. Originally, our goal was to recruit fifteen to eighteen lay persons who would agree to be trained, supervised and available for three or four hours each week. We reasoned that this would greatly assist our pastor in his counseling ministry.

The needs in the church and the community, and the obvious resource of the lay people also influenced us to develop this ministry. We were also strongly committed to the New Testament ministry profile and to the fact that the command and commission of Jesus was to the entire Church. It was evident to us that lay counseling was a ministry Jesus desired for His Church.

The registration response for the first class was overwhelming. It led us to believe that this ministry was unique in itself. Since the initial class, the ministry has continued to grow without persistent recruitment or promotion. Its uniqueness, I believe, lies in the reality that the ministry touches people at their point of need and gives lay people the message from leadership: "I trust you, God trusts you, and your ministry is vital to His Kingdom."

SUGGESTED GUIDELINES FOR ESTABLISHING A LAY COUNSELING MINISTRY

During seminary study, a fellow student and I investigated a number of lay counseling programs in Southern California. From our research, we developed guidelines for use in setting up a lay counseling ministry. Slightly modified, these became the guidelines for the Neighbors Who Care ministry. They are reprinted here in their original outline form. The italics are used to indicate how the guidelines have been implemented in the Neighbors Who Care ministry.

Philosophy
A clearly articulated statement of philosophy should be developed. Such a statement should include the following:
1. A descriptive theological and psychological view of man.
2. Justification for the ministry of counseling with reference to Christ's love, the ministry of believers, and the body concept as outlined in 1 Corinthians 12 and 1 Peter 5:9–10.

Purpose
The purpose of the counseling program would be as follows:
1. To provide an opportunity for people in the Bellevue area to receive Christian counseling; that is, experience Christ's love in time of need and crisis.
2. To extend the ministry of counseling to the Body of Christ at The Neighborhood Church by means of trained lay counselors and professionals who may be available in the congregation.

Organization
1. The congregational leadership should assume full responsibility for the program with regard to finance, legality, facility, and organization.
2. The pastor will appoint a director of counseling or minister of counseling who would be responsible to him and the church board. The director would also be responsible to recommend and train lay counselors for this ministry program. *The recruitment and training of lay counselors in the Neighbors Who Care ministry was delegated to the Director of Counseling.*
3. One professionally qualified person from the congregation or community should be identified as the consultant to the counseling program. That individual's services could be secured on a retainer basis so that he or she would be available for critical cases and for training.
4. Every attempt should be made to use the professional people now affiliated with the congregation for assistance in training and supervising the counseling ministry. Such persons could form a committee to review the program as it develops and could give meaningful guidance. *In the Neighbors Who Care ministry, this committee is called "The Counseling Advisory Council." It meets monthly to review ministries, refine procedures, and give oversight to ministry structures. It is composed of the Pastor, the Director of Counseling, counseling professionals, and supervisory persons in the ministry.*
5. Serious consideration should be given to some secretarial assistance with regard to scheduling, correspondence, reports of counselors, etc. *From the inception*

of the ministry, the secretarial responsibility has required at least one half-time person.

Resources

1. *Finances.* Ordinarily, the responsibility of the sponsoring organization would be met by donations based on a sliding scale related to the counselee's ability to pay.

2. *Facilities.* There will be a need for several rooms that are relatively soundproof and adequately furnished with chairs. One room should be larger so it could be used for group meetings.

3. *Library.* Some basic books which could be used for training of lay counselors could be placed in the church library. These could also be made available to counselees. *A special section of the church library has been designated for counseling. Several copies of regularly used volumes are available. They are available to both counselees and counselors.*

4. *Information tools.* Some basic forms and tests should be available which could be developed for use in a lay counseling program. *The Taylor-Johnson Temperament Analysis Test has been used regularly. Supervisory personnel are responsible for administration and interpretation. Special forms have been developed for intake, homework, and process records as needs have arisen. Some standardized tests for career and vocational counseling have also been used.*

5. *Lay personnel.* Personnel for the program would be selected by the pastor and the coordinator of counseling from members of the congregation. Some screening would need to take place, as well as having an acknowledged commitment from the counselors. *Each person in the ministry is asked to sign a Statement of Ethics (adapted from that used by the American Association of Pastoral Counselors) and a Statement of Commitment affirming a willingness to be in ongoing training, supervision, and availability of three to four hours per week.*

6. *Supervision and referrals.* Professional resources in the congregation should be used for supervision and referral of difficult cases. *Supervisory people oversee ongoing counseling, do intakes, assign lay counselors to counselees, meet with lay counselors and counselees every three to four weeks to give guidance, and serve on the Counseling Advisory Council. They also approve all referrels to other counseling resources.*

Counselor Acquisition

1. *Qualifications.* The following qualifications should be considered in the selection of lay counselors as relevant to the philosophy of the program:

    a. Spiritual and personal maturity

    b. Commitment to the Christian community and its ministry—especially in terms of time, finances, and personal growth

c. Teachability
d. Ability to relate to others—authority figures, peers, and people in need.
2. *Selection.* The following procedures are suggested in the actual selection of lay counselors:

a. Appointment by the congregational leaders. *The Senior Pastor and Director of Counseling appoint lay counselors at The Neighborhood Church*

b. Careful screening for the above qualifications by means of testing, personal interview, and biographical analysis.

Counselor Training
1. The training should be conducted by qualified professional people from the congregation and community.
2. Initial training should be at least 8 to 12 weeks in duration. *The Neighbors Who Care initial training includes three hours per week over a period of 14 weeks. One and one-half hours are spent in teaching and one and one-half hours in small group experience. The groups are facilitated by two lay counselors each. This gives group members an opportunity to work on personal growth and counseling skills.*
3. The acquisition of knowledge should include: (a) spiritual implications of the counseling process; (b) therapeutic models—e.g., Transactional Analysis, Reality Therapy, Integrity Therapy, Prayer Therapy; (c) evangelism techniques; and (d) basic reading in counseling.
4. The development of skills should include competence in displaying (a) accurate empathy, personal genuineness, and non-possessive warmth; (b) active listening skills; (c) problem-solving skills; (d) testing (administration and interpretation); and (e) diagnosing of cases and presenting case histories.
5. Personal growth experiences should be provided by role playing, case history discussion, and group and/or individual therapy.
6. Continuous training ideally should be on a weekly basis and should cover the following areas: education of items listed under 2 above, and discussion of case problems.

Counselor Supervision
In planning the supervision of lay counselors, it is helpful to consider both the personnel and the responsibilities.
1. The ongoing coordination (administration, scheduling, training, recruiting) should be the responsibility of an experienced person, thoroughly trained in the task. *The Director of Counseling carries this responsibility.*
2. The ongoing case supervision should be the responsibility of a qualified professional. *Professionals from the congregation are appointed to assist with this task.*
The following items should be considered in scheduling counselees: (a) the

nature of the program; (b) the case load per lay counselor; (c) the availability of facilities; (d) the length of counseling sessions; and (e) the availability of secretarial support (church secretary, answering service, etc.). *All of the scheduling is done by the receptionist, under the direction of the Director of Counseling.*

Advertising

Before the program is advertised, the leadership should investigate (through the Office of the Secretary of State) the legal requirements of lay counseling services. *The legal ramifications of the program were investigated and it was found that if (a) we did not claim to be professional or call ourselves such; and (b) we did not receive a required fee, that there were no restrictions.* Those seeking to establish this kind of ministry should investigate the specific laws in their own state.

In presenting the lay counseling program to the community, it is suggested that discretion be taken in *accurately representing* the nature and purpose of the program.

Public media should be used in a limited way so as not to "cheapen" the program. *Over the years, only the training times have been announced. The counseling ministry has been promoted entirely by word-of-mouth.*

CONCERNS

In extending this discussion, let us consider some of the questions that need to be addressed before beginning this kind of ministry.

Can Lay Persons Really Be Trusted to Help Hurting Persons?

Yes, this is demonstrated not only biblically, but in terms of counseling research. They can be trusted and are even more effective in providing high levels of therapeutic empathy, warmth, and genuineness than are some professionals.

What About Confidentiality?

Most lay persons who are asked to make a commitment to confidentiality in a relationship are both capable of and faithful in carrying it out. This kind of commitment should be required and enforced by the program's leadership.

Will a Lay Counseling Program Open the Doors to More Problems in the Church?

Certainly the risk of problems is present; this is true in any ministry. Care needs to be taken to reduce the risks and teach the lay counselor how to handle them. For example, in the Neighbors Who Care program, the risk is reduced by the following structure.

    1. All counseling is done by appointment, at the church facility, with the oversight of a supervisor, when the office is open, and when the receptionist is on duty.

2. Counselees and counselors of the same sex work together. If an exception needs to be made, a supervisor or another lay counselor is brought into the process.

3. Specific training and instructions are given to the lay counselors in risk areas.

What About Legal Ramifications?

Each state has its own unique laws. In lay settings, care should be taken not to assume the position and liability of a professional. Malpractice concerns need to be addressed; malpractice (professional liability) insurance should be carried for, at least, the remunerated, professional staff. The implications of charging fees or donations also need to be investigated thoroughly.

Do Lay Persons Risk Getting in Over Their Heads?

Yes, this is a risk. Lay counselors need to learn their limitations, function within a structure, and have appropriate support systems. When these objectives are satisfied, the risk is greatly reduced, if not eliminated. The risk is also reduced if the number of counselees and sessions per week for each lay counselor are limited. Agape love demands that we minister within our qualifications, abilities, and energies.

What if Some Lay Counselors Want to Do It Their Own Way?

The leadership needs to be flexible and lay counselors should be encouraged to develop their individual strengths and uniquenesses. On the other hand, some issues such as biblical truth, confidentiality, ethical standards, basic procedures, supervision, and teachability should never be compromised.

Is the Cost of Initiating This Kind of Ministry Extensive?

There is a financial commitment in initiating this kind of ministry. However, it is not unreasonable, nor is it unlike the cost of other ministries. There are costs involved in remuneration to program leaders who provide training, supervision, and ongoing support. Materials, secretaries, receptionists, facility overhead, etc., are additional sources of expense. The cost of long-term availability must also be considered. Hurting people need ongoing, systematic support if they are to be brought to maturity. Potential lay counselors should consider the need to be available for extended periods of time.

Will People Stop Coming to the Church Celebration Times if They See People There Who Know All About Them?

My observation is "No"; not if a loving, trusting relationship is built and maintained. If loving attitudes are openly expressed, the healed and those being healed will rejoice together (1 Cor. 6:9–11).

Where Can We Get Materials?

The materials we have developed and used over the years are now available through the College Division of the International Correspondence Institute in Brussels, Belgium as a three-credit college correspondence course titled "Christian Counseling: Agape Therapy." (Other materials relevant to lay counseling are referenced in Select Bibliography.)

THE CHURCH'S CHALLENGE

The challenge that faces us is clear and forceful. It cannot be dismissed, or ignored, if the Church is committed to the command and commission of Jesus and the prompting of the Holy Spirit to act upon God's Word.

The Need

Perhaps no passage in Scripture sets the need before us so clearly as does Matthew 9:35-38. It gives us a picture of Jesus and His response to the needs He saw:

> And Jesus was going about all the cities and the villages, teaching in their synagogues, and proclaiming the gospel of the kingdom, and healing every kind of disease and every kind of sickness. And seeing the multitudes, He felt compassion for them, because they were distressed and downcast like sheep without a shepherd. Then He said to His disciples, "The harvest is plentiful, but the workers are few. Therefore beseech the Lord of the harvest to send out workers into His harvest." (NASB)

This is an amazing picture, isn't it? The need that so deeply penetrated the heart of the Master is the same one that faces us. Consider the scene. Jesus had been going into all of the cities and villages proclaiming the Good News. His reign of deliverance and life had come to them. He healed (note Gk., *therapeuō,* from which we get the word "therapy") *every kind* of disease and *every kind* of sickness.

See how deeply personal this ministry was for Jesus. The Scripture says, "He felt compassion for them." The word "compassion" here portrays the Greek thinking that the deepest emotions were experienced in the major organs of the body (stomach, intestines, etc). I believe the text literally means that Jesus had a physiological response to what He saw. We should pray to have His compassion in response to the needs around us.

It is interesting and motivating to observe that the term "compassion" is used twelve times in the New Testament either directly or indirectly of Jesus. It describes His response as He met hurting persons and ministered to them. We observe that Jesus saw the people in the totality of their need—physical, psychological, and spiritual. He saw them in their "distress"; this portrays their physical need. He saw that they were "downcast"—dejected, despondent, and emotionally hurting; this was their psychological need. And finally, he saw them as "sheep without a shepherd"; this was their spiritual need. These terms depict the total deprivation of health and wholeness of those whom Jesus encountered. We, too, must see people in their total need. We must see them through His eyes and feel with His compassion.

Finally we observe that Jesus used both human and divine resources to respond to the need of the people. In so doing, He modeled effective interpersonal ministry. He used prayer, the Father's authority, and people to minister to others. Notice the beautiful and inseparable mix of human and divine resources.

The only difference in the need and challenge we face today, as compared to that which Jesus encountered, is that now the multitude is larger. Everything else—the lostness, the total deprivation, the desperation of the people, and the resources which are available—is the same. The response of His Body today needs to be the same as it was then. We must look at people through His eyes, be moved with His compassion, and then use all the resources available to us to bring them into renewal, healing, wholeness, and maturity.

The Command

The command of Jesus dictates that His Church do the love work of His ministry today. As one reads the following command, it should be remembered that the meaning of the word love *(agapaō)* is "to deliberately relate to the person loved in a way that is for their highest good." Consider then the command: "You shall love *(agapaō)* the Lord your God with all your heart, and with all your soul, and with all your mind.... You shall love *(agapaō)* your neighbors as yourself" (Matt. 22:34, 39).

Jesus has told us that this love *(agapē)* was the mark that would set us apart from the world and distinguish us as His very own (John 13:34, 35). Remember, this is a *command*; it is not optional. We must love as He loved, He is our model. The challenge cannot be mistaken: *"Church, love (agapaō) the hurting, lost desperate world!"* This is their only hope. It is the only way to please the Father. We must imitate Jesus! "Therefore, be imitators of God, as beloved children, and walk in love *(agapē)* just as Christ also loved *(agapaō)* us and gave Himself up for us, an offering and a sacrifice to God as a fragrant aroma" (Eph. 5:1, 2).

The Commission

We really do not need any further challenge, but we cannot ignore His commission (Matt. 28:16-20). It, like the command, is not given with options or alternatives. It is a straightforward imperative from Jesus, the Head, for the Church, His Body. The only appropriate response is simple obedience. There are several observations on this commission passage which will enhance its impact upon our lives.

First, all authority in heaven and earth has been given to Jesus. Who could ask for a greater assurance than to know that what you are doing is authorized by the supreme power of the universe and that its success is unquestioned (cf.

Matt. 16:13–20).

Secondly, the function and process of the directive is to make disciples and teach them to observe His commands (Matt. 28:19, 20). In other words, we are to show them how to love *(agapaō)* like Jesus loved. This sets up a love cycle. Love begets love. This is the work of the Church—it is mimicking Jesus. It is loving hurting people, showing them how to love, and repeating the cycle over and over until "all nations" have heard.

Lastly, we observe that Jesus, the Model, the Healer, and the Enabler (the Source of all authority), is with us in this ministry. His presence is promised. He has sent His Spirit to fulfill this promise (cf. John 16:7–13). Think of it, how can we fail? We have His authority, His love, and His presence. Is there any greater enablement? Is there any work more noble? Is there any greater assurance?

Select Bibliography
Additional Resources for Lay Counseling

Adams, J. (1972). *Competent to counsel.* U.S.A.: Presbyterian and Reformed Publishing Co., (Training kit available from National Association of Evangelicals, Wheaton, IL)

Brammer, L. M. (1973). *The helping relationship.* Englewood Cliffs, NJ: Prentice-Hall.

Clinebell, H. J. (1966). *Basic types of pastoral counseling.* Nashville: Abingdon Press.

Collins, G. R. (1976). *How to be a people helper.* Santa Ana, CA: Vision House. (*People helper pak* available through same publisher)

Crabb, L. J. (1977). *Effective biblical counseling.* Grand Rapids: Zondervan.

Drakeford, J. W. (1978). *People to the people therapy.* New York: Harper & Row.

Egan, G. (1975). *The skilled helper.* Monterey, CA: Brooks/Cole.

Miller, P. H. (1978). *Peer counseling in the church.* Scottsdale, PA: Herald Press.

Wright, H. N. (1977). *Training Christians to counsel.* Denver: Christian Counseling and Enrichment.

THEORY

INTRODUCTION

Statements frequently heard as we have listened to pastors who counsel relate to their desire to "get to the root of the problem." They want to know how to strip away superficial distractions and identify the "real" problem.

How do counselors—either pastoral or professional—recognize "the root" of the problem? There are at least four approaches; each reflects its own orientation to understanding human behavior and malfunction.

> 1. A counselor may automatically label all problems as sin, and look and listen until sin is discovered in the life of the counselee—*and it certainly will be!*
>
> 2. A counselor may listen to the counselee or client in a warm, caring way until the Holy Spirit supernaturally reveals the "root" problem.
>
> 3. A counselor may employ psychological diagnosis and prognosis (perhaps based on the DSM III or another diagnostic procedure) in a way which is consistent with a given theory or model of counseling.
>
> 4. A counselor may attempt to combine two or more of these approaches in an informal eclectic system.

Each of these methods of "root" recognition reflects a "way of knowing." Each has validity at certain times.

This section consists of nine chapters which deal directly with major counseling theories, followed by one summary chapter. Each of the theory chapters attempts to demonstrate that a given way of knowing in the domain of counseling/ psychotherapy can integrate—or at least find areas of common ground—with Christian theology in general and the theology of the Holy Spirit in particular. I picture this much like two circles.

Figure 1

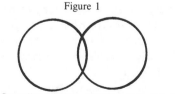

Counseling Theory   Theology of the Holy Spirit

The circles never coincide completely—and should not be expected to do so! Some coincide more than others. Counseling theories which are either interpersonally and socially oriented (e.g. Adlerian Therapy), or expressly theologically based (e.g. Integrity Therapy), *should* "fit" better with some aspects of the theology of the Holy Spirit than theories which are clearly individualistic (e.g. Behavior Therapy), or intrapsychically and dynamically oriented (e.g. Psychoanalysis). These differences in the fit of the circles are reflected in the following chapters.

Multiple volumes have been written about each of these theories and an exhaustive review is not feasible in the limited number of pages alloted to each chapter. Practitioners of a given theoretical model may object to either an omission or overemphasis of some topics relevant to the theory. Further, some theologians may object to the limited theological "proofs" offered for key points. This unavoidable limitation results from employing authors who are adept at theory, but who are not professionally trained theologians. However, for those scholars interested in further exploration of the "fit" between things psychological and things theological, the following chapters should prove challenging and stimulating.

Certainly, as Korzybski stated, "the map is not the territory"; but without an accurate map the territory is unpredictable and perhaps frightening. These chapters are written for those who hold not only a secular "map" or model, but for those who also see the territory with spiritual eyes—who know the reality of the supernatural and who seek to encompass that reality into their helping of others. Elisha's servant (2 Kings 6:16–17) drew a much clearer map after seeing the *whole* territory! We believe that the Holy Spirit (when invited to do so) will enlarge the perception of the counselor and psychologist to see both the spiritual and the psychological territories in the therapeutic interaction.

In Chapter 8, Dr. Larry Bass discusses the *Psychoanalytic Theory* of Freud. Dr. Bass serves as chairperson of the Board of Examiners for Psychologists in the state of Missouri; in addition, he maintains a thriving private practice in Springfield, Missouri.

Chapter 9 surveys *Client-Centered Therapy* and was written by Dr. Fred Greve, recently retired chairperson of the Department of Psychology at Southern California College, Costa Mesa, California. Dr. Greve has lectured and published extensively in Europe as well as in the United States.

Dr. Michael Rapoff, author of Chapter 10, is professor of Behavioral Medicine in the Department of Pediatrics at the University of Kansas Medical Center in Kansas City. His discussion of *Behavior Therapy* presents a fascinating insight into the integration of psychology and theology from an experiential perspective. Widely published in scholarly journals, his research has focused primarily on behavioral treatment of children.

I have written three chapters in this section; Chapter 11, addresses *Reality Therapy*, Chapter 13 discusses *Adlerian Therapy* (individual psychology), and

Chapter 14 examines *Systems Theory*. I approach these chapters from my experiences as a doctoral student under professors holding Adlerian, Reality and Systems Therapy orientations. I also draw upon experiences at the Christian Center Counseling Services in Sioux Falls, South Dakota, and at Evangel College, where I was assistant professor of psychology and director of institutional research. (Dr. Gilbert is now a missionary to Kenya, East Africa.)

Cognitive Therapy is presented by Dr. Lannes Baldwin in Chapter 12. Dr. Baldwin is a clinical psychologist with Veterans Administration in Tulsa, Oklahoma. Before joining the V. A., Dr. Balwin was assistant professor of psychology at Evangel College.

John Drakeford's unique style of *Integrity Therapy* is reviewed in Chapter 15 by one of his students, Everett Bartholf. Bartholf studied with Drakeford at Southwest Baptist Theological Seminary in Ft. Worth, Texas, while serving as dean of students and assistant professor of psychology at Southwestern Assemblies of God College in Waxahacie, Texas. Currently, he is in private practice as a counselor in San Jose, California, and is also a doctoral student at San Francisco State University.

The final theoretical discussion is that of *Actualizing Therapy* formulated by Dr. Everett Shostrom. I first became acquainted with Shostrom through the book he and Dr. Dan Montgomery co-authored, *Healing Love*. In Chapter 16, Shostrom and Montgomery present the unique concepts of *Actualizing Therapy*. Both are psychologists in private practice and have active writing and lecture schedules. Shostrom is also professor of psychology at the University of California-Irvine.

To conclude this section, we have asked Dr. Edwin Anderson, a licensed psychologist and director of Renew Ministries in Minneapolis, Minnesota, to share his reflections on the *practical integration of theory and the theology of the Holy Spirit*. In Chapter 17, he draws not only from his psychological practice and extensive theological training, but also from an active speaking schedule in which he relates to singles and couples in retreat and workshop settings.

As the reader reexamines the theories of psychology treated in this book, it is my prayer that the Holy Spirit will assist each one in a lucid appraisal of theoretical psychological content and that He will highlight those concepts which only He can bring to the mind of the counselor during therapy sessions. Let all truth that is God's truth operate in counseling, guidance, and psychotherapy!

Marvin G. Gilbert

8

PSYCHOANALYTIC THEORY

Larry Bass

INTRODUCTION

There is little question of the importance of the Psychoanalytic Theory (hereafter PT) in the development of all forms of current psychotherapy and counseling. It probably can be accurately stated that any therapy practiced today has been influenced to some degree by psychoanalytic thinking. Many counseling and psychotherapy approaches have developed either as *reactions to* or as *extensions of* the psychoanalytic model. Consequently, an adequate understanding of the psychoanalytic model is necessary in order to appreciate the present state of the art or science of psychotherapy and counseling.

HISTORICAL PERSPECTIVE

Unquestionably the father of psychoanalytic model of psychotherapy is Sigmund Freud. Freud, a physician in Vienna, became interested in the value of hypnosis as a treatment for certain neurological disorders. One of the difficulties any student of PT experiences is understanding the processes of change in the theory over time. Freud was a man who allowed for change in his theory as he encountered new data and new insights. It is important to keep these changes in mind, or one can become overwhelmed and confused. This is precisely what has happened to many of Freud's readers; the process of confusion has given rise to many differing theories and techniques of psychotherapy.

An Elementary Textbook of Psychoanalysis, by Charles Brenner (1974), cogently summarizes the psychoanalytic theory and helps to clarify its developing changes. Brenner discusses the various concepts which have evolved out of the PT and also effectively notes the changes which Freud and, later, other psychoanalytic theorists have made in those concepts.

Early in his thinking, Freud relied heavily on a physical model to explain psychic phenomena. He described the function of psychic apparatus according to a dynamic model. This meant that there were pressures and forces operating within a person which required discharge and release. Failure to discharge adequately resulted in an accumulated buildup of pressure.

Freud developed a schema to account for the different qualities of thought processes which he believed expressed, managed, and controlled various psychic phenomena. This schema included the concepts of the unconscious, preconscious, and conscious experiences and the id, ego, and superego. A complete discussion of these concepts can be found in Brenner (1974); only a brief overview is presented here.

Mental Processes

Freud categorized mental processes according to types of psychic experiences. Unconscious experience refers to any psychic experience (a thought, feeling, memory or behavior), "registered" in the brain as having occurred, but no longer remembered directly by the person, such as a painful or very embarrassing event which occurred but is subsequently "forgotten."

Preconscious experience refers to a thought, feeling, memory, etc., which can be recalled if attention is focused on it. A person may not be aware of these psychic phenomena until his or her attention is directed to them. For example, most of you are probably not thinking about your birthdate as you are reading right now. But if you were asked to tell what your birthdate is, you could do so. This information is stored in what Freud termed the preconscious experience.

Conscious experience, according to Freud, is composed of thoughts, feelings, memories, or behaviors which a person is aware of at any given moment.

Principles of Motivation

Freud later speculated that basic impulses give rise to motivation and organization of behavior in the human being. He hypothesized that such instinctual impulses could be distilled to two governing principles. These instinctual impulses are initially expressed in the infant according to what Freud terms the "pleasure principle" (Freud, 1911/1955). The *pleasure principle* suggests that the goal of human behavior is to discharge the instinctual impulses which results in the experience of pleasure or gratification.

As the infant grows and develops, however, continuous, immediate discharge of impulses and constant gratification is impossible. Reality intrudes and the infant must begin to deal with and account for the experience of reality which blocks discharge and immediate gratification. Freud consequently termed this response as the "reality principle." The *reality principle* was supposed to describe the way the human being must learn to delay gratification of instinctual impulses and to take into account the pressures from the outside world.

Structure of Personality: Id, Ego, and Superego:

The recognition of the need to deal with the outside world heightened the development of the concept of the *ego*. The ego refers to any mental process which helps the person adapt to and deal with the external world as well as the internal world of feeling, thinking, remembering, intellectual functioning, evaluating, and planning. In short, any function which aids the organism in living, growing, adapting, or surviving is an ego function.

The concept of *id* refers to those mental processes involved in the expression or experience of instinctual impulses. Id processes are involved in immediate gratification of those pleasurable instinctual impulses.

The *superego* includes those processes associated with morality, choices between good or bad, right or wrong, with guilt, or what ideally "should" occur in thought, feelings, or behavior.

The id, ego, and superego concepts form what has been called the *structural theory* and can be found more fully discussed in Freud's essay, *The Ego and the Id* (1923/1961).

The thinking which grew out of the concept of ego functioning became extremely important to the further development of PT. A group of theorists focused on the importance of the ego and thus became known as "ego psychologists." Some important summaries of their thinking can be found in Hartmann (1958), Hartmann, Kris, Lowenstein (1946), and Anna Freud (1966). A more complete summary appears in Blanck and Blanck (1974, 1979). These theorists turned their attention away from instinctual impulses, and focused instead on the way the person, through the ego processes, learns to take into account reality and adapts to this reality. Thus, adaptation became the primary focus of psychoanalytic thinking. At this stage of development of PT, it was important how the person adapted to the world.

Additional Theoretical Topics

Psychoanalytic Theory has always been concerned with the concepts of healthy as well as pathological functioning. Health was viewed by Freud as a result of being able to find ways of *appropriately* gratifying the demands from the instinctual impulses requiring constant discharge or gratification. Pathology was understood as a failure to find these appropriate means of instinctual discharge; such failure brings the person into conflict with the outside environment on the one hand, or internal restrictions—such as guilt feelings—on the other.

A further development in psychoanalytic thinking examined how a person experiences the *self* and how the self relates to other persons. These concepts form the basis of what is termed *object relations theory*.

The emphasis in object relations theory is on how the developing infant relates to other persons in the environment. The word "object" refers to any person who interacts with the developing infant. Special emphasis is placed on the mother-child interaction and the father-child relationship. These early relationships are thought to influence profoundly the child's self concept, and later the quality of adult relationships. The ability of the person to develop healthy, mature, and meaningful interpersonal relationships greatly depends on the quality of the relationship between the infant and parental figures.

Any adult relationship characterized by relating to another only for what he or she can provide is immature and suggests probable arrests or blockages in the development of healthy object relationships. The *healthy* object relationship is characterized by the ability to relate to another human being as a separate person entitled to his or her *own* thoughts, feelings, and desires, and who is not to be experienced only for personal advantage or satisfaction. A good summary of object relations theory can be found in Mahler, Pine and Bergman (1975), and Horner (1979).

EARLY APPLICATIONS

Freud originally used the psychoanalytic model to treat hysterics who presented various neurological and physical complaints. He developed the tool of "free association" and used it to discover unconscious, repressed, or conflicted thoughts, fantasies, and feelings which were being withheld from conscious experience in order to avoid the pain of acknowledgement (Brenner, 1976).

Freud primarily treated what were then diagnosed as neurotic individuals. He maintained that the psychoanalytic technique would not be appropriate in treating more seriously disturbed persons, such as those diagnosed as suffering from psychoses and character disorders. Subsequently, however, theorists and therapists have applied the psychoanalytic technnique to a wide variety of pathological groups (Boyer & Giovacchini, 1980).

As other therapists began using the model, various adjustments and changes in interest or attention developed. Although basically psychoanalytic in attitude, these therapists found themselves differing on many issues. The theorists largely responsible for expanding psychoanalytic thinking include Jung, Rank, Adler, Horney, Sullivan, and Klein. It is beyond the scope of this chapter to review all of the changes resulting from these diverse points of view. An excellent summary of these various approaches can be found in Wyss (1973).

PSYCHOANALYTIC VIEW OF THE NATURE OF HUMANITY

Developmental Processes

Psychoanalytic thinking contends that Man is born with various "instinctual" urges and impulses which demand gratification. The infant is perceived as experiencing no sense of self or separateness; rather, the infant is thought to experience a oneness with the environment. At this point of development, psychic functioning cannot be classified into id, ego, and superego. Gradually, however, these various experiences of psychic processes do emerge.

The developing infant soon becomes aware of the inability to experience immediate gratification of all needs. Gradually it develops a sense of self separate from the mothering figure attending to its needs. A very important work in psychoanalytic literature describing the process of the development of self and separateness is *The Psychological Birth of the Human Infant* by Mahler et al. (1975).

Two primary processes occur simultaneously in the development of the personality. The process just described, termed the *birth of the self*, allows for the experience of the self as a separate person, and it permits the ability to relate to other objects (persons) as separate entities.

The second process is the development of *ego functioning*. This process describes the ways developing persons learn to adapt to the outside world while still being able to meet appropriately the instinctual needs of the self.

Essential Drives: Motivation

The instinctual needs refer to the need to experience pleasure and gratification as well as the need to survive. Freud postulated that sex and aggression—*dual drives*—are inherently present to some degree in *all* behavior. Freud's concept of the sexual drive has been greatly misunderstood. By the *sexual drive* Freud did not mean the narrow sense of adult, genital sexual pleasure; rather, he meant a broad sense of pleasure experienced by the developing infant. This includes eating, sucking, and touching; in short, any experience judged pleasurable by any of the senses—sight, sound, touch, smell, and taste—is referred to as sexual.

By the *aggressive drive* Freud referred to any impulse that is present to preserve the self and continue survival, whether it be the need to destroy, control, dominate, or overpower.

Thus, the theory of *dual drives* is more complex than what is usually connoted in the simple meanings of sex and aggression. The theory suggests that both of these drives are present in *all* behavior, and although they may not necessarily be experienced in equal amounts, both drives motivate behavior.

This theory suggests that no matter how tender or loving a behavior may seem, aggression has played a small role in motivating the behavior. Likewise, no matter how mean, aggressive, or destructive a behavior may seem, it is prompted to some degree by pleasurable motivation.

The theory of *dual drives* may be illustrated by looking at some very common, but telling, verbal expressions. A mother may be hugging her infant and in a very tender way say, "I could just squeeze you to death," or "I could eat you up." The mother is not likely saying that she wants to hurt or destroy her baby; rather, she is overtly expressing how much she loves the baby and how much pleasure she is experiencing.

Psychosexual Stages

Freud described a typical sequence in which the sexual and aggressive drives become manifested in behavior as the child develops. He first outlined the sequence in *Three Essays on the Theory of Sexuality* (1905/1953). It is important to note that Freud believed that this sequence reflects what occurs in *normal* childhood development and does not indicate illness or pathology. Pathology results only when this normal process is thwarted or blocked due to some type of trauma interrupting the normal developmental process. Examples of such trauma might include the death or illness of a parent, birth of a sibling, or illness in the developing child.

It must also be remembered that these stages are not discrete events, even though they may be described as such; on the contrary, the stages flow smoothly into one another such that the transition is very gradual. Freud also suggested an age period during which a given stage is likely to occur; however, these age periods are only approximations.

Oral stage. The first stage of psychosexual development occurs approximately during the first year and a half of life. The infant's mouth, lips, and tongue serve as the chief sources of pleasure and excitement. During this stage, the activities of sucking, mouthing, and biting appear to be especially important as the infant uses these activities to explore and experience the environment.

Anal stage. From approximately age one and a half to age three, the anus becomes the most important area for the expression of bodily tensions and pleasure. Pleasurable and unpleasurable sensations are associated with both the retention and elimination of feces. During this stage, the child usually develops keen interest in the process of bowel movements, feces, and fecal odors.

Phallic stage. As the child reaches age three, the primary site of pleasurable sensation becomes the genitals; these remain the primary focus thereafter. Freud termed this stage *phallic* for both males and females because he believed that the penis is the principal object of interest for the child of either sex. In addition, Freud believed that, for the little girl, the clitoris is the primary site of pleasurable sensation during this period; Freud posited that the clitoris is embryologically the female analogue to the penis.

Genital stage. The phallic stage merges into the stage of adult sexual organization at puberty. This is the stage of normal adult development, and represents psychosexual maturity.

SOURCES OF CONFLICT

Psychoanalytic thinking posits several sources of conflict in the development of psychopathology. One source of conflict lies within the experience of the sense of self. One part of the self may not be comfortable with or acceptable to another part. As the sense of self develops, integration may not be experienced, since parts of the self may be in conflict with each other. Rather than wholeness, integration, and self-acceptance, a person may experience self-derogation, self-hatred, and nonacceptance of the self.

Self-Other Conflict

Another source of conflict is in the experience of the self in relationship to other persons—in psychoanalytic terms, a conflict in object relations. These conflicts are experienced as fears, feelings of inadequacy or inferiority, and feelings of disapproval by others.

As mentioned above, PT suggests that, at birth, there is no awareness of self as distinguished from non-self. The mothering figure meets the needs of the infant for food, shelter, warmth, physical touching, and clothing. The infant only gradually begins to develop an awareness of the mothering figure's existence separate from itself. The infant at first experiences others as extensions of the self. Others exist for the benefit of the self. The infant begins to develop a relationship with the maternal figure and other persons, which is described as "part-object" in nature. This means that the self and other person (object) are not experienced as two, separate, whole persons with differing wishes, thoughts, or feelings; rather, the other person is viewed as being there only to meet *my* needs.

Only in later stages of development does the self have the capacity for "mature object relationships." These mature relationships are characterized by the ability to view and experience the needs of the self and the needs of the other person as having relatively equal value.

If the child experiences anxiety or trauma during the process of differentiating the self from the object, the child may remain arrested at the part-object level so that other persons are seen as existing only for the benefit of the child. This blocking of the maturation process results in conflict and anxiety such that the child remains arrested at the earlier level. The capacity to develop mature adult relationships remains thwarted.

Developmental Failure

A third source of conflict or psychopathology occurs in so called developmental failures. Freud's hypothesized psychosexual stages were briefly discussed earlier in this chapter. These stages were further described, substantially modified, and expanded by Erik Erickson (1963). Erickson suggested there were certain developmental issues of primary importance at each stage. If trauma, conflicts with others, or fears within the self prevent successful resolution of the issues at any stage, certain types of psychopathology and conflict will likely develop. In addition, if an earlier stage is not resolved successfully, the chance for successful resolution of later stages is adversely affected.

Fixation and Regression

Freud postulated the concepts of fixation and regression, which are important for understanding the effects of conflict in the development of personality (Brenner, 1974).

Fixation refers to the idea that some energy remains attached to each psychosexual stage as it is experienced. Thus, oral and anal activities continue to be pleasurable as attention is shifted to other modes (zones) of gratification, e.g., phallic or genital. This occurs in normal personality development, but if significant difficulties are encountered at a certain stage the person may remain "fixated" at that stage and continue to experience primary gratification at the earlier level, rather than in more "age appropriate" ways. This second use of the term "fixation" describes more neurotic or pathological functioning.

Regression refers to a process which may occur if a person encounters severe conflict or trauma while in the process of maturing through the sequence of psychosexual stages. Under such conditions, a return to earlier—and often more "immature"—modes of pleasurable gratification may occur. An example of regression is the return of thumbsucking behavior in a seven-year old child confronted by the birth of a sibling. Regression implies that thumbsucking was an earlier mode of gratification no longer experienced by the seven-year old child, but which returns when a sibling is born. Regression is closely related to fixation, since when regression occurs, it is usually regression to an object or mode of gratification to which the person was already fixated.

Defense

No discussion of psychoanalytic thinking concerning conflict and psychopathology would be complete without a discussion of the concept of defense. A defense mechanism is developed as a part of ego functioning to help the self experience less inner conflict, while still allowing some degree of expression or gratification of an impulse demanding discharge. Consequently, the defense provides a mechanism allowing continued functioning, while "disguising" or changing an inappropriate id impulse. Defense is present in all individuals since it allows for appropriate functioning. However, defense structures can also become quite inhibiting and may interfere with effective functioning. Many types of defenses have been described by Freud and other theorists. (For a listing of various defenses and a discussion of their functions, see *The Ego and the Mechanisms of Defense* by Anna Freud [1966].)

GOALS OF PSYCHOANALYTIC PSYCHOTHERAPY

The particular goals of a psychoanalytically oriented psychotherapy vary according to the personality structure of the patient and the reason why the person is entering therapy.

So called *insight therapy* has as its goal the person's gaining understanding or insight into the *why* of his or her behavior. With this therapy, there is a desire to understand the causes of certain behavior so the behavior can be changed or accepted and understood.

Supportive therapy, on the other hand, does not have the primary goal of insight or understanding. It is directed towards "shoring up" or building more effective defensive structures in the person, thus permitting a higher level of functioning. Individuals who have structural deficiencies in their personality or who have had a collapse of effective defenses due to prolonged stress or trauma are placed in a supportive therapy.

A therapy is rarely purely insight-oriented or supportive. Most therapies are characterized by a shift of emphasis between these two goals throughout the therapy. The shifts are always dictated by the best interests of the patient.

Regardless of whether the primary focus in the therapy is *insight* or *support,* there are common goals present in any psychoanalytically based therapy. One such goal is to aid the process of growth and maturation in the client. Whatever the reason for coming for therapy, the client faces roadblocks to personal growth because of anxiety, fear, trauma, or environmental influences. One goal of the therapy is to discover, understand, and remove these roadblocks so that the person can continue the growth process toward becoming a healthy, appropriately functional, and effective person. No person escapes these roadblocks, so in a very real sense every person can profit from this kind of therapeutic interaction.

Another goal of psychoanalytically oriented psychotherapy is to identify developmental failures preventing successful resolution of conflicts and thus hindering further growth. Once identified, these difficulties can be confronted and the person encouraged through the therapy process to proceed to higher, healthier, and more mature levels of functioning.

An additional goal of therapy is to improve the quality and nature of object relationships. Healthy, appropriate functioning depends greatly on the ability to relate to other people in order to meet one's own needs, while at the same time meeting the needs of another person and valuing the other person as whole and separate.

The ability to develop healthy relationships especially depends on the sense of separation of oneself as a unique, whole person. Other people must also be recognized as separate persons in their own right, and not just objects available for personal gratification who can be discarded when their usefulness diminishes.

A very significant goal in psychotherapy is to assess and correct faulty or inhibiting self-percepts. *Self-percept* refers to the way in which a person views and experiences the sense of self. Is this person able to view himself as good *and* bad or is there a tendency to focus only on the good or bad to the exclusion of the other? A lifestyle characterized by overemphasis on good or bad tends to be fraught with difficult interpersonal relationships or inadequate and deficient functions which are results of depression and/or inhibition.

PSYCHOANALYTIC TECHNIQUE

Contracting

The techniques of psychoanalysis or psychoanalytically oriented psychotherapy can be described as a prescribed relationship between the analyst or therapist and the patient. A contract is established whereby the patient agrees to pay a fee, to attend regularly prescribed sessions; moreover, he or she further agrees to say whatever thoughts, feelings, or fantasies occur during the session. The analyst or therapist agrees to listen with "free floating attention" and to keep the patient moving toward a greater understanding of his or her behaviors, thoughts, and feelings.

Utilizing Regression

As this interaction occurs, there is a natural tendency for the patient to regress in the presence of an "all-understanding," "nurturing" figure. Regression here refers to a return to infantile desires, wishes, and impulses which have previously experienced frustration or have not been permitted expression. The regression allows the therapist to see various unresolved issues and conflicts, which may be contributing to the patient's current dysfunctions.

The regression, in order to be therapeutically helpful, must occur "in the service of the ego" (Greenson, 1967). This means that the ego allows for the regression while maintaining control; consequently, by the end of the therapy session the patient can leave and carry on the necessary functions of living.

Transference and Countertransference

There are two occurrences in psychodynamic therapy that are extremely critical to the therapy process. *Transference* and *countertransference* provide much of the "meat" of the therapeutic interaction. Transference refers to the feelings or thoughts that the patient develops toward the therapist as the therapist reminds the patient of important (i.e., significant other) past relationships. Thus the patient "transfers" onto the therapist various expectations, feelings, or ideas that were experienced in these past relationships (Brenner, 1976; Langs, 1973, 1974, 1981a; Menninger & Holzman, 1973).

Countertransference occurs when the therapist develops thoughts, feelings, and expectations toward the patient which arise out of relationships the therapist has had in the past (Langs 1973; Menninger & Holzman, 1973). It is important to note that countertransference is not "bad," but it must be acknowledged and controlled so that its issues will not interfere with the process of therapy. Because of these countertransference issues, it is imperative that a therapist who attempts to use the psychoanalytic model have a personal therapy, or at the very least a significant period of close supervision by a trained therapist.

Resistances

As transference issues emerge, and as the remainder of the therapeutic work continues, resistances often occur (Langs, 1981b, 1982). Resistances surface due to that part of the patient which is afraid to confront issues and which wants to avoid pain. Resistances may occur such as maintaining a long silence, "forgetting" an appointment, arriving late for an appointment, or waiting until the end of a session to mention an important issue so that there is no time to discuss it in detail. The therapist takes note of these resistances and confronts the patient with them.

Interpretation

Interpretation is another important tool in psychoanalytic therapy (Menninger & Holzman, 1973). Interpretation is rarely a single pronouncement by the therapist presenting insight and understanding to the patient; rather, *the* interpretation can be considered a *series* of small interpretations, which, over a period of time (weeks, months, or years), gradually lead the patient into insight or understanding of behavior or feelings. The timing of interpretation is critical, since making an interpretation *before* the patient is ready to hear it is rarely helpful, and may even increase the resistances (Langs, 1974, 1982).

CURRENT PRACTICE

The type of clientele treated with psychoanalytically oriented psychotherapy is much more varied today than in the early developmental years. With the current understanding of *object relations theory* and the structure of ego functioning, diagnostic formulations have been refined and techniques expanded so it is possible to apply the psychoanalytic technique to a broader range of psychopathological functioning.

The goal of insight therapy is to analyze defensive structures and loosen them so that functioning can occur with more comfort and less anxiety. Thus, neurotic individuals can profit from an insight-oriented therapy since their defensive structures seem to be too rigid to allow for a more comfortable, healthy level of functioning. Insight-oriented therapy is often not appropriate for psychotic individuals, however. Psychotic individuals have faulty, inadequate defensive structures to begin with; an insight-oriented analysis and breakdown of what defensive structures are present could result in further decompensation.

This issue points up clearly why it is so vitally important to have an adequate and thorough evaluation when beginning to work psychoanalytically with a patient. An assessment of ego strengths and the quality of object relations can provide the therapy focus and alert the therapist to the basic goals needed to be accomplished during the therapy. Attempting a therapy without this evaluation can be frustrating, at the least, since the therapy may become stalemated due to inappropriate goals. At worst, failure to evaluate the patient properly and failure to treat the patient appropriately can contribute to further deterioration and decompensation of personality structures.

Character-disordered individuals tend not to do well with psychoanalytically oriented psychotherapy since their motivation for change and desire for insight and understanding tend to be the least of all the patients who come for psychotherapy.

There is a special group of persons who tend to reveal serious character pathology but developmentally present a different picture from the more obvious character-disordered individuals. This special group can be treated with psychoanalytic techniques as long as these techniques are applied in a special manner. This group includes those persons diagnosed as having borderline personality organization. The special technique used to treat this group has been presented in Kernberg (1976; 1980), Kohut (1971), and Masterson (1976; 1981).

SETTINGS

Psychoanalytic psychotherapy is practiced by a trained therapist who may be a psychiatrist, psychologist, or social worker. The training is often obtained as part of a degree program supplemented by clinical supervision in a clinical training facility.

Psychoanalytic psychotherapy is often conducted at least once a week up to three to five times a week for more intensive, insight-oriented work. Occasionally the therapy is conducted less than once a week, but this would probably be supportive therapy or would occur during the ending stages of therapy.

Hospitalized patients receive this type of psychotherapy, as do patients seen in a private practice setting. With inpatients, the therapy may be given in conjunction with medication. The use of medication becomes an important issue for discussion in the therapy and the medication must be used judiciously so as not to interfere with the therapy process. For example, some anxiety is necessary to motivate the patient to work in therapy. If the patient is medicated to the extent that the anxiety is mostly controlled and/or the mentation processes are slowed to the extent that productive thinking is minimal, psychotherapy of the psychoanalytic type is not usually effective.

The psychoanalytic model has also been integrated with other therapy approaches. For example, Wachtel (1977) discussed the integration of psychodynamic treatment with a behavior therapy approach, and Stierlin (1977) presented an integration of the psychoanalytic framework with a family therapy model (see also Chapter 14: Systems Theory).

Research

Research into the effectiveness of psychoanalytic psychotherapy has not been plentiful. Strupp (1973) has attempted to look at some data regarding the outcome of psychotherapy. The variables and issues related to psychoanalytic psychotherapy are so complex and difficult to quantify that well-designed and scientifically rigorous research is very rare. The interaction effects between patient and therapist are so complex that specificity of controlled research variables is very difficult to achieve.

What supportive evidence there is for psychoanalysis exists primarily in the form of case studies. There are many case study-type research discussions in such journals as *The Psychoanalytic Study of the Child* and the *Journal of the American Psychoanalytic Association.*

INTEGRATION

Freud was generally criticized for viewing religious experience as only a defensive need having no reality of its own. However, an exploration of object relations theory reminds one of quite consistent concepts of God's relationships with Man and the teachings of Christ regarding appropriate human relationships.

Small (1974) suggested that Man as created in the image of God is best understood in view of the fact that God is a relational being. Small said that God is a Being-in-Relation (Father, Son, and Holy Spirit) and Man is a Being-in-Relation (male and female). God is a Triune Being and Man is a Biune Being. Smedes (1976) echoed these concepts.

Object relations theory suggests that healthy relationships are those which exist between two whole, separate, human beings who view each other with mutual respect and acceptance. Christ seems to epitomize this style of relationship as He describes and models appropriate relationships. For example, consider how He related to the woman at the well (John 4:7-30), to social outcasts (Matt. 9:10-13; 11:19), and even to Judas Iscariot (John 13:18-38). Christ seemed to leave the person's identity intact and yet confronted the person with the relational ideal. In view of these Scriptures, one can conclude that it is *never* appropriate to relate to another person as a part-object, or anything less than a whole human being. All human beings have equal worth and value. We are each separate and deserving of mutual respect and consideration.

The therapeutic stance of the psychoanalytic therapist demands respect for the patient. The patient is accepted and understood in terms of all the influences, past and present, which determine current feelings, attitudes, and behavior. The therapist works to confront the patient with patterns of behavior that are either adaptive and healthy or self-defeating, conflict-ridden, or self-destructive. The maladjustive behaviors do not lead to further growth and healthy change.

The relationship between the therapist and patient as suggested by PT provides an opportunity for the Holy Spirit to work to inspire personality growth. A Christian therapist who allows therapy experiences to be avenues for ministry can provide a very unique way for God's relational ideal to be modeled. Any roadblocks which prevent a healthy view of the self and/or a healthy experience of interpersonal relationships, can also be discovered and removed, or at least reduced, by the believing therapist.

It would be helpful if various Christian theorists and psychotherapy theorists could stop focusing on the differences in their belief systems or theories and note the similarities and commonalities in their approaches to problems. Learning is usually a complex process involving a variety of experiences. The various theorists and therapists can learn from one another. Appelbaum (1982) challenged the psychoanalytic theorists to guard against defensive rigidity when comparing other approaches to the psychoanalytic technique. He encouraged theorists to continue to explore and use data from whatever source, as long as the data continue to build toward greater understanding.

Therapists are not the only ones who need to be concerned about helping other people grow and develop. M. Scott Peck in *The Road Less Traveled* (1978), reminded us that we need to cultivate therapeutic interaction outside the formal relationship of therapist and patient. The therapist-patient relationship is a model for the many therapeutic relationships that all of us need to experience during our lifetime. Christ suggested that we, as His Body, need to exemplify appropriate therapeutic relationships with each other. A full understanding of the psychodynamic perspective and especially object relations theory can help us to experience more fully appropriate interactions in our families, friendships, churches, and neighborhoods. Only then can we really appreciate the value and worth of others as human beings as well as accept the self as a special, unique person created by God.

9

CLIENT-CENTERED THERAPY

Fred J. Greve

INTRODUCTION

Carl Rogers did not originally call the therapy for which he is best known "client-centered therapy," but he did say as early as 1942, that "the individual and not the problem is the focus" (Rogers, 1942, p. 28). Thus he indicated his view of the preeminence of the individual and the locus of the therapeutic encounter.

By 1951, however, *Client-Centered Therapy* had become the title of his now-famous book. That the *individual* was of central importance was indicated in this book when he said, "the primary importance here is the attitude of the counselor to the worth and the significance of the individual. Do we see each person as having worth and dignity in his own right?" (Rogers, 1951, p. 20).

This was a profound switch in perception and in the assignment of status. The client was not just a wretched and sick supplicant—coming to a majestic therapist who was powerful, arrogant, and superior. The client was a fellow human being who, though troubled, was no less human than the therapist. Rogers stated, "It is fortunate that imperfect human beings can be of therapeutic assistance to other imperfect human beings" (in Nye, 1975, p. 101).

In 1942, Rogers laid down postulates which not only characterized his therapy, but which have become incorporated into many other therapeutic practices today. These postulates include: (a) Therapy is not a matter of doing something *to* the individual, it is a matter of freeing the client for normal growth; (b) maladjustments are not failures in *knowing*; rather, knowledge is imperfect because it is blocked by the emotional satisfactions of the present maladjustments; (c) warmth and responsiveness from the counselor help to create rapport, which gradually develops into a deeper emotional relationship; and (d) the counselor does not have the answers; however, the counseling situation does provide a place where the client can receive assistance to work out problems. Implicit in Rogers's scheme was that, given a place of safety from threat, the client could express problems, and feelings about those problems, and that something in that process would bring healing.

These ideas, so central and in some ways so utilitarian, have puzzled some Christian thinkers, then and now. But it was not these constructs which so deeply bothered serious theologians; it was and remains Rogers's avowed "humanism." Rogers holds that human beings have a capacity to move toward growth and fulfillment. He stated, "Human beings are viewed as essentially growth oriented, forward moving.... If individuals are not forced into socially constructed molds but rather accepted for what they are, they will turn out 'good' and live in ways that will enhance both themselves and society" (in Nye, 1975, p. 82).

Can there be any *rapprochement* between such a philosophy—both implicit and explicit in Rogers—and the convictions of the Christian thinker and practitioner, who hold as an absolute theological maxim that humanity is sinful by nature, is bent on doing wrong, and is proceeding toward destruction? The answer may be the essential admission by Rogerian and Christian thinkers alike: the person is the center of the therapeutic enterprise in general, and is the focal point of the immediate therapeutic experience in particular.

HISTORICAL DEVELOPMENT

Rogers's influence has been so broad and his writings so prolific that the therapy we call "client-centered therapy" has acquired an almost universally recognized associated term, "Rogerian counseling." Yet early on, Rogers confessed a debt to many therapists and theorists.

Influence of Psychoanalysis

It should be recalled that when Rogers wrote *Counseling and Psychotherapy* in 1942, Sigmund Freud had only recently died (1939). Freud's influence was still great, and psychoanalysis was an entrenched method of therapy. The place of therapist-as-physician was strong; interpretation (of dreams, of transference, of "slips," of resistance) was crucial, necessitating long-term, professional training with a high degree of specificity. The person in need of help was a *patient* in the medical tradition.

But some psychoanalysts challenged that tradition. Karen Horney had written *New Ways in Psychoanalysis* in 1939, a work to which Rogers ascribed intellectual and practical debts. She later (1945) wrote *Our Inner Conflicts*, in which she stressed the therapeutic function of social relations. Otto Rank, one of the members of Freud's original inner circle who had broken with Freud over the "birth trauma," had come to America and had begun to think of therapy as relationship.

In his autobiography (1973), Rogers wrote of Rank's influence: "At about this time came a brief two-day seminar with Otto Rank, and I found in his therapy (not in his theory) he was emphasizing some of the things I had begun to learn. I felt stimulated and confirmed" (p. 9).

Rogers also acknowledged the indirect influence of Rank because of the contacts Rogers had had with persons whom Rank had trained.

[There was] a somewhat similar therapeutic approach stemming directly from
the work of Otto Rank (work which had also influenced the present writer)
being practiced by social workers, psychiatrists, and psychologists who had
received their training in Philadelphia under such workers as Jessie Taft,
Frederick Allen, and Virginia Robinson. This was about the extent of any
practical experience which relied primarily upon the *capacity of the client*
[italics mine]. (Rogers, 1951, p. 10)

Influence of Phenomenological Psychology

The influence of the German *gestalt* psychologists and of *field theory*
psychologists provided important antecedents as well as theoretical undergirdings.
Rogers acknowledged that client-centered counseling "has been indebted to Gestalt
psychology, with its emphasis upon the wholeness and interrelatedness of the
cluster of phenomena which we think of as the individual" (Rogers, 1951, p. 4).

This is phenomenology: the whole person responds to given situations as they
are perceived. Phenomenology stresses the importance of the individual's
immediate conscious experience in determining reality. Rogers maintained that
knowledge of these *individual perceptions* of reality is necessary for understanding
human behavior. He suggested that all of us behave in accordance with our
subjective awareness of ourselves and the world around us.

Rogers (1951) listed 20 "Propositions," many of which reflect *gestaltism* and
phenomenology. Some of the more important of these propositions include the
following:

(I) Every individual exists in a continually changing world of experience of
which he himself is the center. (II) The organism reacts to the field as it is
experienced and perceived. This perceptual field is, for the individual,
"reality." (III) The organism reacts as an organized whole to this phenomenal
field. (VII) the *best point* [italics mine] for understanding individual behavior
is from the internal frame of reference of the individual himself. (VIII) A
portion of the total perceptual field gradually becomes differentiated as the
self. (XVII) Under certain conditions, involving primarily complete absence
of any threat to the self-structure, experiences which are inconsistent with
it [the organized self] may be perceived, and examined, and the structure
of self revised to assimilate and include such experiences. (pp. 483–517)

Philosophical Orientation of the Counselor

As Rogerian thought progressed, concern grew that the counselor (or the
counselor-in-training) had to have a special perception of his or her role. The
counselor had to provide emotional warmth. In the warmth of the relationship,
the client would experience emotional safety. Rogers (1951) suggested that

the client begins to experience a feeling of safety as he finds that whatever
the attitude he expresses is understood in almost the same way that he perceives
it, and is accepted. He then is able to explore, for example, a vague feeling
of guiltiness which he has experienced. In this *safe relationship* [italics mine]
he can perceive for the first time the hostile meaning and purpose of certain
aspects of his behavior. (Rogers, 1951, p. 41)

Rogers called this "non-possessive warmth." But because it is conceivable that a therapist could be "warm" and yet could manipulate and "own" the client, Rogers (1965) was constrained to reiterate:

> It means that the therapist cares for the client in a non-possessive way, as a person with human potentialities. It means that he prizes the client in a total rather than a conditional way. By this I mean that he does not simply accept the client when he is behaving in certain ways [but accepts at all times without reservations]. (in Huber & Millman, 1972, p. 130)

Clinebell (1966) reported that by 1961 Rogers had identified three crucial counselor characteristics, which some have called "The Therapeutic Triad." They are (a) congruence, (b) unconditional positive regard, and (c) empathic understanding; these constructs are discussed in detail later in this chapter.

The Counselor's Role

In the history of client-centered therapy and its reception by the community of scholars and therapists, there has been an ongoing misunderstanding of the idea of "non-directive therapy." It was assumed that this denoted a *laissez-faire* role for the counselor. Rogers (1951), aware that his work was being criticized along these lines called this interpretation a "misconception." In the first place, such passivity and seeming lack of interest or involvement would be experienced by the client as rejection. Furthermore, such a posture would not in any way indicate to the client that he is regarded as a person of worth. Rogers continued:

> Hence the counselor who plays a merely passive role, a listening role, may be of assistance to some clients who are desperately in need of emotional catharsis, but by and large his results will be minimal, and many clients will leave both disappointed in their failure to receive help and disgusted with the counselor for having nothing to offer. (Rogers, 1951, p. 27)

Beyond Rogers

Client-centered therapy is by no means limited to Carl Rogers. Carkhuff and Truax—jointly and independently—have pushed the client-centered idea into new and creative expressions. Together they proposed concepts and conducted research leading to programs which would train lay workers in the basic Rogerian "Therapeutic Triad." Evidence indicated that these trained lay persons had results comparable to licensed therapists at statistically significant levels (cf. Chapter 7 by Rosell).

Carkhuff (1972) conceived his "folk model" of counseling and counselor training and, through extensive and rigorous research and practice, forged it into a scientifically acceptable model. Not only did Carkhuff spell out the demands which were characteristic of each stage of the model, but he also delineated the subskills needed for each function. He carefully devised training programs (e.g., "accurate empathy") and trained persons in these skills until they were effective helpers.

It remained for Egan (1975) to develop even further specific programs and exercises for training both lay counselors and advanced graduate students in counselor training. These programs were extensions of Carkhuff's "folk model." It would seem that this "folk model" provides one of the better avenues for meeting the immense mental health needs of our country and our world: lay counselors helping other lay persons. Further, this "folk model" is a substantial validation of the Rogerian model: i.e., the client-as-center.

THE CORE CONDITIONS OF CLIENT–CENTERED THERAPY

For Rogers, theory did not always precede practice. Some techniques were experiential, experimental, and practical, although Rogers had always laid strong claims to a scientific bias. As a practicing therapist, he could identify constructs and concepts, adopt a tentative theory, submit such theory to the scrutiny of new and emerging research data from his and other persons' practices, and then revise and validate the theory. Nye (1975) analyzed it in this way:

> Some of the ideas, and a realization of their uniqueness, crystallized for Rogers in 1940. He then continued to observe and to attempt to empathize with clients' difficulties and progress, meanwhile developing and nurturing various theoretical assumptions. There was an interplay between therapy and theory as he formulated hypotheses from his clinical practice and then attempted to substantiate these hypotheses in further clincial work. (p. 86)

One risks oversimplification when attempting to identify any "minimum core" of a therapeutic philosophy or paradigm. But Rogers (1957, 1972) himself noted that "The Therapeutic Triad" was central to his theory. Truax and Carkhuff (1967), Carkhuff and Truax (1969), Egan (1975) and others not only found these variables to be central, but they were able to train lay persons for specific skills in these areas.

Unconditional Positive Regard

We have already noted that Rogers saw the need for *non-possessive warmth*. But it seems that as he saw more clients and deliberated about the process that "unconditional positive regard" was a better term. What does this mean?

In the development of the child and in the development of the person in a counseling relationship, a need exists for *positive regard* from others. Significant other persons in the developing child's life—parents, teachers, Sunday school teachers—can strongly influence the individual by giving or withholding love and acceptance. In other words, to be accepted and to gain needed love and affection the child may be forced to please parents and other significant persons by *ignoring his or her own inner experience*. If other persons determined what is "right" and "wrong," the role of the individual's valuing process is usurped. We have all seen this in the "Christmas Syndrome" in which the little boy is told that if he is *good*, he will get certain gifts. He cannot possibly "get" everything, so he concludes that he has failed, that he is *not* good. This is *conditional regard*, a situation which Rogers also termed "conditions of worth."

In the counseling setting, the counselor must give his "regard" (i.e., love) without condition. Unconditional positive regard is received when a person perceives that all self-experiences (feelings, thoughts, sensations, and so on) are worthy of positive regard from the significant other (the counselor).

Rogers (1959) thus answered his most severe critics who had questioned the word "acceptance." He suggested that "acceptance" and "prizing" are synonymous with "unconditional positive regard." If another person is *accepted*—the *person* must be accepted, *not* the behavior—and prized, that person is valued unconditionally and is allowed awareness of the full range of inner experiencing.

On a practical level, unconditional positive regard is more difficult to achieve consistently from one situation or client to another. In the face of the child's (or the client's) annoying and disrupting behaviors, we tend to get angry and may even threaten to withdraw love, affection, or even acceptance. Yet anger does not have the ill effects associated with the withdrawing of love; it is possible to "prize" others even after having been angered by them (Nye, 1975).

This idea of "outrage reaction" is somewhat new in Rogers's paradigm. While it did not emerge as a formal answer to his critics, it is this one point, perhaps, with which his critics have had their greatest difficulties. In earlier writings, Rogers seemed to have a rather even tempered approach to others—especially pertaining to therapists' attitudes toward clients. But Frick (1971) stated that

> more recently he (Rogers) seems to be saying that *within the context of an accepting relationship* a variety of emotions can be expressed mutually and productively even if anger or annoyance is involved.... A parent, teacher, or friend can convey to a child, a student, a peer that love and acceptance are *not* at stake, despite the fact that annoyance, anger, or disapproval of a particular *behavior* is expressed. It is important that the respect for the person and their thoughts and feelings be maintained regardless of the specifics of the interaction at a given time. (p. 102)

The client who throughout life had received attention and some kind of regard *on condition* is now free to express any inner feelings in safety—provided that the regard now being received in the therapeutic setting is, indeed, *unconditional*.

Congruence

Congruence is a state of consistency or harmony; incongruence is a state of discrepancy or disharmony. *In the client*, incongruence develops over a lifetime as a result of subjugating inner, organismic experiences (because it is sensed that it is expected), which further leads to a disharmony between one's *experiencing self* and one's *self-concept*. Therapy moves the client from a state of incongruence to an increasing congruence between the *experiencing self* and the *self-concept*.

In defining congruence, Rogers stated:

> We coined the term ''congruence'' to try to describe this condition. By this
> we mean that the feelings the therapist is experiencing are available to him,
> available to his awareness, that he is able to live these feelings...and able
> to communicate them to the client. (in Huber & Millman, 1972, p. 125)

This process can occur because the counselor or therapist is *congruent*. The
congruence here is not between the persons in the relationship but *within* the
therapist. The counselor *is* what he or she *is*. The congruent counselor is genuine,
unified, integrated, and without defensive facades. As such, available feelings
may be ''lived out,'' and the counselor may be free to communicate them to the
client, if such communication seems appropriate.

On a practical level, whatever the therapist *is* will be communicated. Because
of the nature of interpersonal relationships, insincerity and incongruence will
always be transmitted. Inner, invisible, and unconscious attitudes will form and
project unmistakable cues which the other person will inevitably perceive. The
therapist must be genuine and congruent. Being genuine, open, and congruent
may seem to be insurmountably difficult (and Rogers admits that it is not always
possible, but these characteristics are corollaries of ''unconditional positive
regard.''

Empathy

The therapist must experience an accurate empathic understanding of the client's
inner world. Empathy entails sensing the client's inner world of private meanings
as if they were one's own, without ever losing the ''as if'' quality.

Several closely related definitions of empathy have appeared in the literature.
Gazada (1975) described empathy as ''putting oneself in the shoes of another''
and as ''seeing through the eyes of another'' (in Greve, 1980). Blocher (1974)
provided a terse but adequate definition of empathy: ''Empathy involves at least
two components. One is a cognitive component that involves psychological
understanding. The other is an affective component of feeling *with* an individual''
(p. 175).

Rogers explained his understanding of this concept:

> To sense his anger or his fear or his feelings of being persecuted as if it were
> your own, and yet without your own anger, fear, or suspicion getting bound
> up in it, this is the condition we are endeavoring to describe. When the client's
> world is clear to the therapist and he can move about in it freely, then he
> can both communicate his understanding of what is already known to the client,
> and he can also voice meanings in the client's experience of which the client
> is scarcely aware. It is this kind of sensitive empathy which seems essential
> to therapeutic change. (in Huber & Millman, 1972, pp. 131–132)

THE CLIENT

The notion of a ''client-centered therapy'' has the implicit implication that the client is, indeed, the center of therapy—both on a philosophical level and a practical, procedural level. Nye (1975) is very helpful at this point: *Not sick but "injured by sin"*

> The term "client" is used because it emphasizes the person's active, voluntary, and responsible participation; also, it suggests equality between the therapist and the person seeking help, avoiding the implication that the individual is sick or that he or she is being experimented upon. (p 86)

Some persons—both supporters and critics of Rogers—have had difficulties with the term "client." Rogers seems to have had an ongoing struggle with the term, too, because even though he used it extensively in his 1942 book, he provided a long footnote in his 1951 book to explain the term and to give a rationale for its adoption:

> What term shall we use to indicate the person with whom the therapist is dealing? "Patient," "subject," "counselee," and "analysand," are terms which have been used. We have increasingly used the term client, to the point where we have absorbed it into the label of "client-centered therapy." It has been chosen because, in spite of its imperfections of dictionary meaning and derivation, it seems to come the closest to conveying the picture of this person as we see it. The client, as the term has acquired its meaning, is one who comes actively and voluntarily to gain help on a problem, but without any notion of surrendering his own responsibility for the situation. It is because the term has these connotations that we have chosen it, since it avoids the connotation that he is sick, or the object of an experiment, and so on. The term client does have certain legal connotations which are unfortunate, and if a better term emerges, we shall be happy to use it. (Rogers, 1951, p. 7, n. 1)

Because of the inherent connotational difficulties, Rogers in later writings has been referring to "help-seeker," "person," and "person-centered therapy." Frequently Carkhuff referred to the client as "helpee," but that term can be very patronizing and even pejorative. Gibb, on the other hand, believed that role-laden terms do not fit, and so he suggested that if single words fail, we can turn to phrases such as "the person coming for help," or "the person you are trying to help" (Gibb, 1968).

The Client and Therapy

Client-centered therapy focuses on clients' efforts to come to grips with their true experiencing and to develop more meaningful and satisfying ways of living. *Purpose of story: one's life* Rogers believed that individuals have the inherent capacity to discover the source of their unhappiness and to bring about changes within their lives.

Some have said, in criticism, that the so-called non-directive approach essentially fails because it does not imply *responsibility*. But the client, seen in the locus or "the center (of the counseling process)" must discover experientially the causes of intrapsychic pain and "bring about change(s) in his life"; this *is* heavy responsibility.

The therapist has clear responsibility, too, to provide a warm, accepting atmosphere within which the client can be openly expressive. In client-centered therapy, the therapist avoids offering advice or "setting the client straight"; rather, the therapist provides acceptance, understanding, and occasional clarification during the client's struggle toward greater awareness (Nye, 1975). This is a very big job!

The task of the Rogerian counselor demands a very heavy professional responsibility. It requires personal and professional restraint of a very high order not to give the client a ready-made answer. The counselor must truly believe in the worth of the client in order to remain silent and permit the client to achieve personal understanding or insight.

Insight

Rogers had much more to say about insight in his 1942 writings than at any later time. This could mean that having said it, he did not deem it necessary to repeat it. Perhaps he was more significantly constrained because he was expounding a new theory—set against the then prevailing theory of psychoanalysis—and he may have wanted the nuances of meaning in his use of the construct to be very distinct from its Freudian definition. In Freudian theory, insight came as a function of the psychoanalyst's interpretations; it was a lengthly process. With Rogers, insight could emerge at any moment—even at a time when the client might be reflecting on a completed session.

> It may be adequate to say that [insight] implies the perception of new meanings in the individual's own experience. To see a new relationship of cause and effect, to gain a new understanding of the meaning of behavior symptoms have had, to understand the patterning of one's behavior—such learnings constitute insight. (Rogers, 1942, p. 174)

I have had the experience of working with a client for several sessions or for several weeks. I began to see patterns of thought, behavior, and attitudes emerge into a theme, and I believed that we were approaching an answer to the client's dilemma. But, quite suddenly, the client seemed to grasp these things for himself, and a full and accurate answer came forth. Rogers used expressive literary language at this point when he said,

> And in this type of situation, insight and self understanding come *bubbling through* [italics mine] spontaneously. Unless he has watched insight develop, it is difficult to believe that individuals can recognize themselves and their patterns so effectively. (Rogers, 1942, p. 40)

Insights include: (a) the perception of relationships; (b) new acceptance of the self; and (c) the element of choice. These often occur in a way similar to "problem solving" or "creativity." Insight is much like the solution to a puzzle. Various elements have been observed. Suddenly a new relationship, which provides the solution, flashes into consciousness. Rogers (1942; 1951) sometimes labeled this an "Aha" experience because of the sudden flash of understanding which accompanies it.

The value of "insight" is that it *belongs* to the client. We might have stated our insight conception of the problem during the very first session—but the client would not "own" it nor would he or she be ready to comprehend it. I remember trying to tell a native in Africa that his sins could be "as white as snow." He stared blankly. This word-picture was "mine," not his. I went into a residence, got some ice cubes, and shaved them up and then showed the man the pristine whiteness. He exclaimed "My sins *as white as snow!*" He then "owned" the understanding.

Relationship

Semantically and syntactically, there are at least *two* persons connoted by the term "client-centered therapy." It was Rogers's belief that in the context of a meaningful and deepening relationship between the client and the therapist, essential insight and ultimate healing would occur.

All that has been said about unconditional positive regard, congruence and empathy are necessary parts of this relationship. To illuminate the counseling relationship, Rogers began by telling what a therapeutic relationship is *not*: (a) it is not a parent-child relationship; (b) it is not the relationship of friend to friend; (c) it is not a typical teacher-pupil relationship; (d) it is not a physician-patient relationship with its characteristics of expert diagnosis with authoritative advice on the part of the physician and submissive acceptance on the part of the patient; (e) it is not the relationship of a leader and follower; and (f) it is not even a pastor/priest and parishioner relationship.

The client-centered relationship is characterized by a counselor's warmth and responsiveness, which make rapport with the client possible and which will gradually develop into a deeper emotional relationship. The expression of emotion and feelings is accepted in the client-centered relationship. While characterized by such a freedom of expression, there are definite *limits* of action. There are *time* limits—the client may not be late, may not overstay. There are also *behavior* limits, as with a child who might accidently break a doll, but who may not throw a brick through a window. Coercion finds no place in a genuine client-centered relationship. Furthermore, the relationship is one in which the client and the therapist mutually experience meaningful situations, in which *both* may grow and change. Rogers (1961) poignantly stated:

> I launch myself into the relationship having a hypothesis, or a faith, that my liking, my confidence, and my understanding of the other person's inner world will lead to a significant process of *becoming*. I enter the relationship not as a scientist, not as a physician, but as a person entering into a personal relationship....
>
> I am often aware of the fact that I do not *know*, cognitively, where this

immediate relationship is leading. It is as though both I and the client, often fearfully, let ourselves slip into the stream of becoming, a stream of process which carries us along. (pp. 201–202)

The Therapy Session

Much has been said of the non-directive nature of the Rogerian session. The rationale of this cognitive and affective set is that Rogers saw the client as able to gain an insight, which was then "owned." This demands great appreciation and acceptance of the client. It requires great self-discipline to refrain from giving "professional advice." It necessitates very concentrated listening because the counselor must listen not only to *all* the words and statements of the client, but he or she must simultaneously eavesdrop on the underlying emotions. Rogers, in fact, held that emotions are more important than the statements, but one cannot "hear" the emotions if one is not listening to the statements. Furthermore, this approach demands that the therapist listen to "silences"—noting the occasion of the silences, and "hearing" what the silences are saying.

Critics have said that the counselee (client) wants an answer. But it must be remembered that if the counselor immediately gives an answer, the client will not "own" it. Critics have felt that Rogers is evasive when he foregoes *interpretation* and says things such as, "Do I hear you say that you are angry at your mother?" (He may even make some wordless sound, now and then, such as "Umhum!")

But all this is a function of a philosophy, a belief, a respect for the counselee. If one has observed Rogers in a counseling situation (through film or video-tape) what is most noticeable are the profound *changes* in the client's nonverbal behavior—happier expressions, widening of the eyes, assumption of an erect posture—as the client begins to be knowing [continuous action verb] what he or she is experiencing and what is bothering him or her and what the solutions are.

THE SELF AND SELF–ACTUALIZATION

The notion of self or self-concept is so important to Rogers's psychology that his theory is often referred to as a "self-theory."

The "self" is not a theological entity; it is simply the person one is "becoming." The self is an outgrowth of certain aspects of individual experiencing. The newborn infant is an organism whose inner experiencing—reality—is a relatively undifferentiated composite of sensations and perceptions. As the infant develops and as innate potentialities emerge, it will have interaction with significant other persons (e.g., mother and father and other caregivers). As this happens, a part of the infant's experiencing differentiates into a "self" and a "self-concept." Certain sensations and perceptions become discriminated as "I," "me," "myself." Each child grows increasingly aware that there is a *me*.

As this self emerges, the child will feel happy, insecure, angry, and so on.

Some persons are able to be in touch with honest feelings; others deny them. Rogers proposed that life is best experienced when the self is honest (congruent).

Rogers also believed that the one central motivating force in all individuals is "self-actualization"—the unfolding of innate and latent potentials. The person does not "do" this—does not try in the usual sense of consciously trying—to achieve fullness. The whole organism strives to become all that its potentialities portend. One does not have to subscribe to this *motivational* bias to accept the idea that each human is uniquely endowed. The theologian—philosophically worlds apart from Rogers—believes that each person should become *what God intended him or her to be.*

Self-actualization, then, means the total development of one's potential. The client-centered counselor believes that if the person can be rid of "hang-ups," can become unstuck, that person will tend more nearly to become all that he or she could become. The client, moving into a developing, safe relationship, can, in that context, be honest with personal feelings as well as cognitions, and can achieve those insights which characterize what Rogers called a "fully functioning person." The therapist; having invested trust and honest appreciation in a client, can see that client's life become increasingly full and meaningful.

The Holy Spirit and Client–Centered Therapy: A Synthesis

This section will demonstrate the existence of a correspondence between the Person and work of the Holy Spirit and the work and practice of the effective counselor. Hopefully, counselors (and counselors-in-training) will be assisted in finding concepts, constructs, and skills which can increase their effectiveness as those skills are anointed by the Holy Spirit.

The Spirit-filled counselor—anointed and actuated by the Holy Spirit—can see clients as God sees those persons, and can become an agent in the healing process because of "power from on high."

This discussion is certainly not an attempt to justify the philosophy of Carl Rogers or client-centered therapy as practiced by secular therapists. And, above all, this discussion will not attempt to answer the critics of client-centered therapy. Some of these persons are very sincere and their function has been useful; the critics have caused therapists who are Christians to be cautious about some blanket and uncritical espousal of a secular system.

The point is this: there are some analogues between scriptural truths and the client-centered therapy. There are even precedents and antecedents in the Holy Scriptures which can enhance the healing relationship.

The Client-as-Central

I have long believed, even as a parish pastor, in the priesthood of believers (1 Pet. 2:5). Long before I began formal training in counseling, it seemed that every person I came in contact with was, in God's sight, my equal. The relative worth of each person is indicated in Philippians 2:3, "But in all humility consider others better than yourselves" (NIV). Peter had said at the house of Cornelius, "Stand up, I am only a man myself" (Acts 10:26, NIV).

When I heard during my training as a counselor that there was a systematic counseling approach in which the client was perceived as the center of the counseling situation, I was very interested. Perhaps in this context, the scriptural truth that seemed most important was that, in His incarnation, Jesus Christ took on himself the image of humanity:

> Your attitude should be the same as that of Christ Jesus:
> Who, being in very nature God,
> did not consider equality with God something to be grasped
> but made himself nothing
> taking the very nature of a servant
> being made in human likeness.
> And being found in appearance as a man
> he humbled himself
> and became obedient to death—
> even death to a cross. (Phil. 2:6–8, NIV)

Picture a counseling session either in a pastor's office or the plush suite of a professional, licensed counselor. Who is the most important person in that setting? The *client*! We care and work as skilled counselors in reference to the client and the client's hurtings.

I never deny that I am a licensed professional counselor, trained to be skillful; neither will I deny that I am an ordained minister in a fellowship committed to the ministries of the Holy Spirit. But, at the same time, I consider the person with whom I am counseling to be equal with me in God's sight. Christ died for all. "God does not show favoritism" (Rom. 2:11, NIV). I deeply believe that if that person were to go to Jesus, Jesus would receive him or her caringly.

This viewpoint places *me* in perspective: since I do not regard myself to be superior to a client, I am driven to trust the Holy Spirit for wisdom, for the right words at the right time, for the gift of healing to flow through me—an instrument— into the hurting person. The client is the center; the Holy Spirit is the acting Agent, the Activator and Energizer of the situation.

Relationship as Central

Humphries (1979) concluded the article, "Is Psychotherapy Unbiblical?" with the words, "But there is also a place for therapy that occurs within a caring relationship and has as its goal the enhancement of the patient's capacity to give and receive love" (p. 473). There are several such "caring relationships" which merit special discussion.

The Church is described in the Bible as the Body of Christ: many members, one Body. The principle within this theological viewpoint is that members are interdependent, mutually responsible, and fused into one. Health is implicit in this relationship: if the body is functioning according to God's plan, the interdependent parts are in a state of wellness. If one extends the analogy with the human body, there are "repair mechanisms," "defense-against-noxious-infection mechanisms," and "health-restoring mechanisms." Here is relationship at its full function: we can care for one another in a healing way.

There is the believer-to-Christ relationship. Joined are they; caring is He. This relationship is such that the believer and the Lord are *one*, and the person *shares* his or her hurtings with the "loved one." Such intimate sharing brings health and restoration to the believer. All this is activated and perpetuated by the work of the Holy Spirit.

There is the husband-wife relationship. This original human relationship, formed to provide the man with a helper, involved much more: it was to be a meaningful symbol of the union of Christ and His Church. But the *function* was the key: "It is not good for man to be alone. I will make a helper suitable for him" (Gen. 2:18, NIV). The persons in an enduring marital relationship "heal" each other as they intimately (without guile and without disguise) share hurtings. The key concept at work here is disclosure. When one spouse is hurting (becoming the client) he or she becomes the center, and the counselor (the caring one) is totally devoted to the restoration, well-being, and fulfillment of the other. Even secular theorists—utilizing client-centered theory—have recognized this potential source of healing (e.g., Rappaport, 1976).

There is the disciple-to-disciple relationship. It is no accident that our Lord on earth sent out His disciples two by two. These two, walking together ("Can two walk together except they be agreed?" Amos 3:3) would thus be available for "sharing and caring" for one another. These two would have with them the *Presence* of the Lord. "For where two or three come together in my name, there am I with them" (Matt. 18:20, NIV). And they have the promise of His intervening answer: "Again I tell you that if two of you on earth agree about anything you ask, it will be done for you by my Father in heaven" (Matt. 18:19, NIV).

It is not without significance that the two disciples, walking along in discouragement, defeat, and depression on the Emmaus road, were joined by a third Person, the Lord Himself! (Luke 24:13–32). And they were changed!

Further, any of these scriptural relationships have the possibility of being characterized metaphorically as "flowing." Rogers spoke of himself (as therapist) and the person (as client) as being in a *"lived"* relationship. Such a *lived* relationship was not static but dynamically fluid and could lead to a significant process of becoming (cf. Chapter 5: "Personal and Spiritual Growth"). Any meaningful, intimate relationship generates an element of risk. Yet the client and the therapist, meaningfully interacting, both become different persons. This happens in the Church, in mature and meaningful marriages, and between disciples. And while the Lord, immutable as He is, is not changed by relating to us, *we* certainly are changed by relating to Him!

Crucial Counselor Characteristics

I have mentioned Clinebell's discussion of the three essential keys to greater counselor effectiveness (Clinebell, 1966). With calculated redundancy, I restate them: *congruence, unconditional positive regard,* and *empathic understanding.*

Congruence. This term means inner genuineness, integration, and openness. The counselor, consciously and unconsciously, puts aside false facades and is "transparently real." The client, seeing this genuineness, is free to *become* himself or herself.

Now this is a formidable assignment. We are human, and that is precisely the trouble: we are human—imperfect. But God, through the Holy Spirit, would have *us* to be *us*! The Spirit-filled counselor can have a self-concept through a relationship with God which is so adequate that there is no need to fake anything. One can be authentic before God and the client. Then, through the anointing of the Holy Spirit, the counselor can be guided by the enabling of the Holy Spirit. Thus anointed, the counselor can accomplish what one's own expertise cannot. He or she can do what a secular counselor would like to do but can never quite achieve. Since the Holy Spirit knows the thoughts and intents of the heart of both the client and counselor, He can reveal insights which meet the needs of the hurting client (John 16:13; Heb. 4:12).

Unconditional positive regard. Clinebell (1966) stated that to experience unconditional positive regard is to experience grace in a relationship. He quoted Rogers:

> Actually it is only the experience of a relationship in which he is loved [something very close, I believe, to the theologians' *agape*] that the individual can begin to feel a dawning respect for, acceptance of, and finally, even a fondness for himself. It is as he can thus begin to sense himself as lovable and worthwhile, in spite of his mistakes, that he can begin to feel love and tenderness for others. (p. 295)

Unconditional positive regard is a blend of warmth, liking, caring, acceptance, interest, and respect for the person. This is acceptance to the degree that the counselor can be angry at bad behavior and even point out personal disappointment and displeasure without having a diminished regard for the other person.

I have always marveled that a secular counselor could, indeed, have a high degree of regard for a client. But, as a Christian, I know that it is impossible to have *agape* love without the work of the Holy Spirit in my life. Many times, as I have been in counseling with hurting clients who have said very nasty things to me, I have felt a surge of divine *agape* love. I knew the Holy Spirit was loving them through me. The counselee would sense "something different about this counselor" and break into tears at the realization that nothing had separated him or her from my love.

Empathy. Empathic understanding means entering into the person's inner world of meanings and deep feelings—experiencing and feeling as though it were my own world. Here again the Holy Spirit is the Enabler. "But when he the Spirit of truth is come, he will guide you into all truth" (John 16:13, NIV). When I cannot quite *know* what the client is going through, the Spirit can show me. Furthermore, the Christian counselor, by sovereign design, may be taken through experiences in his or her own life which better prepare him or her for the understanding what a particular client may be going through. Notice this emphasis in Paul's statement:

> Praise be to the God and Father of our Lord Jesus Christ, the Father of compassion and the God of all comfort, who comforts us in all our troubles, so that we can comfort those in any trouble with the comfort we ourselves have received from God. For just as the sufferings of Christ flow over into our lives, so also through Christ, our comfort overflows. (2 Cor. 1:3-5, NIV)

The Counselor and Insight

Insight comes when a stubborn problem suddenly becomes resolved. This happens frequently in counseling sessions. There are times, however, when insights come to the Christian counselor as a sovereign work of the Holy Spirit. If the client is a believer, the requisite *two* are there for the Lord's being among them (Matt. 18:20). It is apparent that the Lord would, in that situation, reveal the answer to one or both of them. If only the counselor is a believer, the Holy Spirit can bring insight which integrates methodology with theology.

I had a client in her very late teens who was deeply troubled and did not know why. She had suffered such profound pain as a young girl that her memory had blanked out the incident. Suddenly she knew! An older relative had sexually molested her when she was only nine years old. With tears of praise, she thanked the Lord for showing her the problem *and also providing a divine solution.* She received a genuine psychological healing and she was given the power to forgive the offender.

This *insight*—both for the client and for the Christian therapist—is like being given a mighty tool. It cannot be obtained in graduate professional training, nor is it granted with one's state licensure; rather, it is a manifestation of the gifts of the Holy Spirit.

Self-Concept and Self-Actualization

Jesus knew mankind. He not only knew the appearance of people before he had seen them (see John 1:48), but he knew what was in their hearts. He saw Pharisees with a cloak of religiosity covering bland, blank, and sinful hearts. He knew these men could be more than they were. He knew that if the rich young ruler would sell all he had (his facade) he could *become* a real person. This is the sort of potential self-concept that is tied to omniscience (all knowing).

Apparently, therefore, God—through Christ—would help us know *who* we are.

But great saints have had to struggle before finally finding themselves in a liberating, freeing way. Furthermore, it must be subsumed under omniscience that the sovereign God has a plan for the "fully functioning person." The promise of John 10:10 is, "I am come that they might have life, and have it to the full" (NIV).

Why would the Lord invest us with potential if that potential could never become realized? It is His will to release it. Today, we call fulfilled potential the "actualization" (i.e., made actual instead of potential) of the self.

Secular counselors report persons becoming more than they were, growing into much of what they could be, by the phenomenon of those persons sensing an empathic and loving relationship in which they do not have to be afraid to be themselves. As a Christian counselor, I seek to provide a setting—a milieu—of genuine loving and caring. In that context, the Holy Spirit, *through the union of myself and the client,* can release those seeking help: they become filled and fulfilled. This is the work of the Holy Spirit.

Synthesis

From these considerations, it seems clear that the tenets suggested in the last section of this chapter (based on client-centered therapy and theory) are not only compatible with the work of the Holy Spirit, but they can actually provide a vehicle for doing the work of God on earth as it is in heaven.

At this point, I am not certain what Jay Adams (1970, p. 103) meant when he stated, "Rogerianism, therefore, must be rejected *in toto.*" If he meant the secular humanistic premises should be rejected, I would agree. If he meant the "client-as-center" must be rejected, I cannot agree. I will continue to value and love those clients whom God sends my way. I believe that as *I believe in them* they will sense God in me and healing will come.

SUMMARY

This chapter has investigated the tenets and premises of client-centered therapy in an attempt to provide a lucid exposition of its principles and practices. The various ideas were explored in the light of the Holy Spirit at work within the client, within the counselor, and within the relationship between the two. It is my conclusion that secular therapists accomplish results which are measurable and effective for the client. However, the Christian counselor, empowered and enabled by the Holy Spirit, can have added dimensions of understanding and powerful healing interventions within the warm and loving and empathic setting formed for and with the client in the counseling relationship.

10

BEHAVIOR THERAPY

Michael A. Rapoff[1]

INTRODUCTION

Behaviorism has often received "bad press." Behavioral approaches to therapy and education have been characterized as simplistic, dehumanizing, and as portraying people as robots, puppets, or machines (Skinner, 1974). These and other negative connotations may stem from reactions to an inaccurate association of behavioral techniques with interventions such as psychosurgery, brainwashing and torture, and to inaccurate media dramatization of behavioral control, such as in the movie *A Clockwork Orange* (Kazdin & Cole, 1981). These types of negative associations can often be "conditioned" by critics of behaviorism. Bandura (1971) stated, "by associating the term 'behaviorism' with odious images of salivating dogs and animals driven by carrots and sticks, critics of behavioral approaches skillfully employ Pavlovian conditioning procedures on their receptive audiences to endow this point of view with degrading properties" (p. 14).

The issue of control is often at the heart of the negative reactions to behavioral approaches. To illustrate, the jacket of a book on behavior modification written for lay audiences stated that people who use this approach to therapy and education assume "that man is a soulless machine and seeks to control his behavior in schools, prisons, corporations, armies, hospitals, in much the same way they would program a computer" (Hilts, 1974).

Even Christian writers have "sounded the alarm" regarding behaviorism, in particular, the "radical behaviorism" of B. F. Skinner. In a pamphlet entitled *Back to Freedom and Dignity*, Francis Schaeffer (1972) warned Christians about the prospects of biological, chemical, genetic, and behavioral engineering. Schaeffer stated that (according to Skinner) those people who oppose Skinner's viewpoint are the "enemy" and must be "wiped out" or at least removed from places of influence (p. 44). Schaeffer also noted that the behaviorist's position is that man is a "machine"; he voiced concerns about what will happen when behaviorists no longer operate on the basis of Judeo-Christian values and ethics—as Skinner does.

One is left with the prospect that it would be extremely difficult, if not impossible, to be either a humanist or Christian (unlikely bedfellows) and a behaviorist. So, then, what is a chapter on behavioral approaches to therapy doing in a book such as this? One answer might be that it is important to "know your enemy." Behavioral approaches to therapy are now in the mainstream of psychological therapies. Scores of clinicians employ behavioral procedures in a variety of settings, including mental health centers, hospitals, and yes, even churches. It behooves us to know what they are up to!

Another position—the one I will take—holds that one can be a practicing behavioral psychologist and a practicing Christian, with a minimum of overt and covert (internal) contradictions. One can acknowledge that there are laws of behavior, use principles based on these laws, and yet reject some of the philosophical assumptions of behaviorism that are incompatible with the Christian faith.

Whichever position the reader takes (accommodation or opposition), an intelligent understanding of the basics of behaviorism is necessary. This chapter provides a brief introduction to the major conceptual approaches to behavior therapy, including the basic principles of respondent and operant conditioning. Examples of therapeutic procedures derived from these approaches will be discussed. There will also be an examination of how it is possible to be a "Christian behaviorist."

DEFINITIONS

The field of Behavior Therapy (hereafter BT) has been defined by "the behavior of those professionals who identify with it and by the historical context within which these people work" (Krasner, 1982, p. 17). Although this definition could be applied to other approaches to therapy, it does convey the idea that there are diverse opinions regarding concepts and techniques within the field of BT. Some professionals within the field believe that cognitive processes are important determinants of human functioning (Mahoney, 1977); others agree that cognitive processes are important, but that such processes are best addressed in therapy by treating *behaviors* directly (Ledwidge, 1978). This diversity within BT will be elaborated upon further in the section on conceptual approaches.

Rejection of "Medical Model"

In spite of the variation in concepts and techniques of application, behavior therapists share a common core of fundamental assumptions which can be contrasted with traditional personality theories. Other theories (Freudian, neo-Freudian, etc.) depict behavior as being determined by "inner forces," i.e., needs, drives, and impulses, that often operate below the level of consciousness (Bandura, 1971). The "medical model" is a prime example of an approach to therapy that is the antithesis of behavioral approaches (Ullman & Krasner, 1965). The medical model assumes that problem behaviors (e.g. depressive behaviors) are symptoms of an underlying pathogenic condition in much the same way that high fevers indicate viral or bacterial infections (Stuart, 1970). To continue the analogy to medicine, unless the pathogen is removed, there is a greater probability of more severe symptoms. Although this model has worked well in medicine, behavior therapists would argue that it is *not* a defensible position—on theoretical and especially empirical grounds—when applied to psychological problems.

In contrast to these traditional approaches, BT considers symptoms (behaviors) to be the proper focus of therapy. It focuses on current determinants of behavior rather than historical events, and avoids traditional constructs (such as the unconscious) to explain the emergence and continuation of problem behaviors (Ledwidge, 1978).

Acceptance of Scientific Methodology

Behavior therapists are committed to scientific method, measurement, and evaluation (Agras, Kazdin, & Wilson, 1979). Problem behaviors and treatment approaches are described with sufficient detail to allow them to be measured reliably, and for the treatments to be replicated by others. In addition, acceptable experimental designs (within-subjects and between-subjects) are used to identify causes and effects (cf. Mahoney, 1978). Even though there are differences in conceptual and treatment approaches within BT, a basic commitment to the scientific method as a route to solving problems of human functioning remains. The following statement by Skinner (1953) could still be affirmed by those identifying with BT:

> The methods of science have been enormously successful whenever they have been tried. Let us then apply them to human affairs. We need not retreat in those sectors where science has already advanced. It is necessary only to bring our understanding of human nature up to the same point. Indeed, this may well be our only hope. (p. 5)

The last sentence may be a point of disagreement for some of us who identify ourselves as behavior therapists. With apologies to the philosopher Bertrand Russell, science may be our only hope if there were "no allies in the sky." Rumors abound among Christians that suggest the opposite!

THE BASICS: CLASSICAL AND OPERANT CONDITIONING

Before discussing the major conceptual approaches in BT, some basics are in order. Many therapeutic procedures in BT have been derived from the theoretical writings and research of the developers of classical and operant conditioning. These theories of conditioning are the foundation upon which BT has been built.

Classical Conditioning

Classical or respondent conditioning elicits behavioral responses by introducing stimulus changes in the environment. While working on studies of digestion, the famous Russian physiologist Pavlov discovered and formulated the law of conditioned reflex. Simply stated, this law holds that "if you pair a neutral stimulus with an eliciting stimulus a few times, this previously neutral stimulus will come to evoke the same sort of response" (Keller, 1969, p. 9). The "neutral" stimulus is often called the "conditioned stimulus" (CS), the "eliciting" stimulus is called the "unconditioned stimulus" (UCS), and the "conditioned response" (CR) is the response which is made to occur by the pairing of the CS and UCS. In Pavlovian terms, the CS (or previously neutral stimulus) is followed or "reinforced" by the UCS.

The following example, taken from Keller (1969), illustrates the process of respondent (classical) conditioning. If a person's hand is immersed in a pitcher of ice water (UCS-also painful!), there will be a drop in the temperature of the immersed hand due to constriction of blood vessels (UCR or reflexive behavior). If one presses an electric buzzer before each dip in the water (at a rate of a dip each three to four minutes), by the twentieth pairing of the buzzer and dip in the water, the drop in hand temperature will occur when the buzzer is sounded alone. The buzzer in this example is the conditioned stimulus and the drop in hand temperature, when elicited by the buzzer alone, is the conditioned response. This example is intended to be straightforward. The process is not usually this simple, however, since the degree of conditioning depends on a number of factors, including how instructions are given, the physiological state of the person, and the timing of the CS-UCS presentation (Keller, 1969).

There are more familiar examples of respondent behaviors such as contracting pupils when a light is flashed in the eye and salivation at the sight or smell of food. Emotional responses are often thought to be classically conditioned; positive emotions are associated with songs and symbols used in religious and patriotic education (Skinner, 1953). Irrational or unadaptive behaviors and emotions also can be classically conditioned; a child attacked by a dog may fear and avoid all dogs.

Although irrational behaviors and emotions can be classically conditioned, the good news is that the same principles can be used to "uncondition" or reduce these unwanted responses. The heart of BT treatment procedures for irrational fears involves using the principles of classical conditioning. Joseph Wolpe's (1973) "systematic desensitization" treatment for fears includes gradual exposure to the feared object (s), while using a response which inhibits anxiety (e.g. relaxation). This type of treatment "breaks the connection," in a sense, between the conditioned stimulus (all dogs) and the conditioned response (fear).

Operant Conditioning

Operant conditioning is a process whereby the strength or frequency of a behavior is altered by the consequences or events which follow the occurrence of the behavior (Keller, 1969). Edward Thorndike is credited with formulating the "law of effect," which is the basis for operant conditioning principles. Simply phrased, this law states: "an act may be altered in its strength by its consequences" (Keller, 1969, p. 13). The principles of operant conditioning have been refined in the laboratory and applied to practical problems by B. F. Skinner and his students.

The term "operant behavior" emphasizes the fact that "behavior 'operates' upon the environment to generate consequences" (Skinner, 1953, p. 65). The most common example of operant conditioning involves the use of food as a reward (which is why behavior modification is often unfairly associated with just dispensing M & M candies). A pigeon will engage in a variety of behaviors (such as pressing a lever) when food is presented following these behaviors. The food is a "reinforcer," presenting the food when a response is emitted is the "reinforcement," and the change in the frequency of the behavior is the process of operant conditioning (Skinner, 1953).

There are basically two types of reinforcers, positive and negative. Positive reinforcers are those stimuli which, when presented, act to strengthen the behavior they follow. Negative reinforcers are those stimuli that strengthen responses that act to remove the negative reinforcers (Keller, 1969). However, what is one person's positive reinforcer may be another person's negative reinforcer. For example, reading is a positive reinforcer for me; I may do a lot of other things (like writing) in order to engage in reading behavior. In contrast, some teenagers may do other things (like cruising the local hamburger joint) in order to remove opportunities to read.

The basis of operant conditioning assumes that people behave in ways which "pay off" and/or avoid "punishment." The extent of conditioning depends on a number of factors such as the kind, amount, and immediacy of reinforcement (Skinner, 1953). The only way to determine really if a stimulus is reinforcing is to observe the frequency of a behavior, make some event contingent (dependent) upon it, and then observe any change in frequency. A less elegant way is to observe a person's everyday behavior; if a person engages in certain behaviors frequently, these behaviors are positively reinforcing for that person.

There are also "generalized" reinforcers or events/objects which have been paired with primary reinforcers (such as food and sexual behavior). *Money* is exchanged for a variety of reinforcers, such as food. *Attention* from others— such as parents for young children—is reinforcing because people who give attention also give other reinforcers. *Affection* is also reinforcing because of its primary connection with sexual behavior and because people who show affection also supply other reinforcers. These generalized reinforcers continue to alter behavior effectively, even though the primary reinforcers upon which they are based no longer accompany them (Skinner, 1953).

Principles of operant conditioning have been employed extensively in behavioral approaches to therapy and education. In the area of child behavior therapy, parents have been taught to reinforce appropriate prosocial behaviors in their children and to remove reinforcement or punish negative behaviors (Sulzer-Azaroff & Pollack, 1982). "Teaching machines" were originally developed to give immediate positive feedback to students attempting to master academic subjects (Skinner, 1968). Incentives have been used in industry, mental health, and hospital settings to encourage desirable behaviors by workers and consumers. (See recent issues of *Progress in Behavior Modification*.)

To have a complete understanding of the field of BT, it is important to have some basic knowledge about classical and operant conditioning. For a more complete coverage of these topics, the reader is referred to several excellent texts (Kazdin, 1975; Rachlin, 1976; Whaley & Malott, 1971). With this brief background we can now proceed to describe the major conceptual approaches within the field of BT.

CONCEPTUAL APPROACHES

There are four major conceptual camps within the field of BT, and each differs in its emphasis on what variables in human functioning should be the focus of assessment and treatment: *neobehavioristic theory, applied behavior analysis, social learning theory,* and *cognitive-behavior theory.* The first two approaches adhere to the tenets of classical and operant conditioning, respectively. The last two introduce other variables which are thought to influence behavior change, such as cognitions. This is admittedly a simplistic and arbitrary division of these approaches, since all of these approaches address cognitions and other "mediating" variables in some fashion. However, the more traditional BT approaches (neobehavioristic and applied behavior analysis) see cognitions and other such internal, "private events" as behaviors which are subject to the same laws of learning as overt (public) behaviors (see Skinner, 1974; Wolpe, 1978).

Neobehavioristic Theory

Behavioral clinicians sympathetic to this position are concerned with the "application of the principles of conditioning, especially classical conditioning and counter conditioning, to the etiology and treatment of abnormal behavior" (Agras et al., 1979, pp. 8, 9). This approach to therapy is based on Pavlovian classical conditioning studies with animals and on some of the initial clinical applications and writings of the "father of behaviorism," J. B. Watson. Watson's basic position argued that behavior is largely determined by habits acquired by classical conditioning, that language, emotional, and motor habits are conditioned, and that inappropriate habits can be eliminated through counter conditioning procedures (Eysenck, 1982).

The most notable application of this approach has been the treatment of phobias through systematic desensitization, a set of procedures developed by Wolpe (1973). Systematic desensitization is based on the premise that one emotion (relaxation) can be used to counteract another (anxiety), while allowing the person to approach threatening situations gradually. Children, if allowed to, often follow this approach in dealing with threatening situations. My daughter Lindsey taught me this on the playground when she was two years of age. She learned to enjoy swinging in a fairly systematic fashion. First, she watched other children swing, then she asked to be put in the swing with me close by. Gradually, she asked me to push her higher and higher and also asked that I move further and further away from her. She also asked questions ('I'm okay, huh Dad?'') seeking reassurance, and made positive comments ("I'm swinging high! I'm a big girl!''). In the same way people with phobias can be taught to overcome their fears by learning to relax and to expose themselves gradually to fearful stimuli, first in imagination and then in live situations. (The interested reader is referred to practical manuals of systematic desensitization by Weinrich, Dawley, and General [1976] and Wolpe and Wolpe [1981].)

Although neobehaviorists still adhere to the basic tenets of classical conditioning, particularly in the treatment of phobias, they have broadened their position in response to research findings. For example, there is some evidence that physiological reactivity may be higher in people with complex fears than in people with simple monosymptomatic fears (Eysenck, 1982). In addition, neobehaviorists would admit that the principles of operant conditioning may better account for how behaviors are maintained (Eysenck, 1982). A fear may be classically conditioned but maintained by operant conditioning, perhaps in the form of special attention, when the person shows fearful behavior. For a more detailed account of the neobehavioral approach to therapy, see Eysenck (1960) and Wolpe (1958).

Applied Behavior Analysis

Researchers and practitioners who identify with this approach are concerned with the ''application of behavioral methods to modify behaviors of personal and social importance'' (Agras et al., 1979, p. 7). Applied behavior analysts (abbreviated ABAs) work in a variety of applied settings (homes, schools, hospitals, and community groups) to modify behaviors using procedures derived from operant conditioning principles. They study ways to modify behaviors which constitute personal or societal problems rather than study behaviors which are convenient to study or of primarily theoretical interest (Baer, Wolf, & Risley, 1968). As an example, my colleagues and I are studying ways of improving compliance with medical treatment by children with acute and chronic disease. This represents a major personal and societal problem; children who do not adequately comply with treatment are likely to have a poorer prognosis and may need to have further treatment. This results in increased medical costs for the family and for society as the costs to insurance carriers are passed on to other consumers (Rapoff & Christophersen, 1982).

Other distinctive features of the applied behavior analysis approach are summarized eloquently by Baer (1982). ABAs are concerned with principles and techniques which show how to translate problems into observable behaviors that, if changed, constitute a solution to a problem. Translating complaints into observable behaviors is considered a crucial step. The techniques used to alter behaviors utilize powerful environmental variables (such as positive reinforcement), which produce effects large enough to be of practical value (Baer et al., 1968).

In evaluating the effects of these techniques, individuals are intensively studied using repeated measures and single-subject (within-subject) designs that experimentally correlate a particular response with environmental stimuli that precede and/or follow the response (Baer, 1982; Hersen & Barlow, 1976). After repeated demonstrations that the techniques "work" with a small number of people, the techniques are applied with larger groups of people by trained personnel. In this way, a "technology" of behavior change for particular problems is developed, and through manuals, workshops, and on-site training, the technology is disseminated to people who can employ it in their respective settings.

Of all the approaches within BT, this one is most directly and almost exclusively (with the exception of a few "renagades") identified with Skinnerian or operant psychology. The focus is on overt behaviors, and procedures are developed from animal and human research of operant conditioning. Some would say that within this approach, cognitive processes and other covert (private) events are *not* considered to be a proper subject of a scientific analysis (Agras et al., 1979).

One of the premier examples of the applied behavior analysis approach to a socially important problem is the Achievement Place program for juvenile delinquents. Montrose Wolf and his colleagues at the University of Kansas have developed and disseminated a group home program for delinquents that utilizes reinforcement procedures to teach social skills and decrease delinquent behaviors (Willner, Braukmann, Kirigin, & Wolf, 1978). The components of this program have been carefully studied, packaged and distributed through a graduate training program, workshops, on-site training, and in written form (Braukmann et al., 1975). For example, the procedures for teaching conversational skills to delinquents—an important but noticeably absent skill for many delinquents—have been experimentally studied and found to be effective (Minkin et al., 1976). The procedures included giving instructions on conversational skills (asking questions and providing positive feedback), modeling these skills, and giving positive feedback for practicing these skills. (For more information about ABA, see Ramp & Semb, 1975.)

Social Learning Theory

This approach within BT is most closely identified with the work of Albert

Bandura and his colleagues. Bandura (1971; 1977) maintained that traditional behavioral theories can be faulted for an *incomplete*, rather than an *inaccurate*, account of human behavior. He asserted that human beings are not driven by inner forces, as in psychoanalytic theory, nor "buffeted helplessly by environmental influences," as in traditional behavior theory (Bandura, 1971). The social learning perspective admits that behavior is influenced by classical and operant conditioning (Krasner, 1982). However, behavior change involves more than can be accounted for by conditioning theory. Bandura argued that most behaviors are learned through "examples," either deliberate or inadvertent. People can learn by observing other people's behavior and the consequences which others experience. Thus, to a large extent, behavior is regulated by anticipated consequences of actions. Bandura (1971) termed this a cognitively mediated learning process.

Within social learning theory, "modeling" or "observational learning" is an important process in human learning. The social learning explanation of how modeling influences behavior change is different from the operant view. In operant conditioning theory, behavior is modeled, the person displays the behavior and is reinforced. According to Bandura (1971), this position does not account for situations when behaviors are copied long after the original modeling occurs, and when overt reinforcement is not given (which occurs in varying degrees when children develop language). The social learning position is that observational learning occurs when people attend to the relevant features of modeled behaviors, code the modeled behaviors in their memory, retain what is coded, have the motor skills to perform the behaviors, and are reinforced sufficiently for exhibiting the behaviors (Bandura, 1971). Thus "cognitive" as well as behavioral factors interact to produce behavior change.

The concept of reinforcement is also expanded from traditional behavioral conceptualizations to include cognitive or symbolic processes. According to Bandura (1971), reinforcement serves an "informative" as well as response-strengthening or motivational function. Reinforcement is informative in the sense that people develop hypotheses (thoughts) about what types of behaviors are more likely to succeed—that is, what they must do to obtain positive outcomes and avoid negative ones. Reinforcement also serves a motivational function, as in traditional BT. Bandura (1971), however, maintained that most behaviors are *not* controlled by immediate consequences, but by "anticipated" consequences. People can represent outcomes symbolically. Thus, future consequences can influence behavior just as actual consequences do, such as when people buy fire insurance before experiencing the tragedy of a fire in their home.

Applications of the social learning theory to clinical practice have centered on the use of modeling as a therapeutic technique to help children and adults with phobias and deficient social skills (Perry & Furukawa, 1980). For example, in O'Connor's (1969) study, socially withdrawn children were shown a film depicting a child who gradually moved from isolated to nonisolated play patterns and was appropriately reinforced by his peers for more socially interactive play. The withdrawn children who viewed the film displayed more socially active play in their school setting as compared to withdrawn children who viewed a neutral film.

Cognitive-Behavioral Theory

Like social learning theorists, those who identify with this approach emphasize the importance of symbolic or cognitive factors in human learning. Cognitive-behavior therapists are characterized as the "thinking behaviorists" and their premise is that individuals respond "not to some real environment—but to a perceived environment" (Mahoney, 1974, p. 5). For example, a frightened airline passenger reacts not just to external stimuli (loud noises at take-off) but to the perception, or internal labeling, of the stimuli ("We've lost an engine!"). Cognitive-behavioral theory, like social learning theory, asserts that traditional BT does not go far enough in accounting for behavior change.

According to Mahoney (1977), there are four general assertions of the cognitive-behavior perspective: (a) people respond primarily to cognitive representations of their environment rather than the environment *per se*; (b) these cognitive representations are functionally related to the processes and parameters of learning; (c) most human learning is cognitively mediated; and (d) thoughts, feelings, and behaviors are causally interactive. However, there is still a major emphasis on empirical research and the importance of "observable anchors" (reliable assessment of overt behaviors) in psychological research consistent with traditional behavioral theory (Mahoney, 1974).

The hyphen in the label "cognitive-behavioral" reflects the composition of this group of therapists. They have been identified with either cognitive or behavior therapy positions and more recently those who have been trained to combine these approaches. The cognitive therapists, most notably Beck (1976) and Ellis (1962; 1977), attempt to modify behavior and emotion by influencing the client's pattern of thought (Ledwidge, 1978). (Note: see Baldwin's chapter in this volume for a detailed discussion of Cognitive Therapy.)

Like traditional Behavior Therapy, Cognitive-Behavior Therapy is set apart from traditional psychotherapy in that it is complaint-oriented, it does not focus on distant historical antecedents, and it avoids traditional constructs like the unconscious (Mahoney, 1974). Cognitive and *some* traditional behavior therapists have shared principles and techniques. Certainly, cognitive factors have not been ignored by behavior therapists and theorists, such as Bandura. Behavioral journals and conferences are now replete with examples of the merger between cognitive and behavioral approaches. In my own graduate training, I participated in workshops with Albert Ellis and traditional behavioral practitioners under the auspices of the Association for the Advancement of Behavior Therapy (the largest professional organization for behavioral *and* cognitive-behavioral clinicians).

In clinical applications, cognitive-behavioral procedures have been applied to a variety of problems with children and adults, including anxiety and pain disorders (Mahoney, 1974; Meichenbaum, 1977). For example, people with chronic pain problems have been taught to control their pain using coping skills which combine cognitive and behavioral elements (Fordyce, 1976; Turk, Meichenbaum, & Genest, 1983). People who interact with chronic pain patients (medical staff and significant others—especially family members) are instructed how to reinforce adaptive behaviors (such as engaging in an appropriate exercise regimen) and to avoid reinforcing verbal and nonverbal displays of pain. Cognitive coping skills involve having the patient monitor thoughts which may exacerbate pain (e.g. ''I can't stand this!'') and to challenge and replace these negative thoughts with more adaptive thoughts (e.g. ''I don't like this but I can stand it! I can use my relaxation skills to reduce my pain'').

Evaluation of Conceptual Approaches

As can be seen from this brief review, there are differences within BT concerning the role of cognitive factors in human learning. These differences have been ''aired'' in the psychology literature, with traditional behavior therapists challenging the cognitive trend in BT on both conceptual and empirical grounds. The traditional behavior therapists contend that there is no evidence that the addition of cognitive therapy procedures adds to the effectiveness of behavioral treatments, in particular for the treatment of ''neurotic'' disorders such as phobias (Ledwidge, 1978, Wolpe, 1978). On conceptual grounds, the traditional behavior therapists argue that cognitions are behaviors and are subject to the same behavioral processes as overt behaviors (Wolpe, 1980). This position has been stated most eloquently by Baer (1982):

> Radical behaviorists do not ignore, escape from, or avoid descriptions of private behaviors observable only to their possessor; they do, however, strenuously avoid any implication that such private events are different in kind or function from observable behaviors. (p. 278)

Those favoring the cognitive trend within BT argue that cognitive interventions should not be disqualified on an *a priori* basis, since there is evidence that they may contribute to the clinical effectiveness of behavioral and other psychological treatments (Beck & Mahoney, 1979). They also state that the ''cognitive movement'' gives proper attention to exclusively human functions of speech and abstract reasoning and has appropriately turned away from strictly ''infrahuman analogues'' (Lazarus, 1979). This reference to ''infrahuman analogues'' implies that classical and operant conditioning theories were built on research with animals, and that more complex models are needed to account for human learning.

Clearly, BT has advanced beyond the ''M & M'' days when simpler applications of behavioral technology were attempted with people in institutional settings. Those who would continue to describe BT as simplistic have apparently not kept up with recent advances in the field. Although there are differences between behavior therapists regarding cognitive factors, there still remains a basic commitment to experimental methodology. Part of this commitment involves defining clinical problems and their solutions in specific, operational terms. One of the attractive features of BT is the emphasis on translating information into common language. Behavioral principles and procedures have been well specified and are teachable to people of various socioeconomic backgrounds. C. S. Lewis (1970, p. 98) noted "that if you cannot translate your thoughts into uneducated language, then your thoughts are confused. Power to translate is the test of having really understood your own meaning." Behavior therapists are often quite good at translating theory and technique into understandable language (Kanfer & Goldstein, 1980).

THE MAKING OF A CHRISTIAN BEHAVIORIST

When asked to write this chapter, I had more than a few reservations. Besides the usual concerns about how much time and effort would be necessary, I knew I would have to struggle in a public way with how to reconcile the apparent philosophical differences between behaviorism and Christianity. As it turned out this was not too difficult, as is true of most things one dreads in life. I decided that, in the broader sense, I could not resolve philosophical differences between two apparently opposite views of mankind. What I decided to do instead was to write about how one person—namely me—can function as a behavioral psychologist and as a Christian.

The Adoption of a Behavioral Position

I became a Christian at least six years before I became a practitioner of behavioral psychology. In fact, during my undergraduate studies, I was quite anti-behavioral. I found some old sermon notes where I had spoken against Skinner's "ratomorphic" view of mankind. This was a homiletical reference to Skinner's work based on studies with animals (actually pigeons, not rats), and how he viewed human beings as admittedly more complex, but *not unlike* other animals. Through my undergraduate work, I found the phenomenological and humanistic psychology positions (e.g. Rogers, Maslow, May, Frankel) more compatible with my Christian faith than behavioral psychology. Now I think one has to edit and rework *any* position in psychology to fit one's religious beliefs better.

My disdain for behavioral psychology changed to appreciation as a result of a practical challenge I faced when beginning graduate studies in special education. During my first semester, I was assigned to work two hours a day, four days a week, with a small, attractive little four-year-old girl who was autistic. Each day in a small trailer, I was alone with this beautiful, but disturbed little girl who spent most of her time aimlessly moving about the room screeching in a high pitched voice. This little one had no language, no eye contact with others, and was totally unresponsive to my efforts to form a relationship with her. My background in humanistic psychology was of little help as I struggled to find a way to reach this self-absorbed child. In conference with some of my professors, I began to read some of the behavioral psychology literature on how to teach autistic children. To my relief, the procedures were well specified. By trial and error, I was able to teach this little girl (through primary reinforcement and extinction procedures) to sit in a chair, establish eye contact with me, and to imitate motor movements. I was hooked! The procedures were understandable, could be applied humanely, and were quite effective. In behavioral terms, my adoption of behavioral principles and techniques was positively reinforced by her changed behavior. It was also negatively reinforced, as any humane way to avoid high-pitched screaming is reinforcing!

Areas of Acceptance and Integration

So, there are indeed practical considerations that allow for the possibility that someone can be a Christian behaviorist. This is also possible to some extent on a more philosophical level. I do not find much difficulty in accepting the conceptual or theoretical premises of BT. In a general sense, BT is an ''environmentalistic'' position; events or interactions with others play a larger role than genetic or intrapsychic factors in determining how people behave. As a Christian, I can accept this. Because I believe in this environmental position, I want my children exposed to people who model and reinforce behaviors that are characterisic of followers of Jesus Christ. We as Christians believe environmental influences are important as we take great care to create educational, social, and interpersonal environments that encourage caring and nurturing behaviors. We also go beyond behavioral theory in claiming the existence of supernatural as well as natural influences on the behavior and ultimate eternal destiny of people. The activity of the Holy Spirit in convicting unbelievers (negative reinforcement) and guiding and empowering Christians (positive reinforcement) is a clear example of such supernatural influences.

As a Christian, I do not have any more difficulty in accepting that there are laws of behavior than that there are laws of the physical sciences. Extrapolating from Lewis's (1966) comment about psychoanalysis, there is no problem with Christian acceptance of behavioral sciences, ''so long as it remains a science and does not set itself up to be a philosophy'' (p. 180). The fact that there are empirically verified laws of behavior does not preclude the presence of phenomena that are outside of the laws of nature. As also noted by Lewis (1969), ''experiment finds out what regularly happens in Nature: the norm or rule to which she works. Those who believe in miracles are not denying that there is such a norm or rule: they are only saying that it can be suspended. A miracle is by definition an exception'' (p. 244). As Christians, we do not have to be anti-science, since the order and predictability necessary for science are God's business. It is also His business to circumvent or go beyond His natural order to influence the affairs of men and women.

The cognitive trend in BT is also not a problem for me as a Christian. The philosophical roots of the cognitive therapies are traceable to the Stoic philosophers. The philosopher Epictetus (AD 60) is often quoted by cognitive-behavior therapists: "Men are disturbed not by things, but by the views they take of them." Although as Christians we would not embrace Stoicism, there are truths in it as there are in many philosophical positions. Proverbs 23:7 states, "As he thinketh in his heart, so is he." Also, Paul reminds us that our thoughts are important in spiritual growth, as even our thoughts are to be subject to Christ (2 Cor. 10:5).

The Scriptures are clear that the thoughts as well as the behaviors of people are to be subject to the influences of the Holy Spirit. Christian counselors are using cognitive-behavioral methods to help people challenge negative, unadaptive thoughts and replace them with positive, coping thoughts which lead to more adaptive functioning—the writings of Schuller and Stoop (1982) are notable examples. Christian counselors also use traditional behavioral techniques such as positive reinforcement to help people develop more adaptive coping strategies. For example, the Christian psychologist James Dobson (1970; 1978) has written books for parents which describe the use of behavioral techniques in child-rearing.

Areas of Concern and Reservation

In spite of my conciliatory remarks about BT, there are legitimate criticisms about a behavioral position that need to be addressed. A number of these criticisms—such as, it "dehumanizes man"—have been eloquently described and countered by Skinner (1974). My own reservations are *not* about a *science* of human behavior, but a *philosophy* of human behavior which is developing out of the science. Unquestionably, a variety of human behaviors can be changed by using behavioral techniques; it would be hard to argue against the scientific evidence for this. However, one can (and should) question the *value judgments* inherent in deciding what people "ought" to do or not do. Lewis's (1966) comments about psychoanalysis are equally relevant to behavior therapy:

> Insofar as [psychoanalysis] attempts to heal, i.e. to make better, every treatment involves a value-judgment. This could be avoided if the analyst said, "Tell me what sort of a chap you want to be and I'll see how near that I can make you;" but of course he really has his own idea of what goodness and happiness consist in and works to that. And his idea is derived, not from his science (it couldn't) but from his age, sex, class, culture, religion and heredity, and is just as much in need of criticism as the patient's. (p. 180)

Thus psychological treatments involve value judgments which need to be critiqued as thoroughly as the scientific evidence for the treatments.

Although some behavior therapists argue that deciding "what" values are taught is not part of BT, most would disagree. Most would argue that therapists have social responsibilities (Krasner, 1982). Skinner (1971) rejected the notion that behavioral scientists (like physical scientists) have no answers about what people ought to do. He maintained that things are "good (positively reinforcing) or bad (negatively reinforcing) presumably because of the contingencies of survival under which the species evolved" (Skinner, 1971, p. 104). For example, the value of "being truthful" means that if you find the approval of others reinforcing, then "you will be reinforced when you tell the truth" (Skinner, 1971, p. 112).

According to Skinner, the ultimate—if there *is* an ultimate—or primary value is survival. He argued that "survival is the only value according to which a culture is eventually to be judged, and any practice that furthers survival has survival value by definition" (Skinner, 1971, p. 136). Skinner rhetorically raised the question, "Why should one be concerned about survival?" His answer was that "there is no good reason why you should be concerned, but if your culture has not convinced you that there is, so much the worse for your culture" (Skinner, 1971, p. 137). This position is similar to the one expressed by Ellis (1977, p. 108) regarding the "worth of individuals":

> Perhaps the only sensible way of making a global rating of an individual is on the basis of his aliveness: that is, assuming that he is intrinsically good just because he is human and alive (and that he will be nongood or nonexistent when he is dead).

These philosophical positions expressed by Ellis and Skinner should not come as a surprise to Christians. They are based on a naturalistic position which denies or (at best) seriously questions the possibility of supernatural influences. What else is one left with from their perspective? "Aliveness" or "survival of the species" are all that remain!

As Christians we can and do take a different position about ultimate values, but we can still learn from those who differ from us. The Christian position holds that our self-worth as human beings is tied to the sacrifice and worth—in God's eyes—of our Savior, Jesus Christ. I am worthwhile, you are worthwhile, everyone is worthwhile because He who is completely worthy, has, through His sacrificial death, affirmed our worth. Now some behavioral scientists (of all theoretical persuasions) would have major reservations about this position; they have a right to, just as we have the right (and spiritual mandate) to challenge their position.

My training in behavioral psychology, although technically excellent, did not fully prepare me to answer questions about the ethical basis for decisions about what behaviors ought to be modified. This perhaps would be too much to expect of any psychology program. Of course, we dealt with professional ethics, which simply reflected the "majority opinion" or the mores and norms of my culture: e.g. one should not have sex with one's clients. There is no problem with following cultural norms as long as they are consistent with the Judeo-Christian value position. However, Christians have raised and will continue to raise objections when the majority accepts a position contrary to the teachings of Christ. At this time I have found few, if any, ethical positions among my behavioral colleagues that require me to take an opposing position. This is probably the case because they—as well as I—have been taught values consistent with the Judeo-Christian ethic. However, as noted by Schaeffer (1972), there are potential conflicts if and when people no longer function on the basis of the Judeo-Christian tradition.

It is possible for me to be a Christian behaviorist by adopting the scientific and clinical approach of BT while questioning and sometimes rejecting the philosophy of behaviorism. I have found behavioral approaches to be quite useful in helping people define their problems and apply practical techniques to solve them. I also recognize the limitations of this approach to therapy. Many problems presented to therapists involve issues of self-esteem and, ultimately, self-worth. This is where my Christian faith affords me a basis for affirming the worth of human beings. My faith facilitates a base that is "revealed truth," rather than scientifically verified truth or knowledge. This revealed truth is only available to those who would know Christ, who is Truth. It is made available to us by the ministry of the Holy Spirit as He illuminates our minds as we read Scripture, as He speaks directly to us in times of prayer, and as He gifts other Christians to minister to us.

CONCLUSION

As Christians we can object to a science of human behavior on philosophical grounds ("to control others' behavior is to rob them of freedom of choice") or on conceptual grounds ("a science of human behavior is simplistic and not possible"). However, this does not change the fact that a technology of behavior change has been developed and is continuing to expand. This technology has been useful in reducing the psychological suffering of people with unwanted habits, fears, and self-destructive behaviors. As with any technology, there are potential dangers. Skinner has been quoted as saying that "a science of human behavior is just as dangerous as the atom bomb" (in Evans, 1968, p. 54). This technology could be used by those who are oppressive and seek to control others for their personal benefit (Skinner, 1948).

The techniques of behavioral engineering are indeed available. What, then, are we as Christians to do with this technology? I would argue that we cannot afford to be ignorant of these techniques. We will be in a better position to influence our culture in a positive way if we can understand and can employ these techniques for behavior change. The best defense is a good offense. As Skinner (1974) noted, "we cannot choose a way of life in which there is no control. We can only change the controlling conditions" (p. 190). Christian behaviorists can be in a unique position to teach people to recognize and control behavioral processes in ways consistent with the traditional Christian position of respect for the rights and worth of individuals.

[1]The assistance of Rosa Meagher in the preparation of this manuscript is gratefully acknowledged.

11

REALITY THERAPY

Marvin G. Gilbert

INTRODUCTION

In 1965, a small book appeared on the market which was destined to have considerable impact upon future counselors, mental health workers, teachers, and others concerned with human psychology. *Reality Therapy: A New Approach to Psychiatry* by William Glasser has since become a best seller and has rocketed Glasser to a place of prominence in the mental health field. This chapter reviews Glasser's own writings and the scant amount of research of others which has focused on this method; it then examines the integrative fit between Reality Therapy (hereafter RT) and the Scriptures in general and the Holy Spirit in particular.

HISTORICAL DEVELOPMENT OF THE THEORY

William Glasser

William Glasser is the undisputed "founding father" of RT; although some would argue that many of the principles of RT are generously borrowed from preexisting therapeutic systems (Rozsnafszky, 1974). Interestingly, Glasser did recognize the contributions of other theorists and therapists. He stated, "I'm sure it [RT] has roots in other therapies; it has ties to Adlerian Therapy because Adler broke with Freud along similar lines and to Albert Ellis's Rational-Emotive Therapy" (in Evans, 1982, p. 461). Glasser does not claim to have originated the concepts of RT; nevertheless, his unique and simple style of expression make his books enjoyable reading, and make him a very popular author.

Glasser is a psychiatrist with deep academic roots in psychology. He completed all of the coursework for a Ph.D. in clinical psychology before entering medical school at Case Western Reserve University. He finished the M.D. degree in 1953 and went on to complete a psychiatric residency at the U. C. L. A. Medical School in 1957.

It was during this crucial residency that he experienced growing conflict with the model of psychiatric intervention which he was being taught. He came to believe that the psychoanalytic (i.e. Freudian) emphasis upon feelings, past trauma and conflicts, and insight simply aided patients in avoiding personal responsibility for life and for their behaviors. Such questioning hardly made him popular; one gains the impression that Glasser rather enjoys the image of maverick and nonconformist. He later stated that the lack of referrals from his medical colleagues was due to his lack of acceptance of the Freudian medical model.

In more than one of his books he acknowledges the gratitude he holds for G. L. Harrington, a supervisor and teacher during his psychiatric residency, for supporting his questioning and experimentation with new ideas of intervention. Apparently, even after Glasser finished his residency, Harrington continued to play a behind-the-scenes role in developing what later became RT.

Discouraged from waiting for referrals to come flooding in from medical doctors, he accepted a position as head psychiatrist at California's Ventura School for Girls. Working with juvenile delinquent girls at Ventura, Glasser perfected his straightforward approach with a most difficult clientele. Yet in the context of a program committed to excellence, Glasser's unique combination of caring and a no-nonsense approach gained him the respect of the girls and administrators. The recidivism rate for the school was remarkably low during Glasser's employment there.

After leaving Ventura, Glasser became involved in a number of projects which allowed him to apply and further develop RT concepts on an ever widening scope. However, as popular as *Reality Therapy* and his other books were, it was not until he began training people at the Institute of Reality Therapy that his method really began to be used on a large scale. Even as recently as 1981 (in Evans, 1982), he estimated that there were only 300 or so certified Reality Therapists, though many others have received training from him without completing the certification process.

Early Applications

In *Reality Therapy*, Glasser identified four distinct settings as illustrations of the practice of his new approach. The first was the previously mentioned delinquent girls' school, the Ventura School. This school received the most difficult of delinquent adolescent females in California. Glasser noted it was really a prison, but because of a dedicated staff, it was able to maintain a school atmosphere. As he later coined the term, Ventura School was a "school without failure."

The reader of *Reality Therapy* will note that he writes in the present tense; apparently he still worked at the Ventura School while preparing the manuscript. The things which characterized his working with girls there characterize the therapy; he did not concern himself with the girls' delinquent history. Reasonable rules were enforced and discipline was firm and consistent. "We have discovered that unless we have high standards, the students conclude that we are 'phoney' and don't really care for them. However, once they are aware of the high standards we maintain by enforcing strict, consistent rules, they realize, perhaps for the first time in their lives, that real care is implied by discipline'' (1965, p. 87). Through personal involvement with these girls Glasser and staff created an atmosphere in which responsible behavior was reinforced and irresponsibility was punished. He documented several cases of successful outcomes including some written correspondence between the girls and himself.

The second area of early application, discussed at length in Chapter 4 of *Reality Therapy*, was the treatment of hospitalized psychotic patients. Glasser recounted the change introduced in a V.A. hospital psychiatric unit in Los Angeles, under the direction of his mentor, G. L. Harrington. Harrington moved away from the goal of maintenance *within the hospital* (Glasser, 1965, p. 131) to stressing responsibility for behavior and believing that the patients could do more than lie around and vegetate. As a beginning point, "Harrington carefully taught and retaught each staff member to forget the concept of schizophrenia and mental illness, and to consider the patients as people who are behaving this way because that is the best they have been able to do up to now. He instructed them...to treat each patient as if he is capable of not being crazy now'' (1965, p. 133). As with the previous example, RT in a psychiatric unit stressed involvement by staff and therapists with the patients on a person-to-person basis. Irrational ("crazy'') behavior was not tolerated, while responsible behaviors resulted in increased amounts of personal freedom, benefits, *and obligations*. Glasser's firm conviction is that psychiatric patients do not behave as they do because they are crazy, their behavior *is* their craziness. Thus, in his view, there is no such thing as "mental illness,'' only grossly irresponsible behaviors which can be changed.

A third application of RT presented in the book centered on the private mental health practitioner. Little new information is shared in this chapter; illustrative case studies of selected clientele in private practice are presented. As with the other two areas of application, this chapter emphasized the need for the therapist to become personally and warmly involved with clients, and to insist upon responsible behavior.

The final area, and concluding chapter of *Reality Therapy*, was basically a plea for the public schools to accept the principles of RT as a preventative program of mental hygiene. Glasser recognized that the public schools are the most logical place for implementing a large scale preventative psychiatric program, but he also knew that many school administrators and teachers would be hesitant to accept his ideas for a variety of reasons. Two of his more recent books, *Schools Without Failure*, which is an outgrowth of his consultation and intervention in a Watts school district, and *Positive Addition*, express, respectively, Glasser's concern with preventative mental health issues in the school and in general life settings. His most recent area of application, "Take Effective Control'' seminars, further underscore his concern with mental health education and prevention of psychiatric problems (see Glasser, 1981).

The Nature of Personality

Theoretically oriented mental health professionals find Glasser's books, with the possible exception of *Stations of the Mind*, frustrating and shallow; RT, in original form, represents a *method* without strong theoretical underpinnings.[1] Only by "reading between the lines" and attending training seminars sponsored by the Institute for Reality Therapy can one gain an understanding of Glasser's views of human personality structure and function. This section represents such an extrapolation.

Glasser clearly reacted against and rejected Freud's structure or components of personality: id, ego, and superego. In contrast, his holistic treatment of people reflects a belief in the indivisibility of personality.

In rejecting psychoanalysis, Glasser also rejects the idea that we are controlled or strongly influenced by unconscious motivations. His writings are almost totally silent regarding the unconscious; his therapeutic interventions are overtly conscious and rational. In absolute conflict with many models of psychotherapy—particularly those with a psychodynamic foundation—he indicates that he believes what his clients say about themselves and their problems.

Somewhat related to the rejection of the unconscious is his rejection of the past as a major influence upon present behavior. Although he acknowledges that the past—he prefers the term "history"—can influence us in unique ways, it plays a minimal role in RT.

Glasser is clear and direct in discussing what we as human beings are capable of experiencing.

> I think behavior is made up of three things: How you feel? What you think? What you do? *[sic]* I think there's always a combination of those. In Reality Therapy we emphasize the physical behavior. We talk about what you're thinking and what you're feeling, but the emphasis is always on...what can be changed. (in Evans, 1982, p. 461)

Thus, current, consciously controlled behavior is that expression of personality with which RT deals most.

Glasser does provide a somewhat crude classification of personality. He claims that people can be differentiated according to their identity: failure or success. For Glasser, a failure identity is synonymous with mental problems and psychopathology, while a success identity is the essence of mental health. He claimed that "a person functions at any time feeling either that he is a success and enjoying the psychological comforts of success or that he is a failure and desperately trying to avoid the attendant psychological discomforts. Rarely does he feel both strongly; one usually dominates the other" (1969, p. 15). He further implies that people who hold success identities are those who have found ways of increased development and satisfaction through habitual involvement in positive activities, hence the book title: *Positive Addiction (1976).*

Glasser acknowledges the importance of the family and the school in personality development. However, he writes more about the role of the school than the role of the family in contributing to the development of the child's identity. He concluded that "*if* the home is successful, the child may succeed despite the school, but that is too big an *if* to rely upon" (p. 14). Those parents and teachers who interact and influence the child according to the principles of RT help to develop a success identity in the child.

Motivation

Glasser clearly identifies two sources of motivation in human personality. He describes them as basic needs: the need to be loved and to love, and the need to feel worthwhile to oneself and to others (1965, p. 10). Glasser believes all behavior is motivated and purposeful, the purpose revolving around satisfaction of these two needs. In this light, Glasser's thinking clearly reflects the influence of Adlerian psychology, particularly the innate drive for social interest.

Without question, some people are more successful than others in meeting these basic needs; such people develop success identities. Glasser believes that love and self-worth are the two pathways that lead to successful living. "If a person cannot develop an identity through the two pathways of love and self-worth, he attempts to do so through two other pathways, delinquency and withdrawal" (1969, p. 15).

Thus, whether positively motivated to fulfill our basic needs, or negatively motivated by discouragement and frustration in reaction to our inability to fulfill them, we are motivated beings. In *The Identity Society* (1972), however, Glasser tied these basic needs into a large motivation. He claimed that our culture has, for the past twenty years (over thirty years now), been experiencing a new phenomenon: the quest for personal identity as a primary motivation. The big questions of life no longer are concerned with physical or economic survival. Thus *role* ("Who am I?") precedes *goal* ("Where am I going?"). In contrast to the survival goals of an earlier age, the goals arising out of the quest for identity "may or may not lead to economic security, but they do give people verification of themselves as human beings" (1972, p. 28). The movement of people away from a singular concern for the size of their pay check to a greater concern for finding "meaningful" employment and enriching avocational pursuits illustrates this essential motivator from Glasser's perspective.

Sources of Conflicts and Psychopathology

The failure identity has already been mentioned as the primary source of what Glasser would label psychopathology. People develop failure identities because of their failure to satisfy their basic needs of love and self-worth. Failure identities lead to a variety of maladaptive behaviors, which perpetuate the failure identity.

Simply failing at a given task, e.g., failing a school exam, will not automatically doom a person to a failure identity. Glasser suggests that a failure identity develops in a cumulative fashion. Task failures, as they accumulate, contribute more and more to a failure identity unless they are countered with interpersonal successes in the home or in the classroom. Once a failure identity is formed, with its self-defeating, negativistic behaviors, it becomes very resistant to change. At extreme levels, psychotherapy may be needed to break that vicious cycle.

Writing about psychopathology from a RT viewpoint is somewhat challenging because Glasser firmly and consistently rejects the idea of "mental illness." He views that concept as a principal roadblock to effective therapy. According to Glasser, the mental illness model posits that behaviors are caused by some specific, identifiable, medically treatable illness which is comparable to a physical illness. Thus, the attention of the traditional therapist is diverted from the dysfunctional behavior to some causal entity in the mind—the "root of the problem," which must be removed. "We believe that there is no noxious psychological causative agent to remove. Our job is to help the patient help himself to fulfill his needs right now" (1965, p. 56).

Psychopathology, then, expresses a person's inability to fulfill the basic needs; it consists of behaviors which, in turn, block further attempts to fulfill those needs. It is not an entity to be treated medically; it more appropriately could be described as a collection of irresponsible behaviors which must be changed to responsible ones. In Glasser's system, psychopathology and irresponsibility appear to be functionally synonymous.

THE GOALS OF COUNSELING AND THE NATURE OF CHANGE

Counseling Goals

If the essence of all emotional and interpersonal problems in life is a failure identity, then it is clear that a global counseling objective for the Reality Therapist is the client's development of a success identity. People with a success identity can face and accept reality responsibly; they involve themselves with others and they generally find constructive ways of meeting their basic needs of love and worth.

However, in order to be effected, these large, global goals must be translated into behavioral specifics. This is certainly consistent with the emphasis on behavioral change repeatedly stressed by Glasser (e.g. 1981, p. 269). Session after session, the client is encouraged to plan for and to engage in new, more effective and responsible behaviors. Completing the weekly plans becomes a *formative* goal for the therapy, while the *summative* goal remains the development of a success identity.

Steps Involved in Client Change

Glasser (1965, 1972) must be complimented for the clarity with which he has outlined the steps involved in moving the client from a failure identity to a success identity. There are eight steps, each of which merits some discussion.

1. *Involvement.* By involvement, Glasser means that the therapist becomes involved with the client as a person of worth and value. The therapist foregoes the unrealistic belief that therapeutic objectivity should be maintained by interpersonal distance between therapist and client. In expressing and building involvement, the therapist discusses anything that is of value to the client: hobbies, relationships, fun, etc. This does not mean that the therapist exercises no control over the conversation. Glasser concluded that it "is unwise to talk at length about a patient's problems or his misery....Talking at length about a patient's problems and his feelings about them focuses upon his self-involvement and consequently gives his failure value" (1972, pp. 110–111). By becoming actively involved at the beginning of the relationship, the therapist accomplishes two things: first, he begins building rapport which becomes crucial later in therapy, and second, he models responsible interpersonal involvement which is a skill the client must also develop.

2. *Current behavior.* Glasser effectively makes the point that many people are not aware of what they do and how their behavior influences others. Thus, a husband who complains about the miserable behavior of his wife is directed to look upon his own behavior. Glasser stresses that it is impossible to change the behavior of another; it is also impossible to effect much change in "reality." Only personal behavior is open to personal change. In emphasizing current or present behavior, the therapist might ask: "What are you doing?" Implied in this question is a de-emphasis of feelings. The fact that the Reality Therapist is not greatly interested in hearing about emotions often comes as a surprise to the client. Part of Glasser's rationale is that people "often avoid facing their present behavior by emphasizing how they feel rather than what they are doing" (1972, p. 114). Although emotions are not disregarded, they are not dwelt upon, particularly early in the therapy relationship.

3. *Evaluating behavior.* After telling a caring human being *what* they are doing, clients then respond to the question: "Is this behavior working for you?" The therapist has an opinion about a client's behavior, but the client's own judgment is more crucial. If the client responds "yes," the therapist, as a reflector of reality, may challenge this statement by pointing out ways that the client's behavior appears to be preventing satisfying living. If the response remains "yes," the Reality Therapist can do little for the client. However, the "yes" may simply be reflecting the client's pessimism about ever finding a more effective way of behaving and living. The effective therapist must present an optimistic, hopeful message to the discouraged, failing client.

4. *Planning responsible behavior.* If any single step is key to RT, it is the

emphasis upon clients making realistic plans for future change. If client and therapist agree that the client's current behavior is not helping, they can—together—search for realistic alternatives. The therapist is free to make suggestions, but the plan must ultimately be the client's. The therapist has the exciting and often demanding task of insuring that the plan is realistic; often clients who finally begin to believe that life can be different want immediately to attempt major changes. This is a set-up for continued failure. As clients learn the process of establishing realistic goals, they experience more frequent success, which further reinforces future change.

5. *Commitment.* "To give the person greater motivation to fulfill the plan, we ask him for a commitment to us....a commitment is often stronger if it is in writing" (Glasser, 1972, pp. 125-126). In my experience in requesting a commitment to a plan from clients, I have often heard the phrase, "Well, I'll try." My response is to challenge this as a premature admission of failure. The commitment works much more effectively if the client states, "I will." Following this commitment with a specific time at which the planned behavior will be initiated ("When will you do it?") further crystallizes the plan and the commitment to it.

6. *No excuses.* Glasser is emphatic on this point; if the client *for any reason* does not complete the plan, the therapist must not accept any excuse. "I think you're playing God when you accept an excuse. What right do I have to accept an excuse from you....People who accept excuses from anybody...really are saying, "OK, I'll allow you to be miserable and as ineffective as you are" (in Evans, 1982, p. 462). When a plan is not completed, the therapist re-poses the original question: Will you do it? The therapist must also be sensitive to the possibility that the plan needs to be changed or modified in some way, or an entirely new plan may need to be developed. However, if the plan appears reasonable, "the therapist must insist that a commitment made is worth keeping" (Glasser, 1972, p. 128).

7. *No punishment.* The important other side of the coin of "no excuses" is the total avoidance of punishment. Glasser defined punishment as "any treatment of another person that causes him pain, physical or mental" (1972, p. 129). The therapist, although confrontive at times, does nothing which would threaten the relationship or cause the client to feel like a failure. Punishment is so devastating because it breaks the involvement necessary for the patient to succeed or want to succeed. The therapist does not, however, shield the client from experiencing the natural consequences of irresponsible behavior. Clients have to understand that they are responsible for their behavior and choices.

8. *Never give up.* Closely related to Step 7 is the therapist's deep and lasting commitment to the client. Related to this step, Glasser stated, "In Reality Therapy—the way I do it—there's always tomorrow. There's no such thing as, 'You've got to do it now or the world comes to an end' " (in Evans, 1982, p. 462). If the therapist gives up and says, "I can't help you," the client perceives

the therapist saying, "*You* have failed as a client," and the failure identity is perpetuated and deepened. RT is a method for patient, optimistic therapists.

Setting and Clientele

Reality Therapy is currently used in many of the settings discussed by Glasser in *Reality Therapy*. It has been reported to be effective with retarded adolescents (Dolly & Page, 1981) and adults (Zapf, 1976), and in psychiatric and other institutional settings (German, 1975; McMordie, 1981; Schuster, 1978–79). However, many of the reported applications have been in the public schools. It has been used with underachievers (Holleran, 1981; Margolis, Muhlfelder & Brannigan, 1977) and with general disciplinary problems (e.g., Atwell, 1982; Brandon, 1981; Cherry, 1976; Dakoske, 1977). In addition, it has been utilized with special student populations, including children with learning disabilities (Fuller & Fuller, 1982), black students (Burkley, 1975) and college students experiencing emotional difficulties (Martig, 1979).

Glasser acknowledges that RT has not become a widely encountered method of treatment; few Reality Therapists operate in private practice (Evans, 1982; Glasser, 1965). There is essentially no literature other than Glasser's (1965) on the application of RT in the private practicioner's office.

Research

A total of 13 empirical studies of the effectiveness of RT were reviewed in writing this chapter. Of these, 10 were doctoral dissertations; this indicates that RT is not a topic frequently addressed in the professional journals. The overall evaluation of RT emerging from these empirical reports suggests that it is of mixed effectiveness. Two studies reported completely positive results, three studies found completely negative outcomes, and eight studies reported mixed outcomes on two or more dependent variables.

In some of the studies (Dakoske, 1977; German 1975) self-concept improved, while in others (Shearn & Randolph, 1978; Browning, 1979) there was no positive change in self-concept. Similarly mixed outcomes were reported in student studies for such variables as grade point average (G.P.A.), amount of time spent on task (completing assignments), and changes in locus of control. One fairly consistent finding was the positive impact of RT training on those most closely involved with the target populations (Gang, 1974; German, 1975; Schuster, 1978–79). Those who received adequate training in the principles of RT felt better about themselves and the RT intervention program in which they participated.

One possible explanation for the mixed, inconclusive, empirical outcomes is the frequency with which weak research designs have been used. Atwell (1982) and Zapf (1976) both reported extremely small sample sizes; Zapf's study was further confounded by difficulties in collecting meaningful data. The study by Dolly and Page is amazingly weak—perhaps having been totally confounded by major errors in original design and analysis. Only the study by Browning (1979) clearly demonstrates adequate planning in terms of sample size, RT training, and research design. Browning's results were mixed: student G.P.A. and student attitude toward school improved, but there was no change in self-concept and the number of disciplinary incidents.

The conclusion is that RT has not been effectively evaluated empirically. Long-term, systematic evaluation is needed. It seems reasonable to look to the Institute for Reality Therapy and to Glasser himself for direction in developing such an evaluation program. In the meantime, the effectiveness of the approach remains tentative; it is supported more by case studies than by data from large scale studies.

CONTROL THEORY: STATIONS OF THE MIND

Glasser's (1981) recently published book, *Stations of the Mind*, details his thinking about how the brain operates to motivate behavior. A detailed review of this book is beyond this chapter's scope; only a brief distillation is presented in hope of capturing the essence of this complicated theory.

Control theory reaffirms that all behavior is internally motivated. The motivation arises out of perceptual errors when what we think we want (internal world) is compared with what we perceive to be reality in the external world. "All my behavior is initiated by the error signal caused by the detection of an error in an open comparing station (in the brain). When there is perceptual error there is always an error signal, and I must do something. It is a neurological fact of life" (Glasser, 1981, pp. 51–52).

Thus, we attempt to control our perception of reality; we do this as our behavioral system (output) attempts to correct the external reality. We also do it as we selectively perceive that reality by attending to selected elements in raw sensory input and by organizing that input in individually unique ways. Glasser proposed that we have 10 orders or levels of perceptions, arranged hierarchically from crude, simple detection of sensation to very complex, mystical experiencing. Each higher perceptual order represents a more complex way of organizing and deriving meaning from external stimuli.

In *Stations of the Mind*, Glasser expanded his original list of two basic needs—love and worth—to four needs: (a) belonging and love and cooperation, (b) self-esteem and power and competition, (c) fun and freedom, and (d) security and survival. This list is reminiscent of Adler's proposed need for social interest and the striving for superiority (essentially the same as Glasser's competition). It also resembles Maslow's hierarchy of needs, although no hierarchy is proposed among the four needs in Glasser's system. It is in reference to what we believe will satisfy these basic needs that the comparison of perceptions of reality is made and errors are detected.

One of the most meaningful contributions of Glasser's version of control theory is that emotional states, which are generally viewed as involuntary (e.g. anxiety, depression), are viewed as active behavior choices in response to error signals. These emotions are simply attempts by the person to get what he or she wants, or to control life so that it does not get any worse. Hence, in Glasser's terms, people are said to be "depressing" instead of "being depressed," and even "headaching" instead of "having a headache."

The strongest connection between this theory and RT appears to be at Steps 2 and 3 of the classic eight steps of the therapy. When clients are asked, What are you doing? and Is it working for you? they are really being asked about their behavioral output system—including emotions as behaviors—and their understanding of their perceptual errors, respectively. Beyond this, however, little apparent connection exists between the theory and the method; any heuristic contributions of the theory to the practice of RT remain to be demonstrated in future publications.

INTEGRATION

A recent computer search of the RT literature revealed that there are no articles or books which have attempted to integrate this therapy approach with biblical theology. While computer searches are not infallible, it is presumably safe to state that this section represents one of the very few—if not the only—attempts at such an integration.

Theoretical Integration

Glasser originally proposed two basic needs in human beings: the need to love and be loved and the need to feel worthwhile to oneself and to others. Any meaningful integration must examine scriptural teaching in relation to these needs: does the Bible present a picture of these needs in us?

One of the clearest thoughts communicated in the early passages of Genesis is that human beings are created in the image of God—presumably a finite reflection of God's nature and character. The relevant question then becomes: Is God characterized by the need to love and be loved? From a non-theologian's viewpoint, this is a very difficult question to answer. It is abundantly clear, however, that God *does* love, and does so very effectively (John 3:16; 1 John 4:7-9). Thus, while it may or may not be appropriate to speak of God needing to love and be loved, it is certainly appropriate to speak of Him *being* love. If we indeed have a need for love, it ultimately must be considered an expression of the God-nature in us, with Him being the foremost focus of our need. John beautifully stated that our place of utmost satisfaction and contentment is in God: "And we have come to know and have believed the love which God has for us. God is love, and the one who abides in love abides in God, and God abides in him" (1 John 4:16).

If it seems inappropriate to speak of God needing to love and be loved, it seems absurd to think of God needing to feel worthwhile. Yet the Scriptures abound with verses which speak of such a need in *us*. An essential beginning point for grasping an integrated view of worth is God's "good news" that, though we were dead in sin, strangers and aliens from God, He valued us, considered us such worthwhile people that Christ died that we might have life (Eph. 2:1–7; Rom. 5:8). Glasser's distinction between a "failure identity" and a "success identity" is clearly relevant here. While in sin, we *are* failures; in Christ, we are successes, even though some Christians have difficulty translating that fact into a reality in their own identity. With my worth as a person firmly established in God's view of me as a worthwhile person, I am free to live out that worth without continually, neurotically striving to maintain it.

The preceding paragraph alluded to a factual failure, the failure resulting from sin. It should not be particulary surprising that Glasser does not include the concept of sin in his therapy. Yet the Christian sees sin as a condition of life with devastating consequences. Even for the most moral person, sin eventually will result in selfish, irresponsible behavior. It is an enormous threat to all of God's best for us, a deep trap from which the highest of responsible behavior in our interactions with others cannot extract us (Rom. 7:24). Here, the role of the Holy Spirit is evident, because He convicts us of sin and points us to Christ and to freedom from the power of sin. To apply Glasser's terms, the Spirit confronts us with the irrationality of our behavior and the reality of our sin and its consequences. He is the facilitator of the most beautiful of all plans—salvation!

The fit is not exact between theology and Glasser's insistence upon dealing only with present behaviors. First, while Glasser acknowledges that human experience consists of thoughts, emotions, and behaviors, the latter is the element of utmost importance. This is not true of Christ's teaching in the Gospels. Matthew records that the thoughts and intents of the heart—viewed only by God—are ultimately most important to God (Matt. 12:34–35). While what we do is clearly important to God (James. 2:14–26), it is not of exclusive importance. In fairness to Glasser, behaviors were not exclusively important to him either; they only represented the medium of fastest change. Through the Holy Spirit, change can occur even faster in the heart. Attitudes and motives thus changed by the Spirit transcend our own efforts to effect such a change. Had Saul of Tarsus simply stopped persecuting the infant New Testament Church (Acts 9:1–2), one would hardly want to argue that his heart—i.e., his mind and emotions—would also have changed.

Second, Glasser's emphasis upon the present, while certainly important in the Bible, is not the entire biblical perspective. We will be judged for past behaviors and inner thoughts. Yet, it seems that Glasser's stress on the present is similar to Paul's statement: "forgetting those things which are behind (past), and reaching forth unto those things which are before (future), I press (present behavior) toward the mark for the prize of the high calling of God in Christ Jesus'' (Phil. 3:13-14). The present is important from God's perspective, though not exclusively so.

A final theoretical note should be mentioned. Glasser refused to divide people into parts or elements of personality; he treated whole people. Though the New Testament speaks of human beings consisting of body, soul, and spirit (1 Thess. 5:23) and body and soul (Matt. 11:28), such a trichotomy or dichotomy is rarely relevant to the way God relates to us. In an interesting integration of the biblical concept of the soul and personality theory, Jackson (1975) stated:

> Personality can only be understood in terms of community—the community of man to man and man to God. This is included in the idea of wholeness which is basic to both a psychological and theological anthropology. Man's redemption is never considered apart from his corporeal nature and must include the total man, and no part of man has any existence in its own right in isolation. The soul cannot be equated with id, ego, or superego but with the total ''person.'' (p. 9)

Certainly, Jackson and Glasser's views of the essential nature of personality are similar. When Christ redeemed us, it was a total restoration and healing for the entire person (1 Pet. 2:24-25).

Practical Integration

Consideration of integration on a practical or applied level effectively can be focused on the eight steps of RT. The role of the Holy Spirit at each step of therapy is examined, as He influences both the counselor and client.

Step 1: Involvement. Paul, in Romans 5:5, stated ''the love of God has been poured out within our hearts through the Holy Spirit who was given to us.'' As the counselor receives the gift of the Holy Spirit, he or she also receives the love of God; it is poured into the heart in such measure that relating warmly and compassionately to the hurting client is not unnatural. Genuine involvement with the client is easier for the counselor who is willing to be a mirror of God's own love and concern. Such a counselor will not be rushed into a premature confrontation or hastily considered technique in order to produce quick results.

Step 2: Current behavior. The Spirit-filled counselor who asks *What are you doing?* does so with a divine perspective; at least part of what the client is doing has spiritual ramifications. Further—and unique to a Pentecostal theology—the counselor may be gifted by the Spirit with a word of knowledge or discernment regarding the client's lifestyle and behavior. Although such divine insight may not be the norm (and is certainly at the discretion of the Spirit), it may be helpful as the counselor aids the client in determining current behavior (cf. Chapter 3).

Step 3: Evaluation. The counselor must not determine for the client if the behavior is working. Yet the counselor should be a reflector of reality as the client struggles to evaluate the behavior. For the Spirit-directed therapist, reality must include the Scriptures—God's perspective. Reading scripture passages relevant to the client's behavior is certainly appropriate in this regard. If our basic needs are best met in a harmony of relationship with God and fellow human beings, God's Word cannot be omitted from this evaluation stage.

Step 4: Plan. Here the leading and direction of the Spirit are most pertinent. Jesus promised that the Spirit would be our guide, would direct our decisions, and would give wisdom. While the plan of altered behavior must be the client's plan, the counselor can make suggestions and help the client consider the available options. The Spirit-guided counselor can be used by God to help the client identify new, more productive directions for living.

Step 5: Commitment. Jesus spoke on a number of occasions about commitment. For instance, He used the parable of the sower and the seed to describe the varied levels of commitments which people make in response to the Gospel (Matt. 13:3–9). Those commitments range from no response at all, to a temporary response that is never developed, to an effective, fruitful commitment. While the Spirit never forces His will upon any of us, He is obviously involved in the process of drawing us to God. As such, He is a master of aiding us to make and to keep our commitments, not only to God, but to others and ourselves.

Steps 6 & 7: No excuses/No punishment. As absurd as it appears, human beings have offered excuses to God for irresponsible, sinful behavior since the beginning of human history (Gen. 3:11–13). Certainly, we have become experts in excusing our actions to others and even to ourselves. Psychoanalysts refer to this as ego defense mechanisms, which include projection and rationalization. In not accepting any excuse for failure to complete a plan, the counselor simply reflects God's perspective on the failure. As the counselor acknowledges the role of being an instrument of God's healing, he or she can refrain from ego involvement in a given plan. Thus, the client's excuses are not accepted, but the client will not experience anger from the counselor, either. The counselor used by the Spirit in counseling will not seek to hurt or punish the client for failure, realizing that God does not punish or hurt when we fail Him with our sin. No reason for behaving sinfully removes the guilt of the sin, just as no punishment— from God or ourselves—atones for it!

Step 8: Never give up. This is perhaps the most challenging of Glasser's steps. Many times I have reached the point of saying, "This just isn't working. This person is going nowhere." At such times I desperately need to communicate again with the Holy Spirit. To be renewed in Him is to experience afresh that beautiful mixture of *hope* for future change and *patience* for continuing in the present to work for that change. It is frankly difficult for me to understand how a non-Christian counselor, without the Holy Spirit as a personal and professional resource, can withstand the pessimism and discouragement which inevitably touch all counselors.

Summary

Reality Therapy offers a present-tense, easily mastered method of helping people change their lives. Little in this approach would conflict with a biblical theology, and much recommends it for a variety of counseling problems ranging from delinquent acting out to some psychosomatic problems.

Although it is not exclusively a lay person's counseling approach, RT does not require extensive psychological training. With the focus of the therapy being present behaviors and responsibility for actions, there appears to be little danger in well-trained and supervised lay counselors using it.

The Spirit-filled counselor who uses RT may not appear to be radically different than any other Reality Therapist. The difference would be primarily an internal one—drawing on the strength, power, and inspiration of the Spirit to remain optimistically on target. Thank God, He empowers us with divine strength so that we can fulfill Paul's admonition: "let us not lose heart in doing good, for in due time we shall reap if we do not grow weary. So then, while we have opportunity, let us do good to all men, and especially to those who are of the household of the faith" (Gal. 6:9–10, NASB).

[1]Control theory, borrowed from John Powers and explained in *Stations of the Mind*, represents Glasser's most in-depth theoretical thinking. Because the theory followed the method by some 16 years, and because the theory, in my view, does a poor job of predicting or directing the method and techniques of the therapy, I have chosen to avoid extensive integration of the theory with the rest of Glasser's writing. Control theory is reviewed as a distinct topic in this chapter.

12

COGNITIVE THERAPY

Lannes Baldwin

INTRODUCTION

Cognitive Therapy, (hereafter CT) as defined by Aaron Beck (Beck, Rush, Shaw, & Emery, 1979, p. 3), is an "active, directive, time-limited, structured approach used to treat a variety of psychiatric disorders....It is based on an underlying theoretical rationale that an individual's affect and behavior are largely determined by the way in which he structures the world." His cognitions (inner thoughts or internal dialogue) are based on attitudes or assumptions (schemata), developed from previous experiences. For example, if a man interprets all his experiences in terms of whether he is competent and adequate, his thinking may be dominated by the schema, "Unless I do everything perfectly, I'm a failure." Consequently, he reacts to situations in terms of adequacy even when they are unrelated to whether or not he is personally competent.

Albert Ellis (Ellis & Grieger, 1962) described Rational Emotive Therapy (hereafter RET)—one of the cognitive therapies—by stating simply that people do not directly react emotionally or behaviorally to the events they encounter; rather, people cause their own reactions by the way they interpret or evaluate the events they experience.

HISTORICAL DEVELOPMENT

Although Ellis and Beck were both developing their theories during the 1950s, both traced the philosophical origins of CT to the Stoic philosophers in the fourth century B.C. and credited Epictetus (ca. AD 60) with the statement: "Men are disturbed not by *things* but by the views which they take of them" (Beck et al., 1979; Ellis & Grieger, 1977). Eastern religions such as Taoism and Buddhism emphasize that human emotions are based on ideas, and control of most intense feelings may be achieved by changing one's ideas. Ellis gave credit to a number of people who "employed their own brands of active-directive, cognitive-oriented therapy years before I did" (Ellis & Grieger, 1977, p. 4); among those he listed Adler (1927, 1929), Horney (1939), Berne (1957), Meyer (1948), Salter (1949), and Sullivan (1947.

During the early part of the twentieth century, psychological thought was dominated by Freud and psychoanalysis, which taught that behavior, symptoms, and affect were controlled by the unconscious. In psychoanalysis, therapy was long and tedious and involved exploring dreams and fantasies; it dealt with the past, and sought to produce insight into the unconscious motives (Hall, 1954).

Behavior modification was primarily developed when B. F. Skinner adapted learning theory to therapy (Hill, 1971). Psychoanalysis was then criticized as being unscientific, unsubstantiated by research, filled with concepts which could not be validated, and focused upon a client's past rather than the present. Skinner and his followers reacted to the extremes of Freud by attending only to behavior which could be observed and measured; they considered thoughts or consciousness too subjective and mentalistic for study.

Behaviorism has made a great contribution to psychology by pulling away from the unproven (and perhaps unprovable) presuppositions of psychoanalysis. However, in the process, behaviorists shifted to the other extreme by stating that internal thoughts and motivations are unimportant, by treating human beings as nothing more than animals, and emphasizing empirical research as the only appropriate method of learning. Thus, research became the god of the learning (behaviorial) theorists.

Another important influence was the phenomenological approach to psychology; this taught that we should not describe people as an outsider sees them, but try to understand their behavior from their own point of view. Thus, the objective is to observe a person's world as he or she perceives it. This view says that we behave according to how we view our environment, regardless of whether we are right or wrong. If I *think* you don't like me, I will *behave* as if you don't like me, regardless of whether or not that belief is accurate. Combs and Snygg (1949, p. 11) said, "we run very hard from the danger we think is there and ignore the danger we do not know exists." Thus, phenomenology says that we respond according to how we view or structure our environment.

At the same time Ellis was developing RET, Beck and his colleagues were working on his cognitive views at the University of Pennsylvania. In 1963 Beck (1967) began writing about his cognitive model for the treatment of depression. While Ellis was loud and abrasive (Hauck, 1972), and claimed that RET was useful for almost every known disorder, Beck focused on the disorders of mood. He used more tact than Ellis, which earned greater respectability for CT.

Both Ellis and Beck stated that they have always used behavioral techniques in their therapy; during the past one or two decades a number of behavioral psychologists have also begun to accept some of the cognitive tenets, thus producing what is now called "cognitive-behavioral" therapy. Kendall and Hollon (1979) referred to cognitive and behavioral psychology as "bidirectional movements" which

involve behavior therapists' increasing concern with mediational therapeutic approaches and cognitive therapists' growing recognition of methodological behaviorism....cognitive-behavioral interventions appear to be the infant offsprings of a paradoxical but successful marriage. (p. 2)

Further, Kendall and Hollon believed that this results in a

greater flexibility in terms of models and approaches, without sacrifice of rigorous standards of assessment and evaluation....Cognitive-behavioral therapy is not a retreat to mentalism but is, instead, an attempt to include within behavior therapy terms that were once in the closet. (p. 2)

The reader is referred to Rapoff's chapter in this volume for a thorough discussion of cognitive-behavior theory.

RET: An Example of Cognitive Therapy

During the past few years, RET has lost some of its identity as a major force in therapy; it is now considered merely one form of CT. However, despite the abrasiveness of Ellis, his descriptions are clear and simple. I will, therefore, use RET as a detailed example of CT.

We human beings seem to have a predisposition toward denying personal responsibility for what happens to us (perhaps inherited from Adam and Eve?). We tend to project blame onto others or onto circumstances, to rationalize, and to exaggerate (either over or under) what happens to us. We habitually make such statements as, "*He* made me mad," or "This rainy weather *makes* me depressed," or "I lost my temper *because* she lied about me." Thus, we say that the circumstances or behavior we do not like *caused* our response, and imply that there is nothing we can do about it.

The ABC Theory of RET

In RET, Ellis (1962) postulated what he called the ABC theory of emotional and behavioral reactions. He asserted that we do not directly react emotionally or behaviorally to the events we encounter; rather, we cause our own reactions and moods by the way we interpret or evaluate the events we experience.

Because of our innate and acquired tendencies, we largely (though not exclusively) control our own destinies, particularly our emotional destinies. We do this by our basic values or beliefs, by the way we interpret or look at the events that occur in our lives, and by the responses we choose to make to the environment. For example, if my wife burns my toast, spills coffee on my new suit, and tells me she is tired of me; she does not *make* me mad or depressed. Although I may have no direct control over what she does or says, I do have total control over how I respond to her. There are dozens of ways I could respond, but the one *I choose* depends on how I *interpret* her behavior and how I *choose* to respond to my perception.

The ABC theory of RET states that at point *A* (an *Activating* experience or

Activating event) something occurs; my wife burns my toast, spills coffee, and tells me she is tired of me. At point *C* (an emotional and/or behavioral *Consequence*) I react to the events at point *A*, and I feel angry and depressed.

Since the emotional and/or behavioral *Consequence (C)* immediately and directly follows after the occurrence of the Activating experience *(A)*, we frequently (but falsely) assume that *A caused C*. I therefore erroneously tend to conclude that my wife treated me horribly, and that *A made* me mad and depressed. Actually, according to RET, this conclusion represents a *non sequitur*. If my son were killed on the other side of the world, and I did not learn about it for three days, I would not become sad at the moment he was killed, but rather, after I received the news. This illustrates what really happens; we become upset only by all the internal cognitions or *Beliefs (B)* we have about *A*. Within the first seconds of hearing of a problem *A* there are many internal thoughts or inner speech going on. In the case of my son, I might say to myself: ''Why? This can't happen. He's only twenty-one. This is unfair.'' In the case of my wife I might be saying to myself: ''This is horrible. She is always doing things like this to me. Isn't it pitiful what I have to put up with.''

RET says that it is not *A* (wife's behavior) that leads to *C* (anger and depression); instead, it is all the *irrational Beliefs (B)* about *A* which leads to my choice of reactions. For example, had I thought *(B)*:''She really had a bad night nursing our sick baby. This is not like her; she must be under an awful lot of stress. Maybe I could get her some help for a day or two''; then my reactions would be all together different. Thus, my reactions *(C)* are never caused by circumstances *(A)*, but by my beliefs or internal thoughts *(B)* about the event *(A)*.

Personal Control of Our Responses

We can rationally accept the fact that external events (no matter how unpleasant they may be) significantly contribute to, but do not actually cause, our feelings or emotions; rather, our feelings are largely the result of what we think about the events. Howard Rutledge (Rutledge & Rutledge, 1973) was a POW in North Vietnam; Corrie ten Boom (1971) was in a German concentration camp. They certainly were not in pleasant environments. But their survival—physical, emotional, and spiritual—was attributed to the fact that they did not dwell on the ''Why,'' but focused their attention on the positive side. They maintained their communication with God and filled their thoughts with positive things. (For example, most of the surviving POWs used their imagination to do such things as play golf, taking hours to visualize every shot; or they may have planned the construction of a new dream home by taking months to imagine every piece of lumber and every nail.) These people knew that, while we cannot control circumstances and events, we can control how we react to circumstances.

Ellis referred to the inner thoughts or dialogue that goes on within us (when an Activating event happens) as being either Irrational Beliefs or Rational Beliefs.

Rational Beliefs are based on reason and an accurate assessment of data. Irrational Beliefs are distortions and exaggerations of the truth, and are often filled with "shoulds," "musts," or "oughts." Ellis (Ellis & Grieger, 1977, p. 9) called these "MUSTurbatory," and said they usually fall under three major ideologies:

> 1. "I *must* do well and *must* win approval for my performances, or else I rate as a rotten person."
> 2. "You *must* act kindly and considerately and justly toward me, or else you amount to a louse."
> 3. "The conditions under which I live *must* remain good and easy, so that I get practically everything I want without too much effort or discomfort, or else the world turns damnable, and life hardly seems worth living!"

One of the conclusions we make, which is a major reason for our negative emotions, is "awfullizing." This is not merely a generalization, but an over-generalization. It goes far beyond the actual facts and distorts reality, making it appear worse than it actually is. When circumstances are not what we desire, we frequently call them "awful" or say "I can't stand it." Again, this distorts reality. Unless it literally kills us, we *can* stand it—no matter how painful, undesirable, or unpleasant. Most of the unpleasant things that happen to us, which we label as "awful," are actually very "common to man" (1 Cor. 10:13), and thus are a part of being human.

Eleven Irrational Beliefs

Ellis described "Eleven Irrational Beliefs" as being the most typical examples of how we produce negative emotions and behaviors. The destructive nature of these beliefs is summarized by Hauck (1972, pp. 31–45):

1. *It is a dire necessity for an adult human being to be loved or approved by virtually every significant other person in his community.* Not being loved or liked is *not* a dire catastrophe. Life is always nicer when people we love return that love. But if they do not, we need not feel it is the end of the world. A person who gives a speech or bakes a cake would like very much for other people to appreciate and applaud the effort, but if they do not, it is not the end of the world.

2. *One should be thoroughly competent, adequate, and achieving in all possible respects if one is to consider oneself worthwhile.* Hauck (1972, p. 33) called this "the most strongly indoctrinated ideas our society supports." In the case of Irrational Belief #1, people evaluate themselves by the reactions or opinions of others while with Irrational Belief #2, people evaluate themselves on the basis of their own skills. This internal criticism of ourselves is usually the result of our internalizing the criticism from our parents, or significant others, i.e., it is learned. In both of these Irrational Beliefs, it is assumed that one's *value* as a person should be judged by one's *achievements*. The greater the achievement, the more worthwhile and superior the person is; while failure is regarded as proof of one's inferiority. However, the student who makes A's is not a better person

than the student who makes D's—he or she is only a better student.

3. *Certain people are bad, wicked, or villainous and they should be severely blamed and punished for their villainy.* Blame is here defined as a criticism of, and anger over a person's unacceptable behavior, *and the person as well.* A distinction should be made between disapproving a person's behavior and rejecting that individual as a person. Hauck (1972, p. 35) said the person may commit wrong deeds because of (a) mental retardation, (b) ignorance or lack of training in the area, or (c) a "neurotic personality."

4. *It is awful and catastrophic when things are not the way one would very much like them to be.* We think things "should" or "ought" to be just the way we want them to be, and if they are not, we get mad, depressed, or upset. We get upset if it rains (if we planned a picnic), or if it does not rain (when we want our lawn watered).

5. *Human unhappiness is externally caused and people have little or no ability to control their sorrows and disturbances.* This belief is based on the false assumption that our happiness and unhappiness are caused by external events. Happiness is neither dependent on our environment, nor is it a destination (e.g. "I will be happy when..."); rather, happiness is an attitude or a way of life. The happy person is not the one with fewer crises, disappointments, or sorrows, but the one who counts the blessings rather than the disappointments. Robert Schuller told of a disasterous year on their Iowa farm when the entire crop of corn was less than one wagon load. While their neighbors were counting up their "losses," his dad thanked God because they had lost nothing—they got back the same amount of corn they had planted. Disappointments are as natural to a human as breathing, but how one reacts to disappointments is a matter of personal choice. We can either count the thorns or the roses on the bush; the choice is ours.

6. *If something is or may be dangerous or fearsome one should be terribly concerned about it and should keep dwelling on the possibility of its occurring.* Many people seem to think that worry is essential to the eventual solution of their problems. Worry does not solve anything. Anxiety is the result of a person focusing on all the anticipated bad things of the future. We tend to focus on *why* something happened, rather than considering possible solutions.

7. *It is easier to avoid than to face certain life difficulties and self-responsibilities.* The alcoholic and drug addict are prime examples of people who are unwilling to tolerate frustration; they insist upon having immediate gratification. When we avoid our responsibilities because of the unpleasant nature of the task, we are assuming that everything should be pleasant or easy. The truth is that life's tasks do not *have* to be pleasant. Ellis and Knaus (1977) indicated that procrastination involves: (a) indecision (deciding not to decide), (b) often an excessive expectation (the "shoulds" and "oughts") of perfectionism, and (c) self-downing or self-criticism. Thus, the procrastinator says "I must have outstanding accomplishments and acclaim; and if I don't have such guarantees,

I might as well put off tough jobs.''

8. *One should be dependent on others and should need someone stronger than oneself on whom to rely.* Excessive dependency stems from two sources: lack of self-confidence and the belief that failure proves one's worthlessness. Yet, relying too much on others tends to perpetuate both conditions. Fear of failure and letting others make decisions for us assumes that failure is catastrophic, but this is not true. Thomas Edison is said to have failed at more things than any other man, but he also succeeded at more. He felt that when he failed at an experiment, he then knew what would not work. It is also said that few baseball players ever struck out more times than Babe Ruth, one of the greatest hitters in the history of the game.

9. *One's past history is an all-important determiner of one's present behavior, and that because something once strongly affected one's life, it should indefinitely have a similar effect.* We often tend to think our behavior or personality is fixed. Many times we hear people say: "I can't do math.""I inherited my mother's fiery temper." "I've just never been able to sing." "I can't change now." "He'll never amount to anything." Such statements imply the person is unchanging and unchangable.

10. *One should become quite upset over other people's problems and disturbances.* This is a problem many parents have with their children (especially teen-agers), or toward other family members. Some people feel a tremendous need to control the lives of others, or at least to "give them advice." Even if we are "right," the other person still has the right to be wrong.

11. *There is invariably a right, precise, and perfect solution to human problems and it is catastrophic if this perfect solution is not found.* This is all-or-nothing thinking. Many people continually postpone decisions and actions, waiting for some feeling of certainty that they have arrived at the one perfect decision. In the religious community, we may feel that there is only one right, correct, God-given answer to a problem, and that unless we choose that one correct answer, we are doomed. However, this is not true with most problems; God has set some broad parameters in the Bible, and we have freedom to choose alternatives within those parameters.

BECK AND COGNITIVE THERAPY

Beck and Ellis differ in terminology and in tone, but very little in substance. Beck focused on disorders of depression, and talked about "dysfunctional beliefs," but the basic concepts of the two are similar. While Ellis (Ellis & Grieger, 1977) referred to the therapeutic technique of Debating or Disputing *(D)* the client's irrational beliefs, Beck (Beck et al., 1979) referred to the therapist "questioning," "challenging," and "collaborating with" the client. Thus, Ellis's language suggests argumentation, while Beck's language connotes working along with the client.

Cognitive Techniques

The therapeutic techniques described by Beck et al. (1979) were designed to identify, reality-test, and correct distorted conceptualizations and the dysfunctional beliefs underlying those cognitions. The goal of Beck's therapy included the development of five behaviors for the client: (a) monitoring negative, automatic thoughts; (b) recognizing the connections between cognition, affect, and behavior; (c) examining the evidence for and against the distorted automatic thoughts; (d) substituting more reality-oriented interpretations for the dysfunctional cognitions; and (e) learning to identify and alter the dysfunctional beliefs which predispose the client to distort experiences.

The cognitive therapist might take a client's statement, "no one cares about me," and phrase it in the form of a hypothesis to be tested. Collaborating with the client, the therapist might ask such questions as: "How strongly do you believe that no one cares?" "What evidence is there that your position is true?" "What evidence is there that it is not true?" In this way, Beck described the therapist as being active, directive, and structured in working with the client.

For Beck, CT was a time-limited procedure. Therapy was usually limited to fifteen to twenty-five sessions, with perhaps some "booster sessions" later.

Behavioral Techniques

Initially, the cognitive therapist offers an explanation and description of the rationale of CT. Clients are taught to recognize and monitor their automatic thoughts. Such behavioral techniques as the Daily Record of Dysfunctional Thoughts (Beck et al., 1979) are used in which the client is asked to record his or her upsetting thoughts, then describe the feelings and the negative events that trigger those thoughts.

Behavioral techniques refer to goal-directed activities prescribed for therapeutic results. These may include such things as bibliotherapy, graded task assignments, or counting certain behaviors. The behavioral techniques are like "works" which are to be expressed with our "faith." Beck (Beck et al., 1979, p. 118) stated:

> The ultimate aim of these techniques in cognitive therapy is to produce change in the negative attitudes so that the patient's performance will continue to improve. Actually, the behavioral methods can be regarded as a series of small experiments designed to test the validity of the patient's hypotheses or ideas about himself.

RESEARCH

The various aspects of CT have been subjected to so many research studies that only brief mention of them is made here.

Ellis (Ellis & Greiger, 1977) reported 987 references to research, covering 32 clinical and personality hypotheses of CT. Some of the hypotheses included: (a) ways in which thinking creates emotions, (b) the effect of cognitions on biofeedback and physiological processes, (c) internal versus external locus of control, and (d) field dependency versus field independency. DiGiuseppe and Miller (in Ellis & Greiger, 1977) reported numerous outcome and comparative studies with RET, and determined that the results were positive and hopeful, but inconclusive. Beck et al. (1979) reviewed several controlled studies of the treatment of depression with student volunteers and clinical patients. They reported cognitive therapy with depressed patients was more effective than treatment with antidepressant drugs.

RECENT TRENDS IN APPLICATION

The basic ideas in cognitive psychology continue to expand. This expansion is evident, not only in the area of psychotherapy, but also in the numerous programs of self-improvement, positive mental attitude, and the "self-talk" used in sports and sales. Some of the more popular books which present the cognitive approach to laymen are the books by David Burns (1980), Wayne Dyer (1976, 1978, 1980), and Jerry Schmidt (1983). The emphasis on biofeedback has shown the effect of cognitions on physiological processes. Such programs have brought about a greater emphasis on preventative mental health.

INTEGRATION

Ellis is one who many Christians have difficulty listening to or reading because of his abrupt, bold, abrasive speech, not to mention some of his personal views. Hauck (1972, p. 13) put it very mildly when he said: "because of Dr. Ellis's antireligious opinions and unorthodox sexual views, to say nothing of his startlingly emotive language, it is difficult to see clearly what he is offering."

However, in order to evaluate CT (or any other theory), one must separate the personalities from the theory, and the essential from the nonessential presuppositions. If the personal beliefs of Ellis were essential to the theory, we, as Christians, would have to reject the theory. However, as Christians, we object when the non-Christian picks out an "Elmer Gantry" (e.g. Jim Jones) and reacts as if he were typical of all Christians. While I personally cannot accept many of Ellis's personal views, these views are not essential to an understanding and use of CT.

Many Christians have difficulty relating their religious views to secular theories. To me, it is very simple. As a Christian, I start with my belief in God as Creator of the universe and Man; this is my foundation. I then examine any theory as to whether it will fit on this foundation. If it does, I consider it. If it does not, I reject it.

Cognitions Are the Key to Emotions

The first, or primary, assumption of CT argues that our cognitions (inner thoughts) are the key to our emotions. What could be more scriptural than this? The writer of Proverbs knew the importance of our cognitions. He exhorted:

"Keep thy heart [or mind] with all diligence; for out of it are the issues of life" (Prov. 4:23). "For as he thinketh in his heart [or mind], so is he" (Prov. 23:7). Paul advised that we bring into "captivity every thought" (2 Cor. 10:5). In the Sermon on the Mount, Jesus' whole emphasis was on the importance of the heart, or the inner person. Perhaps we could also substitute the term "cognitions," since our inner thoughts reflect our true motives. Jesus emphasized that it is not just the outward keeping of the letter of the law, but the motives of the heart which are most important. For example, the giving of alms and praying are of value only when done with the right motive.

In Philippians 4:4-13, Paul clearly enunciated cognitive concepts. He said:

1. "Rejoice in the Lord alway: and again I say rejoice." He did not say we should deny the existence of problems and unpleasant circumstances. Instead, he reflected that our mood and happiness depend on what we focus on most of the time. This also suggests that we tend to achieve the goal we set our sights on; we tend to move in the direction of our dominant thought. It was said of Jesus (Heb. 12:2) that "for the joy that was set before him [He] endured the cross"; thus, He endured because He kept His eyes on the goal.

2. "Be careful for nothing," really means "don't get all uptight" or "don't work yourself up into a frenzy by spending all of your time worrying about the problems; think of the solutions." Jesus said the same thing in Matt. 6:25-34.

3. Then Paul related the rewards which follow this behavior: "the peace of God, which passeth all understanding, shall keep [guard or protect] your hearts and minds." In Deuteronomy (28:1-2), Moses expressed it as "all these blessings shall come on thee, and overtake thee"...[i.e. they will almost run over you].

4. Paul then exhorted that we always keep our attention centered on those things which are true, honest, just, pure, lovely, and praiseworthy. Again, this does not mean we should ignore problems, act as if they do not exist, and then expect them to go away miraculously. On the contrary, if we have a problem, we should do something to solve it; let us forget about the parts we can not change, and spend the majority of our energy on the solutions and the positive things.

5. Finally, Paul knew the true meaning of contentment (Phil. 4:11-13; 1 Tim. 6:6-8; Rom. 8:35-39). The often repeated prayer expresses it clearly: "Lord, help me to change the things that need to be changed; to endure the things which cannot be changed; and the wisdom to know the one from the other."

How could Paul be calm and happy in prison? How could Paul and Silas sing at midnight after being beaten and chained? How could Stephen be so peaceful and serene as he was being stoned? How could John, imprisoned on a barren island with convicts, be "in the Spirit on the Lord's day" (Rev. 1:10)? In every case, these men directed their attention upon their relationship and fellowship with God. Had these men spent their time thinking about what they did not have, or worrying about what might happen in the future, or feeling sorry for themselves, they would have all been depressed and miserable. Caleb and Joshua did not deny any of the data ("facts") described by the other ten spies; they just looked at the data through the promises of God and concluded that those "facts" were not the most important measure of reality. Peter (1 Pet. 4:12, 13) said that we are not to be surprised when trials and disappointments come, because these are a part of being human. Contrary to popular thought, Scripture does not teach us to be thankful for trials, disasters, and pain; Paul said (1 Thess. 5:18) "*in* everything give thanks," not *for* everything.

Emotions Can Be Controlled

Closely related to the first assumption, and yet with an important difference, stands the assumption that we can control our emotions by controlling our cognitions. Thus, we are responsible for our reactions and we *can* change. Scripture is full of references (with emphasis added) to our choice. "*Choose* you this day whom ye will serve" (Josh. 24:15). "*Let* the peace of God rule....*Let* the word of Christ dwell in you..." (Col. 3:15, 16). (Note also: Deut. 30:19; Luke 10:42; John 3:16; Rev. 3:20.) Even Ephesians 5:18, "be filled with the Spirit" (although emphasized in a different way by Pentecostals), suggests a choice. By filling our minds with godly thoughts we accomplish this exhortation. We cannot be "filled with the Spirit" while our minds are filled with negative thoughts or dysfunctional beliefs.

What is worship—especially corporate worship? It is coming together with a joint purpose, centered on God, His gift, and His love. It is giving praise. We spend all week in the world, listening to news of wars, political problems, corruption, crime, the threat of economic collapse or nuclear destruction. When we gather for worship, we willfully turn our thoughts from these things, and redirect our attention (cognitive control) on divine things. (One can be driving down a highway, start singing a hymn or chorus, and immediately experience a change in affect or mood.) One of the purposes of singing, praying and worshipping is to become recharged with divine energy, or regain proper perspective—to see our problems through the eyes of God.

In Psalm 73, the psalmist said (in an informal paraphrase) he was so discouraged he was about to give up. The wicked were prospering; the godly were afflicted; politicians were getting more corrupt; inflation was getting higher; Communism was spreading faster; and prospects for peace in the Middle East were getting less likely! He continued that it was getting harder and harder to live a Christian life, and he was becoming envious of the prosperity of the wicked. These feelings were getting almost too hard to deal with; "Until I went into the sanctuary of God; then understood I their end." Thus, Scripture teaches us that we control our affect with our cognitions, and that we are responsible for exercising such control.

The Source of Dignity and Self-Esteem

A third area of concern has to do with the dignity of humanity and the source of self-esteem. One of the things which permeates Ellis's views, and is expressly stated in Irrational Belief # 3, is his disbelief in the concept of sin. Throughout his writings, Ellis made clear his belief that nothing is "right" or "wrong," and nothing is evil, sinful, or wicked. He proposed that guilt results from neurotic religion. Even Hauck (1972), writing from a pastoral perspective, referred to "neurotic personality," but not to sin. These ideas are totally unacceptable to any conservative Christian. However, acceptance of these views is not necessary to accepting CT. True religion does not condemn mankind; rather, humanity is condemned already (John 3:18).

As Christians, we are likely to be so turned off by Ellis's rejection of the concept of sin that we fail to see a workable truth. The dignity of a human being is not determined by deeds, behavior, material possessions, education, or position. Dignity arises from the fact that we are persons. The *Wesleyan Bible Commentary* on 1 Peter 2:17 states:

> The inherent dignity and worth of every human being, especially his capacity for redemption, reconciliation, and regeneration undoubtedly prompted the exhortation to "honor all men." Every heathen soul, by the mere title of humanity, had a right to be regarded with honor. (Ball, 1966, p. 261)

If value were determined by behavior, the newborn infant, the mentally retarded, and the elderly, bedridden person would have no value.

After talking about the ways our society rewards performance, Dave Grant (1983) told of warning his four-year-old not to pick the flowers in the flower bed. Later, on his birthday, she sang "Happy Birthday" and gave him a handful of rosebuds. He said he paddled her as he had promised, but also reaffirmed his love for her, so she would know that: "Love for the *person* is *unconditional*. Discipline of *behavior* must always be *conditional*" (p. 44). Grant then continued (1983, p. 53):

> Have you ever considered how the biblical concept of unconditional love breaks the performance-to-be-loved syndrome? God doesn't love us *if* we are good, or kind, or decent. He doesn't love us *because* we are moral, or honest, or religious, or generous to charities. He doesn't love us *as soon as* we are good enough to measure up. He simply loves us because He is love....When we accept our self-worth and adequacy as a gift, we immediately perceive a new standard of achievement. It is not performance but our measure of faithfulness to our gifts. Faithfulness is the only adequate, all-inclusive definition of success.

The Bible clearly tells us the source of our value as a person. It tells us that we were created in the image of God. Thus, we bear some characteristics of our Father. God "breathed into his nostrils the breath of life; and Man became a living soul....And God blessed them...and God saw every thing that he had made, and, behold, it was very good" (Gen. 2:7; 1:28, 31). In Hebrews 2:7, we are told, "Thou madest him a little lower than the angels; thou crownedst him with glory and honour, and didst set him over the works of thy hands." Jesus was speaking of the value of humanity when He said God so *loved* the world that He *gave* (John 3:16). God had such respect for His creation! Should not we also?

Peter referred to Christians as a "chosen generation," while Paul called them "heirs of God and joint heirs with Christ." Of all the creation of God, only Man was given a brain with such tremendous powers to use, to think, to choose, and even to rebel. In the parables of the talents and pounds (Matt. 25), we are told that God has endowed us with abilities, but He has left to us a choice as to what degree we will utilize those abilities.

We humans tend not only to determine the dignity or value of other people according to their performance, but we also tend to tie our self-esteem to our own performance. This can drive us to a perfectionism which says: "that's not quite good enough." In a taped sermon entitled "Damaged Emotions," David Seamands (see Seamands, 1981, ch. 7) referred to this perfectionism as the "terrible tyranny of the 'oughts'." He said that it is the feeling of always striving; never quite being able to achieve—never quite good enough. Just when we think we have reached the top of the ladder, we find there is something else that must be done to be "good enough." In essence, we say to ourselves, "I am worthwhile and valued *if* my behavior is perfect, and *if* other people praise me."

If I give a speech to which the audience applauds and people tell me it was the greatest speech they have ever heard, am I of more value? Or, if I give the same speech, and the crowd tells me it was boring, am I worth any less? Despite the fact that we often respond that way with others, and feel that way about ourselves at "the gut level," we could never acknowledge it. For, if we did, we would also have to say that Christ was more successful at the "triumphal entry" than on Golgotha! If I measure my worth as a person by the opinions of other people, my self-worth "barometer" will be constantly going up and down. Instead, my self-esteem can be determined by the degree to which I am pleased with my own efforts and motives, and the degree to which I am using my abilities to please God.

The Source of Pathology

The final assumption to be discussed concerns the source of pathology. Most theorists would probably say that the etiology of pathology is biological, cultural, and learned. Cognitive therapists would emphasize the latter two. Many Christians think that mental illness is always the result of sin; thus, they equate sin with mental illness. Such a view was exemplified by a well-educated friend who spoke of visiting someone in a mental hospital. She described the visit by saying, "you could just feel the powers of the devil." Some pathology is clearly the result of sin. For example, there is biological and psychological pathology which is the result of venereal disease. Guilt also plays a large part in pathology, but, to state that mental illness is always a result of sin would be erroneous. Christians as well as non-Christians suffer from emotional problems.

One can accept the biblical view of humanity and sin and still believe that many of our problems are learned, or come from dysfunctional ways of handling common stress. When Adam and Eve listened to Satan, they not only sinned themselves, but also transmitted the sin nature to all the human race. One part of that sin nature might be thought of (at least partially) as the predisposition to project blame, to deny responsibility, and the inclination to rebel. Certainly, the Bible indicates that one of Satan's activities is to be the "accuser of the brethren" (Rev. 12:10). He not only accuses us to God, but also accuses God to us, and suggests to us ulterior motives in our neighbor's behavior. Thus, Satan does anything that will foster dissension, distrust, and doubt. So, perhaps we could also say that Satan promotes the kind of thinking that cognitive therapists call "irrational" or "dysfunctional" beliefs.

One final note on the source of pathology must be mentioned. All of us have experienced emotional stress with which we cope in various ways. We live in very stressful times. Tremendous political pressures, threats of wars, economic uncertainties, and volatile social pressures confront each of us. One of the greatest present stresses is the rapidity of change in our society; this makes it difficult to adjust to the pace of life. Cetron and O'Toole (1982) and Naisbitt (1982) have described the trends of the past decade and have made projections for the future. Whether we like it or not, we are now in a world economy; we are greatly affected by events in small remote countries. Social and moral changes are creating both traumatic pressures and tremendous opportunities for Christian service, for the greater the problems, the greater the opportunity for victory.

STRENGTHS AND WEAKNESSES OF COGNITIVE THERAPY IN INTEGRATION

So far, in evaluating CT, the focus has been on the ways in which this theory fits our theology. Perhaps no theory of psychotherapy more closely coincides with Scripture than CT. Does this mean that every Christian therapist should practice CT? Should it be used with all clients? Absolutely not. Each client possesses individual needs and problems which warrant customized attention. Let us now look at some of the advantages and disadvantages of CT, and when it could be used appropriately.

While one should be cautious in interpreting research, even the most cautious clinician would agree that research is supportive of the use of CT, at least with affective disorders. CT is especially useful with verbal, intellectually bright, and motivated clients. Claims by Ellis (Ellis & Grieger, 1977) of its usefulness with almost every disorder, including psychoses, are probably overstated. Therapists with stronger orientation toward a behavioral therapy will be more inclined to use it to treat anxieties, fears, phobias, habits (such as eating and drinking), and for assertiveness training and pain control. Most therapists could find it useful with "preventive therapy" and with many marital problems. Such behavioral techniques as bibliotherapy, exercises, and homework function as useful adjuncts to most forms of therapy.

Although there are exceptions to every rule, the following cautions about the use of CT must be highlighted. As a general rule, it should not be used with to treat emotional problems such as psychoses, schizophrenia, paranoia, or bi-polar (manic-depressive) disorder. Further, it should not be used to treat clients with lower than average intelligence, and those with brain damage. These people may have problems with their thought processes, and frequently may misinterpret the therapist.

One of the greatest dangers of the use of CT may be with clients who are "intellectualizers" and manipulators. Many clients like to play games or to talk *about* therapy—and they do so for years without change. (This is also a major problem with the use of Transactional Analysis, if the therapist is not highly skilled, so as to prevent the client swapping one type of game for another.) Clients often know they "ought" to change, but have other motives (perhaps subconscious) not to change. Some of the military veterans I work with in psychotherapy (which is a very skewed sample of all veterans), have an intense conflict. If they were to "get well," they would lose their financial compensation. So, they have to be sick, either to begin receiving compensation, to have their compensation increased, or to maintain it. A large number of people seek psychological help because of pressures from a spouse, parent, employer, or court. One common example is when a spouse threatens to get a divorce unless the other partner gets "help."

THE HOLY SPIRIT IN THERAPY

One of the first things to note in evaluating any model of psychotherapy is that the practice of therapy is more an art than a science. Knowing the facts, the details, or what the textbook says about therapy is simply not adequate. Therapy is the interaction between two people, the therapist and client; and the interaction between them is at verbal and nonverbal levels. Therefore, for the therapist seeking to integrate faith and theory, success depends, in part, upon the degree to which the therapist is in tune with God (filled with the Holy Spirit), and in tune with the soul of the client (some degree of rapport or empathy). In this position, the therapist is a kind of mediator or conduit through which the client can more clearly see God. (e.g. Paul said in 1 Cor. 11:1, "Be ye followers of me, even as I also am of Christ.") The secular therapist, however, might refer to this as the client seeing the therapist as a father/mother figure or authority figure.

The therapist must not only know what to do, but when, in what way, with which clients, and with what exceptions. Two surgeons may use the same operating room, the same surgical tools, and the same nursing staff, and yet produce vastly different results—all because of the difference in their skills. Two musicians with similar voice qualities can sing the same song with quite different results. In the religious community, I have seen one church look at a very successful neighboring church, and try to copy the successful church's methods, only to find that those methods do not work in another setting. The key lies not so much in the precise plan, but how one works the chosen plan.

Only the very naive person thinks that human problems can be simply categorized, labeled, and "solved." Rarely does a client come in and divulge directly the real nature of the problem. It takes considerable knowledge of human behavior, plus the wisdom of the Holy Spirit, to know how to work effectively with people. It is not a matter of one or the other; it takes both. The therapist must separate the symptoms from the problems, see behind the defenses and facades, and find a way to spark motivation in the client. Sometimes this requires instilling hope or faith that will inspire the client to risk change. Some have mistakenly thought that for a person to be used by the Holy Spirit in this way, they need not study or prepare. The Holy Spirit cannot use or bless what we do not have. Jesus said the Holy Spirit would "bring all things to your remembrance" (John 14:26). But, He will not bring to our remembrance what we have not learned.

Through the influence of the Holy Spirit, the therapist may be prompted to go beyond his training, or take advantage of the "exceptions to the rule." No matter what books or theorists say, there are exceptions to all rules of counseling intervention—the "shoulds" and "musts" of psychotherapy. However, when I talk about exceptions, there is danger that a naive, unskilled therapist may think he or she can make such exceptions every day. One cannot follow every impulse and claim this as being the leadings of the Holy Spirit!

Only the truly skilled therapist can afford to risk making exceptional interventions. One example of an exception might be where there are schizophrenics in good remission (or borderline personalities), who could profit from CT. Some therapists are so skilled in a given model that they might be successful with that model when most others would not. At times I have gone contrary to all my training to do or say something as I followed the leading of the Holy Spirit.

The key to therapy lies more in the therapist than in the technique, whichever model is used. E. M. Bounds (1946, pp. 5-6), writing to preachers, said:

> God's plan is to make much of the man....The Church is looking for better methods; God is looking for better men....What the Church needs today is not more or better machinery, not new organizations or more and novel methods, but men whom the Holy Ghost can use—men of prayer, men mighty in prayer. The Holy Ghost does not flow through methods, but through men. He does not come on machinery, but on men. He does not anoint plans, but men—men of prayer.

The same thing Bounds said about preachers can be said about therapists. The person (the character of the therapist) is more important than the model used.

I am not sure that the Holy Spirit uses a *model* of psychotherapy, but I know He uses the *person* using the model.

The key qualities of a successful psychotherapist have frequently been called warmth, empathy, and genuineness. Phrased differently, we might say they are genuine concern, caring, and love for the client. When a loving therapist shows non-judgmental acceptance, he or she becomes transparent and allows the characteristics of God to be seen. The therapist need not play the role of judge, for John 16:8 says that it is the Holy Spirit who reproves of sin. Frequently, the therapist will feel frustrated, will feel like giving up on a certain client, or will have difficulty relating to a client in the first place. For the counselor who welcomes such assistance, the Holy Spirit will provide the divine love necessary to overcome such difficulties.

In John 14:26 and 16:13-14, Christ foretold the coming of the Holy Spirit, and said, "He will teach you all things; He will bring all things to your rememberance; He will guide you into all truth; and He will show you things to come." In the clinical training of a therapist, the supervisor often observes through a one-way mirror and/or gives feedback by telephone. For the Christian therapist, the Holy Spirit can be like a divine Supervisor or Consultant to come alongside and provide direct assistance and feedback.

13

INDIVIDUAL PSYCHOLOGY:
THE THEORY AND PSYCHOTHERAPY OF ALFRED ADLER

Marvin G. Gilbert

INTRODUCTION

Individual Psychology is the term coined by Alfred Adler to represent his contribution to psychological theory and to the alleviation of mental and societal distress. It is a term which hints at the deep respect Adler had for the uniqueness of each individual, which is a cornerstone of his writing. Although "Adlerian Psychology" is the more popular expression, "Individual Psychology" is more correct and more faithfully represents Adler's writings and thought.

HISTORICAL DEVELOPMENT OF THE THEORY

The historical development of Individual Psychology (hereafter IP) cannot be discussed cogently without discussing the life of Adler himself. In a description of Adler, Ansbacker (in Adler, 1973) recounted that Adler was born in 1870 in a Jewish Viennese family. While growing up he suffered some early illnesses and experienced the death of a younger brother, events which presumably influenced his later thinking. He graduated from medical school, specializing in psychiatry, and began a colleagueship with Sigmund Freud. This relationship developed coincidently with the famous Vienna Psychoanalytic Society.

His association with Freud may have been both a blessing and a curse. His formal association with Freud began in 1902. Prior to his departure from the presidency of the Vienna Psychoanalytic Society in 1911 (followed by Carl Jung's formal departure in 1914), there may have never existed in one association such a psychological brain trust. The people associated with Freud were intellectual giants in their own right—Adler included. Yet, by and large, Adler remained in Freud's shadow. This pattern has continued, despite the aggressive work of Adlerians to change the psychological world's understanding of the relationship between Adler and Freud and to highlight Adler's contribution.

Apparently Adler never considered himself a student or disciple of Freud, even though he was fourteen years younger. Adlerians point with obvious pride at the direction "neo-Freudians" such as Horney and Sullivan have taken in revising

Freud's original psychoanalytic principles. They have emphasized the social nature of humanity and pathology, in contrast to Freud's intrapsychic view of personality. This shift in emphasis echos Adler's thoughts.

As is true of most personality theories, IP evolved and developed over time, particularly since Adler's early writing during the 1920s. Overall, however, it remains a self-consistent apologetic for the social nature of human beings.

EARLY APPLICATIONS OF INDIVIDUAL PSYCHOLOGY

Furtmuller's biographical essay provides rich detail of the early applications of IP in Europe and the United States (in Adler, 1973). In that biographical sketch, the areas of therapeutic and educational activities which consumed Adler's apparently enormous energies are highlighted.

Adult Education

After his resignation from the Vienna Psychoanalytic Society, Adler looked for opportunities to share his views. The doors which opened were primarily educational. One of the first was a lectureship at an adult educational facility in which professional and nonprofessional people voluntarily attended lectures. His lecture style developed there, as did his reputation as a person who could speak both intelligently and understandably about human behavior and motivation.

Teacher Education

Somewhat later, Adler joined the faculty at a teachers' college in Vienna. He did not view his involvement with educational settings as second best or necessitated by financial hardship; rather, it reflected his basic belief in the power of education to change human beings and it demonstrated his reformist's orientation. Social reform activities were a well-documented part of his early professional life, even before his association with Freud. Adler's lectures were essentially a call for more humane treatment of children in the classroom.

Child Guidance Clinics

The close association with parents in the adult education lectures and with teachers in the college created a demand for application of IP to child-rearing (and educational) problems. Adler responded by establishing in Vienna, and other locations somewhat later, a number of child guidance clinics where parents and teachers could consult with Adlerian-trained psychotherapists. It was in his own work in one of these clinics that Adler stumbled upon what is now a trademark of Adlerian consultation: *public treatment*. Furtmuller stated:

> Adler decided to use his work in the clinic as a demonstration, and therefore held his interviews with child and parents not in privacy but before a restricted audience....Adler's skill in handling people made the children as well as the adults soon feel at home with him, so they did not take account of, or soon forgot the audience. (in Adler, 1973, pp. 380–381)

Thus he successfully combined treatment with training in a socially supportive atmosphere.

Lectures

The later part of his life was spent in public and university lecture halls, both in Europe and the United States, trying to establish on an international scale a foothold for IP within a profession dominated by psychoanalysis and behaviorism. Since he attracted very zealous disciples, such as Dreikurs, Ansbacher, and O'Connell, his efforts may be viewed as somewhat successful. It was during this extended time of lecturing—of attempting to express concisely the details of the theory—that he began placing increasing emphasis upon prevention and mental health principles, in contrast to psychotherapy. In 1935, he stated, "a great improvement in the next generation can be assured by preventative work" (Adler, 1935/1982, p. 6), although he recognized the importance of continued training in and application of psychotherapy.

Types of Problems Treated and Therapeutic Method

The range of problems addressed in Adler's writings is quite large; it includes neurotic behavior of various types, sleeplessness, suicide attempts, psychosomatic dysfunctions, and delinquency (Adler, 1973; Ansbacker & Ansbacker, 1956). Adler's writings, however, leave a distinct impression that neurotic behavior and parenting difficulties (including teacher-student problems) were a major focus of his practice, particularly in his later years.

It is interesting to note Adler's then novel approach to psychotherapy: he talked to people! His method was didactic, rational, and at times confrontive (Rozsnafszky, 1974). He replaced the Freudian couch with chairs; he and the patient sat, looked at each other, and talked. It must be understood, however, that what is now standard procedure for most counselors was then a very revolutionary concept.

UNDERLYING THEORETICAL ASSUMPTIONS

In this section, Adler's thinking about the nature and structure of personality is addressed in some detail. It considers Adler's view of Man as a social, responsible, motivated being; it discusses Adler's classification of personality types; it explores the sources and expressions of psychopathology; and it concludes with a discussion of the change process from the viewpoint of IP.

Man as a Social, Communal Being

In sharp contrast to Freud, Adler stated that human beings have an innate need to belong to a larger group and to cooperate and contribute to that group. Life is best lived with an awareness that, as individuals, we are part of a larger whole called humanity. We need not be at war continually with society (and ourselves) as Freud had proposed; we can live in harmony.

Man as a Responsible Being

Adler stressed in many ways that human beings must be held responsible for their behavior, i.e., for their choices (Rozsnafszky, 1974). We are responsible, Adler argued, because we have freedom of choice—within the parameters of certain biological givens (Adler, 1929a). Such a view was certainly out of step with psychoanalysis and behaviorism, both of which argued for its own deterministic view of human behavior. This personal responsibility and its concomitant requirement for freedom of choice lends to IP an optimism regarding human existence (Leibin, 1981) that permeates both theory and practice.

Man as a Unified, Goal-Directed Being

In contrast to the various reductionistic psychologies prominent in the early part of this century, Adler believed that a human being is best understood as a unified whole, not as a composite of so many parts. Ansbacker and Ansbacker (1956), in an edited quote from Adler's *The Science of Living*, stated: "In real life we always find...the whole commands the parts....Very early in my work, I [Adler] found man to be a self-consistent unity. The foremost task of Individual Psychology is to prove this unity in each individual" (p. 175).

Thus, "style of life" was for Adler that facet of personality which unifies all actions, thoughts, and intents, and is an expression of the person's unique goal in life. The concept of style of life is further expanded in the following section. Perhaps his often quoted statement, "whether, not whence" (Adler, 1973) best expresses briefly the goal-directed, teleological view of human behavior.

Motivation

Adler held that the basic push in life came, not from sexual or biological needs, but from a basic, unavoidable sense of *inferiority*. This originates primarily from the small child's actual size in comparison to adults, and from any bodily organ weakness, handicap, or inferiority (Maddi, 1972).

Rozsnafszky (1974) stated: "Adler sees the basic dynamic force behind behavior, not as sex, but as the striving of humans to move from a feeling of inferiority towards superiority which is normal and inevitable because a young child is actually inferior" (p. 69). Thus faced with inevitable feelings of inferiority, accentuated by any biological inferiority, the child experiences the great "upward striving": the drive for "superiority" or "perfection" (Adler, 1973, p. 31).

The Adlerian concept of "superiority" need not be one of domination of others, a "one-up-manship" which crushes others; rather, it reflects, at its best, a striving to compensate for the inferiority. Superiority may express itself through a variety of mediums: academic performance, athletic ability, personal appearance, artistic expression, work, etc. Adler (1929) believed that the goal of complete superiority does not come from reality. Instead, it is a fictional thing, an expression of the imagination. Although ridiculous from the viewpoint of reality, this goal becomes the principal motivating factor of our lives.

All of life, then, for Adler, expresses the striving for superiority. But because superiority is a fictional thing, created in the imagination, the details of its expression are unique to each person. That is, we *create* with our "creative selves" the content of our striving for superiority. The goal may be fictional, but the behaviors are real; their pattern reveals the life style. The style of life is developed as early as age four or five years, when presumably the child is feeling inferiority intensely, while beginning to fantasize about being an adult and role playing adult behavior.

Gentry, Winer, Sigelman, and Phillips (1980) quoted an earlier definition of life style by Frederick Thorne, who said the life style was "the distinctive schema...which each person develops very early in life...(it is) the organization of acquired dispositions and attitudes...the functional totality of attitudinal constellations of a person toward the problem of how to get along with life" (p. 36). That each child (person) develops a unique style of life must be underscored. In this regard, Adler (1929b) proposed that, although the feelings of inferiority and strivings for superiority are universal, people are not created equal in how they experience and cope with inferiority. The life style can be either good or bad, depending upon the person's unique interpretation of life. He stressed, however, that as long as a person is in a favorable situation, it would be difficult to see the style of life clearly. In new situations, however, where the person is confronted with difficulties, the style of life appears clearly and distinctly.

A final motivation must be considered, in that it formed the essence of Adler's view of the individual and society. That motivation is *gemeinschaftsgefuel* or "social interest." Adler viewed social interest as an innate drive or need in all human beings. It was a drive to be connected with others, to work toward the common good, to belong, and to contribute. However, at various times in his writings, social interest appeared to be either an undeniable drive, or a disposition which must be developed in order to be effective. It appears that Adler believed that the drive toward social interest was present in all human beings, but played a meaningful role in life for only some. Those who expressed their striving for superiority *with* social interest were said to be on the "useful" side of life, those who did not were on the "useless" side of life. He stated, "the individuals who lack social interest are...[the] criminals, insane persons, and drunkards" (1929b, p. 40). "Social interest is a slow growth. Only those persons who are really trained in the direction of social interest from their first childhood and who are always striving on the useful side of life will actually have social feelings" (Adler, 1929b, p. 232).

Classification Systems of Personality

Adler's holistic treatment of individuals functionally prohibited a detailed classification of the substructures of personality, e.g., Freud's id, ego, and superego. He did, however, develop two relatively distinct systems for classifying people. This may appear somewhat contradictory to his disapproval of psychological diagnosis and his appreciation for uniqueness. The solution, if indeed there is one, lies in Adler's belief that his classifications actually guided his treatment, whereas psychoanalytic diagnosis was not necessarily useful in a similar way. He stated: "We do not consider human beings as types, because every person has an individual style of life. If we speak of types, therefore, it is only as a conceptual device to make more understandable the similarities of individuals" (Ansbacker & Ansbacker, 1956, p. 116).

Character types. The first system of classification focuses upon the outgrowth of the life style, i.e., given a certain expression of life style, what kind of person is this individual likely to become? Adler (1935/1982) stated there were four possible types, and he labeled them the "ruling" type, the "getting" type, the "avoiding" type, and "the socially useful" type. The *ruling* type expresses a life style in which striving for superiority is expressed by power. This person feels a need to control, to manipulate, to be in charge, in compensating for inferiority. The *getting* type of person is a most dependent type who expects everything from others and leans upon them. Adler viewed this getting type as the most common, related directly to being pampered as a child. The third type, *avoiding*, tries to run from life and its demands and responsibilities, instead of facing them with courage. The courage to face life's problems is the thing most characteristic for the fourth type; *the socially useful person* has, in contrast to the first three types, a keen sense of social interest which motivates behavior. This person solves life's problems in ways which benefit others.

Degree of activity. The second method used to classify personality involved identifying where, on a continuum between activity and passivity, the life style best fit (Ansbacker & Ansbacker, 1956). Although this method of classification did not play as prominent a role in Adler's writings as did character types, it is nonetheless instructive. In addition to the activity continuum, Adler also added a second variable, that of constructiveness versus destructiveness. With these two variables considered simultaneously, then, a life style could be classified as (a) active constructive; (b) passive constructive; (c) active destructive; and (d) passive destructive. The first two represent life styles which evidence social interest, while the latter two clearly show an absence of it. The person displaying the greatest amount of courage in life would have a style of life which could be classified as active constructive, while the most discouraged person would adopt a passive destructive life style.

SOURCES AND EXPRESSIONS OF PSYCHOPATHOLOGY

Lack of Social Interest

Adler's writings clearly posit that mental dysfunction results from a lack of social interest. This lack results in the development of a life style which is mistake-oriented and maladaptive. The errors are mistakes in interpretation as the person creatively seeks to make sense out of the world. To say that the world is a cruel place filled with uncaring people would be, to Adler, a basic mistake in interpretation. Out of such a mistake emerge patterns of behavior (life style) which would be oriented toward *ruling, getting, or avoiding*. That is, not only is the interpretation a mistake, but the goal for upward striving is also mistaken.

Mistaken Goals

Dreikurs (1964, 1968) developed an easily understood classification of these mistaken goals. His application centered upon work with children, although he claimed the concepts apply to adults as well. The goals were (a) attention-getting, (b) power, (c) revenge, and (d) withdrawal or inadequacy. The relationship to Adler's four character types is clear. Selection of any one of these four goals, with attention-getting as the most common, is declaring, in effect, "I can find my place of superiority and specialness through this door, not the one marked 'social interest'. " Thus, the discouraged child who does not have a developed drive of social interest may choose to be *perfectly* bad, a child whose misbehavior is *superior* to that of any other child.

Adler believed that the individual who feels overwhelmed by the problems of life and who adopts an assumption which protects him or her from such a sense of powerlessness by avoiding full participation in life is the individual who is constructing a basic mistake. He believed that all such basic mistakes share a common reliance on some external rule or principle as an assurance of successful, meaningful living. Such mistakes all constitute attempts to find an external source of power for coping with the problems of life. This hiding from the stress of life, from its "basic questions" (discussed in the following section) is pathological, whether the form taken is alcoholism, psychosomatic illness, neurosis, or psychosis. For Adler, the basic problem was clear: a life style empty of social interest, and thus void of courage. Adler (1929a) concluded that to cure a neurosis or a psychosis, it would be necessary to change completely the whole up-bringing of the patient and to turn the person definitely and unconditionally back into human society as a useful, contributing courageous member.

THE GOALS AND TECHNIQUES OF INDIVIDUAL PSYCHOLOGY

If the basis of all psychological problems is a lack of social interest, the remedy is the development of social interest and the courage to face life fully. Adler stated, "all of my efforts are devoted towards increasing the social interest of the patient.

I know that the real reason for his malady is his lack of cooperation, and I want him to see it too. As soon as he can connect himself with his fellow men on an equal and cooperative footing, he is cured'' (Ansbacker & Ansbacker, 1956, p. 347). Thus, for Adlerians, individual adjustment is social adjustment, because all conflicts are really interpersonal conflicts; hatred and fear of others are masked by drives for power, dependency, or avoidance.

Adler and others (e.g. Kazan, 1978) recognized that social interest cannot be taught; it is, rather, a by-product of useful activities and meaningful relationships. IP, then, seeks to generate useful activities and to develop meaningful relationships both within and beyond of the counseling room so that social interest is developed in the client.

THE BASIC QUESTIONS OF LIFE

Individual Psychology stresses the need for courage to face the realities and difficulties of life. Adler defined these as the questions of life, and listed four in his writings (1929b; 1935/1982): How does the person deal with the issue of (a) work and occupational selection, (b) social relationships, (c) love and sex, and (d) creativity and art. These basic questions guide Adlerian diagnosis, allowing the therapist to understand where the patient has and has not been successful in life, and permitting the therapist to understand to what degree therapy has been successful when completed.

RESPONSIBILITY

Responsibility for improvement, for therapeutic progress, rests with the client or patient, not the therapist. In a sense, no other position is possible, given a belief that any psychological malfunction is an expression of avoidance of responsibility. The therapist makes it clear that the patient is responsibile for his or her own cure. Rozsnafszky (1974) labeled this client responsibility as one of the two main pillars of IP, the other being the client's freedom of choice or free will. The therapist communicates in a caring, albeit a sometimes forceful way, belief in the client's ability to and responsibility for change.

STAGES OF TREATMENT

Nikelly (1971) briefly outlined four phases or stages of the IP therapeutic process. During the first stage, beginning with the first session, a cooperative relationship is sought, one marked by mutual trust, equality, and respect. It is facilitated by a search for a common purpose or goal for the therapeutic relationship.

The second stage involves exploration of the current life situation of the client, with emphasis upon current behavior. How the individual is functioning in relationship to the four basic questions of life is discussed. The client's birth order and family constellation are reviewed, giving the therapist information regarding the formation and content of the life style.

During the third stage, the therapist extracts from these characteristics an underlying pattern of behavior. This pattern is explained (interpreted) to the client, and the client's intentions, private logic, and mistaken goals are pointed out. This is often a painful time of increased self-understanding which requires a well-established therapeutic relationship.

The final stage is often referred to as a "reorientation," that is, reorientation to the useful side of life. The greatest degree of behavior change occurs in this final stage. Ideally, increased social interest and more effective handling of the basic questions are evidenced prior to termination.

SUMMARY

The summary of Adler's therapy provided by Rozsnafszky (1974) is most relevant here. She stated Adler's method was didactic, rational, ego- or conscious-oriented and was, essentially, a reeducation of the client along more socially useful paths. In both education and in therapy, he operated in a positive, directive way. He believed that, if presented intelligently and with social interest, such directive, perhaps coercive, reeducation would be readily received by the client.

CURRENT PRACTICE

This section provides a brief overview of clientele and settings normally associated with applied IP. It also reviews Adlerian research efforts during the last decade.

Clientele

As one examines the current Adlerian literature, it is clear that Adler's interest during the early part of this century has been faithfully maintained by his disciples. Four areas of treatment are observable: (a) parent-child consultation, including parent study groups; (b) teacher-student-family consultation; (c) marriage counseling; and (d) other areas such as the school reform movement labeled "individual education."

Parent-child consultation. Adler's early work with parents and children in front of a supportive group of trainees, parents, and teachers continues (e.g. Willingham, 1980). In this setting, a therapist or consultant (terms vary in the literature) work through—at least to some extent—the four phases of the helping process outlined earlier in this chapter. The concern is not an in-depth analysis of the life style or a personality reconstruction. Rather, the purpose is to explore the current situation, to disclose the child's probable mistaken goal, and to examine what the parents (and to some extent, the child) can do to encourage the child to move toward the "useful side of life." During my training in such consultation groups, I observed that, if presented properly, the entire consultation process is relatively low in threat, yet effective as a means of parent reeducation and family change. Dreikurs's (1964) extremely readable and practical text on child psychology is often used as source book in such groups.

Teacher-student-family consultation. Dreikurs (1968) and Dinkmeyer and Carlson (1973) have provided excellent manuals for teachers, school counselors, and school psychologists who wish to apply IP to the classroom. By providing volunteer training for teachers and student teachers, Adler's method continues to be applied (Willingham & Chambliss, 1974). As with the parent study groups and parent-child consultation, the structure for such consultation often involves a group setting with "live" work with teachers and their "problem students," although the consultation process works just as well with private meetings (Dinkmeyer & Carlson, 1973). Perhaps the most beneficial aspect of such consultation is not only that it allows teachers to understand children's motives and goals better, but that it also permits teachers to understand their own contributions to the situation, since teachers often perpetuate the problems they seek to eliminate from the classroom. As the consultant communicates respect, trust, and caring—carefully avoiding a "one-up" position—the frazzled teachers are often very receptive to suggestions.

Marriage counseling. One of Adler's four great questions of life was: How does the person deal with sex and love? Thus, marriage counseling has always played an important role in IP. Dinkmeyer and Dinkmeyer (1982) have provided an excellent review of Adlerian principles and techniques in marriage counseling. One of the interesting contributions of that article involved linking emotions to the four mistaken goals identified by Dreikurs (1946). Thus, when spouses feel (a) *annoyed*: it reflects an objective of attention-getting; (b) *angry*: it expresses a goal of power; (c) *hurt*: this is linked to the goal of revenge; and (d) *like giving up* (e.g. divorce): this expresses inadequacy or withdrawal. Given the importance of understanding and disclosing to the client the nature of the mistaken goals, such a schema certainly appears promising.

Other areas of involvement. It should not be construed that Adlerians confine themselves to only those areas addressed by Adler. Adler's disciples have zealously applied IP to almost every conceivable area of human interest. Therapeutically, IP has been applied to marriage enrichment (Hawes, 1982), to juvenile delinquency (Hirschorn, 1982), as well as to a host of physical and psychomatic illnesses and their related psychological distresses. The individual education movement, briefly mentioned above, illustrates Adler's original concern for school reform. It is being applied to entire schools and school systems (Krebs, 1982) with positive results. Theoretically, Adlerians have attempted to integrate IP with a wide range of other disciplines and theories: (a) existential psychology (Maddi, 1978); (b) Jungian psychology (O'Connell, 1978); (c) cognitive behaviorism (Dowd & Kelly, 1980); (d) systems theory (Amerikander, 1981); (e) reality therapy and R.E.T. (Rozsnafszky, 1974); (f) pastoral counseling (Brink, 1977); and (g) even Zen (Croake & Rusk, 1980). In most cases, it appears that these authors are arguing that ideas germinal to the other theory or therapy were either borrowed or stolen from Adler, and if the other systems would only adopt the label "Adlerian," everything would be fine!

Research Related to Individual Psychology

Individual Psychology has not been characterized by a prodigious amount of research; the emphasis has traditionally been on application first, then research. This situation has produced criticism by non-Adlerians, which has apparently motivated the increase in the number of published empirical studies (Watkins, 1982; 1983).

Type of studies. Watkins (1983) has provided a most useful overview of the kinds of Adlerian studies reported in the *Journal of Individual Psychology* from 1970 to 1981. A total of 75 studies were printed, with studies of birth order, social interest, early childhood recollections, and life style representing the bulk (72%) of the studies. In a year-by-year analysis of these publications, Watkins concluded that birth order studies were more numerous during the first five years of this period, while studies of social interest were being published with growing frequency during the last four years. The increase in birth order studies was attributed to the availability of increasingly sophisticated instruments designed to measure social interest. Early recollections and life style studies *combined* represented only 13% of the total studies.

Study outcomes. Those few authors who have summarized Adlerian-based studies have generally agreed that the studies supported the theory. This should not be surprising, given that the authors are almost all Adlerians; yet their conclusions cannot be discounted for that reason. Watkins (1982) concluded that findings in the area of birth order, social interest, and early recollection were particularly consistent with the theory. In a more narrow review, Manaster (1977) discussed the difficulty in conducting birth order research, given the large number of variables inherent in family constellation possibilities. Despite these statistical and research design problems, and the criticisms of birth order research by non-Adlerians, he concluded: "in the face of...skepticism, birth order research continues with significant results in specified areas...and with increased respectability when...various critical factors are controlled" (pp. 5-6).

The vast majority of the empirical studies conducted by Adlerians have focused upon validation of Adlerian *concepts* or constructs. What seems to be missing are large numbers of studies validating the *therapeutic outcomes* of IP. Such studies exist, but not in convincing enough numbers to address adequately the criticisms by non-Adlerians who value applied research.

INTEGRATION

Before detailing areas of similarity and potential integration of IP and a biblical view of the Holy Spirit, a brief review of Adler's perspective of God and religion seems appropriate. Adler wrote extensively of the relationship between his theory and religion. The book which he co-authored with the Rev. Ernst Jahn, a Lutheran minister, attempted an early integration of his psychology with Christianity (Jahn & Adler, 1933, in Ansbacker & Ansbacker, 1956).

View of God and Religion

For Adler, God was an idea, an idea of ultimate and eternal perfection which had found concrete expression in religion. God, for him, was an idea which emerged out of humanity's great upward striving—the striving for perfection. In this sense, humanity created God! He stated that mankind "once put into the world...must strive incessantly toward self-preservation and ascendency. In this manner he found God" (Adler, 1973, p. 277). Notice that humanity finds God; how different from the biblical view of God reaching out, searching for, finding, and redeeming us (Rom. 5:8-10).

Adler's view of religion was consistent with his theory; religion functioned to bring people together in harmony. "The primal energy which was so effective in establishing regulative religious goals was none other than that of social feelings (interest). This was meant to bind human beings more closely to one another" (Ansbacker & Ansbacker, 1956, p. 462). The emphasis is upon restoration to fellow humans, never to God. In this light, Jahn commented:

> For Adler, the meaning of life is the experience of fellowmanship and the courage for it. There are, however, human problems which can be solved neither by fellowmanship nor by courage...there can be no courage for life without faith in God. (in Adler, 1973, p. 274)

The thoughts on integration which follow should not be construed as an attempt to minimize the differences between IP and a biblical view of the Holy Spirit. Ansbacker and Ansbacker (in Adler, 1973) have noted that, although Adler made an adult conversion from Judaism to Christianity, it was a liberal Christianity that was much more humanistic than theistic. IP is not a Christian system, yet it may have much to offer the Christian counselor. Adler stated, "I regard it as no mean commendation when it is emphasized that Individual Psychology has rediscovered many a lost position of Christian guidance" (Ansbacker & Ansbacker, 1956, p. 463). The following section examines the extent to which this statement may be relevant.

Theoretical Integration

Adler stated that the basic motivator in life was a feeling of inferiority. Inferiority is experienced by all, and all strive (either usefully or uselessly) to overcome it. The Bible speaks of guilt over sin—godly sorrow—as a universal human experience. Though Adler did not write extensively of sin, the close relationship between this state of inferiority and mankind's state of fallenness is intriguing.

If, however, Adler were forced to identify a synonym for sin in his system, it would probably be a lack of social interest—or inordinate self-interest. Such a lack led clearly to the "useless side of life"; it denied our essential social nature. We would certainly concur that sin results in a similar denial, since humanity's essential nature is a pale, imperfect reflection of God's own image.

Adler posited that striving for superiority or perfection in response to feelings of inferiority, or inferiority complexes, pulled mankind upward; ascendency became the goal. Behavior was viewed as purposeful and goal-directed. Through the work of the Spirit, we are redeemed and are filled with such a sense of purpose and "calling" that, for the sincere believer, all of life is spent in being led of the Spirit (Rom. 8:4) and striving to do the will of the Father. Such passages as 2 Corinthians 5:14 speak of the "compellingness" of God's call.

That the final goal of this upward striving, perfection, is only a myth to Adler must not deter us from considering that the biblical goals of complete sanctification or perfection only await us in the life hereafter. In this sense, Paul spoke of running a race which was to last for a lifetime (1 Cor. 9:24-27). In one of his more memorable passages, Paul recognized that he had not yet arrived at that state of perfection, yet it still motivated and pushed him to continue the race (Phil. 3:10-14). While Adler would label Paul's belief in a future prize as fictional, we Christians are persuaded otherwise: consequently we live our lives with eternity in view. Interestingly, Adler acknowledged the benefit of viewing life from an eternal vantage point, *sub specie aeternitatis* (1973, p. 283), while presumably believing that eternity was only fiction.

One of the passages of Scripture most quoted and appreciated by Pentecostal believers is Acts 2:1-4, the account of the first outpouring of the Holy Spirit. How refreshing it has been for me, after immersing myself in Adler for days, to read once again that first verse: "And when the day of Pentecost was fully come, they were all with one accord in one place." That this verse is saturated with "social interest" must not be overlooked by the serious student of Pentecost. This brief passage is the first of many that link human love and unity with the supernatural power of God. Acts 2:43-47 is another example; it pictures believers holding all things in common and having daily fellowship with one another. *Furthermore*, signs and wonders were performed, with the Lord daily adding people to the Church.

This same linking of social interest and the power of Pentecost is evidenced most clearly in Acts 4:31-35. In fact, this passage alternately describes the power of God upon the disciples and their sharing all their worldly possessions with one another. As a statistics teacher, I know the temptation to infer one thing causes another simply because they are related, and I know how important it is in most cases not to make that mistake, but in this case I shall yield to the temptation. *I believe the power of Pentecost can only be experienced fully when God's people are committed totally not only to God but to one another.*

The story of Ananias and his wife Sapphira is illuminated by Adlerian concepts. In the middle of people sharing openly, contributing all they had to the group, in short, experiencing social interest at a peak level, two people emerge with a mistaken goal of attention-getting! They wanted to be approved by the group more than by God; they lied about the amount of the purchase price received for land they had sold, and thus moved to the "useless side of life." So much did God perceive this attitude and behavior as a threat to the new Church, that, at Peter's anointed word, they were struck dead by God. Peter described their awesome sin as lying "to the Holy Ghost" (Acts 5:3, 4). In Adlerian terms, their mistaken goal threatened the social interest of the group, and threatened to lessen the power and operation of the Spirit. Certainly, His power is restrained whenever sins of pride, deceit, coveteousness, and pompousness enter our hearts—His Church.

The term "Individual Psychology" underscores Adler's appreciation for individual uniqueness. Without doubt, God appreciates each of us as individuals, recognizes our strengths and weaknesses, and places us individually into the Body of Christ as pleases Him. Jesus made it clear that God knows each of us personally (Matt. 10:29–30). Paul applied this in describing the Church as a physical body. Certainly God knows us better than life style analysis could ever accomplish. And on the basis of this knowledge, the Holy Spirit distributes gifts to each of us, so that the entire body will profit from our individual contribution (1 Cor. 12:7). *All* have something to contribute, and *all* profit by the contribution of each individual.

Brink (1977) provided a final insight into theoretical integration in his discussion of works and grace as related to IP. He concluded that the Adlerian pitfall lies in works as a solution to the problem of inferiority, i.e., sin. The person striving for superiority to compensate for inferiority remains self-bound. It represents an "I can do it myself" attitude; an attitude ironically labeled "masculine protest" by Adler! In contrast, Brink presented the life of reliance upon God's grace. This would involve acceptance of inferiority and recognition of failures and limitations, while still striving for perfection. The striving for perfection would, then, reflect a striving for a closer relationship with God, to reflect more fully Christ's image, while resting in God concerning guilt over sin and moral wrong. I am at rest when I realize that nothing I can do will ever make God love me more—or less!

Implications of a Practical Integration
Belief in free will, given certain biological and environmental realities, is a basic tenet of Adlerian counseling. With an integrated theory-theology, the Spirit-filled counselor in an Adlerian setting could feel quite at home in stressing to clients a belief in their free will and freedom to choose to be different and to behave differently. Similarly, insisting that the counselor should not assume responsibility for client change would be consistent with a biblical view of ministry to others

Admittedly, the preceding paragraph reflects a non-Calvinistic bias. Whether or not we are "free" to respond to the invitation to the Holy Spirit to accept Christ is a question which is beyond the psychological scope of this chapter. However, a rejection of psychological, if not theological, determinism makes for a much more optimistic counselor and client, and presumably produces faster therapeutic change.

The Pentecostal counselor could easily use Adler's four basic questions of life (love, work, social relations, and the arts) as a basis for understanding clients, but he or she would probably insist upon a fifth question: "How is the relationship with God?" To know how a person relates to God is a critical element of analysis for the Spirit-filled helper.

One temptation faced by Spirit-filled counselors is an overreliance upon the Holy Spirit. I realize this sounds heretical; please permit an explanation. Reliance upon the Holy Spirit for guidance, supernatural wisdom and knowledge, and for power to break through resistance is a dynamic potential of great importance in counseling. The danger lies in communicating to clients that they are utterly helpless to change their lives (thoughts, behaviors, emotions), and that they are, consequently, totally dependent upon the Spirit to provide that change for them. In this situation, responsibility for change would be taken from the client and placed upon God, and to some degree on the counselor, to produce spiritual power and deliverance in the counseling session. Only as responsibility for change rests primarily upon clients' shoulders will they develop the courage to seek changes in their own lives. Such change, obviously, should involve prayer and spiritual devotion by the client. The counselor must resist the temptation to become the dispenser of God's power if exercising that role would rob the client of self-reliance and the personal discovery that God is the source of strength, power, and encouragement.

SUMMARY

Alfred Adler provided the psychological world with an approach to understanding human behavior which is socially and, to some degree, morally oriented (Dreikurs, 1952). By stressing the importance of social interest, he touched the essence of humanness, and perhaps has provided a dim, incomplete picture of the image of God in us. By stressing the creative development of the life style, he portrayed Man as a being of dignity, creativity, and purpose. By detailing the nature of mistaken goals, he accounted for psychopathology and defined it in terms of the good of society.

That Adler was not an Evangelical Christian should not deter the Christian from giving serious consideration to the implications of helping others from an Adlerian viewpoint. The preceding integration section, albeit incomplete, does illustrate the viability of viewing truth from both a psychological and theological framework. However, such a synthesis must remain centered in God, not Adler. Thus social interest is not a complete explanation for the miraculous events which occurred in the early Church, or in the twentieth century Church. Nonetheless it may serve to remind us that in the counseling setting, praying for divine intervention in another's life, without being willing to risk mutual trust, respect, and involvement, may not be effective in moving that person to the "useful side of life," nor in bringing divine intervention. Adler stated:

> Since Individual Psychology is not interested in the verbal expression of feelings, but only in the intensity of the movement by which they are expressed, it will evaluate the members of various religions not by the way they represent their feelings, but by the movement of the whole individual follower, i.e. by their fruits. (in Ansbacker & Ansbacker, 1956, p. 463)

As Spirit-filled helpers, we have the responsibility not only to have the fruit of the Spirit in our own lives, but to bear much fruit in lives touched by God, encouragement and usefulness.

14

SYSTEMS THEORY

Marvin G. Gilbert

HISTORICAL DEVELOPMENT OF SYSTEMS THEORY

Writing this chapter has posed a unique challenge. So closely intertwined are Systems Theory (hereafter ST) and marriage and family therapy that teasing them apart to discuss the theory without majoring in its applications is a difficult task. I have concluded that an adequate presentation of this theory must include at least some substantive reference to marriage and family systems (and therapy). Redundancy between material in this chapter and those chapters in Volume II which focus on specific aspects of marriage and family therapy will be held to a minimum, but presumably cannot be completely eliminated.

Development of General Systems Theory

What the counseling literature refers to as ST was initially labeled General Systems Theory by its first major proponent, Ludwig von Bertalanffy. In lectures at the University of Chicago in 1937, von Bertalanffy, a biologist, proposed an alternative view to the then dominant mechanistic-reductionistic approach to biology and other natural sciences (von Bertalanffy, 1968). Essentially, he proposed that true scientific understanding could be best achieved by looking larger, not smaller. That is, any biological entity could be better understood by examining the functioning of the entire entity (whether human being, dog, or neuron cell) instead of analytically breaking that entity down into smaller and smaller units for study until, at an extreme, the entity is reduced to a biochemical mass.

Von Bertalanffy labeled all such entities "systems." He defined a system as a number of parts which are relatively organized so that a change in one or more of the parts is usually accompanied by a change in the other parts of the system. Since General Systems Theory was first introduced, a number of formal definitions of a system have appeared in the literature. Among the best of these is found in a family theory text by Kantor and Lehr (1975, p. 10):

A system (is) a set of different things or parts...that meet two requirements: first, these parts are directly or indirectly related to one another in a network of reciprocal causal effects, and second, each component part is related to one or more other parts of the set in a reasonably stable way during any particular period of time.

Thus a system can be any entity which has or is capable of having parts and which is itself part of a larger whole (system). As an example, a nuclear family system is an entity having subsystems, and which is, in turn, part of a larger kinship network or system.

General Systems Theory was first embraced in the natural sciences including biology, physics, chemistry, and applied mathmatics. Social theorists such as Buckley (1967), and Anderson and Carter (1974) soon recognized the theory's potential as a means of understanding social systems, including small groups, families, and larger complex organizations.

As the influence of ST has spread from the natural to the social and behavioral sciences, critics have argued that ST is *not* a theory at all, but is instead a collection of loosely defined terms and concepts. Interestingly, those who defend ST agree, at least in part. Buckley (1967), Dell (1980), and Kantor and Lehr (1975) have all agreed that ST is more a means of viewing reality than a true theory in the hypo-deductive tradition. Buckley admitted that "the modern systems approach aims to replace the older analytic, atomic...technique with a more holistic orientation to the problem of complex organization" (1967, p. 39).

SYSTEMS THEORY'S INFLUENCE UPON PSYCHOTHERAPY

Systems Theory's principal impact has been felt in the field of family therapy, and more recently marital therapy, rather than in academic psychology. The mechanistic-reductionistic approach to science, which served as the background for the theory's emergence, had thoroughly dominated the medical professions, including psychiatry. Psychiatry adhered to the medical sequence of diagnosis, prognosis, treatment, and evaluation, with causes of emotional and mental dysfunction viewed as *intra*-psychic phenomena. Murray Bowen, one of the most influential of the systems therapists and theorists, stated that ST stands in contrast and opposition to the linear, cause-effect thinking which forms the foundation for the "medical model." Systemic theorists recognize the potency of the familial and cultural systems to impact beneficially and destructively upon individuals, and they acknowledge the individual's ability to impact upon the family and culture (Bowen, 1978). The linear, cause-effect thinking is discarded in favor of a dynamic, cybernetic understanding of behavior.

Although the roots of ST may be traced to the Child Guidance movement in the early part of this century, ST's first psychotherapeutic application occurred during the 1950s. Guerin (1976) and Olson (1970) have provided excellent reviews of the development of family therapy (i.e. Systems Therapy). Both stated that family therapy emerged out of trial-and-error work by a number of therapists in various parts of the country working with hospitalized schizophrenics. Guerin stated that

> family research with schizophrenics was the primary focus of a majority of the pioneers in the family movement: Bateson, Jackson, Weakand and Haley in California, Bowen in Topeka and Washington; Lidz in Baltimore and then in New Haven; Whitaker and Malone in Atlanta; Scheflen and Bird-Whistle in Philadelphia. (1976, p. 3)

One of the interesting things about this list of pioneers is the diversity of disciplines represented: psychiatry, communicology, anthropology, linguistics, and psychology.

Thus, in the crucible of psychiatric hospitals, researchers and therapists (in the early days of family therapy, the two terms were functionally synonymous: Wynne, 1983) broke with the dominant psychiatric model and began treating schizophrenia by treating the *family* of the schizophrenic. While this was occurring covertly in some hospitals; little publication of this therapeutic approach was seen. Both Guerin and Olson accused psychoanalysts of inhibiting these burgeoning ideas and techniques. Olson (1970) stated that these early therapists "were generally afraid to report their experiences because of the strong Freudian tradition which dictated treating only the identified patient....the [psycho]analysts in this country have played a suppressive role regarding the development of marital and family therapy" (p. 17). It was not until the late 1950s and early 1960s that the leaders in Systems Therapy learned of each other's work and began finding national mediums for expression. Thus, it is not surprising that, in 1962, von Bertalanffy stated that few attempts had been made to apply General Systems Theory to the theory of human behavior.

It should not be concluded, however, that psychoanalysis played an insignificant role in the development of family therapy. Nathan Akerman remained committed to a psychoanalytic perspective until his death in 1971. With his death, "the family movement lost its most creative and zealous psychoanalytic proponent, and after it, the center of the field moved swiftly toward systems" (Guerin, 1976, p. 7). Since 1971, ST has evolved, diversified, and to some degree polarized around the work of Salvador Minuchin, Murray Bowen, Carl Whitaker, Jay Haley, and Virginia Satir. It has, in fact, now become an international movement with major contributions to theory and practice coming principally from England and Italy. It should also be noted that there are continuing attempts to integrate ST with preexisting modes of therapy, e.g. systems-psychoanalysis (Pincus & Dare, 1978; Skynner, 1976), and systems-behaviorism (Lester, Backham, & Baucom, 1980).

A SYSTEMS VIEW OF THE NATURE OF HUMANITY

Many of the popular theories of counseling or psychotherapy have emerged concomitantly with personality theories. Nevertheless, ST is not, and probably never will be, considered a theory of personality. Like true theories of personality, though, it abounds with unique terms and explanations for human behavior. A comprehensive review of all systems concepts is beyond the scope of this chapter and only selected constructs can be discussed in detail. (For a full discussion of the components of ST, see Buckley's [1968] *Modern Systems Research for the Behavioral Scientist: A Sourcebook.*)

It should be clear that, in the systems view, each individual composes a system, and that, in turn, a collection of individuals (e.g. marriage, family, church, counseling office) comprises a larger system composed of "individual" parts or elements. Thus, this discussion may consider alternatively human beings and systems; within a systems perspective the terms are interchangeable.

Human beings are socially oriented beings, with much of "self" emerging out of contact and interaction with others. Pre-systems theory social scientists, such as W. I. Thomas and G. H. Mead, theorized at length about such social influences and shaping processes. Fogarty (1976) stated that one of the basic assumptions of ST is that all people seek closeness—a merger with others to become a part of a larger social system. Thus humans are relational beings.

ESSENCE OF A SYSTEM

Energy

Energy comprises the basic "stuff" of any system. In biological systems, energy is defined biochemically: cells receive "energy" from digested food and from oxygen via the blood system. In photosynthetic systems, energy exists in the form of the sun's rays. In social systems, energy consists of information, i.e., communication, which occurs between the various *sub*-systems or subgroups, and between the entire system with other, external systems (Anderson & Carter, 1974). As an example, energy is transmitted *within* a church body as members talk to and fellowship with one another. Energy is also transmitted *into* the church system by evangelists, television programs viewed by members, films, and other outside influences.

Boundaries and Systemic Change

Not all systems are equal in their receptivity to energy, either from within or from without. Systems may thus be classified as relatively *open* or *closed*; this indicates the degree to which the system is utilizing the energy sources within it and around it (von Bertalanffy, 1968). Open systems, because their boundaries are relatively permeable, are more efficient in receiving and utilizing energy. The open system obtains what von Bertalanffy (1968), Anderson and Carter (1974), and others have labeled a "steady state." This is a dynamic equilibrium in which, though changes are occurring, adaptation to the changes produces a balance that maintains the system's identity despite its modification. An example is again seen in the local church where, despite pastoral or parishioner turnover, the church remains the church and keeps its identity and purpose. A closed system, by contrast, is relatively isolated from external influences, and may even be closed to contributions from its own subsystems. In the face of inevitable change, it is unable to maintain a "steady state," and may experience decay or even collapse.

In this respect, two terms are crucial: *morphogenesis* refers to a process of change in or elaboration of the system's structure and organization; in contrast, *morphostasis* denotes a process of maintaining a system's structure or form. If a system fails to develop beyond its earlier form, it is *morphostatic*, and presumably is experiencing some degree of entropy or decay. "Steady state" expresses the concept of a balance between these two processes, and thus reflects a system's ability to change (evolve) over time while maintaining predictability in form and structure (Andolfi, 1980).

One of two conditions of energy may develop within a system over time. First, systems which are relatively closed, unable to receive and/or utilize the energy available to them, will experience a reduction of energy—*entropy*. At extreme levels of entropy, the system collapses and ceases to function. An example of an entropic system is an aging wild animal that is no longer able to run and capture game (energy). If that state persists, it will die.

The other condition occurs when a system is open, particularly with reference to subsystem communication or energy transfer. It is called *negative entropy* (von Bertalanffy, 1968) or *synergy* (Anderson & Carter, 1974). In such high energy systems, more energy is actually being produced than is being utilized. This results in elaboration of the system, increasing complexity and diversity of subsystem functions, in short, growth and high morale.

Paul's description of the Body of Christ in 1 Corinthians 12 and 14 illustrates synergistic church functioning. Synergy occurs most frequently in cybernetic systems in which *feedback* of communication (energy) to the sending subsystem or external system is permitted and facilitated. In less theoretical terms, an organization of any type experiences growth and its members feel good about belonging to the organization when they can talk to each other and influence the direction and goals of the organization. If, however, the talking to each other is hurtful or destructive, people will stop communicating and the entire organization will suffer a drop in energy as internal boundaries become thick and rigid.

A further word about systemic boundaries is needed at this point, particularly as this concept serves as a focal point for the Structured Family Therapy of Salvador Minuchin (1974). A system's boundaries function to protect the differentiation of the system, i.e., to define it (Barnard & Corrales, 1979). Minuchin stated that boundaries may be defined as being *clear, enmeshed,* or *disengaged. Clear* boundaries allow the system or subsystem to function without undue interference, while still allowing contact with other systems. The clarity of boundaries within a family is a useful parameter for evaluating family functioning. The other two possibilities reflect either a closed system *(disengaged)* with too little contact with others, or an open system with *too much* contact or closeness, which smothers individuality *(enmeshment)*. These two conditions are dysfunctional, and are discussed later in this chapter.

Organization

This term refers to the grouping and arranging of parts to form a whole. Systems can be highly organized or highly disorganized; each reflects the system's ability to utilize available energy. The measure of effectiveness of an organization is its capacity to fulfill its goals as well as the goals of its parts or subsystems. *Dis*-organized human systems are generally incapable of fulfilling their goals and are uniquely dissatisfying for their members.

Motivation

Systems Theory is one of the few theories of human behavior which overtly accounts for goal-directed or purposeful behaviors and intentions (Buckley, 1967). Anderson and Carter (1974) stated: "One of the characteristics of living systems is the purposefulness of activities. They operate in a *goal-directed* manner" (p. 14). Every system has goals and behaves in a manner more or less consistent with those goals, whether the goal is survival for an individual lost in the wilderness, profit for a company, or caring, loving and evangelizing for a church congregation.

The motivation is reflected in the system by the way in which its subsystems are organized and by how it expends energy (Anderson & Carter, 1974). The activities of any system, whether simple or complex, reflect an attempt to balance forces which would keep the system as it is (morphostatic) and which would change the system (morphogenic). Thus, systems are motivated to do both. This results in a dynamic tension in healthy systems. Too much status quo and too much change and unpredicability may be defined as pathological states for any system.

THE NATURE OF PSYCHOPATHOLOGY

Within a systems framework, the intrapsychic pathology prominent in Freudian-based therapeutic approaches loses much of its viability. At a most elementary level, a system is said to be dysfunctional—pathological—when there is too much (enmeshment) or too little (disengagement) connection or communication between a system's subsystems or members.

Fusion

Fogarty (1976) used the term "fusion" in place of Minuchin's (1974) "enmeshment," stating that fusion is an abnormal amplification of a basic pull in human beings toward closeness. It can occur either through continuing conflict between two people, as illustrated by the mother and daughter who are in a regular state of conflict over the daughter's style of dress or friends, or by the development of emotional or physical symptoms in one of the two fused people. This latter situation may be illustrated by the couple who are pathologically fused over the husband's alcoholism.

The interesting, if not paradoxical, thing about fusion is that the fused people need not like each other; the only requirement is that they are "stuck" with each other. Fogarty stated that, over the lifetime of the fused relationship, the identity of each person becomes blurred. A similar concept forms the basis of much of Bowen's family therapy. He believed that the lack of differentiation of the self in the context of the family system is a primary cause of individual psychological problems. This lack of separation was called the *undifferentiated family ego mass*. Whether this condition describes the over-involvement of spouses with each other, or the blurring of distinction between parent and child (particularly problematic with teenagers), it speaks of a loss of self as a distinct entity. Individuals in such families live only for the family; children experience great conflict over the issue of leaving home and starting lives of their own as adults.

Fogarty (1976) added that the reaction to fusion may be distancing. Often one person may begin to feel smothered in a fused relationship, and will seek "breathing room." The other(s) may perceive this to be a threat and may experience emptiness. This results in increased efforts to bring the other close again. Thus, the destructive cycle is evident, with one person in the role of pursuer, and the other trying to distance himself or herself from the pursuer. The factor that distinguishes this situation from the break-up of a relationship is the sense of bonding to each other which *both* feel, and the refusal by the distancing person to run too far. Thus, we hear such mournful statements as "I can't live with her and I can't live without her."

Barnard and Corrales (1979) and others have noted that such pathological relationships are rarely noticed in the community until a crisis point is reached. Often these crises are predictable, following the transition points in the family life cycle. A clear example is an increase in marital distress when the youngest child leaves home. Such distress may serve to "pull" that child back home, or to take up residence in the same community to lessen the impact of leaving.

Triangulation

Another key term related to dysfunctional systems is "triangulation." Bowen (1978) proposed that the smallest stable emotional or relational unit is the triangle, not the dyad. He elaborated:

> A two-person emotional system is unstable in that it forms itself into a three-person system or triangle under stress....As tension mounts...it is usual for one to be more uncomfortable than the other, and for the uncomfortable one to "triangle in" a third person by telling the second person a story about

the triangled one. This relieves the tension between the first two, and shifts the tension between the second and third. (p. 478)

The goal of triangulation is tension reduction within the dyad, so that (in psychoanalytic terms) the negative emotions can be projected onto the other outside of the important dyadic relationship. Although triangulation serves the system's goal of survival, it is a pathological strategy for two primary reasons. First, it "short-circuits" attempts at genuine problem-solving within the dyad; the precipitating conflict is never faced directly and, hence, never resolved. Second, often the triangulated person is a family member (most frequently a child), and thus is labeled the "true" source of family conflict and difficulty. Bowen used the term "scapegoat" to describe the symptom-bearer in the family who, because of personal problem(s), allows the *family* to be seen as relatively normal.

GOALS OF COUNSELING

The goals of systems counseling or therapy relate directly to the definition of the problem. In almost every case, therapeutic intervention may be seen as an attempt to modify or alter the system's boundaries—both external and internal.

This emphasis upon restructuring a system's boundaries is perhaps most clearly seen in Minuchin's goals of therapy. In describing the process of change in family therapy, he stated:

> As a result of therapy, the family is transformed. Changes are made in the set of expectation that governs its members' behavior. As a result, the extracerebral mind of each family member is altered, and the individual's experience itself changes. This transformation is significant for all family members, but particularly so for the identified patient, who is freed from the deviant position....the transformation of structure is defined as changes in the position of family member vis-à-vis each other, with a consequent modification of their complementary demands. (Minuchin, 1974, p. 111)

Subsystems which were previously disengaged or enmeshed develop clear boundaries. Children become children again, not pseudo-parents or "parentified children," spouses relate openly and exclusively to each other, and the family as a whole seeks levels of involvement with the larger community appropriate to its goals and identity.

Although the specific techniques involved in eliciting these changed relationships vary from one systems therapist to another, altered patterns of distancing, roles, and involvement within the system is a common therapeutic goal (Barnard & Corrales, 1979, p. 95).

SYSTEMS THERAPY CLIENTELE AND THERAPEUTIC EFFECTIVENESS

Clientele
One of the truly unique contributions of ST is the definition of the "client."

Barnard and Corrales (1979) stated: "the client is the family, not just one member of that family" (p. 95). Minuchin (1974) concurred: "The target of...intervention is the family. Although individuals must not be ignored, the therapist's focus is on enhancing the operation of the family system. The family will be the matrix of the healing and growth of its members" (p. 111).

Thus, the system is the target of intervention, even though the system may have presented one of its subsystem members as the "problem." Although technically an individual seeking help could be appropriately viewed as a system, this is rarely the case in practice. Thus, Bell (1975) proposed that individual pathology is *usually* seen as an indication of a deeper level of disturbance within the family group. Not all individual symptoms are viewed as being family related; some may be organic or in other ways physical. But insofar as it is suitable to say that an individual's difficulties are created by or are the product of the family life, it is appropriate to say that the family is disturbed. The individual, presenting symptom is only a starting point for family interaction in therapy. While not dismissing the presenting symptom as unimportant, it is not the focus of the therapy.

Research

Gurman and Kniskern (1978) provide an exhaustive review of the empirical effectiveness of marital and family (essentially systems) therapy. They concluded that a conjoint systems therapy approach to working therapeutically with an "individual" problem is at least as effective, if not more so, than traditional individual therapy approaches. If, indeed, some individual problems are symptomatic expressions of dysfunctional systems, then changes in the system eliminate the need for the symptom. Even such "individual" problems as asthma, obesity, and anorexia nervosa have been treated very effectively and *indirectly* (i.e., not as the focus of treatment) by treating the larger system in which the individual problem is seen as functional (Minuchin, 1974).

Gurman and Kniskern also concluded that a conjoint systems approach to the treatment of marital problems is much more effective than working with only one spouse or seeing both spouses separately. It produces faster change, and involves less risk of divorce than individual treatment, particularly when both are motivated to seek change.

Thus systems therapy, with its theoretical emphasis upon relationships and role modification, creates a setting in which systemic change can occur. Its major stress has been upon altering dysfunctional marital and family relations, although some have expanded this scope to include larger social systems (e.g. Bell, 1978).

The approaches which fall under the systems "umbrella" range from those which are relatively structured and inactive (Bell, 1975; Skynner, 1976) to those which are much more "free-wheeling" and active (Napier & Whitaker, 1978). Their effectiveness lies, perhaps, not so much in the specific techniques of the therapist, as in their ability to tap the potency for self-healing inherent in any system, particularly kinship systems.

INTEGRATION

With its roots in biology and other natural sciences, there is little obvious relationship or easy integration of ST with the theology of the Holy Spirit. There are some ways, however, in which ST can be related to the Pentecostal counselor's understanding of God and to the practice in the counseling office. These are reflected in the following pages with the hope that such an attempted integration represents more substance than trivia.

Integration at the Theoretical Level

Systems theorists have stressed that a system can exist at any level of organization. What is a system at one level is a subsystem at a higher level or larger viewpoint. Thus, a person is a system, yet is also a subsystem of a marriage, a family, a work force, etc. In this sense, it is reasonable to view the Holy Spirit as part of a larger system—a "suprasystem" to use systems terminology—in which we are a subsystem. Paul reflects this perspective on Mars Hill in Athens when he states that God is, "not far from every one of us: for in him we live, and move, and have our being" (Acts 17:27-28). The implication is, of course, that even if we insist on focusing upon ourselves—our own system—we are nonetheless still part of a greater system, God's system. The flexibility provided by a systems viewpoint allows us to redirect our attention and perspective quickly to reaffirm that we are "in Him"—in His system.

The Holy Spirit, for those who will risk acknowledging His reality and their own role in this larger system, is not a silent, passive subsystem. He is a communicator, and as such, He touches us with His energy and power. The systems principles relevant here are: (a) energy is the basic ingredient of any system; (b) energy for human systems (and also for this larger God-Man system) exists primarily in the form of communication; and (c) transmission of energy (communication) from one system to another is essential for the survival and maintenance of systems. Throughout the revelation (communication) of God to humanity called the Bible, God has revealed Himself as a communicator. He spoke the world into existence (Gen. 1:3). He "spoke" with Moses (Gen. 3:4-22), and "spoke" through the prophets to Israel and other nations. He "called" Abraham on more than one occasion (e.g. Gen. 12:1). In the New Testament, after Christ's ascension into Heaven, most of God's communication came through the ministry of the Holy Spirit in supernatural ways (1 Cor. 14). The role of the Holy Spirit in the process of inspiring certain men to write the various books of the Bible further illustrates His variety in methods of communication to our "systems."

In every case, when He communicates there is an energizing element present; in some cases, this energizing element transcends anything previously known to human beings (Acts 2:7-8; 4:31). Scriptural examples of this energizing via communication with the Holy Spirit would be helpful. In 1 Corinthians 14:4, Paul states that speaking in an unknown tongue, by the direction and enabling of the Spirit, serves to edify, build up, or strengthen oneself. Energy is transmitted in the form of unknown communication; Jesus described this energy as "power" in Acts 1:8. However, Paul further states that the person who prophesies edifies the entire church. If the perspective is held that prophecy is God the Holy Spirit speaking supernaturally through an individual, then the same energizing-communicating process is evident. In this case, however, the entire church (system) is energized or built up. Additional illustrations are evident in 1 Corinthians 12 and 14, and throughout the book of Acts, where the Spirit energized normal people to accomplish supernatural feats.

If the Holy Spirit can touch my life—my system—and can change me by communicating with me, then it is imperative that I must not neglect those normal means by which He does so: praying in private, reading the Scriptures which He inspired, and listening to preachers who are anointed by Him to speak to me. All three means are undeniably biblical and essential for the Spirit-led counselor.

A systems concept particularly relevant to the present discussion is *synergy.* Synergetic systems enjoy expansion, increased differentiation, and growth. Individuals, marriages, families, churches, and counseling systems are all capable of being synergistic. I would not argue that a system must encounter and communicate with the Holy Spirit in order to be described as synergistic. Communication with Him, however, whether in individual prayer, in family devotions, or in prayer at the start of a counseling session, will flood our lives with His divine power, and will transform us into growing, synergetic beings. The word-picture Christ painted of a river of living water flowing and flooding out of us is most descriptive of the synergistic nature of the Spirit-filled life (John 7:38-39).

A final aspect of the work of the Holy Spirit from a systems viewpoint must be noted. It was mentioned earlier in this chapter that a systems definition of pathology lay in the dysfunctional nature of the system's boundaries (internal and external). Given this, if the Spirit's activities have relevance from a systems view, there must be evidence of His ability to reorganize boundaries either by His direct influence or by the work of those to whom He gives gifts and direction. The Scriptures, in my view, do provide such evidence.

When Jesus commanded His followers to wait in Jerusalem for the outpouring of the Holy Spirit following His ascension to Heaven, He left behind a group of bewildered, somewhat fearful believers. They could not doubt the reality of Christ's resurrection, yet they could not fully believe it either. In sum, they were ineffective in living the kind of life Jesus had stated would be descriptive of His disciples (Mark 16:17-18). Their system was clearly an entropic, dying one. Yet with the outpouring of the Holy Spirit on the day of Pentecost came a restructuring of the nature of this system. They were no longer closed to the outside community because of fear and confusion. Instead they boldly, dynamically, and supernaturally proclaimed the glory of God in diverse native languages for the benefit of foreigners present to hear them. With great anointing Peter preached that salvation came only through the name of Jesus—the very Person brought to the Cross by some of those listening! The external boundary of the infant Church's system was opened by the Spirit. And with fear replaced by power, the disciples impacted the larger system in Jerusalem, and later in the entire known world.

In systems terms, the early Church, empowered by the Spirit, was clearly *morphogenic*. It grew in membership (Acts 2:41; 5:14), and in diversity of function (Acts 6:1-7). The structure of the Church was changing, yet it remained the Church; it achieved that dynamic balance called "steady state." On an individual level, the same "steady state" is possible; we can remain ourselves in the sense of being self-consistent even while adapting to changes in society, family, and our own bodies through maturing and aging. In theological terms, being led by the Spirit (Rom. 8:4-14) would certainly produce a steady state balance between stability and predictability (Ps. 1:3), and continual change and transformation (2 Cor. 3:18). It results in continual modification of our systems structure, organization, and nature, by the influence of and our communication and fellowship with the Spirit. The Holy Spirit is indeed an expert change agent!

Application and Implications of an Integrated Theory
The contributions of various social theorists to a systemic understanding of the emergence of a sense of "self" out of social contact with significant others have been highlighted previously. If the self is shaped by the opinions and views of others, and if this is a lifetime shaping process as the theorists imply, then the counselor would be well advised to share with the seeking client God's perspective as revealed in the Scriptures.

Reading scriptural passages during a counseling session and assigning homework consisting of Scripture reading is not only "spiritual," but it makes sense theoretically because the person would be hearing directly from the One who is (or hopefully would become) the most "significant" Other.

A most obvious application of this integration is that the Spirit can actually become part of the therapeutic system. This would be predicated upon the helper's belief (and perhaps the client's also) that He is a reality, is truly transcendent, and is interpersonally effective. Systemically, this would be labeled as an open boundary between the human therapeutic system and the divine suprasystem. This openness can be facilitated by the counselor's private prayer before the session, by meditation upon those Scriptures which the Spirit illuminates as relevant to the client's problem, and by actually inviting the Spirit to "join" the system at the start of the counseling session. It may also be expressed by the counselor's stopping during a critical point in the counseling hour and praying for supernatural wisdom and guidance.

The preceding discussion introduces one of the Holy Spirit's specialties which is extremely relevant for counseling. The Spirit is the Person who convicts us of sin and draws us to God the Father. As such, He is an expert at overcoming resistance. Client resistance, ranging from passive quietness and withdrawal to active belligerence and intimidation, is a topic which is regularly addressed in counseling and psychological journals, books, and seminars. Often, people do find themselves in a counselor's office without being wildly enthusiastic about it! This is particularly true when the counselor is working with a couple (one spouse wants help desperately, the other appears to be uncaring), a family ("just fix our kid, there's nothing wrong with us!"), and in those situations in which a single client is being forced or coerced to seek help by a school system, legal system, pastor, etc. A number of effective therapeutic techniques have been developed for use in such cases. But the counselor who relies upon additional help and guidance from the Holy Spirit is inviting the aid of a resistance expert.

If the counselor actively seeks the involvement of the Spirit of God in the counseling process, it is only reasonable that the gifts of the Spirit, discussed in Chapter 3, may also be a part of the helping process. The counselor may be supernaturally gifted at a given time with divine knowledge, wisdom, discernment, or faith to pray for emotional healing. There have been some times (perhaps too few) when I have been keenly aware of a need to explore an area in a client's life which we had not previously discussed. There have also been times when I have requested that my client pray for me, and have seen God touch both of our lives in a deep, powerful way.

The counselor must recognize that the ultimate in boundary transformation and reorganization of an individual's systems is acceptance of Jesus Christ as personal Savior, made possible by the work of the Spirit. It is tempting for psychologically and diagnostically oriented helpers to overlook the impact of sin in emotional distress, or to nullify it by never mentioning and confronting it during the counseling session. If the counselor invites the Spirit to participate actively in the session—to be a part of the therapeutic system with an unbeliever—then the work of the Spirit in redemption and transformation from darkness into light must remain a real possibility and priority for the therapist.

Related to the difficulty of system boundaries being too open or too closed, Forgarty, Bowen and others have indicated that the essence of emotional dysfunction lies in fusing (too close) or in distancing (too far). A relevant question for the counselor is, "How does the Holy Spirit impact upon these extremes?" A partial answer is seen in 1 Corinthians 12, which is a beautiful description of a close, unified body, with distinct members, each of whom functions uniquely yet interdependently. With the Spirit directing the Church, we do not become a single cell—some giant amoeba—in which identity and separateness are lost, submerged into a great "us"ness. Neither are we drawn into a totally separate isolation and self-sufficiency. The Spirit calls us into a dynamic tension of respecting individuality *and* functioning as a part of a larger system. Thus, He balances the tendency to move toward undifferentiation at one extreme and isolation at the other. At a practical level, the client can say "I need your help" without the threat of loss of self, and the counselor can insist that the client work toward self-reliance, while providing needed, temporary assistance. Dealing with the client's potential overdependence upon the counselor (fusion) or premature termination of counseling because of struggles related to dependence (flight) is potentially made much easier with the counselor's reliance upon the Spirit as an additional member of the therapeutic team.

SUMMARY

Systems Theory provides a view of reality which places the context of psychological dysfunction in social and family relations. It stresses the importance of patterns of behaviors as indicators of systemic organization and goals. Communication is a key barometer of the health of a system; both destructive and constructive communication patterns can be observed, particularly within family systems.

Many points of similarity exist between ST and a biblical understanding of the Church and the manner in which the Holy Spirit functions within the Church. By implication and extension (because counseling as such is not discussed in the Bible) these similarities may also be appreciated in understanding the way in which the Spirit operates within the counseling setting.

The systems perspective of reality does, however, have a weakness for the Spirit-filled counselor; it lies in the absence of the construct of sin in explaining human behavior and mental distress. The destructiveness of sin, evidenced throughout history and in the lives of biblical characters (e.g. David with Bathsheba) stands apart from the contributions which systems thinking can make to the Spirit-filled counselor.

The strength of a systems approach lies primarily in alerting the counselor to the complex interpersonal dynamics to be dealt with and (hopefully) to be understood. This is particularly true of family dynamics; a systems view will guide the counselor in determining who should be a part of the therapeutic system at any given time. The evidence, both theoretical and empirical, is simply too strong to continue to believe that individual counseling, with an underlying assumption of *intra*-psychic conflict, is the treatment mode of choice in many cases. With the aforementioned limitation noted, the Spirit-filled counselor could generally profit by adopting a systemic view of reality.

15

INTEGRITY THERAPY

Everett W. Bartholf

HISTORICAL DEVELOPMENT

Boisen

Integrity Therapy emphasizes action on the part of the *counselee*. As a theory, it has its origins in the experiences and writings of Anton Boisen, but it has been expanded by Mowrer and Drakeford.

One of the first advocates of a departure from a Freudian-based "impulse theory" was Anton T. Boisen. As a result of his stay in a mental hospital, Boisen saw an opportunity for ministers to be involved in the treatment of those with emotional difficulties; he established the Clinical Pastoral Education movement to facilitate ministerial involvement in psychotherapy. He contended that during his hospitalization the doctors continually disregarded his conscience and attempted to lower his values in order for him to be able to accept his behavior.

Boisen (in Drakeford, 1967) recounted a conversation with his doctor, "the very charming young doctor pointed out that one must not hold the reins too tightly in dealing with the sex instinct. Nature, he said, must have its way" (p. 28).

Boisen believed his hospitalization was shortened when he came to see that his *behavior* was inappropriate, not his *value system*. In establishing the Clinical Pastoral Education movement, his hope was that ministers and therapists would again recognize the importance of one's behavior being in compliance with one's values. He lamented that, in psychiatric facilities, there was a

> tendency to accept Freudian doctrine on authority without scrutinizing it closely, and a failure to ask the questions which are of first importance to the student of religion. I was especially troubled by a tendency to accept the easy solutions to some of the perennial problems of sin and salvation. Take, for example, a patient who is torn with conflict between the demands of conscience and his erotic desire and impulses. The solution offered by some of our chaplain-supervisors was that of getting rid of the conflict by lowering the conscience threshold. (in Drakeford, 1967, p. 139)

Mowrer

Although Boisen's influence on the mental health community did not meet with his expectations, another period of hospitalization was to effect yet another, more prolific writer: O. Hobart Mowrer. Mowrer was president of the American Psychological Association in 1953, and for many years was a research psychologist at the University of Illinois. He had undergone several years of psychoanalysis and eventually succumbed to severe depression resulting in his hospitalization during the year he served as president of the American Psychological Association.

Mowrer (1964) began to theorize that his depression was a manifestation of guilt for past actions. He came to see guilt as a useful and trustworthy mechanism for reminding one of past misconduct which must be resolved rather than rationalized. Mowrer began to tell his story to others and, through this process of openness, he found freedom from his depression. He found not only relief for himself, but discovered that those with whom he shared also began to tell their story. He reinterpreted the role of the conscience, and the guilt arising from its violation, as healthy rather than neurotic.

He set out to confirm his findings and to have other professionals evaluate them. His work took him to the State Research Hospital at Galesburg, Illinois, (under provisions of a grant from the Eli Lilly Foundation), where he worked with psychologists, therapists, ministers, seminary professors and former mental hospital patients.

Flying to Galesburg on one occasion, several of the Lilly Fellows discussed a name or phrase that would describe this new approach to counseling. "Integrity Therapy" evolved from the discussion. On the plane that day was John W. Drakeford, a seminary professor from Texas. He has since become the leading spokesman for Integrity Therapy as a psychotherapeutic intervention.

Drakeford

Drakeford's contribution includes several books delineating the principles of Integrity Therapy. Perhaps the two most significant are: *Integrity Therapy* (1967) and *People to People Therapy* (1978). Drakeford's research and teaching have systematically applied the principles of Integrity Therapy to a wide variety of settings including marriage counseling and pastoral counseling.

For centuries, theologians have claimed that sin is the cause of humanity's difficulties, while guilt is the great motivator of human behavior. Freud, however, told the world that the conscience was antiquated and the concept of guilt was destructive; both were relics from Man's ancestral past. Freudianism was a relatively new approach which saw feelings and self-expression as the ultimate in human virtue; putting limitations on the conscience was harmful and restricting. Thus, Freudianism is often placed in opposition to the teaching of Christianity.

In order to reconcile their theological position with that of the counseling world, many Christian counselors began to call for a distinction between "real" guilt and "false" guilt (Narramore & Counts, 1974). The distinction was presumably that "real" guilt was initiated by the Holy Spirit in response to acts which violated

God's law, while "false" guilt originated in the oversocialized superego of the believer in response to unexpressed desires.

Today, pioneered by such men as Mowrer and Drakeford, Integrity Therapy offers the Christian counselor a new perspective in understanding the work of Freud, one in which the Christian counselor need no longer leave his convictions about the nature of humanity behind. Mowrer (1964) stated:

> In essence, Freudian theory holds that anxiety comes from evil wishes, from acts which the individual would commit if he dared. The alternative view here proposed is that anxiety comes, not from acts which the individual would commit but dares not, but from acts which he *has committed* but wishes that he *had not*. It is, in other words, a "guilt theory" of anxiety rather than an "impulse theory." (p. 184)

BASIC POSTULATES OF INTEGRITY THEORY

To explain the nature of humanity, Integrity Therapy draws from both the dynamically oriented and behaviorally oriented theories of personality. It recognizes the tremendous power of the unconscious, yet does not yield to the tempting view that the unconscious rules us without the possibility of intervention by our will. Integrity Therapy also recognizes the influence of society and "significant others" as we observe and learn from their behavior. This learning process is recognized and accepted as valid without overriding the will.

The postulates of Integrity Therapy can be expressed in the following seven principles proposed by Drakeford (1964) [italics added for emphasis].

> 1. *Integrity therapy rejects all deterministic theories which would make man a victim of heredity, environment, or any other force. Every individual is answerable for himself, and exercises his responsibility in making his personal decisions* (p. 9).

It is not so much what happens to a person as it is how the person responds to what has happened that determines the consequences of a given event. Integrity Therapy does not reject the influence of one's life history; rather, it maintains that we have the resources, through responsible living, to overcome life's difficulties.

> 2. *Each person has a conscience, or value system, the violation of which gives rise to guilt. This condition is not a sickness but a result of his wrongdoing and irresponsibility* (pp. 9-).

Integrity Therapy sees the value system as being an important factor in shaping personality. Much of our behavior, conscious and unconscious, is directly attributable to the voice of conscience. Shakespeare illustrated the motivating force of the conscience in *Macbeth*. The murderous deeds of Macbeth and Lady Macbeth cause their consciences to revolt so violently they both fall prey to neurotic delusions. After killing Banquo, Macbeth has delusions of seeing him at a feast while Lady Macbeth compulsively washes her hands again and again imagining they are still stained by the blood of those killed.

Rather than being our enemy, the conscience is seen by the integrity therapist as a friend. The conscience may be seen as consisting of values emerging from two separate sources. The first is the internalization of society's values. Significant others influence the values we hold as we learn from their actions, opinions and beliefs. The socializing process broadens from the individual to family and on to other social groups such as school, church, etc. However, the process of socialization is not completed with society's influences. A second source of values has been called the "voice of Transcendence" (Drakeford, 1964, p. 17).

Integrity Therapy is concerned with two aspects of the violation of our value system: (a) the *frequency* with which one violates his value system, and (b) the *degree* to which one violates his value system. Although irresponsible behavior need not be drastic to produce guilt, the consequences are the same. When one violates one's value system to a lesser degree, but does so frequently, the resulting neurosis may be of similar severity as when a significant violation has occurred only once.

> 3. *The typical self-defeating reaction to personal wrong doing is concealment. In this secrecy, guilt throws up symptoms of varying degrees of severity, from vague discomfort to complete immobilization* (pp. 9-10).

Conscience has often been referred to as a "still small voice" that lets us know when we have done something wrong. When our behavior is inconsistent with our values, this voice becomes the all too familiar twinge of guilt.

Cecil Osborne wrote concerning guilt, "either we must secure a sense of forgiveness and cleansing, or we find a way to be punished, or to punish ourselves" (1967, p. 99). Typical self-defeating reactions to guilt are rationalization, denial and repression. Even when denied or repressed, guilt continues to speak to us, becoming increasingly distorted as time and rationalization enhance its message.

When we ignore the still small voice of conscience it must speak to us in other ways. Conscience is skillful and creative in its attempts to communicate with us. Belgum (1960) has referred to this process as "the amplified and distorted voice of conscience" (pp. 306-307). This distortion may take many forms, but Drakeford (1967, pp. 23-27) grouped them into the following categories:

Organ language. Here, conscience expresses itself through the organs of the body, bringing pain and discomfort. Psychosomatic illnesses serve as the receptors for the conversion of guilt into pain and punishment. Treating these symptoms ultimately may only add to the discomfort in that we are not listening to the voice of conscience.

Affective language. This is often experienced in a state where individuals simply do not feel good about themselves. With depression, anxiety, and low self-concept, life often seems pointless and hopeless. Listening to conscience and resolving the guilt will lead to the extinction of such feelings.

Sensate language. When ignored long enough, guilt may distort the sensory process in such a manner that voices or other hallucinations are experienced.

Behavior language. One's behavior may become inappropriate in an attempt to punish oneself or in an attempt to be detected by others and eventually punished. At times behavior may become compulsive in what is often seen as meaningless acts. Rather than being meaningless, however, many compulsive acts are distortions of the original behavior which produced the guilt. Now the behavior has been amplified and distorted by the conscience in an attempt once again to be heard.

Dream language. Perhaps one of the earliest and least distorted mediums our conscience uses to speak when we have ignored guilt is through our dreams. Here, either veiled in symbolism or at times overtly realistic, we are warned that certain actions may "catch-up" with us, or in other ways "threaten our existence."

An understanding of the motivation of personality may be gained by thinking of a dynamic relationship between the id, ego and superego. Freud hypothesized that the superego, or conscience, requires the ego to strive for unattainable perfection while not allowing the id to manifest itself.

Mowrer (1964), although a disciple of Freud for many years, has come to reject this approach. He described the alternative position in the following diagrams.

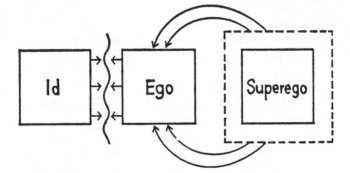

Fig. 1. Representation of the "dynamics" of neurosis, as conceived by Freud. A "hypertrophied" superego, or conscience, supposedly lays siege to the ego and takes it captive. Then the superego forces the ego to reject the claims of the id for any expression or satisfaction of its "instinctual demands." The result is that a sort of "iron curtain" is constructed between ego and id (see wavy line) and dissociation or "repression" results. Neurosis proper ("anxiety") consists of the "unconscious danger" that the force of the id will succeed in breaking through this "wall" and overwhelming the ego; there is a constant, devitalizing expenditure of energy by the ego to keep up its "defenses."

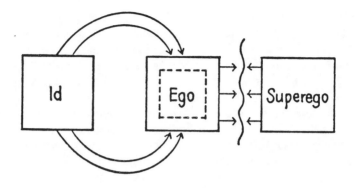

Fig. 2. A modified interpretation of the state called neurosis. Here it is assumed that the ego is taken captive, not by the superego, but by the id. It is now the "voice of conscience" that is rejected and dissociated. "Anxiety" thus arises, not because of a threatened return of repressed energies of the id, but because of the unheeded railings and anger of conscience. Here it is assumed that there is no difference in the "size" or strength of these three aspects of personality, unless it is that the ego is somewhat weak and undeveloped.

4. *As secrecy brought on his trouble and separated him from his fellows, so openness with 'significant others' is the individual's first step on the road back to normality* (p. 10).

Harry Stack Sullivan, whose theory has influenced the writers of Integrity Therapy, maintained that an individual learns to behave in a particular way as a result of interaction with people, not because he or she possesses any innate dispositions toward a certain type of behavior. Integrity Therapy, then, maintains that interpersonal relationships are a major force in shaping personality. As long as our behavior is in compliance with our value system, we interact in a normal and sufficient manner with those around us. We maintain an adequate self-concept as well as intimate relationships with others.

When our behavior conflicts with our values, we tend to withdraw, in ever increasing intensity, from those who are closest to us in an attempt to cover our weakness and mistakes. Our behavior becomes increasingly distorted and disruptive in order to maintain this robe of secrecy.

In order to remove the symptoms from a person's life, it is important to retrace the steps which caused the abnormality. This route requires the person to become open with significant others, thus revealing the irresponsible actions. Thus freed from the need for secrecy, the person begins a renewal of relationships and positive self-concept.

Mowrer suggested that all therapies encourage some form of confession. One of the unique characteristics of confession in Integrity Therapy is the emphasis on the confession of *behavior* rather than *emotion*. It is irresponsible behavior which has caused the dilemma and it is this behavior which must be confessed. The question asked is "What did you do?" not "What did you feel?"

> 5. *The process of socialization involves a group which could be called a microcosm or small world exercising both a corrective and supportive function for the growing individual* (p. 10).

Mowrer and Drakeford both have heavily emphasized group therapy. There is great value in groups and often openness is facilitated as group members model behavior by telling their own story. In addition, groups provide an opportunity for participants to receive corrective feedback. Integrity Therapy groups become an excellent place to learn new patterns of living.

Whether openness begins in group therapy or with an individual counselor, confession and restitution must extend beyond the counseling session to those who have been directly affected by the irresponsible action. It is confession, restitution, and a lifestyle based on integrity which is central to the process of Integrity Therapy. These principles bring wholeness and healing, whether learned via group or individual therapy.

> 6. *Openness by itself is not enough and the individual is under an obligation to undertake some activity of restitution appropriate to his acknowledged failure in life* (p. 10).

Confession brings with it only a temporary release from guilt and its symptoms. For permanent relief, one must take some appropriate action which amends for past misconduct. This is not action for action's sake, but activity which will set straight or make amends for our irresponsible behavior.

The theoretical matrix of such action is that people destructively pay for guilt through their symptoms. Confession and restitution allow payment to be made in a *constructive* manner, thus the guilt is appropriately resolved and the need for symptomatic payment ended. Here it is important to understand that I am not describing a process of paying for sin and thus being accepted by God through our own efforts. Rather, we are describing a process whereby one establishes and maintains a right relationship with himself and his fellow Man. Matthew 6:14, much of Matthew 18, James 5:16, and other Scriptures speak of the importance of confessing our faults to others and seeking forgiveness.

As a result, the emphasis of Integrity Therapy is on action, i.e., changing behavior. If behavior is the origin of our trouble, then behavior is also the solution to our trouble. A common axiom of Integrity Therapy comes from E. Stanley Jones who said that it is easier to *act* yourself into a new way of thinking than to *think* yourself into a new way of acting (in Mowrer, 1964, p. 68).

7. *The only way to continue as a truly authentic person is not only to remain open and make restitution but also to feel a responsibility to carry the message of integrity therapy to other needy people (pp. 10-11).*

Newly authentic persons begin to share their experiences with others as they integrate the principles of Integrity Therapy into daily living. As these principles begin to permeate all of our experiences we continue to live our lives in accordance with our values and continue the process of becoming a fully functioning person.

GOALS AND TECHNIQUES OF COUNSELING

The goals of counseling through the process of Integrity Therapy can be summed under the following headings:

Establishing Dialogue

Mowrer (1969) stated that he knew of no form of psychotherapy which did not desire the counselee to be open and honest. Openness on the part of the counselee is a major factor in the therapeutic process; therefore, the counselor should attempt to bring about this openness as quickly as possible by establishing rapport with the client.

In an effort to reduce the amount of time needed for a counselor to develop rapport with a client, thus enabling the client to be open and honest, Integrity Therapy utilizes a technique known as "modeling the role." In this process, the counselor shares an experience of his own life which demonstrates an area of irresponsibility, thereby placing himself on the same plane as the counselee and opening the way for an honest interchange between them. Mowrer (1969) reported:

> When I was as honest with others about my life as I was trying to get them to be with me about theirs, they gave me more material in one two-hour interview than I had previously gotten in months of conventional therapeutic sessions; and I could work with people in this context with ease and a sense of joy rather than strain. The results were little short of miraculous! (p. 24)

According to Drakeford (1967) much of the time spent in counseling is wasted until a distinction is made between the *presenting* problem and the *real* problem. He cited an example of a counselee who told him, "I talked with the psychiatrist and he said he was a man like me, but it was all so vaguely stated. You told me about that crummy thing in your life and I felt I could share my experience with you" (p. 84).

The technique of modeling the role quickens the pace of openness and honesty in dialogue between counselee and counselor as the therapist takes a calculated risk to initiate openness by showing himself worthy of trust, making a gesture of openness toward the counselee.

Accepting Responsibility

The first step in helping counselees accept responsibility is to show them that they and they alone are responsible for their current situation in life. On the surface, this appears to be a rather harsh position for the counselor to hold. However, if we are held responsible for our own condition, then we alone hold the key to the solution. If others, on the other hand, are held responsible for the condition, then those others also hold the key to the solution.

Integrity Therapy does not ignore the effects of the actions of others, nor does it maintain that the counselee is responsible for the action of others. What is held is that individuals are responsible for their own actions in response to the behavior of others. In this regard, Mowrer wrote, "neurotic difficulties commonly, if not invariably, have their roots in unresolved personal guilt, rather than in the unfortunate or traumatic things which have happened to us" (1964, p. 94).

Openness/Confession

Once people have accepted personal responsibility for the present problem, it is important that their confession, which begins with themselves and the counselor, or a therapy group, be broadened into ever widening circles, letting significant others know of the irresponsible actions. A common question of the integrity therapist is, "Who else needs to know about this?"

Mowrer (1964) suggested, "letting others, *significant others*, know our weaknesses and needs involves 'coming out into the open' and is the only thing that is radically—and relatively swiftly—curative, corrective, redemptive" (p. 93). The process of confession to significant others involves confession of specific behaviors (not thoughts or feelings) to those who have been directly deceived or affected by our behavior. Indiscriminate confession to anyone who happens to be listening is not suggested. However, the broader the openness on the part of the troubled person, the more solid the recovery.

Confession, according to Integrity Therapy, must go beyond mere words of regret. Appropriate and responsible action, free of deception, must follow in order for confession to be complete.

There is always some risk in confession. There appear to be two important causes of rejection of the one confessing. These occur when the action has been rationalized rather than confessed or when the other person is experiencing a similar or identical problem which he or she is unwilling to face. In the latter case, the other person may project unresolved personal guilt onto the confessor. The risk seems small, however, in comparison to the possibility of a life of openness and integrity, free from the pangs of guilt and its distortions.

Restitution/Positive Action

After the counselee has opened his life to the counselor and significant others in his life, the next step in the process of Integrity Therapy is to undertake some form of positive action. This positive action may be constructing a plan insuring the irresponsible behavior does not occur again. Or, in some cases, actually undertaking restitution may be needed in order to make amends, thereby restoring the relationship with the offended person.

Learning New Patterns of Living

In its purest form, Integrity Therapy is not a temporary alleviation of symptoms but a long-term commitment. Although its principles often bring quick relief of symptoms, this is not adequate. Once past areas of irresponsibility have been resolved, it is important that clients learn to live in compliance with their value system in order to become fully functioning persons.

Since people often react from habit, clients must literally learn new patterns of living. Here Integrity Therapy relies upon many of the techniques of behavior therapy. The clients are encouraged to forsake old habits, replacing them with responsible behaviors in accordance with their value system. Drakeford (1967, p. 124) stated:

> It is sometimes said that integrity therapy is the fastest and the slowest, the shortest and the longest of all types of therapy....The price of meaningful living is commitment to the ideals of integrity therapy. It is never just a respite from symptoms but means entering on a new way of life. Commitment to the life of openness often entails a fundamental change of character structure.

INTEGRATION

Restoration and Regeneration

It is especially crucial for the counselor utilizing Integrity Therapy to integrate this therapeutic intervention with the power of the Holy Spirit. This section discusses several ways in which such an integration can be accomplished.

In recognizing irresponsible behavior as the source of personality disorder, and in stressing the resolution of symptoms by confession and restitution, it would be easy to slip into the trap of trying to pay for sin, thus "*earning* a right relationship with God." Through sensitivity to the leading of the Holy Spirit, the counselor can assist the client in understanding that payment for sin has been made through the sacrifice of Christ and a right relationship with God comes through accepting the atoning work of Calvary.

The need for confession and restitution in alleviating personality disorder is a *sociological* process which restores relationship with oneself and with one's fellow human being. It is only a process which opens the possibility for one to become fully human and must never be considered a means of *spiritual* regeneration.

Conscience

As a major influence in personality, conscience is "awesome in its power but persuasive in its influence, rewarding in its returns for cooperation, and exacting in its penalities for indifference'' (Drakeford, 1967, p. 14). Conscience prompts, prods, and encourages us toward behavior which is consistent with reaching God's ideal. Where, then, does this mechanism of personality have its origin?

As noted previously, the conscience is shaped by the processes of socialization and the ''voice of Transcendence.'' For the believer, the voice of Transcendence may be the most important element in shaping the conscience. Here, the Holy Spirit operates quite independently of any reliance upon society or the Church. He works in individuals to ''show that the requirements of the law are written on their hearts, their consciences also bearing witness, and their thoughts now accusing, now even defending them'' (Rom. 2:14-15, NIV).

The Holy Spirit, through the inspired Scripture, has provided a pattern for living by which we may measure the appropriateness of our values. Paul, in writing to the Romans, stated, ''Therefore no one will be declared righteous in his sight by observing the law; rather, through the law we become conscious of sin'' (Rom. 3:20, NIV). Scripture then becomes a handbook of daily living. It is our guide to appropriate human behavior according to God's perfect and holy standard. The psalmist must have had this in mind when he penned, ''Your word is a lamp to my feet and a light for my path'' (Psalm 119:105, NIV).

A word study of the word ''conscience'' leads to the Greek word *suneidēsis*, which literally means ''a knowing with'' (Vine, 1966, p. 238). More than simply an indication of joint knowledge, the concept is one of knowing together with something or someone. It implies a knowledge of right and wrong in relationship to God's law. Conscience, then, in the biblical view, is ultimately a knowledge, prompted by the Holy Spirit, by which we know if we are conforming to moral law and to the will of God.

It is only as we live in accordance with moral law and the will of God that we have the potential of becoming fully functioning human beings. Therefore, just as the Holy Spirit is involved in forming the conscience, He, too, is involved in alerting us to violations of our conscience. Integrity Therapy is rooted in the assumption that God has created us with the capacity for guilt—an early warning mechanism designed to indicate when our behavior is less than that which is required to experience life as God intended.

The Apostle John indicated that the Holy Spirit is a Comforter in the life of the believer (John 14:16ff.). What better comfort can He bring than to enlighten us to areas in our life which are not pleasing to God and which will lead us into sin or personality disorder?

Agape Love

In a theoretical sense, the Holy Spirit may be seen to be integrated with the process of Integrity Therapy through shaping the conscience and by prompting us, through guilt, to change our behavior when it is inappropriate. In a practical sense, the Spirit participates in the counseling session, providing guidance and wisdom to both the counselor and counselee.

It is important for the counselor to see the client in a positive and meaningful manner. Carl Rogers has emphasized that the client should be able to expect unconditional positive regard from the therapist. For the Christian counselor, unconditional positive regard is not sufficient; he must go beyond this and respond to the client with agape love; i.e., seeing that person from God's perspective.

Through the power of the Holy Spirit, the therapist is able to respond to the client positively. This response is not based on the client's history, but on the future: the client's potential to become fully human. It is the power of the Holy Spirit which provides new life, and through sensitivity to the Spirit, the therapist is able to see the potential of the client's new life.

The therapist, through the power of the Spirit, is able to respond to the past only in the context of helping alleviate its influence through confession and restitution. From that point, the therapist responds as though the irresponsible behavior had not occurred and in that sense models for the client the unconditional agape love with which God responds to us.

> One cannot "learn" to love in this way through reading or academic training. A person can only achieve a genuine agape love through contact and fellowship with the Source of such love—God himself. And this contact and fellowship is possible through the presence and power of the Holy Spirit within us. (Crane, 1970, p. 31)

As we walk with people through their most intimate hurts and failures, only the counselor who genuinely understands agape love can gently but realistically encourage acceptance of personal responsibility for irresponsible action and, at the same time, demonstrate unconditional positive regard toward the client. "There is no substitute—not even the best clinical training can take the place of a genuine concern for people in need" (Crane, 1970, p. 32).

Modeling the Role

Fearing rejection or judgment by others, people continue in their secrecy and deception, hiding failure and weakness. Yet it is this very secrecy which begins to separate them from others. Just as sin and irresponsible behavior resulted in Adam's hiding from God, we continue to hide from one another. Concealing our wrong alienates us, intensifies anxiety, and may keep us from the social support vital for correcting an irresponsible view of life.

Because openness and integrity are essential for wholeness in life, God has provided us with a principle which eases the fear of confession. In the Gospels, He instructs us to treat others in the manner in which we want to be treated. At the heart of Integrity Therapy is a process which implements this principle; the counselor models the role for the counselee by opening his own life and sharing an area of irresponsible behavior, its consequences, and the process of remediation.

Modeling the role is a process where the Holy Spirit at times, through the gift of wisdom or knowledge (1 Cor. 12), may prompt the counselor to share an area of life which, on the surface, may seem unrelated, but is later discovered to correspond with an area of irresponsibility in the life of the counselee. Having experienced this gesture of openness from the therapist, the client is freed to risk removing his own veil of secrecy. Prompted and supported by the Holy Spirit, the client now is able to share personal experiences.

The attitude of the integrity therapist is reflected in a statement attributed to John Bunyan. Upon seeing an alcoholic staggering along the road he commented, "There, but for the grace of God, go I."

Confession and Restitution

Another avenue of the Spirit's intervention in the counseling process is that of providing wisdom and direction in confession and restitution. Isaiah wrote, "Whether you turn to the right or to the left, your ears will hear a voice behind you, saying, 'This is the way; walk in it' " (Isa. 30:21). Through the leading of the Spirit, the counselee can be directed in the appropriate content of confession and led in discerning to whom confession can appropriately be made.

When restitution is needed, we can confidently rely upon the Holy Spirit to direct us in the same manner; we can effectively decide to whom restitution needs to be made and what activity will set the matter straight once again.

Just as Zacchaeus (Luke 19) was prompted to make restitution, the Holy Spirit is eager today to prompt the heart of the repentant person toward positive action which will mend broken relationships and restore integrity.

CONCLUSION

At His ascension Jesus, the Master Counselor, told His disciples that He would not leave them alone but would send another Comforter and Counselor, the Holy Spirit. With the coming of Pentecost, the greatest power in all of God's creation was made available to all believers. That power which created and now sustains the entire universe is accessible in each counseling session to provide guidance and direction. The Holy Spirit can influence the mind and change the will of any who allow His intervention. "So do not fear, for I am with you; do not be dismayed, for I am your God. I will strengthen you and I will help you; I will uphold you with my righteous right hand" (Isa. 41:10, NIV).

It is the work of the Spirit which produces such positive character traits as love, joy, peace, patience, kindness, goodness, faithfulness, gentleness, and self-control (Gal. 5:22-23). He "is capable of working in counselees to accomplish everything that could be desired by a counselor who has genuine concern for the growth and maturity of those who come to him with problems" (Crane, 1970, p. 20).

It is impossible to separate psychology and theology as they relate to the counseling process. The object of counseling is a human being created in God's image; wholeness is achieved only when life is lived in the manner which He intended. Therefore, it is not a question of whether therapists rely upon the Holy Spirit or upon their counseling skills. We must equip ourselves with the best tools available, while being certain that the presence and the power of the Holy Spirit permeates our personalities as counselors as well as the methods and techniques used in the counseling process.

16

ACTUALIZING THERAPY

Everett L. Shostrom and Dan Montgomery

HISTORY

Actualizing Therapy (hereafter AT) emerged through the close personal friendship of Everett Shostrom and Abraham Maslow. Maslow (1954) proposed self-actualizing as a reasonable goal of therapy. Shostrom designed a system of concepts and techniques capable of assisting a client along the journey of actualizing. Shostrom and Montgomery (1978) extended the theory to religious life through a comprehensive integration of AT with Christian spirituality.

Essential Elements of Personality

The theoretical underpinnings of AT came from research at the Institute of Personality Assessment at Berkely by Leary, Barron, MacKinnon, and Coffey (Leary, 1957). Factor analysis of personality traits in a sample of over 5,000 cases showed that two dynamic polarities form the core of personality. These traits were labeled assertion-love, and strength-weakness. Other polarities labeled masculinity-femininity, dominance-submission, and independence-dependence were also found to be significant. For simplicity and to provide key reference points of latitude and longitude in the domain of feeling, assertion-love and strength-weakness were chosen by Shostrom to be the core elements in AT. These compass points of the self correspond to Maslow's classic research on personality (1954); he found that actualizing people express tender love and assertion with ease, and that they are competent and strong, yet keenly aware of weakness.

A superb example for understanding the actualizing life is Jesus Christ. He possessed a capacity for spontaneity, emotional honesty, and self-trust that awed and inspired the people he met. He was flexible and authentic in expressing himself in each of the four polar modalities. He could be *loving* enough to restore and free a woman caught in the act of adultery when her accusers wanted to stone her to death. He could be *assertive* enough to make a whip and physically drive the animals from the temple and overturn the tables of the moneychangers. He could surrender to being put to death and buried in another man's tomb. He could be strong enough to rise from the grave, a victor over death itself.

A Spiritual Core

In addition to the concept of rhythmic self-expression modulated along the four polarities, Shostrom and Montgomery (1978) added a second key concept, that of a *spiritual core* which is energized by the *agapē* love of God. The spiritual core lends stability to the ever-evolving nature of the person. The spiritual core is an individual's God-given personhood, one's "God within." The Holy Spirit dwells here. The core reflects the fact that we are made in the image of God, and share with God the capacity for awareness, choice, and intimacy. Whether the potential of the core (one's spiritual identity and calling) can be actualized or "made actual" depends on a person's responsiveness to the promptings, intuitions, and guidance that may be referred to as the "wisdom of the core." Jesus conceptualized trusting the core self as doing the will of the Father, and said He was sending the Holy Spirit to perpetuate this potential in the believing Christian.

The goal of AT is to restore a client's trust in the core being, and to enable the client to become rhythmic and expressive on the feeling polarities in verbal, feeling, and bodily ways. Replacing manipulative survival tactics with actualizing growth-responses enables the client to handle problems of living having to do with creative self-expression, interpersonal effectiveness, commitment to values, and finding one's mission in life.

Influences of Other Psychotherapeutic Systems

An important dimension to the historical evolution of the theory and technique of AT is the close personal association of Shostrom with founders of other schools of psychotherapy. This came about primarily through a series of films which Shostrom produced on each of the following persons and their theories: Abraham Maslow, Rollo May, Carl Rogers, Victor Frankl, Albert Ellis, Fritz Perls, Alexander Lowen, and Arnold Lazarus. In addition to these psychological films, Shostrom produced several films of a more philosophical nature with Paul Tillich, Allan Watts, and Ashley Montague.[1]

In 1962, Shostrom collaborated with Maslow to produce the *Personal Orientation Inventory* (POI), the first psychological assessment instrument for measuring actualizing tendencies. The POI introduced a scientific research orientation to AT. It has generated over 250 published studies and is currently being used in therapeutic, educational, industrial, and religious settings.

Actualizing Therapy is a creative synthesis. From Rogers (1942, 1951, 1961) comes the focus on a client's feelings and the importance of nonjudgmental warmth between client and therapist. From Perls (1951, 1969, 1973) comes the focus on the client's awareness in the here and now. From Ellis (1961, 1962, 1973) comes the view of therapy as a process of revising assumptions about life. From

Lowen (1958, 1965, 1967) comes the focus on the client's body as a primary tool for diagnosis and therapy. And from Montgomery (1980, 1982; Shostrom & Montgomery, 1978) comes the idea that the spiritual core of the personality is a vital, life affirming energy that needs to be experienced and utilized in the client's life.

By selectively integrating the central aspects of each of the above mentioned systems, AT transcends the limitations of each of the parent systems, and develops an overview theory that deals more comprehensively with the total potential of the client as experienced and expressed in affective, cognitive, visceral, and spiritual dimensions. The Actualizing Therapist, then, develops versatility and flexibility in understanding a particular client's impasse in personal growth, and seeks to intervene therapeutically at the most promising level of client gain, whether it is the client's thinking, feeling, bodily awareness, openness to God, or a combination of some or all of these four aspects of being.

Summary
To summarize the historical synthesis that AT brings to the field of psychotherapy, Corsini (1982) wrote:

> One of my long-term and long-held goals is to write the definitive book on psychotherapy. In this book I will combine everything that I know from both my own experience and the experience of others to generate the final system of psychotherapy. Everett Shostrom and Dan Montgomery beat me to it in their chapter on Actualizing Therapy. Actualizing Therapy is intended to be the final therapy, combining all theories of known value—a synthetic supersystem, if you will, of the best of all known theories and procedures....in my judgment Actualizing Therapy is a step in the direction that we must eventually go to really become a profession based on science.

UNDERLYING ASSUMPTIONS ABOUT THE NATURE OF HUMANITY
Traditionally, psychotherapy has steered away from the suggestions of universal values. However, the polarities of assertion-love, strength-weakness, and the concept of the core self seem to us to come close to a concept of universal values that support personal growth and interpersonal fulfillment through the journey of life.

The Impact of Fear
Fear is the reason so many people get stuck in life and stop growing psychologically and spiritually. Or, more specifically, inordinate amounts of fear cause a person to stop growing. Everyone experiences fear. It is how we handle the fear that is so crucial to our well-being.

Since fear and anxiety are built into human existence, we must all learn to cope with these experiences. Psychoanalyst Karen Horney (1945) has emphasized the disabling power of fear by her term *basic anxiety*, which we define as free-floating fear.

Fear brings resistance to experiencing and expressing feelings. Fear causes us to constrict our feelings, rigidify our behavior, and lose sensitivity to others and to God. Increasing amounts of fear make a person more defensive, more desperate, and more emotionally numb. Fear is similar to cold; too much fear causes us to freeze and become inactive in our cores.

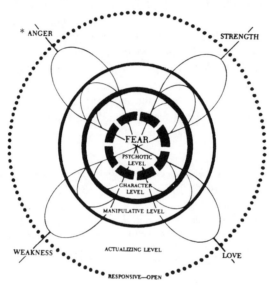

Figure 1: FEARFUL CONSTRICTION OF THE PERSONALITY

* "Anger" here equals "assertion" in the vocabulary
of Actualizing Therapy.

To understand how fear works to constrict the core, we use the analogy of the amoeba, a tiny one-cell animal. If an amoeba is repeatedly pricked by a pin, it permanently contracts itself to survive the attack. If a person is threatened psychologically or physically, especially early in life when basic character is being formed, he or she learns to contract bodily musculature and constrict awareness and expression of feeling. Control, rather than trust, comes to characterize the person's behavior. The stronger the inner fear and accompanying *core pain*, the more rigid and defensive the lifestyle. Core pain is defined as a person's reaction to the denial of a fundamental right to exist and to express his or her being in satisfying ways. At the deepest level of the core, there is hurt and pain reflected in the feeling, "Why wasn't I loved, given freedom to be or permitted the right to exist?"

Unresolved core pain yields defensive, survival-oriented behaviors that can be understood as the person's creative, yet self-defeating, attempts to get along in a world that is perceived as basically hostile. The behaviors can be predicted for each level of fearful constriction by understanding the specific way in which the whole personality was weakened by physical, psychological, or spiritual deprivations. Efforts to over-control organismic responses in life (i.e. feelings, thoughts, spiritual, and bodily responses) as well as fearful calculation in relating to others are the bases of immobility—"stuckness"—and life problems.

Three Levels of Deterioration

When a person is in the state of fear, AT proposes that the person moves headlong into three progressively deteriorating levels. Figure 1 shows the actualizing level as the outermost ring, which is usually experienced as a child. But when an individual leaves the actualizing mode, moved by the fears instilled by parents, teachers, clergy, or society, life becomes increasingly constricted.

As one moves inward from the outer sphere, one enters levels of reduced mobility, increased rigidity, and more severe "shut-upness." As the pattern of fear becomes more and more severe, moving inwardly to progressively more encased inner circles, the experiencing of the primary polarities of love-assertion and strength-weakness become more constrained. The center of the nonactualizing person is filled with *fear*, not trust or love.

Additional dimensions of Figure 1 which must be understood are the circles themselves, which stand for the ego boundaries of the person. The greater the fear a person experiences, the thicker the boundary becomes. For the *actualizing person* (at the outermost circle) the ego boundary is open and permeable, thus enabling the person to be responsive to others and to the many elements of the life situation. Such a person can be emotionally moved by the feelings or experiences of others, and can also react to others with the full intensity of feelings, without cover-up or masking. If such a person becomes indignant, it will show honestly and directly. If he feels loving, those feelings will be expressed clearly. If he chooses not to express a particular feeling, he is still fully aware of it. Vitality is not diminished as it is with the person who is fearfully constricting awareness of all feelings.

The progressive levels in the process of deterioration are termed manipulative style, character disorder, and psychosis. In each of these levels, the ego boundary becomes thicker and more rigid, as though the person were building a coat of armor or wall around the inner self.

The actualizing person is relatively free to experience and express personal fears. Such a person is able to live from within along all the polar axes of his being. Few people remain in the actualizing process all of the time, however. More common is the tendency to be actualizing part of the time and manipulative part of the time. However, if the person remains unaware of manipulative tendencies, such tendencies may grow like weeds and eventually overtake the garden of the personality.

Unfortunately, most people learn to relate at the *manipulative level*. This comes about when experiences that bring pain and fear result in a tendency to live in a more controlled, calculating way. Since the open and direct experience of feelings makes one vulnerable to others, the manipulative person closes up and becomes less straightforward in order to avoid any possibility of being hurt or frightened again. He relates to others primarily in mechanical and unfeeling ways, thus becoming less authentic, less spontaneous, and less creative than the actualizing person.

Manipulative behavior is stereotypic and compulsive, lacking novelty and choice. That is why it becomes a boring and tedious way to live and often leads to depression. As Shostrom pointed out in his book, *Man the Manipulator* (1967), manipulation is a way of using others to get what you consciously or unconsciously want from them. But the person who exploits people as though they were things loses the capacity to enjoy intimacy and love in relationships.

Manipulative patterns are based more on an abnormal level of fear and occasional calculating rather than on genuine, emotionally based responses to others. Persons stuck at the manipulative level are usually not suffering enough to seek professional psychotherapy, but they can benefit from the principles of AT presented in an educational or religious context.

In contrast to the actualizing person, the manipulator invests more energy in fortifying the ego boundary and less energy in living rhythmically and responsively. Even the body becomes tighter and less sensitive. It is as though in pursuit of security, the manipulative person retreats into a walled city and tries to hide there.

Next comes the *character level,* in which the person literally beomes a "character"—that is, someone who reacts in the same narrow, limited way to almost any input from outside. This level of functioning is even more emotionally constricting. The fear is greater than that experienced by the manipulator, and the person is more thoroughly stuck in rigid behavior patterns. There is a real inability to learn from new situations in life. Rather, the person reacts in the same stiff, repetitive way day after day, year after year. This is the level of most neurotic behavior. The games or manipulative patterns now reflect a rather grim, frozen stance against a hostile and threatening world. The walls of the self become still more thick and rigid. This level could be described as further withdrawal into a central fortress within the city walls.

Reich (1949) described a person who has constructed character defenses as one who has developed a coat of armor, much like the knights of old. The armor of this person is so thick and heavy that behavioral flexibility and emotional resiliency have been lost, therefore, the individual is unable to cope with life effectively. Stuck with the illusion that this coat of armor must be worn in order to survive, this person is actually severely impaired in the ability to cope with life.

Figure 1 also illustrates the *psychotic level*—the level opposite from actualizing. The psychotic person has a broken but rather heavy wall, indicating that, at the *chronic* stage, the person is strongly under control and closed to growth and contact with others. At the *acute* stage, however, the psychotic becomes fragile and disintegrative, and the broken wall suggests the chaotic flow from within. Differentiation of self from others is lacking and the self is fragilely defended.

The psychotic level is the desperate "Custer's last stand" against a world that is experienced as overwhelming. Everything is subordinated to the task of psychological survival in this crisis mode of existence. Fear has completely filled the center of the personality. There is no room for love, hope, joy, wisdom, or peace. The muscles remain chronically tensed or flaccid, depending upon the specific form the psychosis takes. The psychotic's behavior is bizarre and extreme. The person may hallucinate, repeat certain phrases incessantly, sit in one position for days, or act out in criminal ways. Meaningful and emotional relationships with others almost completely vanish. The psychotic must construct a new reality out of fantasies and unconscious compulsions.

Research on psychotics by Rothstein and Boblitt (1970), using Wolpe and Lang's *Fear Survey Schedule* (1969), has shown that the most frequently expressed fear among this group is the fear of losing control. This research supports the conceptualization of the psychotic as one who is chronically under strong control or who becomes disintegrative and fragmented in the acute phase.

Bleuler (in Brown, 1940) stated that schizophrenia is the inability to modulate affect. AT holds that actualizing includes the *ability* to modulate affect fully. If schizophrenia is the major mental disorder—and it allegedly accounts for 90% of the people in mental hospitals (Shostrom, 1976)—then it is logical to define actualizing as the opposite of schizophrenia. Indeed, the data of Fox, Knapp, and Michael (1968), based on the POI, demonstrated that hospitalized schizophrenics are extremely low on all scales of actualizing. The actualizing person, in contrast, develops the capacity for a "full feeling repertoire."

Expressions of Actualizing and Deterioration

The fleshing out of AT is shown in Figure 2, where most patients are located at any given time in terms of the *level* or intensity of stuckness, as well as in terms of the *vector* or polarity that undermines their attempts to achieve an actualizing life.

In a study by Karin Montgomery (1981), the researcher examined 35 verbatim transcripts representing 18 major approaches to psychotherapy to determine whether the five actualizing categories of assertion-love, strength-weakness, and the core self could be found in the clinical sessions. Her findings were that all of the client expressions of emotions could be readily placed into these five categories. Her study helped demonstrate the universality of the four compass points of the self and the reality of a central core within the personality.

Ideally, the psychologically and spiritually healthy person has access to all polarities and functions with the genuineness and balance that is described by

Actualizing Therapy

Figure 2

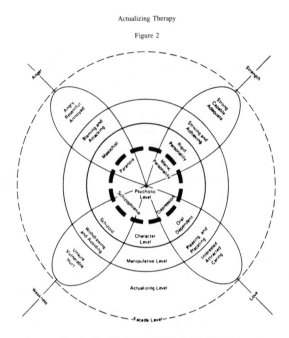

Figure 2: AN ACTUALIZING MODEL OF PERSONALITY

behaviors located in the actualizing level of Figure 2. As one becomes more and more rigid, the repertoire of behavior likewise narrows, and a person generally becomes isolated in a fixed and static position on one of the four polarities. Such a person's behaviors can be accurately understood by using one of the manipulative, character, or psychotic descriptions shown in the diagram.

It must be emphasized that only certain character traits or psychotic behaviors (those most exemplary of behavior on the assertion-love, strength-weakness continuums) are described here. While actualizing theory does not purport to account for all character or psychotic behavior, it does explain much pathological behavior as abortive attempts at actualizing: actualizing theory joins a theory of malfunction with one of healthy functioning.

ACTUALIZING THERAPY AND THE CORE OF SELF

In actualizing theory, it is assumed that energy is present at all personality levels, energy that provides the motivational force impelling the person to action. The more energy invested in fortifying the facade, repressing core pain, and utilizing survival behavior tactics, the less is available for actualizing growth. As an example, repressed feelings require energy investment in chronically tensed musculature.

The actualizing process, then, consists of aiding the person: (a) to become aware of core pain; (b) to express feelings that have been rigidly held back; (c) to experiment with actualizing behaviors, body awareness, openness to life, and expression on the four polarities; (d) to develop a sense of core trust in the self; and (e) to use newfound energies for effective and satisfying living.

In AT, we seek to invite a distressed person back into the warmth of human encounter to "thaw out" the core. We do this through vigorous action techniques that mobilize the person's core feelings and move the person from indifference to caring, from apathy to full feeling and motivation. Psychopathology may be understood in terms of limited or distorted attempts to actualize. Manipulative behavior, character disorders, and psychotic states (see Figure 2) represent survival tactics for getting along in the world when one has been hurt and frightened. Therapy, then, is a system of "rebirth" where the individual reexperiences fears and finds the strength to trust his core in spite of negative influences in life.

We define the core as an untouched, perfectly preserved sense of self—one's spiritual essence. The core may be threatened, resulting in core pain, but can never be destroyed. Individual therapy enables a client to make contact with *re*-pressed core pain. The client *ex*-presses intense feelings of rage, terror, shame, or longing that reside in the core as a residue from past betrayals or rejections. In time the person is invited into group therapy, where he has a laboratory for interpersonal relationships. In a group, the client works through ancillary feelings of embarrassment or guilt by learning to admit his manipulations. The client becomes free to experiment with experiencing and expressing the feeling polarities in the "here-and-nowness" of the group. *Dependence* in asking for help becomes *independence* as the client becomes more expressive at the core level. Finally, the client understands what it means to be *interdependent*: to be strong and yet vulnerable; to be autonomous and yet surrender to feelings of love for others.

TECHNIQUES OF ACTUALIZING THERAPY

Therapy is as much an art as it is a science. The artistic dimension comes from the therapist's ability to orchestrate the client's awareness in feeling, thinking, and bodily aspects of being, so as to transform rigidity into movement, and defensiveness into growth. The following techniques are therapeutic tools for facilitating awareness and change: (a) reflection of feeling and experience, (b) therapist self-disclosure, (c) interpretation, (d) body awareness, and (e) value clarification.

Reflection of Feeling and Experience

This is the reexpression, in fresh words, of the essential attitudes (not so much the content) expressed by the client. It involves observing the posture, gestures, tone of voice, breathing, facial expression, and eye contact of the client *while* he is involved in self-expression, and feeding certain information back to him in order to expand the awareness of what the body is doing. This technique is particularly effective for focusing on contradictions between what the client says he feels and what the therapist sees his total organism saying.

Disclosure of the Therapist's Feelings
The client in therapy is provided with a real human encounter. The therapist needs courage to express perceptions of the client as well as to discuss candidly his own personal weakness and defenses. In so doing he models a basic tenet of AT: Owning your weakness is a precursor of actualizing your strengths.

Interpretation
This is an attempt by the therapist to present the client with a hypothesis about relationships or meanings for the client's consideration. Interpretation brings a fresh look at behavior, a new frame of reference, or a revised outlook on life. It provides the client with cognitive understanding of therapeutic experiences, and facilitates generalizing the client's growth gains to new life situations. Additional techniques for the intellectual approach to therapy can be found in Brammer and Shostrom (1977), Krumboltz and Thoreson (1969), and Lazarus (1971).

Body Awareness Techniques
Such techniques involve giving attention to the body and what it is expressing at the moment. To be able to feel fully requires that one get in touch with one's body. Actualizing Therapy focuses on three aspects of body work: (a) learning to breathe fully from the diaphram, (b) learning to relax body musculature, and (c) learning to express oneself bodily on the feeling polarities (i.e. assertion and love).

Value Clarification
This involves "prioritizing" one's values. Priorities are statements of needs, wants, and desires at any given moment. Priorities also involve a wide perspective of future goals and past learning experiences. A practical method of choosing priorities involves periodically asking the client to arrange the concerns and commitments most important to his life. The actualizing person eventually develops a system in which he is constantly aware of priorities and changes, and is ready to act in terms of committed values.

CURRENT PRACTICE
A study by Shostrom and Riley (1968) confirmed the hypothesis that experienced, seasoned therapists tend to be creative synthesizers. Creative synthesis means that a therapist may use a combination of techniques, or different single techniques, for different clients. For example, the counselor might choose

to use several different approaches with one client. Or he or she might use one model—such as Gestalt Therapy, Rational-Emotive Therapy, or behavior modification—throughout the duration of one client's therapy, but use a different approach with another client.

The strength of AT is its creative synthesis of many therapeutic systems around the central framework of self-actualization as the comprehensive goal of psychotherapy.

Those who seek therapy are most often people who are hurting inside, even though they are not "sick" in the old-fashioned psychiatric sense. In fact, AT has, in our experience, been used most successfully with normal or mildly disturbed persons—referred to in the *Diagnostic and Statistical Manual III* (American Psychiatric Association, 1980) as those with "character disorders." Actualizing Therapy has not been used extensively with psychotics.

Instrumentation

When used for individual or group psychotherapy, the POI provides an objective measure of the client's level of actualizing as well as positive guidelines for growth during therapy. In a study relating changes in POI scores to stages of AT, Shostrom and Knapp (1966) found that all POI scales significantly differentiated a sample of psychiatric outpatients who were just beginning therapy from those in advanced stages of the psychotherapeutic process.

The technical instruments of AT are a set of psychological inventories known as the *Actualizing Assessment Battery* (AAB). These instruments measure the dynamics of *intra-* and *inter-*personal functioning (Shostrom, 1976). The recognition of patterns in the person's historical development, coupled with an understanding of the major survival or growth systems that he or she presently uses, is important in launching AT and in suggesting directions that the client can take in the personal journey of actualizing. In addition to its usefulness in individual therapy, we believe that the AAB is an important research tool for exploring the positive effects of therapy. Inventories from the AAB, including the newly developed *Growth Process Inventory* (Shostrom, 1979), are used to measure survival and actualizing patterns in a wide variety of populations, including college students, church members, delinquents, alcoholics, teachers, hospitalized psychotics, and nominated actualizing persons.

Many psychologists and clergymen have been conducting "marriage enrichment workshops" (Bustanoby, 1974), in which they use the AAB as a basis for discussion of the health or "wellness" of the marriage partners. The AAB is particularly suited for workshops of this kind because it provides a quick evaluation of the actualizing status of the individuals themselves, by the means of the POI (Shostrom, 1963), and of the actualizing status of the relationship, as measured by the *Caring Relationship Inventory* (Shostrom, 1966) and the *Pair Attraction Inventory* (Shostrom, 1970).

The latest psychometric inventory based on AT is the *Manipulative Mastery Inventory* (MMI), co-authored by Shostrom and Karin Montgomery (1984). The MMI registers balance and synthesis in the personality versus fragmentation and unhealthy polarization.

Actualizing Therapy has potential for broad use, even though it is an eclectic system, because the basics can be taught in a two or three week workshop to clinicians, counselors, pastoral counselors, and others who have had a minimum of formal training in psychotherapy. We are actively involved in providing such training.

INTEGRATION OF THEORY WITH THE HOLY SPIRIT

Christianity is in accord with modern clinical psychology in declaring that not coming to grips with basic anxiety and fear blocks growth and fragments relationships.

Manipulative styles, character disorders, and psychoses are maladaptive survival mechanisms based on fear. Much human suffering makes sense when viewed as distorted attempts to survive in a world perceived as painful, frightening, and poisonous to the individual. Fear, the central mechanism that sustains the defensive stance, occupies the center of the personality for far too many people.

The primary teaching of Jesus Christ is not a fear-motivated message; rather, He moved people when He spoke of love, gentleness, and blessedness. The alternative to a fear-oriented religion is a religion based on free will and love. An emphasis on love stresses that Christ must be freely chosen. Too often, Christ is presented in the context of damnation and hell, and the convert becomes the object of fearful coercion.

Psychology has shown time and again that fear is not a permanent motivator. The examples of Hitler and other dictators have shown that people may be temporarily motivated by fear, but in the long run, motivation based on love is much more reliable and permanent.

It is experiencing unresolved fear at the center of the personality that results in the manipulative styles of living that we have examined in this chapter. But *when we feel deeply loved, understood, and accepted in the core of our being, then our fears are healed and we find ourselves on the road to actualizing.*

In AT, we work to generate within clients a potent sense of being understood and accepted. When they feel secure enough, we deliberately use therapeutic techniques to make them "stretch" to acquire the awareness or the coping skills that have been needed all along.

As therapists we do not feel naive in our hope that God can heal and guide people even though they have had their share of the harsh blows that life can sometimes give. As doctors of the soul and students of the psyche, psychotherapists and counselors have a unique opportunity to inspire the brokenhearted, impart courage to the hopeless, and give direction to those who feel lost in life. A Christian

Actualizing Therapist actively trusts the Holy Spirit to inspire these therapeutic encounters.

The presence of a supportive therapist or group makes it safe for the clients to experience strong negative feelings without constricting themselves or distorting reality. In experiencing core pain in an honest and direct way, clients find that it passes through them (emotional catharsis), and that they lose their fear of feeling. Releasing strong negative feelings from the core results in the emergence of strong positive feelings such as trust, harmony, and confidence. Thus, clients come to be more "at home" with all that they are, both the good and the bad, the negative and the positive, the manipulative and the actualizing. They learn compassion and the ability to forgive themselves and others for inevitable mistakes that occur in living. Thus, they mirror the Holy Spirit's life-affirming presence in the core of their personalities.

Individual and group work also seeks to uncover a person's needs at the core level and to satisfy those needs. Most people have their safety and maintenance needs met, but their love needs have been ignored or exploited. Fear can be replaced by trust in one's core as individual or group therapy helps a person surrender to needs for love and to have these needs satisfied in direct, realistic ways. As this happens, the person becomes free to move into esteem needs and self-actualizing needs. Actualizing needs are nurtured by developing a style of emotional expression and interpersonal trust epitomized by Christ's lifestyle of honesty, awareness, freedom, creativity, and mission.

A basic tenet of AT is that energy released from core conflicts becomes immediately available for growth and creative living. Availability of energy for growth, coupled with learning to express themselves along the feeling polarities, offer clients a wide spectrum of actualizing possibilities.

Our central integration thesis is that *perfect love casts out fear* (1 John 4:18, RSV). This *healing love causes the joyful expansion rather than the fearful constriction of the human personality.* The Greek word that is used in the New Testament for this perfect love is *agapē*. This could be translated as spontaneous, altruistic love that involves unselfishly willing the highest good of another. It is a love that cherishes, affirms, and respects the uniqueness of another person. When we say in religious language that "underneath are the everlasting arms," we are symbolizing the agape dimension of love that God has for every person; that love is to be experienced in a person's core (cf. Chapter 7: Lay Counseling).

The center of healthy psychological and spiritual growth is the core, the innermost being of the person. The core is not the raw, chaotic power of the unconscious that Freud portrayed. Rather, it is an innate guidance system energized by the power of God's love. It is out of our core that dignity, courage, and love emerge that we might live life to the fullest. The subtle nuances of guidance that flow from the core enable a person to become truly human, and to fulfill one's unique mission in life.

Maslow described the core *intellectually* as valuing one's own "inner Supreme Court." Rogers described the core as trusting one's own deepest *feelings*. Jesus, however, described the core as *doing* the will of the Father. We might understand the core as the place of divine support within the personality (Tournier, 1968).

Our spirituality is our movement from and into the core. The core is the involuntary energy center *into* which flows the love of God and *from* which flows love for oneself and others. As Paul says, "God's love has been poured into our hearts through the Holy Spirit" (Rom. 5:5, RSV). Thus, love is expressed through the core and love becomes central to our understanding of the core.

We realize that this concept of the Holy Spirit may not have much meaning for some who are oriented primarily to psychology, rather than religion. Consider with us the possibility that the Holy Spirit—this mysterious source of energy and power that may be difficult to understand—is the personal presence of God and the source of inspiration (in a non-theological sense) for growth and fulfillment among human beings; He is a gift from a loving God. Even some Christian readers may have difficulty accepting this premise, because the Holy Spirit has sometimes been viewed as that vague, amorphous Third Member of the Trinity who is spoken of in the Apostles' Creed, but is not experienced directly in daily life. But the Holy Spirit can give us the comfort and the power to live life openly in love, not in fearful hiding (John 16:13; Acts 1:8). "For God hath not given us the spirit of fear; but of power, and of love, and of a sound mind" (2 Tim. 1:7).

As Menzies pointed out in Chapter 2, one of the New Testament Greek words used for the Holy Spirit is *parakletos*. This translates as "One called alongside to help," or "Comforter," or "Companion." These meanings clearly indicate a most personal and intimate role of the Holy Spirit in supporting, nurturing, and guiding a person through life.

In coming home to the core, a person gives up the defensive style of living which is based on fear, manipulation, and pretense, which theologically may be equated with sin. He adopts, instead, a growth-oriented lifestyle based on love, trust, and genuineness. *Perfect love* replaces fear as the motivating dynamic of life.

As we have already pointed out, this process of change is often slow and gradual, for fear is a tenacious guest who is reluctant to be ousted. But given time, even in harsh conditions, the God-inspired personality will still bring forth its bloom in due season. This is a tribute to both the power and resourcefulness of the Holy Spirit and the openness of the person.

Time and again we must plunge beyond our manipulative and character patterns into the stream of energy which comes from the core. This reduces the significance of the defensive structures and opens up the flow of energies from the wellspring of God within our core. The core unifies the polarities and heals the inner wounds of fear, releasing a flow of power that replaces *fear of life* with *faith in life*. Thus, faith plays a vital role in healing, growth, and self-actualization. Sensitivity to and the guidance of the Holy Spirit maximizes this faith.

[1]All of these films are available from Psychological Films, Inc., 1215 E. Chapman Avenue, Orange, California 92666.

17

THE HOLY SPIRIT IN RELATIONSHIP TO COUNSELING: REFLECTIONS ON THE INTEGRATION OF THEOLOGY AND COUNSELING

Edwin P. Anderson, Jr.

INTRODUCTION

Much has been written concerning the activity of the Holy Spirit, but when it comes to the application of that potential dynamic, little guidance has been proffered. This is especially true in the field of pastoral care, where the activity of the Holy Spirit has been generally considered a prerequisite to effective ministry. However, this should not be surprising when one acknowledges that the Holy Spirit is an incomprehensible—yet imaginable—living Being.

Our finite minds have difficulty comprehending the mystical nature of the Holy Spirit. As a result, we are frequently baffled by spiritual interventions in the therapeutic setting. When a rational attempt is made to explain the Holy Spirit's activity, we have few authoritative words to guide us. The situation is further complicated by the reality that our understanding of God's ways is only possible when God chooses to reveal Himself to us.

Communication with the Spirit of God through prayer is essential for the counselor to function in the spiritual domain in a manner which complements rather than competes with God. It is desirable for me as a pastoral counselor and psychologist to begin each day with prayer. I believe that prayer engenders fellowship with God while establishing a partnership for effective counseling. As a result of daily prayer, I am free to operate confidently with my natural counseling abilities, knowing they are being augmented and sustained through a spiritual relationship with God, which, in turn, is maintained and supported by prayer.

Can the counselor who attempts to understand God's purposes and direction function conjointly rather than competitively with God; will he or she permit the Divine to demonstrate healing through human ministry? This is the basic question which this chapter addresses.

DEFINITION

It is helpful to develop a working definition of the Holy Spirit before attempting to apply His activity. A precise definition, of course, is elusive because the word "spirit" describes attributes found on both divine and human levels of existence. Therefore, the issue must be settled by degree of differentiation. "Spirit" is defined as "the activating or essential principle influencing a person" (Webster's, 1967). The term implies existence without material substance; on the highest plane, "spirit" is called God.

A COMPARISON OF HUMAN AND DIVINE ATTRIBUTES
Similarities

People possess a spirit similar to God's, but due to physical, mental, and spiritual constraints, we are confined to our humanity. The human personality is a faint reflection of the attributes of God. God created human beings with a limited ability to do as He does, and to be as He is. This has resulted in temptations for mankind that cannot be ignored. The Christian counselor may find that natural insights and compassion are therapeutic in their own right, and do not necessarily depend upon a continuing relationship with God. Thus, we are tempted to place ourselves in the role of authority while subtly—perhaps even unconsciously—usurping God's authoritative role in the counseling relationship. If we are unable to integrate Him into our counseling relationships and into our personal life dynamics, this powerful asset to therapeutic change goes untapped. Separation, therefore, becomes grossly magnified by our own choosing; the more the Spirit of God is misunderstood or avoided, the less credibility is attributed to Him by the counselor or counselee.

Cooperation

In a more hopeful analysis, the Old Testament gives many examples of people who sought to cooperate with the Spirit of God for ministry. Solomon sought perspective and divine direction to enable him to rule his kingdom in accordance with God's plan (1 Kings 3:5–9). Additionally, the prophets of the Old Testament dedicated themselves to comprehending and elaborating upon God's will for His people. In each of these cases, it was first necessary to perceive what God wanted, then to interpret God's wishes through the personality of the receiver-speaker, who in turn asked the hearer to apply God's message. Application of God's desire begins at the point of reception. What does God want? This question must be answered satisfactorily before attempting to counsel others regarding God's will for their lives. This cannot happen without using the proper channels for communication.

SPIRIT TO SPIRIT SENSITIVITY

How to communicate adequately, and, as a result, to know that what has been perceived, sensed, or felt is genuinely the Spirit of God, depends on another factor: personal commitment to and communication with God. True, the Spirit of God may utilize those who are not spiritually sensitized to accomplish His purposes, but consistent demonstration of the Spirit in one's life depends upon a continual association *with* Him and a willingness to be used *by* Him within the process of discovery and healing.

Counseling necessitates sensitivity to the counselee's need or problem. Without this sensitivity, a struggle ensues both for counselee and counselor. This is not to say that a counselor must identify the specific problem; that may not be possible in the early stages of counseling. The effective counselor will be aware that a problem exists and will be sensitive to the fact that the counselee has come to share a burden with one who is perceived as being sensitive and understanding, yet strong. Additionally, the Holy Spirit may enhance the counselor's sensitivity not only to Himself, but also to others.

I recall a counselee, a man in his late thirties in the process of separating from his wife. He found his feelings entangled in much anger and fear. Sensing his anger but not knowing the root of it, I awaited his response to my inquiry as to why he had to come to see me. He could not answer but sat in stunned silence, breathing heavily, with tense facial muscles; one hand grinding against the palm of the other. I awaited a burst of anger. It came in a flow of tears. My natural response when his sobbing had subsided was to inquire again concerning the source of his problem to determine what elements were contributing to his present dilemma. For some reason, I felt I should wait for Mr. G. to volunteer that information himself. I viewed this silent waiting as a counseling tool which was prompted by the Holy Spirit. A subsequent visit proved the waiting had been beneficial. Mr. G's feelings of anger and fear were now manageable and within his control. He had been able to get out what had been confined for so long. Now he was ready and able to look at the factors contributing to his marital situation and personal pain.

HUMAN RESPONSIBILITY AND DIVINE CHANGE

What element is at work which moves the counselor-pastor or the counselee along a path leading to successful resolution of the problem? It certainly is not tangible or it would quickly be packaged and readily purchased at any price by harried counselors. It is, instead, the grace of God at work—a demonstration of God's love through His Spirit.

The Holy Spirit establishes potential in others by inspiring them to wholeness in spite of their condition. The therapist merely becomes an observer of the living documentation of the Spirit's movement. The life force in the counselee should not be attributed to the counselor, but rather to the activity of the Holy Spirit. This statement may come as a challenge to those who feel they bear the responsibility for resolving their counselees' problems, but it can serve to lighten the burden experienced by those counselors caught up in consciously identifying with their counselees, bearing their loads, taking their steps for them, and finding themselves emotionally and physically exhausted in the process. On the other hand, counselors cannot emotionally divorce themselves from their counselees; instead, they must relieve themselves of the responsibility of bringing clients to emotional health by making their personal abilities available to the Holy Spirit. Counselors must permit the Spirit to deal with the "self" which God imparted through creation. Counselors are resource persons, not slaves or magicians.

I had been working with a female client (whom I shall refer to as "Ms. F") for several months without grasping her real problem. An accurate diagnosis seemed to elude me. Whenever we got close to what I felt was the problem, she would sidestep the issue, suggesting it was useless to work on her problems and that she "shouldn't be this way." I attempted to make clear to Ms. F that she would have to look at how she shirked her responsibility to herself and to God. Something seemed to "click" when her relationship to God, and the possibility of not fulfilling that relationship, was called into question. A life-sustaining force within her seemed threatened. This became her "impetus to wholeness"; her responsibility to God was indeed the therapeutic factor which contributed to a final resolution. I believe that the Holy Spirit's activity within her was important and crucial in bringing about this insight and subsequent change. Had it not been for this identifiable and experiential element, Ms. F would have possibly continued in her depressed state, succumbing to feelings of loneliness, hopelessness and anger.

The Holy Spirit as the Bearer of truth is able to "teach us all things and bring all things to our remembrance" (John 14:26). The counselor is then freed from the need to play God and is able to love as He does. At the same time, the counselor recognizes personal limitations and intensifies his or her reliance upon the Holy Spirit. Neither the expectations of clients nor the counselor's need for approval will necessarily determine the direction of the Holy Spirit's intervention. The activity of the Spirit brings forth the whole truth as He directs the process of discovery from His vantage point. He moves as He wills; His activity is not commanded or demanded. This puts the counselor in a position of waiting for the movement of the Spirit of God; it places the initiative upon God—where it belongs (Ps. 25:5). Thus, the counselor's skills are to be *utilized by* the Holy Spirit rather than the counselor using the Holy Spirit.

THE ROLE OF THE HOLY SPIRIT IN COUNSELING RELATIONSHIPS

When Christ gave His last discourse before His sufferings upon the Cross, He promised His disciples that He would send the "paraclete," commonly translated as "the Comforter" (John 14:16). As expounded upon by Menzies in Chapter 2, the counselor functions in the model of the paraclete by "helping" (Arndt & Gingrich, 1957), or by being someone to lean upon temporarily. The counselor should function catalytically to motivate people to health. Dewar (1959, p. 170), in describing the psychiatrist's method, stated: "he stands by in the same kind of way as the midwife stands by, in order to help to bring them to birth. What could more clearly show the working of the Holy Spirit?"

Another client, Mrs. B, had become increasingly depressed since the death of her infant who had died of an incurable and painful disease. She came to my office with the intention of finding a way to deal with her depression which had begun a month after the child's death. As I listened to her story, I noted there was something missing in her emotional tone; she was detached from the pain of loss. For weeks she had been avoiding an emotional response to her child's death for fear that she "would break down." Her loss had been turned inward. In angry desperation, she had asked for counseling. Her depression had reached the point that she feared she would be overwhelmed by it. It was necessary for Mrs. B to be led into the grieving process. She had avoided grieving because of a need to maintain her composure, "to be strong when everyone else needed her." She ministered to others but suffered within herself because her own wound had not been healed. Consequently, she had begun to withdraw from others, to lose interest in her other child, to become bitter toward her husband and his work. She found herself listless, uncommunicative, and hostile.

We began counseling by discussing the loss of her child and the events which occurred before, during, and after the child's death. I attempted to stay within the model represented by the Holy Spirit in Scripture by standing alongside—not bearing the entire load, but helping her share it. The process of grief began to take effect. She began to understand her depression, the causes for her loneliness and isolation, lack of hope, and anger. It was as if I only had to be there to observe the process of restoration. Some indescribable dynamic was operating during her grief process that eventually enabled her to handle her feelings without excessive fear. I believe the Holy Spirit had provided that helpful dynamic.

Scripture abounds with examples of the Holy Spirit at work in revealing truth and assisting those who are sensitive to the truth. Solomon asked for and received an understanding heart to judge, to be able to discern between good and evil (1 Kings 4:29). Elisha was observed by the Shunammite woman to be a holy man of God (2 Kings 4:9). Nehemiah discerned a false prophet (Neh. 6:12). Jesus sensed the criticism of the scribes and Pharisees (Luke 5:22), and the woman of Samaria perceived Christ to be a prophet (John 4:19). These few examples may only serve to illustrate how observant these people were, but just as easily, they may be interpreted to represent the activity of the Spirit in bringing or revealing the truth to these people. These illustrations may represent the potential interaction of the Holy Spirit with Spirit-directed counselors who, because of faith *and* counselor-training, are set apart to utilize the intuitive function of the Holy Spirit in helping others.

It is important to contrast the *inner strength* of the Spirit operative within the counselor with the *external influences* of the Spirit. We can recognize that the Holy Spirit is demonstrating His power through events apart from the individual *(deus ex machina)*, but we must also remember that the Spirit of God is a necessary factor in ministry. The power of the Spirit is manifested in actions taken by the one who ministers at the Spirit's direction and leading. In other words, the Spirit of God within us can be used to reach out to minister on the physical, tangible levels of human existence. In this manner, there is demonstration not only of one's own spirit of concern, but, through the Spirit-led counselor, the presence of the Holy Spirit stands alongside as a Helper in the therapeutic setting.

SPIRITUAL SENSITIZATION

How does one become sensitive to the Spirit of God? There is always the danger that if something is of value, it will be coveted, that attempts will be made to possess the object without the necessary prerequisites for its utilization. The Bible is clear in the book of Acts that such a procedure is not in keeping with the gift of the Holy Spirit. Simon offered Peter and John money in exchange for the spiritual gift of laying on of hands to bring about the infilling of the Spirit. He was vigorously reproved for his desire because it was apparent to the apostles that Simon's heart was not right with God (Acts 8:14–24).

The Spirit of God is visited upon individuals when their hearts are right with God. If that is so, then such an individual's apparent spiritual sensitivity comes through alliance with God and obedience to His revealed Word, rather than human efforts to be "spiritual." Alliance with God begins with communication and it seems obvious that communication with God begins with prayer (James. 5:16). The Scriptures encourage prayer for spiritual strength (1 Chron. 16:11); prayer is a necessary part of the ministerial role. If prayer is utilized, the counselor may more readily empathize with the counselee due to insight which the Holy Spirit has granted.

HUMANISTIC TENSIONS

Counselors occasionally become inflated with their perceived successes and may unwittingly replace the divine dimension of spiritual anointing in the counseling relationship with learned, human methods. In such cases, the therapeutic relationship tends to revolve around the skill of the counselor instead of the guidance of the Holy Spirit. It is indeed unfortunate when a counseling ministry offers to the public a service that is merely a human interaction without regard for the function—intervention—of the divine.

It is impossible to demonstrate to everyone in the counseling relationship that the counselor accepts and understands them. Unfortunately, counselors do, at times, have difficulty relating in a warm, caring way to clients. The counselor may feel obligated to "manufacture" concern in order to demonstrate acceptance and understanding. In the midst of this absurdity, is it any wonder that the counselee and counselor find they are struggling with a new difficulty—the therapist's incongruence—in adddition to the counselee's presenting problem?

The counseling relationship hits a low point when the counselor's abilities and/or motives are questioned. At this point, the counselee may be thinking of "shopping around" for another counselor, while the counselor may be considering making a referral. Such an unhappy stalemate may be due to the counselor's lack of interest in the counselee, the counselor's inability to deal adequately with his or her own personal limitations, or the counselor's attempt to rely exclusively upon the ministry of the Holy Spirit as a panacea which is void of theological or psychological reality (cf. Integration section, Individual Psychology chapter). It is likely that a referral *is* the best alternative at this point, but had the counselor been aware of these limitations and been sensitive to the Spirit of God, the counseling relationship might have been more productive. Wiksten observed:

> The pastor often panics in the face of the weird assortment of psychopathologies which confront him in people whose longing becomes expressed in personal crisis and breakdown. In his panic he decides that the pastoral counselee is "sick" and must be referred. In so doing he . . . aborts, at least for the time being, a possible birth of the counselee's longing and contributes to the submerging of the only force that might enable the counselee to get in touch with that which will satisfy his longing. (Wiksten, 1969, p. 31)

The focus of counseling cannot be placed on forced feelings for the counselee. Instead, the counselor must be transparently alive, cognizant of personal limitations, and while operating within those limits, he or she must allow the Holy Spirit to pick up where human effort falls short.

REJECTION OF THE HOLY SPIRIT

Counselees often rebel against God or the supernatural without knowing the reason, except that "fate" is against them or their "luck is down." To them, that is enough of an excuse to ventilate anger at any power—recognized or not. They may not name the adversary as God, but unconsciously they need to blame their predicament upon something or someone whom they feel is responsible for their plight. This may be perceived as a justifiable attempt at warding off depression by placing blame on an externalized object, rather than internalizing it to avoid becoming despondent and withdrawn. At this point, the counselor should be sensitive to the counselee's feelings of hostility toward God and offer love and reconciliation as the counselee explores the rebellion and anger. When these unconscious needs or motives are recognized, the counselee will more readily appreciate the presence of the One who has always been there, yet who chooses to work *through* rather than *around* the yielded counselor.

SPIRIT-DIRECTED COUNSELING OBJECTIVES

The objective of the type of counseling described in this chapter should be the experience and outward expression of faith subsequent to the counseling relationship. Through forgiveness and reconciliation, the actual application of that faith begins as one attempts—equipped by the Holy Spirit—to live in the real world. The result of this awakening will be a genuine experience of worship as part of the counseling relationship. This, of course, is contingent upon counselees' discovery that their personal struggles have been a deep longing for God.

Bibliography

CHAPTER ONE

Brembeck, W. & Howell, W. S. (1976). *Persuasion: A means of social influence* (2nd ed.). Englewood Cliffs, NJ: Prentice Hall.

Brunner, J. (1962). *On knowing: Essays for the left hand.* Cambridge, MA: Harvard University Press.

Eliade, M. (1965). *Myths, rites, symbols.* New York: Harper & Row.

_____. (1968). *The sacred and the profane.* New York: Harcourt, Brace, Javanovich.

Greenleaf, R. (1977). *Servant leadership.* New York: Paulist Press.

Jung, C. (1964). *Man and his symbols.* New York: Doubleday Press.

Lamb, W. (1965). *Posture and gesture.* London: Gerald Duckworth & Co.

Maslow, A. (1969). *The psychology of science.* Chicago: Henry Regency.

May, R. (1960). The significance of symbols. In R. May (Ed.), *Symbolism in religion and literature* (pp. 11-49). New York: Braziller.

Ornstein, R. (1972). *The psychology of consciousness.* New York: Harcourt, Brace, Javanovich.

Perls, F. S. (1969). *Gestalt therapy verbatim.* Lafayette, CA: Real People Press.

Ross, R. (1974). *Persuasion: Communication and interpersonal relations.* Englewood Cliffs, NJ: Prentice-Hall.

Schwartz, T. (1974). *The responsive chord.* Garden City, NY: Doubleday & Co.

Tillich, P. (1958). *Dynamics of faith.* New York: Harper & Row.

CHAPTER TWO

Behm, J. (1967). *Paraklētos. Theological dictionary of the New Testament.* Vol. 5 (G. W. Bromiley, Ed. and trans.) Grand Rapids: Eerdmans.

Bennett, D. & Bennett, R. (1971). *The Holy Spirit and you.* Plainfield, NJ: Logos International.

Glasser, W. (1965). *Reality therapy.* New York: Harper & Row.

Harper, M. (1981). *Walking in the Spirit.* Minneapolis: Bethany House.

Horton, S. (1976). *What the Bible says about the Holy Spirit.* Springfield, MO: Gospel Publishing House.

_____. (1981). *The Book of Acts.* Springfield, MO: Gospel Publishing House.

Ladd, G. E. (1974). *A theology of the New Testament.* Grand Rapids: Eerdmans.

Lovelace, R. (1979). *Dynamics of spiritual life.* Downers Grove, IL: Inter-varsity Press.

MacNutt, F. (1977). *The power to heal.* Notre Dame, IN: Ave Maria Press.

Marshall, C. (1978). *The Helper.* Carmel, NY: Guideposts.

Menzies, W. W. (1979). The Holy Spirit in Christian Theology. In K. Kantzer & S. Gundry (Eds.), *Perspectives in evangelical theology* (pp. 67-79). Grand Rapids: Baker Book House.

Morris, L. (1971). *The Gospel according to John.* Grand Rapids: Eerdmans.

Murray A. (no date: pref., 1885). *With Christ in the school of prayer.* New York: Fleming H. Revell.

Schweizer, E. (1978). *The Holy Spirit.* (R. H. Fuller & I. Fuller, Trans.). Philadelphia: Fortress Press.

Williams, R. (1971). *The era of the Spirit.* Plainfield, NJ: Logos.

CHAPTER THREE

Bittlinger, A. (1967). *Gifts and graces.* Grand Rapids: Eerdmans.

Chambers, O. J. (1965). *Workmen for God.* Fort Washington, PA: Christian Literature Crusade, Inc.

Gee, D. (1963). *Spiritual gifts in the work of the ministry today.* Springfield, MO: Gospel Publishing House.

Horton, S. M. (1976). *What the Bible says about the Holy Spirit.* Springfield, MO: Gospel Publishing House.

_____. (1980). Love is indispensible. *Paraclete, 14* (1), 20.

Palma, A. (1974, October). The working of miracles. *Advance,* p. 36.

CHAPTER FIVE

Carter, J. (1974a). Personality and Christian maturity: A process congruity model. *Journal of Psychology and Theology, 2,* 89–96.

_____. (1974b). Maturity: Psychological and biblical. *Journal of Psychology and Theology, 2,* 190–201.

Carter, J. & Narramore, B. (1979). *The integration of psychology and theology.* Grand Rapids: Zondervan.

Freud, S. (1955). Psycho-analytic notes on an autobiographical account of a case of paranoia (dementia paranoides). In J. Strachey (Ed. and Trans.). *The standard edition of the complete psychological works of Sigmund Freud* (Vol. 12, pp. 1-79). London: Hogarth Press. (Original work published 1911)

Gendlin, E. T. (1964). A theory of personality change. In P. Worchel & D. Bryne (Eds.), *Personality change* (100-148). New York: John Wiley.

Holmes, A. (1977). *All truth is God's truth.* Grand Rapids: Eerdmans.

Langs, R. (1973). *The technique of psychoanalytic psychotherapy* (Vol. 1). New York: Aronson.

Robinson, H. W. (1928). *The Christian experience of the Holy Spirit.* New York: Harper & Brothers.

Skinner, B. F. (1971). *Beyond freedom and dignity.* New York: Knopf.

Sullivan, H. S. (1953). *Concepts of modern psychiatry.* New York: Norton.

CHAPTER SIX

Brock, R. T. (1974). Memory and the Holy Spirit. *Paraclete, 8* (3), 23–28.

_____. (1976). The Holy Spirit and perception. *Paraclete, 10* (2), 29–32.

_____. (1983). The role of the Holy Spirit in counseling. In G. Jones (Ed.), *Conference on the Holy Spirit digest* (Vol. 2, pp. 130-135). Springfield, MO: Gospel Publishing House.

Coleman, J. C. (1979). *Contemporary psychology and effective behavior* (4th ed.). Glenview, IL: Scott, Foresman & Co.

Collins, G. R. (1977). *The rebuilding of psychology.* Wheaton, IL: Tyndale House.

_____. (1980). *Christian counseling: A comprehensive guide.* Waco, TX: Word Books.

Conway, J. (1978). *Men in midlife crisis.* Englin, IL: David C. Cook.

Coser, L. A. & Rosenberg, B. (Eds.). (1964). *Sociological theory* (2nd ed.). New York: MacMillan.

Crabb, L. J., Jr. (1977). *Effective biblical counseling.* Grand Rapids: Zondervan.

Czeisler, C. A., Weitzman, E. D., Moore-Ede, M. C., Zimmerman, J. C., & Knauser, R. S. (1980). Human sleep: Its duration and organization depend on the circadian phase. *Science, 210,* pp. 2764–2767.

Edelwich, J. & Brodsky, A. (1980). *Burnout: Stages of disillusionment in the helping professions.* New York: Human Sciences Press.

Faulkner, B. R. (1981). *Burnout in Ministry.* Nashville: Broadman Press.

Foster, R. J. (1978). *Celebration of discipline.* San Francisco: Harper & Row.

Goldstein, E. B. (1980). *Sensation and perception.* Belmont, CA: Wadsworth.

Hendrickson, B. (1979, January). Teacher burnout: How to recognize it; What to do about it. *Learning,* pp. 37–39.

Holmes, T. H. & Rahe, R. H. (1967). The social readjustment rating scale. *Journal of Psychosomatic Research, 11,* 213.

Maher, E. L. (1983). Burnout and commitment: A theoretical alternative. *The Personal and Guidance Journal, 61,* 390–393.

Meier, P. D., Minrith, F. B., & Wichern, F. (1983). *Introduction to psychology and counseling.* Grand Rapids: Baker Book House.

Ragsdale, R. W. (1978). *The mid-life crises of a minister.* Waco: Word Books.

Rediger, G. L. (1982). *Coping with clergy burnout.* Valley Forge, PA: Judson Press.

Sawrey, J. M. & Telford, C. W. (1968). *Educational psychology* (3rd ed.). Boston: Allyn & Bacon.

Schmidt, J. (1978). *New beginnings: Gaining control of your life.* Eugene, OR: Harvest House.

———. (1983). *Do you hear what you're thinking?* Wheaton, IL: Victor Books.

Schmidt, J. & Brock, R. T. (1983). *The emotions of a man.* Eugene, OR: Harvest House.

Silverman, R. E. (1982). *Psychology* (4th ed.). Englewood Cliffs, NJ: Prentice-Hall.

Wagner, M. E. (1975). *The sensation of being somebody.* Grand Rapids: Zondervan.

CHAPTER SEVEN

Barclay, W. (1969). *New Testament words.* London: SCM Press.

Carkhuff, R. R. & Truax, C. B. (1965). Training in counseling and psychotherapy: An evaluation of an integrated didactic and experiential approach. *Journal of Consulting Psychology, 29,* 333-336.

Gilbert, M. G. (1979, Fall–Winter). The therapeutic Church: A theoretical model. *Journal of Pastoral Counseling, 14,* 54–59.

Rogers, C. R. (Ed.). (1967).*The therapeutic relationship and its impact: A study of psychotherapy with schizophrenics.* Madison, WI: University of Wisconsin Press.

Rozell, J. V. (1983). *Christian counseling: Agape therapy.* Brussels: International Correspondence Institute.

Targett, M. (1972). AAPC membership information project, Part 1. Academic and professional background of pastoral counselors; Part 2. Context and clinical dimensions of the professional activities of pastoral counselors; Part 3. Patterns in the receiving and offering of consultation among pastoral counselors. *Journal of Pastoral Care, 26,* 219–244.

Truax, C. B. (1970). An approach to counselor education. *Counselor Education and Supervision, 10,* 4-15.

Truax, C. B. & Carkhuff, R. R. (1967). *Toward effective counseling and psychotherapy: Training and practice.* Chicago: Aldine.

CHAPTER EIGHT

Appelbaum, S. A. (1982). Challenges to traditional psychotherapy from the "new therapies." *American Psychologist, 37,* 1002–1008.

Blanck, G. & Blanck, R. (1974). *Ego psychology: Theory and practice.* New York: Columbia University Press.

_____. (1979). *Ego psychology II: Psychoanalytic developmental psychology.* New York: Columbia University Press.

Boyer, L. B. & Giovacchini, P. L. (1980). *Psychoanalytic treatment of schizophrenia, borderline and characterological disorders.* New York: Aronson.

Brenner, C. (1974). *An elementary textbook of psychoanalysis.* New York: Anchor Books.

_____. (1976). *Psychoanalytic technique and psychic conflict.* New York: International Universities Press.

Erickson. E. H. (1963). *Childhood and society* (2nd ed.). New York: W. W. Norton.

Freud, A. (1966). *The ego and the mechanisms of defense* (rev. ed.). New York: International Universities Press.

Freud, S. (1953). Three essays on the theory of sexuality. In J. Strachey (Ed. and Trans.), *The standard edition of the complete psychological works of Sigmund Freud* (Vo. 7, pp. 125-243). London: Hogarth Press. (Original work published 1905)

_____. (1955). Formulations on the two principles of mental functioning. In J. Strachey (Ed. and Trans.) *The standard edition of the complete psychological works of Sigmund Freud* (Vol. 12, pp. 213–226). London: Hogarth Press. (Original work published 1911)

_____. (1961). The ego and the id. In J. Strachey (Ed. and Trans.), *The standard edition of the complete psychological works of Sigmund Freud* (Vol. 19, pp. 3–66). London: Hogarth Press. (Original work published 1923)

Greenson, R. R. (1967). *The techniques and practice of psychoanalysis* (Vol. 1). New York: International Universities Press.

Hartmann, H. (1958). *Ego psychology and the problem of adaptation.* New York: International Universities Press.

Hartmann, K. & Lowenstein, R. M. (1946). Comments on the formation of psychic structures. *The Psychoanalytic Study of the Child, 2,* 11–38.

Horner, A. J. (1979). *Object relations and the developing ego in therapy.* New York: Aronson.

Kernberg, O. F. (1976). *Object-relations theory and clinical psychoanalysis.* New York: Aronson.

_____. (1980). *Internal world and external reality.* New York: Aronson.

Kohut, H. (1971). *The analysis of the self.* New York: International Universities Press.

Langs, R. (1973). *The technique of psychoanalytic psychotherapy* (Vol. 1). New York: Aronson.

_____. (1974). *The technique of psychoanalytic psychotherapy* (Vol. 2). New York: Aronson.

_____. (1981a). *Classics in psychoanalytic technique.* New York: Aronson.

_____. (1981b). *Resistances and interventions.* New York: Aronson.

_____. (1982). *Psychotherapy: A basic text.* New York: Aronson.

Mahler, M. S., Pine, F., & Bergman, A. (1975). *The psychological birth of the human infant.* New York: Basic Books.

Masterson, J. F. (1976). *Psychotherapy of the borderline adult.* New York: Brunner/Mazel.

_____. (1981). *The narcissistic and borderline disorders: An integrated developmental approach.* New York: Brunner/Mazel.

Menninger, K. A. & Holzman, P. S. (1973). *Theory of psychoanalytic technique* (2nd ed.). New York: Basic Books.

Peck, M. S. (1978). *The road less traveled.* New York: Simon & Schuster.

Small, D. H. (1974). *Christian: Celebrate your sexuality.* Old Tappan, NJ: Fleming H. Revell.

Smedes, L. B. (1976). *Sex for Christians.* Grand Rapids: Eerdmans.

Stierlin, H. (1977). *Psychoanalysis and family therapy.* New York: Aronson.

Strupp, H. H. (1973). *Psychotherapy: Clinical, research and theoretical issues.* New York: Aronson.

Wachtel, P. L. (1977). *Psychoanalysis and behavior therapy.* New York: Basic Books.

Wyss, D. (1973). *Psychoanalytic schools from the beginning to the present.* New York: Aronson.

Chapter Nine

Adams, J. E. (1970). *Competent to counsel.* Grand Rapids: Baker Book House.

Blocher, D. H. (1974). *Developmental counseling* (2nd ed.). New York: John Wiley & Sons.

Carkhuff, R. R. (1972). *The art of helping.* Amherst, MA: Human Resources Development Press.

Carkhuff, R. R. & Truax, C. B. (1969). Training in counseling and psychotherapy: An evaluation of integrated and didactic and experimental approach. In B. G. Guerney, Jr. (Ed.) *Psychotherapeutic agents: New roles for nonprofessionals, parents, and teachers* (pp. 558-564). New York: Holt, Rinehart & Winston.

Clinebell, H. J., Jr. (1966). *Basic types of pastoral counseling.* Nashville: Abingdon Press.

Egan, G. (1975). *The skilled helper: A model for systematic helping and interpersonal relating.* Monterey, CA: Brooks/Cole.

Frick, W. B. (1971). *Humanistic psychology: Interviews with Maslow, Murphy, and Rogers.* Columbus, OH: Charles E. Merrill.

Gibb, J. R. (1968). The counselor as a role-free person. In C. A. Parker (Ed.) *Counseling theories and counselor education* (pp. 19–45). Boston: Houghton Mifflin.

Greve, F. J. (1980). *Counseling.* Brussels, Belgium: International Correspondence Institute.

Horney, K. (1939). *New ways in psychoanalysis.* New York: W. W. Norton.

————. (1945). *Our inner conflicts: A constructive theory of neurosis.* New York: W. W. Norton.

Huber, J. T. & Millman, H. L. (1972). *Goals and behavior in psychotherapy and counseling: Readings and questions.* Columbus, OH: Charles E. Merrill.

Humphries, R. H. (1979, January). Is psychotherapy unbiblical? *Christianity Today,* pp. 26–29.

Nye, R. D. (1975). *Three views of man: Perspectives from Sigmund Freud, B. F. Skinner, and Carl Rogers.* Monterey, CA: Brooks/Cole.

Rappaport, A. (1976). Conjugal relationship enhancement program. In D. H. L. Olson (Ed.) *Treating relationships.* Lake Mills, IA: Graphic Publishing.

Rogers, C. (1942). *Counseling and psychotherapy.* New York: Houghton Mifflin.

_____. (1951). *Client-centered therapy.* New York: Houghton Mifflin.

_____. (1955). Persons or science? A philosophical question. *American Psychologist, 10,* 267–278.

_____. (1957). The necessary and sufficient conditions of therapeutic personality change. *Journal of Consulting Psychology, 21,* 95–103.

_____. (1959). A theory of therapy, personality, and interpersonal relationships, as developed in the client-centered framework. In S. Koch (Ed.), *Psychology: A study of a science* (Vol. 3). New York: McGraw-Hill.

_____. (1961). *On becoming a person.* Boston: Houghton Mifflin.

_____. (1964). Towards a science of the person. In T. W. Wann (Ed.), *Behaviorism and phenomenology.* Chicago: University of Chicago Press.

_____. (1973). My philosophy of interpersonal relationships and how it grew. *Journal of Humanistic Psychology, 13,* 3–15.

Truax, C. B. & Carkhuff, R. R. (1967). *Toward effective counseling and psychotherapy: Training and practice.* Chicago: Aldine.

CHAPTER TEN

Agras, W. S., Kazdin, A. E., & Wilson, G. T. (1979). *Behavior therapy: Toward and applied clinical science.* San Francisco: W. H. Freeman.

Baer, D. M. (1982). Applied behavior analysis. In G. T. Wilson & C. M. Franks (Eds.), *Contemporary behavior therapy* (pp. 277–309). New York: Guilford Press.

Baer, D. M., Wolf, M. M., & Risley, T. R. (1968). Some current dimensions of applied behavior analysis. *Journal of Applied Behavior Analysis, 1,* 91–97.

Bandura, A. (1971). *Social learning theory.* Morristown, NJ: General Learning Corp.

_____. (1977). *Social learning theory.* Englewood Cliffs, NJ: Prentice-Hall.

Beck, A. T. (1976). *Cognitive therapy and the emotional disorders.* New York: The New American Library.

Beck, A. T. & Mahoney, M. J. (1979). Schools of "thought." *American Psychologist, 34,* 93–98.

Braukmann, C. J., Fixsen, D. L., Kirigin, K. A., Phillips, E. A., Phillips, E. L., & Wolf, M. M. (1975). Achievement place: The training and certification of teaching-parents. In W. S. Wood (Ed.), *Issues in evaluating behavior modification* (pp. 131–152). Champaigne, IL: Research Press.

Dobson, J. (1970). *Dare to discipline.* Wheaton, IL: Tyndale House.

_____. (1978). *The strong-willed child.* Wheaton, IL: Tyndale House.

Ellis, A. (1962). *Reason and emotion in psychotherapy.* Secaucus, NJ: The Citadel Press.

_____. (1977). Psychotherapy and the value of a human being. In A. Ellis & R. Grieger (Eds.), *Handbook of rational-emotive therapy* (pp. 99–112). New York: Springer.

Evans, R. I. (1968). *B. F. Skinner: The man and his ideas.* New York: E. P. Dutton & Co.

Eysenck, H. J. (1960). *Behavior therapy and the neuroses.* London: Pergamon Press.

_____. (1982). Neobehavioristic (S-R) theory." In G. T. Wilson & C. M. Franks (Eds.), *Contemporary behavior therapy* (pp. 205–276). New York: Guilford Press.

Fordyce, W. E. (1976). *Behavioral methods for chronic pain and illness.* St. Louis: C. V. Mosby.

Hersen M. & Barlow, D. H. (1976). *Single case experimental designs.* New York: Pergamon Press.

Hilts, P. J. (1974). *Behavior modification.* New York: Harper & Row.

Kanfer, F. H. & Goldstein, A. P. (1980). *Helping people change: A textbook of methods* (2nd ed.). New York: Pergamon Press.

Kazdin, A. E. (1975). *Behavior modification in applied settings.* Homewood, IL: Dorsey Press.

Kazdin, A. E. & Cole, P. M. (1981). Attitudes and labeling bias toward behavior modification: The effects of labels, content and jargon. *Behavior Therapy, 12,* 56–68.

Keller, F. S. (1969). *Learning: Reinforcement theory* (2nd ed.). New York: Random House.

Krasner, L. (1982). Behavior therapy: On roots, contexts, and growth. In G. T. Wilson & C. M. Franks (Eds.), *Contemporary behavior therapy* (pp. 11–62). New York: Guilford Press.

Lazarus, A. (1979). A matter of emphasis. *American Psychologist, 34,* 100.

Ledwidge, B. (1978). Cognitive behavior modification: A step in the wrong direction? *Psychological Bulletin, 85,* 353–375.

Lewis, C. S. (1969). *Miracles.* In *The best of C. S. Lewis.* New York: Iverson Associates.

_____. (1970). *God in the dock.* Grand Rapids: Eerdmans.

Lewis, W. H. (Ed.). (1966). *Letters of C. S. Lewis.* New York: Harcourt, Brace, Jovanovich.

Mahoney, M. J. (1974). *Cognition and behavior modification.* Cambridge, MA: Ballinger.

_____. (1977). Reflections on the cognitive-learning trend in psychotherapy. *American Psychologist, 32,* 5–13.

_____. (1978). Experimental methods and outcome evaluation. *Journal of Consulting and Clinical Psychology, 46,* 660–672.

Meichenbaum, D. (1977). *Cognitive-behavior modification: An integrative approach.* New York: Plenum.

Minkin, N., Brauckmann, C.J., Minkin, B.L., Timbers, G.D., Timbers, B.J., Fixin, D.L., Phillips, E.L., & Wolf, M.M. (1976). The social validation and training of conversational skills. *Journal of Applied Behavior Analysis, 9,* 127–139.

O'Connor, R. D. (1969). Modification of social withdrawal through symbolic modeling. *Journal of Applied Behavior Analysis, 2,* 15–22.

Perry, M A. & Furukawa, M. J. (1980). Modeling methods. In F. H. Kanfer & A. P. Goldstein (Eds.), *Helping people change* (2nd ed., pp. 131–171). New York: Pergamon Press.

Rachlin, H. (1976). *Introduction to modern behaviorism* (2nd ed.). San Francisco: W. H. Freeman.

Ramp, E. & Semb, G. (Eds.). (1975). *Behavior analysis: Areas of research and application.* Englewood Cliffs, NJ: Prentice-Hall.

Rapoff, M. A. & Christophersen, E. R. (1982). Compliance of pediatric patients with medical regimens: A review and evaluation. In R. B. Stuart (Ed.), *Adherence, compliance, and generalization in behavioral medicine* (pp. 79–124). New York: Brunner/Mazel.

Schaeffer, F. A. (1972). *Back to freedom and dignity.* Downers Grove, IL: Intervarsity Press.

Skinner, B. F. (1948). *Walden two.* New York: MacMillian.

_____. (1953). *Science and human behavior.* New York: The Free Press.

_____. (1968). *The technology of teaching.* New York: Appleton-Century-Crofts.

_____. (1971). *Beyond freedom and dignity.* New York: Alfred A. Knopf.

_____. (1974). *About behaviorism.* New York: Alfred A. Knopf.

Stoop, D. (1982). *Life can be great when you use self-talk.* Old Tappan, NJ: Fleming H. Revell.

Stuart, R. B. (1970). *Trick or treatment: How and when psychotherapy fails.* Champainge, IL: Research Press.

Sulzer-Azaroff, B. & Pollack, M. J. (1982). The modification of child behavior problems in the home. In A. S. Bellack, M. Hersen, & A. E. Kazdin (Eds.), *International handbook of behavior modification and therapy.* New York: Plenum Press.

Turk, D., Meichenbaum, D., & Genest, M. (1983). *Pain and behavioral medicine.* New York: Guilford Press.

Ullmann, L. P. & Krasner, L. (1965). Introduction. In L. P. Ullmann & L. Krasner (Eds.), *Case studies in behavior modification.* New York: Holt, Rinehart, & Winston.

Weinrich W., Dawley, H., & General, D. (1976). *Self-directed systematic desensitization.* Kalamazoo, MI: Behaviordelia.

Whaley, D. L. & Malott, R. W. (1971). *Elementary principles of behavior.* Englewood Cliffs, NJ: Prentice-Hall.

Willner, A. G., Braukmann, C. J., Kirigin, K. A., & Wolf, M. M. (1978). Achievement place: A community treatment model for youths in trouble. In D. Marholin, II (Ed.), *Child behavior therapy* (pp. 239–273). New York: Gardner Press.

Wolpe, J. (1958). *Psychotherapy by reciprocal inhibition.* Stanford, CA: Stanford University Press.

_____. (1973). *The practice of behavior therapy* (2nd ed.). New York: Pergamon Press.

_____. (1978). Cognition and causation in human behavior and its therapy. *American Psychologist, 33,* 437–446.

_____. (1980). Cognitive behavior: A reply to three commentaries. *American Psychologist, 35,* 112–114.

Wolpe, J. & Wolpe, D. (1981). *Our useless fears.* Boston: Houghton Mifflin.

CHAPTER ELEVEN

Atwell, B. M. (1982). *A study of teaching reality therapy to adolescents for self-management.* Unpublished doctoral dissertation, University of North Carolina at Greensboro.

Brandon, L. W. (1981). The effects of a reality therapy treatment upon students' absenteeism and locus of control of reinforcement (Doctoral dissertation, Georgia State University, 1981). *Dissertation Abstracts International, 42,* 2380A–2381A. (University Microfilms No. 81-26, 190)

Browning, B. D. (1979). Effects of reality therapy on teacher attitudes, student attitudes, student achievement, and student behavior. (Doctoral dissertation, North Texas State University, 1978). *Dissertation Abstracts International, 39,* 4010A. (University Microfilms No. 78-24, 637)

Burkley, K. W. (1975). The rationale and assessment of the effectiveness of the reality therapy model in the counseling of black youths (Doctoral dissertation, University of Pittsburg, 1974). *Dissertation Abstracts International, 35,* 7052A. (University Microfilms No. 75-4, 081)

Cherry, J. H. (1976). A study of reality therapy as an approach to discipline in the classroom. (Doctoral dissertation, Illinois State University, 1975). *Dissertation Abstracts International, 36,* 7369A. (University Microfilms No. 76-9, 906)

Dakoske, T. J. (1977). Short and long-term effects of reality therapy on self-concept and discipline of selected fifth-graders. (Doctoral dissertation, University of Cincinnati, 1977). *Dissertation Abstracts International, 38,* 2338B. (University Microfilms No. 77-22, 793)

Dolly, J. P. & Page, D. P. (1981). The effects of a program of behavior modification and reality therapy on the behavior of emotionally disturbed institutionalized adolescents. *The Exceptional Child, 28,* 191–198.

Evans, D. B. (1982). What are you doing? An interview with William Glasser. *The Personnel and Guidance Journal, 60,* 460–465.

Fuller, G. B. & Fuller, D. L. (1982). Reality therapy: Helping LD children make better choices. *Academic Therapy, 17,* 269–277.

German, M. D. (1975). The effects of group reality therapy on institutionalized adolescents and group leaders. (Doctoral dissertation, George Peabody College for Teachers, 1975). *Dissertation Abstracts International, 36,* 1916B. (University Microfilms Order No. 75-22, 267)

Glasser, W. (1965). *Reality therapy: A new approach to psychiatry.* New York: Harper & Row.

_____. (1969). *Schools without failure.* New York: Harper & Row.

_____. (1972). *The identity society.* New York: Harper & Row.

_____. (1976). *Positive addiction.* New York: Harper & Row.

_____. (1981). *Stations of the mind.* New York: Harper & Row.

_____. (1984). *Take effective control.* New York: Harper & Row.

Holleran, J. P. (1981). Effect of group counseling on locus of control and academic achievement: Reality therapy with underachieving junior high school students. (Doctoral dissertation, Boston University, 1981). *Dissertation Abstracts International, 41,* 4980A. (University Microfilms No. 81-12, 250)

Jackson, B. (1975) The *psuche* in psychology and theology. *Journal of Psychology and Theology, 3,* 3-10.

Margolis, H., Muhlfelder, C. & Brannigan, G. G. (1977). Reality therapy and underachievement: A case study. *Education, 98,* 153-155.

Martig, R. M. (1979). The behavioral and psychological effects of group reality therapy on male and female college students. (Doctoral dissertation, Florida Institute of Technology, 1978). *Dissertation Abstracts International, 40,* 1902B. (University Microfilms No. 79-23, 319)

McMordie, W. R. (1981). Reality therapy: Icing on the cake of behavior modification. *Journal of Contemporary Psychotherapy, 12,* 137-145.

Rozsnafszky, J. (1974). The impact of Alfred Adler on three "free will" therapies of the 1960s. *Journal of Individual Psychology, 30,* 65-80.

Schuster, R. (1978-79). Evaluation of a reality therapy stratification system in a residential drug rehabilitation center. *Drug Forum, 7,* 59-67.

Shearn, D. F. & Randolph, D. L. (1978). Effects of reality therapy methods applied in the classroom. *Psychology in the Schools, 15,* 79-83.

Zapf, R. F. (1976). Group therapy with retarded adults: A reality therapy approach. (Doctoral dissertation, Boston University School of Education, 1976). *Dissertation Abstracts International, 37,* 1418A. (University Microfilms No. 76-21, 267).

CHAPTER TWELVE

Adler, A. (1927). *Understanding human nature.* New York; Greenberg.

_____. (1929). *The science of living.* New York: Greenberg.

Ball, C. (1966). First and Second Peter. In Carter, C. W. (Ed.), *The Wesleyan Bible commentary,* (Vol. 6, pp. 241–306). Grand Rapids: Baker Book House.

Beck, A. T. (1967). *Depression: Clinical, experimental, and theoretical aspects.* New York: Hoeber.

_____. (1976). *Cognitive therapy and the emotional disorders.* New York: International Universities Press.

Beck, A. T., Rush, A. J., Shaw, B. F., & Emery, G. (1979). *Cognitive therapy of depression.* New York: The Guilford Press.

Berne, E. (1957). Ego states in psychotherapy. *American Journal of Psychotherapy, 11,* 293–309.

Bounds, E. M. (1946). *Preacher and prayer.* Grand Rapids: Zondervan.

Burns, D. D. (1980). *Feeling good.* New York: William Morrow & Co.

Carter, C. W. (Ed.). (1966). *The Wesleyan Bible commentary.* Grand Rapids: Baker Book House.

Cetron, M. & O'Toole, T. (1982). *Encounters with the future: A forecast of life into the 21st Century.* New York: McGraw-Hill.

Combs, A. W. & Snygg, D. (1949). *Individual behavior: A perceptual approach to behavior.* New York: Harper & Row.

Dryer, W. (1976). *Your erroneous zones.* New York: Funk & Wagnalls.

_____. (1978). *Pulling your own strings.* New York: Harper & Row.

_____. (1980). *The sky's the limit.* New York: Pocket Books.

Ellis, A. (1962). *Reason and emotion in psychotherapy.* New York: Lyle Stuart.

Ellis, A. & Grieger, R. (1977). *Handbook of rational-emotive therapy*. New York: Springer.

Ellis, A. & Harper, R. A. (1975). *A new guide to rational living*. North Hollywood, CA: Wilshire.

Ellis, A. & Knaus, W. (1977). *Overcoming procrastination*. New York: A Signet Book.

Grant, D. (1983). *The ultimate power*. Old Tappan, NJ: Fleming H. Revell.

Hall, C. (1964). *A primer of Freudian psychology*. New York: Mentor Books.

Hauck, P. (1972). *Reason in pastoral counseling*. Philadelphia: Westminster Press.

Hill, W. (1971). *Learning: A survey of psychological interpretation*. Scranton, PA: Chandler.

Horney, K. (1939). *New ways in psychoanalysis*. New York: Norton.

Kendall, P. C. & Hollon, S. D. (1979). *Cognitive-behavioral interventions: Theory, research, and procedures*. New York: Academic Press.

Meyer, A. (1948). *The commonsense psychiatry of Dr. Adolf Meyer*. New York: McGraw-Hill.

Naisbitt, J. (1982). *Megatrends*. New York: Warner Books.

Rutledge, H. & Rutledge, P. (1973). *In the presence of mine enemies*. Old Tappan, NJ: Fleming H. Revell.

Salter, A. (1949). *Conditioned reflex therapy*. New York: Creative Age.

Schmidt, J. (1983). *Can you hear what you are thinking?* Wheaton, IL: Victor Books.

Seamands, D. (1981). *Healing for damaged emotions*. Wheaton, IL: Victor Books.

Sullivan, H. S. (1947). *Conceptions of modern psychiatry*. Washington, D.C: William Alanson White Foundation.

ten Boom, C. (1971). *The hiding place*. Old Tappan, NJ: Fleming H. Revell.

CHAPTER THIRTEEN

Adler, A. (1929a). *The practice and theory of individual psychology* (rev. ed.). (P. Radin, Trans.) London: Routledge & Kegan Paul.

_____. (1929b). *The science of living.* New York: Greenberg Publisher.

_____. (1973). *Superiority and social interest* (3rd ed.). (H. L. Ansbacker & R. R. Ansbacker, Eds.) New York: Viking Press.

_____. (1935/1982). The fundamental views of individual psychology. *International Journal of Individual Psychology, 1,* 5–8. (Reprinted in *Journal of Individual Psychology, 38,* 3–6.)

Amerikaner, M. J. (1981). Continuing theoretical convergence: A general systems theory perspective on personal growth and development. *Journal of Individual Psychology, 37,* 31–53.

Ansbacker, H. L. and Ansbacker, R. R. (Eds.). (1956). *The individual psychology of Alfred Adler.* New York: Basic Books.

Bickhard, M. H. & Ford, B. L. (1979). Subjective adaptationism: An Adlerian metapsychology. *Journal of Individual Psychology, 35,* 162–185.

Brink, T. L. (1977). Adlerian theory and pastoral counseling. *Journal of Psychology and Theology, 5,* 143–149.

Croake, J. W. & Rusk, R. (1980). The theories of Adler and Zen. *Journal of Individual Psychology, 36,* 219–226.

Dinkmeyer, D. & Carlson, J. (1973). *Consulting: Facilitating human potential and change processes.* Columbus, OH: Charles E. Merrill.

Dinkmeyer, D. & Dinkmeyer, J. (1982). Adlerian marriage therapy. *Journal of Individual Psychology, 38,* 115–122.

Dowd, E. T. & Kelly, F. D. (1980). Adlerian psychology and cognitive behavior therapy: Convergences. *Journal of Individual Psychology, 36,* 119–135.

Dreikurs, R. (1946). *The challenge of marriage.* New York: Duell, Sloan & Pearce.

Dreikurs, R. (1952). *Character education and spiritual values in an anxious age.* Chicago: Alfred Adler Institute.

Dreikurs, R. (1964). *Children: The challenge.* New York: Hawthorn Books.

Dreikurs, R. (1968). *Psychology in the classroom* (2nd. ed.). New York: Harper & Row.

Gentry, J. M., Winer, J. L., Sigelman, C. K., & Phillips, F. L. (1980). Adlerian lifestyle and vocational preference. *Journal of Individual Psychology, 36,* 80–86.

Hawes, E. C. (1982). Couples growing together: Couple enrichment programs. *Journal of Individual Psychology, 38,* 322–331.

Hirschorn, S. (1982). Pensacola New Pride: An Adlerian-based alternative for juvenile delinquents. *Journal of Individual Psychology, 38,* 129–137.

Kazan, S. (1978). Adler's *gemeinschafsgefuehl* and Meyeroff's caring, *Journal of Individual Psychology, 34,* 3–10.

Krebs, L. L. (1982). Summary of research on an individual education school. *Journal of Individual Psychology, 38,* 245–252.

Leibin, V. M. (1981). Adler's concept of man. *Journal of Individual Psychology, 37,* 3–4.

Maddi, S. R. (1972). *Personality theories: A comparative analysis* (rev. ed.). Homewood, IL: Dorsey Press.

_____. (1978). Existential and individual psychologies. *Journal of Individual Psychology, 34,* 182–190.

Manaster, G. J. (1977). Birth order—An overview. *Journal of Individual Psychology, 33,* 3–8.

Nikelly, A. G. (Ed.). (1971). *Techniques for behavior change.* Springfield, IL: Charles C. Thomas.

O'Connell, W. E. (1978). A re-solution of Adlerian-Jungian opposites. *Journal of Individual Psychology, 34,* 170–181.

Rozsnafszky, J. (1974). The impact of Alfred Adler on three "free-will" therapies of the 1960s. *Journal of Individual Psychology, 30,* 65–80.

Watkins, C. E., Jr. (1982). A decade of research in support of Adlerian psychological theory. *Journal of Individual Psychology, 38,* 90–99.

_____. (1983). Some characteristics of research on Adlerian psychological theory, 1970–1981. *Journal of Individual Psychology, 39,* 99–110.

Willingham, W. K. (1980). A productive consultant-consultee relationship. *Texas Personnel and Guidance Journal, 8,* 19–22.

Willingham, W. K. & Chambliss, E. T. (1974). Teacher study groups solve motivation problems. *Texas Tech Journal of Education, 1* (1), 1–5.

CHAPTER FOURTEEN

Barnard, C. P. & Corrales, R. G. (1979). *The theory and techniques of family therapy.* Springfield, IL: Charles C. Thomas.

Bell, J. E. (1978). Family context therapy: A model for family change. *Journal of Marriage and Family Counseling, 4,* 111–126.

Boulding, K. E. (1968). General systems theory—The skeleton of science. In W. Buckley, (Ed.), *Modern systems research for the behavioral scientist: A sourcebook* (pp. 3–10). Chicago: Aldine.

Bowen, M. (1978). *Family therapy in clinical practice.* New York: Aronson.

Buckley, W. (1967). *Sociology and modern systems theory.* Englewood Cliffs, NJ: Prentice-Hall.

Fogarty, T. F. (1976). Systems concepts and the dimension of self. In P. J. Guerin (Ed.), *Family therapy* (pp. 144-153). New York: Gardner Press.

Guerin, P. J., Jr. (1976). Family therapy: The first twenty-five years. In P. J. Guerin (Ed.), *Family Therapy.* New York: Gardner Press.

Lester, G. W., Beckham, E., & Baucom, D. H. (1980). Implementation of behavioral marital therapy. *Journal of Marital and Family Therapy, 6,* 189–19.

Minuchin, S. (1974). *Families and family therapy.* Cambridge, MA: Harvard University Press.

Napier, A. Y. & Whitaker, C. A. (1978). *The family crucible.* New York: Harper & Row.

Olson, D. H. (1970). Marital and family therapy: Integrative review and critique. *Journal of Marriage and the Family, 32,* 501–538.

Pincus, L. & Dare, C. (1978). *Secrets in the family.* New York: Pantheon Books.

Skynner, A. C. R. (1976). *Systems of family and marital psychotherapy.* New York: Brunner/Mazel.

von Bertalanffy, L. (1968). General systems theory—A critical review. In W. Buckley, (Ed.), *Modern systems research for the behavioral scientist: A sourcebook* (pp. 11–30). Chicago: Aldine.

Wynne, L. C. (1983). Family research and family therapy: A reunion? *Journal of Marital and Family Therapy, 9,* 113–117.

<h3 style="text-align:center">CHAPTER FIFTEEN</h3>

Belgum, D. (1960). *Guilt: Where psychology and religion meet.* Chicago: Scott, Foresman & Co.

Boisen, A. (1936). *The explorations of the inner world.* New York: Harper & Brothers.

Crane, W. E. (1970). *Where God comes in.* Waco, TX: Word Books.

Drakeford, J. W. (1967). *Integrity therapy.* Nashville: Broadman Press.

———. (1978). *People to people therapy.* New York: Harper & Row.

Mowrer, O. H. (1969). *Abnormal reactions or actions.* Dubuque, IA: William C. Brown.

———. (1964). *The new group therapy.* Princeton, NJ: Van Nostrand.

Narramore, B. & Counts, B. (1974). *Guilt and freedom.* Santa Ana, CA: Vison House.

Osborne, C. (1967). *The art of understanding yourself.* Grand Rapids: Zondervan.

Vine, W. E. (1966). *An expository dictionary of New Testament words.* Old Tappan, NJ: Fleming H. Revell.

CHAPTER SIXTEEN

American Psychiatric Association (1980). *Quick reference to the diagnostic criteria from DSM-III.* Washington, DC: Author.

Bonhoeffer, D. (1965). *Ethics* (E. Bethge, Trans.). New York: MacMillian.

Brammer, L. M. & Shostrom, E. L. (1977). *Therapeutic psychology: Fundamentals of actualizing counseling and therapy* (3rd. ed.). Englewood Cliffs, NJ: Prentice-Hall.

Brown, J. F. (1940). *Psychodynamics of abnormal behavior.* New York: McGraw-Hill.

Bustanoby, A. (1974, August). The pastor and other women. *Christianity Today,* pp. 7–10.

Corsini, R. (Ed.). (1982). *Handbook of innovative psychotherapies.* New York: John Wiley & Sons.

Fox, J., Knapp, R. R., & Michael, W. B. (1968). Assessment of self-actualization of psychiatric patients: Validity of the Personal Orientation Inventory. *Educational and Psychological Measurement, 28,* 565–569.

Ellis, A. (1962). *Reason and emotion in psychotherapy.* Seacaucus, NJ: Lyle Stuart.

_____. (1973). *Humanistic psychotherapy, The rational emotive approach.* New York: Julian Press.

Ellis, A. with Harper, R. A. (1961). *A guide to rational living.* Englewood Cliffs, NJ: Prentice-Hall.

Horney, K. (1945). *Our inner conflicts.* New York: W. W. Norton.

Krumboltz, J. D. & Thoreson, C. E. (1969). *Behavioral counseling: Cases and techniques.* New York: Holt.

Lazarus, A. (1971). *Behavior therapy and beyond.* New York: McGraw-Hill.

Leary, T. (1957). *Interpersonal diagnosis of personality.* New York: Ronald Press.

Lowen, A. (1958). *Physical dynamics of character structure.* New York: Grune & Stratton.

_____. (1965). *Love and orgasm.* New York: MacMillian.

_____. (1967). *Betrayal of the body.* New York: MacMillian.

Maslow, A. (1954). *Motivation and personality.* New York: Harper & Row.

Montgomery, D. (1980). *Courage to love.* Ventura: CA: Regal Books.

_____. (1982). Christians are human, too. Mission Viejo, CA: Unpublished manuscript.

Montgomery, K. (1981). A study of verbatim transcripts and actualizing therapy. Unpublished master's thesis, United States International University.

Perls, F. (1951). *Gestalt therapy, excitement and growth in the human personality.* New York: Julian Press.

_____. (1969). *Gestalt therapy verbatim.* Moab, UT: Real People Press.

_____. (1973). *The gestalt approach and eye witness to therapy.* Ben Lomond, CA: Science and Behavior Books.

Reich, W. (1949). *Character analysis.* New York: Orgone Institute Press.

Rogers, C. R. (1942). *Counseling and psychotherapy.* Cambridge, MA: The Riverside Press.

_____. (1951). *Client-centered therapy.* Boston: Houghton Mifflin.

_____. (1961). *On becoming a person.* Boston: Houghton Mifflin.

Schutz, W. C. (1973). *Elements of encounter: A bodymind approach.* Big Sur, CA: Joy Press.

Shostrom, E. L. (1963). *Personal Orientation Inventory.* San Diego: EdITS.

_____. (1966). *Caring Relationship Inventory.* San Diego: EdITS.

_____. (1967). *Man, the manipulator.* Nashville: Abingdon Press.

_____. (1970). *Pair Attraction Inventory.* San Diego: EdITS.

_____. (1976). *Actualizing therapy.* San Diego: EdITS.

Shostrom, E. L. & Knapp, R. R. (1966). The relationship of a measure of self-actualization (POI) to a measure of pathology (MMPI) and to therapeutic growth. *American Journal of Psychotherapy, 20,* 193–202.

Shostrom E. L. Montgomery, D. (1978). *Healing love: How God works within the personality.* Nashville: Abingdon Press.

Shostrom, E. L., Montgomery, D., & Montgomery, K. (1984). Rhythmic relating: The art of marriage. Unpublished manuscript.

Shostrom, E. L. & Montgomery, K. (1983). Manipulation-Mastery Inventory. Unpublished personality assessment instrument.

Shostrom, E. L. & Riley, C. (1968). Parametric analysis of psychotherapy. *Journal of Consulting and Clinical Psychology, 32,* 628–632.

Tournier, P. (1968). *A place for you.* (E. Hudson, Trans.). New York: Harper & Row.

CHAPTER SEVENTEEN

Arndt, W. F. & Gingrich, F. W. (1957). *A Greek-English lexicon of the New Testament and other early Christian literature.* Chicago: University of Chicago Press.

Dewar, L. (1959). *The Holy Spirit and modern thought.* New York: Harper & Brothers.

Webster's seventh new collegiate dictionary. (1967). Springfield, MA: G. & C. Merriam.

Wiksten, D. (1969). The power of pastoral counseling as the work of the Holy Spirit. *Pastoral Psychology, 20,* 28–32, 40–42.

Scripture Index

Index